UNEASY LISTENING

For Sharon and Jake, my favorite listeners

UNEASY LISTENING:
PACIFICA RADIO'S CIVIL WAR

by

MATTHEW LASAR

BLACK
APOLLO
PRESS

First published in Great Britain by Black Apollo Press, 2006
Copyright © Matthew Lasar 2006
The moral right of the author has been asserted
A CIP catalogue record of this book is available at the British Library

ISBN 1 900 355 52 3

Design by DCG Design, Cambridge, UK
Cover illustration by Kaarl Hollis

CONTENTS

The Master said, "Yu, have you ever been told of the Six Sayings about the Six Degenerations?" Tzu-lu replied, "No, never." [The Master said,] "Come, then; I will tell you[:]

"Love of Goodness without love of learning degenerates into silliness. Love of wisdom without love of learning degenerates into utter lack of principle. Love of keeping promises without love of learning degenerates into villainy. Love of uprightness without love of learning degenerates into harshness. Love of courage without love of learning degenerates into turbulence. Love of courage without love of learning degenerates into mere recklessness."

Confucius, *The Analects*, Book XVII, 8

INTRODUCTION

There was a time when we wanted (very seriously) to explain
the *æsthetic* of radio – to describe what it is that makes people
go so foolish and so broke in order to get involved in radio.
– LORENZO MILAM, *THE RADIO PAPERS: FROM KRAB TO KCHU*

Huh?

H ere are the facts of the case. On the afternoon of March 31,
1999, the executive director of the Pacifica Foundation paid a
visit to the general manager of KPFA in Berkeley, California, one of
the foundation's five listener-supported radio stations. Both individuals had long histories of work in public and community radio. The
executive director informed the manager that her services were no
longer necessary, and that she should pack up her personal items
and leave.

The dismissal alarmed the station's staff. They began talking
about it on the air. The executive director promptly fired some of
them for so doing and threatened everyone else with ouster as well,
confirming people's worst fears. Employees and listeners demonstrated in front of the station and continued to talk about the firings
on the air, in defiance of an order to remain silent. In response, the
executive director hired guards, summoned the police, expelled the
entire staff, and bolted the station's doors. The network became
engulfed in a very nasty fight that lasted three years.

By the time the smoke had cleared, 10,000 people had demonstrated for the reopening of KPFA. Dozens of California state

legislators signed a petition denouncing the executive director's actions and had held a legislative hearing on the crisis. Hundreds of academics across the country took sides on the dilemma. Prominent unions passed resolutions on the controversy, as did scores of nonprofit organizations and churches. The mayors of Oakland, San Francisco, and Berkeley spoke out on the crisis. The Attorney General of California authorized about 11,000 of the network's listeners to sue Pacifica's nonprofit foundation board, which happened to be chaired by the head of the United States Civil Rights Commission. The New York City Council debated the crisis. A United States Congressmember made a speech on the matter from the floor of the House of Representatives, which then held a special hearing on the controversy. The foundation hired seven prominent national law firms to deal with the lawsuit, including that of Gregory B. Craig, special counsel to former United States president Bill Clinton. Two major corporate public relations companies and a prominent private investigation firm were hired to help the foundation. Among the celebrities who made public statements on the matter were Danny Glover, Ed Asner, Ralph Nader, Alice Walker, Noam Chomsky, and Joan Baez. The fight received regular coverage from *The New York Times*, *The Los Angeles Times*, and *The Washington Post*, and attention from the *London Independent*, *The Economist*, and *Le Monde*. *Yahoo!* devoted a special web page to news articles about the struggle. Dozens of daily newspapers, weekly newspapers, and national weekly magazines, including *The Nation*, *Time*, *Harper's*, *U.S. News and World Report*, *In These Times*, and *The Village Voice*, published feature stories about the battle. Millions of dollars poured into the conflict for legal and organizing expenses.

The most obvious question is, why? Why did the dismissal of a single general manager spiral into such an uproar? Pacifica is a famously contentious organization, its internal battles chronicled by many scholars of public broadcasting, including this author. But ten thousand people demonstrating on behalf of a radio station? What was that all about? And Gregory Craig, the head of the U.S. Civil Rights Commission, California's Attorney General, the New York

8

City Council, and Congress? Why did the "Pacifica crisis," as it came to be called, spill out into so much of civil society? There were 13,296 radio stations in the United States when the Federal Communications Commission counted in 2002.[1] Pacifica radio owns five. Why did so many people care so passionately about what happened to a tiny handful of local stations? Why did a fight about something so small become so big?

The short answer is that forces within Pacifica came to loggerheads about the organization's future at precisely the same time that Americans became aware of the extent to which their access to the nation's larger broadcasting system had been curtailed. By 1999, twenty years of government policy had permitted a handful of corporations to control most of the nation's radio stations. This crucial form of mass communication became, in consequence, less accessible than at almost any point in the history of broadcasting. It would be an understatement to say simply that the American Left had noticed this. The "crisis of the media," as it was called, had become a central focus of progressive analysis and social concern in the United States. Thus what might have gone down in the annals of listener-supported radio as just another Pacifica squabble was read by a critical mass of people as something much bigger. Thousands of individuals who supported Pacifica radio or had had something to do with the organization at some point in their lives interpreted the Pacifica crisis as part of a larger media crisis and acted accordingly.

Was Pacifica radio's civil war part of that larger crisis? Before offering a fuller assessment, a brief overview of the subject is in order.

A Pacifica Half-Century

It is no overstatement to say that but for the Pacifica network, the American Left would not have been on the radio in any consistent manner. Had Pacifica failed to come into existence, leftists would have been heard sporadically in the United States on the AM or FM dial in the 1950s and early 1960s. Perhaps Michael Harrington,

Norman Thomas, Martin Luther King, Jr., and a few other individuals relatively close to the American center would have been interviewed with some regularity. The doors would have briefly swung wide in the late 1960s, would have remained open with the establishment of National Public Radio in 1971, and would then have narrowed again after the election of Ronald Reagan to the White House in 1980. And that, for the most part, would have been the end of the story.

Pursuing its purposes almost completely alone in the 1950s and 1960s, Pacifica gave the avant garde and the Left a microphone through which to talk on a daily basis to three major U.S. metropolitan areas and then, by the late 1970s, to five. It made it possible for tens of thousands of people not only to hear leftist talk and unconventional culture, but to organize their lives around it. These five boisterous, unstable dispensaries of radical sound did more than just broadcast oppositional ideas – they provided continuous audio validation for generations of people who wanted to live by them. A historian of the Pacifica network can focus on any number of programs or series of programs to explain Pacifica to the reader. Pacifica was one of the earliest organizations to question U.S. involvement in Vietnam, for example. Pacifica remains the only broadcasting network in the U.S. that consistently challenges the government's political and financial support for the state of Israel's illegal occupation of Palestine. But these contributions, while important to note, do not quite get at the central point of Pacifica radio. Pacifica's loyal listeners tuned in to their Pacifica station not just for one particular show, but for the ongoing experience of hearing leftist ideas and nonconformist culture broadcast and validated as an accompaniment to their lives.

Practically all studies and histories of noncommercial and non-state-controlled broadcasting properly credit Lewis Kimball Hill with founding the first listener-supported radio station in the United States and probably anywhere else: KPFA-FM in Berkeley, launched on April 15, 1949. "[T]he longest running example of non-profit, listener supported radio in the world," wrote Peter M. Lewis and Jerry L. Booth in their 1990 survey of noncommercial radio across the globe.[2] The Rousseauean version of pre-Hill radio is well told by community broadcasting pioneer Lorenzo Milam in his marvelous manual titled *Sex and Broadcasting: A Handbook for Starting a Radio Station for the Community*. Radio was born free, Milam suggests, "but then all the toads came along . . . to hawk their awful wares." Following the toads came the "bores" – educational broadcasters with their big Schools of Communication at various institutions of higher education. Finally Lewis Hill and Pacifica came to the rescue, "educating listeners in the widest sense," and inspired further community radio experiments around the country.[3]

The nephew of an Oklahoma oil millionaire, Hill attended Stanford University in the late 1930s and fell in with the then influential pacifist movement. Following the Japanese attack on Pearl Harbor, he registered as a Conscientious Objector (CO) and was sent to a camp for pacifists in remote Coleville, California. Suffering from arthritis of the spine, Hill received a medical release in 1942. He then went to Washington, D.C., to serve as director of the American Civil Liberty Union's National Committee on Conscientious Objectors (NCCO). The National Committee advocated for the many pacifists sent to federal prison during the war because they had been deemed insufficiently pacifist by Selective Service or because as an act of protest they either refused to remain in a CO camp or staged protest strikes at them. Hill also worked part-time as a news announcer for a local D.C. commercial radio station.[4]

Although many of Hill's followers thought otherwise, he did not invent the idea of listener-supported radio, an intuitive concept that visionaries had pursued without success in the pre-World War II years. In the early 1920s, for example, a Kansas City radio station owned by a school for automobile mechanics sold tickets for an "invisible theater." Those "sharing the pleasure" of broadcasting music, explained a brochure, would "pay a portion of the expenses" by purchasing a program book costing from one to ten dollars. The experiment petered out quickly.[5] In the late 1920s, the Chicago trade unionist Edward Nockels attempted to turn his Chicago labor radio station, WCFL, into a listener-supported outlet. Lack of rank-and-file financial support compelled him to accept commercial network programming.[6] In 1935 one F.L. Whitesell, a writer who lived near Scranton, Pennsylvania, asked the Federal Communications Commission (FCC) for a license for a radio outlet funded mostly by listener contributions. The agency turned him down because he "failed to make a proper showing of financial ability to construct and operate the proposed station," perhaps a fair criticism given the Depression-era economy.[7]

But Hill went far beyond these false starts, proving that listener-supported radio could work. He not only organized the first prototype of this kind of broadcasting – KPFA – but proselytized for it as a writer and lecturer. Flexible and adaptable, Hill kept adjusting the station's organizational structure and mission until it reached a self-supporting plateau. He and his anarcho-pacifist associates created the Pacifica Foundation in 1946, a non-profit, tax-exempt institution, to own and run KPFA.[8] Almost all of them conscientious objectors, they hoped to rescue pacifism from the marginality to which it had been consigned during the overwhelmingly popular Second World War.

KPFA quickly built a national reputation as a lively, unconventional force. Hill openly denounced the FBI and U.S. entry into the Korean war.[9] The station's cultural programmers premiered contemporary classical music and poetry on a daily basis.[10] Pot smokers came on the air to extol the virtues of the drug.[11] America's first homosexual-rights activists received sympathetic airtime, as did members of the Communist Party, despite KPFA management's anarchist antipathy toward them.[12]

In his own emphasis, Lewis Hill sought "*a method of sustaining communication for its own sake*," rather than to draw attention to advertisements.[13] He wanted to embed his pacifist ideas within a broadcast schedule of public dialogue that transcended the commercial profit motive. By 1959 Pacifica had built another radio station, KPFK-FM in Los Angeles. Then an eccentric millionaire donated WBAI-FM in New York City to the foundation in 1960.[15] In its first week of broadcasting, KPFK rocked Los Angeles with an interview with notorious anti-Semite Gerald L.K. Smith.[16] WBAI stunned American journalism by putting a disgruntled ex-FBI trainee on the air. His comments provoked the wrath of J. Edgar Hoover, who retaliated with a government investigation of the foundation.[17] KPFA kept up with celebratory coverage of the San Francisco riots against the House Committee on Un-American Activities (HUAC) of 1960, then the Berkeley Free Speech Uprising of 1964.[18] All three stations made themselves beloved by an influential generation of listeners through continuous broadcasting critical of the Vietnam war.[19] Tragically, Hill saw none of this. Afflicted with agonizing arthritis of the spine, he took his own life in 1957.[20]

Pacifica's three radio stations came through the 1960s with younger staffs who spoke in the language of populism. "We have been too academic in the past," declared the head of KPFA's news department, "and now we want to go to the people and get their feelings."[21] The "people" were now often defined as ethnic and cultural minority groups: African-Americans, Latinos, gays, lesbians, and feminist women. They responded with great enthusiasm to such calls, but took exception to the practice of filtering their voices through mediators, usually white, middle-class male public affairs hosts. Pacifica's newest generation of programmers wanted their own airtime and often their own station departments. Through the 1970s the network sustained a series of explosions over this tension: demonstrations, strikes, sit-ins and walk-outs. By the end of this stormy process, Pacifica had redefined itself as "community" radio – an organization dedicated to sharing its resources with a diverse array of cultural constituencies.[22]

Two more radio stations entered the Pacifica orbit during this period. In 1970 public broadcasting pioneer Larry Lee put KPFT on the air in Houston, then reluctantly affiliated it with the Pacifica network in order to obtain nonprofit status. The Ku Klux Klan bombed its transmitter twice.[23] A Texas Congress member named George Bush even requested an FBI investigation.[24] WPFW in Washington, D.C., came less easily to the organization. It took the foundation nine difficult years to obtain a license for a station in the nation's capital. Inaugurated in 1977, WPFW became the network's "black-oriented" station. A "fly in the buttermilk," one broadcasting historian fondly called it, contrasting the frequency's largely African-American listener base with the predominantly white audiences most community radio stations serve.[25]

By the early 1980s, an obvious question bore down upon the organization: what could it accomplish as one united voice? The network's governing board decided not to join National Public Radio (NPR), which began in 1971 with 104 affiliates and by 1980 served 220 public radio stations across the country.[26] Could Pacifica offer a credible alternative? In 1978 it established its own news service. The Pacifica Radio News provided a half-hour of feature stories on national and international events to its licensees and to dozens of community stations elsewhere, which came to be known as affiliates. KPFA's Larry Bensky hosted live gavel-to-gavel coverage of the Iran/Contra hearings in 1987, broadcast to great acclaim across the Pacifica network. The tradition of live alternative coverage of national events continued with the Senate Judicial Committee's hearings on the candidacies of Robert Bork and Clarence Thomas to the Supreme Court.[27] In 1996 the network inaugurated what quickly became the most popular show in the annals of alternative media, *Democracy Now!*, hosted by WBAI's Amy Goodman and Juan Gonzalez of the *New York Daily News*. Then Pacifica launched its own satellite distribution service, allowing its stations and affiliates to uplink and download independently produced radio programs, among them acclaimed physicist Michio Kaku's Explorations, a program on science and technology.[28]

Several years later a prominent audience measurement analyst declared that 800,000 people throughout the United States listened to some portion of Pacifica radio each week. "Pacifica's audience has never been larger," he declared.[29] Although small by corporate media standards, the network's influence on the larger culture had been demonstrated repeatedly, not only by its more daring exploits but by its long history of mentoring hitherto unknown genius – Zen scholar Alan Watts, folk-rocker Jerry Garcia, Firesign Mystery Theater, film critic Pauline Kael, vocalist Bobbi McFerrin, and novelist Alice Walker, to offer only a few examples. Generations of journalists had begun their journey at Pacifica, from CBS's Terry Drinkwater to John Rockwell of *The New York Times*.[30] At age fifty, this remarkable legacy should have been cause for celebration and unity. Instead the organization slipped into a spectacular free-fall. Why?

A Crisis of Containment

In brief, this book argues that the origins of the Pacifica crisis have their roots in an attempt by the American Left from the 1980s onward to transform the Pacifica network into a unified national voice able to compete effectively in an increasingly conservative medium. Superficially, Pacifica, with its five big signal stations and small but passionately loyal audiences, looked like the ideal candidate for this makeover. In reality, it was anything but the right institution for the job. Decentralized in its operations yet paradoxically undemocratic in its legal structure, divisions and internal contradictions denied the five-station Pacifica confederation anything even remotely resembling a legitimate stratum of leadership.

By the 1990s the foundation faced another, even bigger problem. Thanks to the gradual abandonment of public service requirements for radio from the 1980s onward, most radio stations across the country, both "public" and commercial, adopted formats and schedules that excluded local musicians, local activists, local opinion makers, indeed, local *anyones*, in favor of highly automated, satellite-driven schedules designed to feed the bottom line. This left the Pacifica network's five locally driven stations with the privilege of carrying on the tradition of local, democratic communications, along with the debilitating burden of serving dozens of cultural and political broadcasting missions relinquished by the rest of radio. The public service deregulation and subsequent monopolization of radio left Pacifica "contained" – to borrow an old Cold War term – packed with people with few better places to go and few resources with which to grow.

Those who favored centralizing the organization anyway failed to gauge the extent to which this external reality would block their project. They also ignored early signs that further attempts at removing and restructuring network personnel in the interests of a more compelling national sound would produce ever more explosive results. Their unwillingness to look closely at Pacifica's adaptability was understandable. First of all, "they" were a disjointed succession of governing board members, managers, and staff who often had little sense of the institution's recent history, let alone its origins. Second, the urgent necessity of finding a more effective broadcasting voice for the Left made Pacifica's governors willing to tackle obstacles that, given the organization's containment, turned out to be social landmines. Unifying Pacifica both programmatically and structurally required collective "housekeeping," as one journalist close to the organization would put it: the elimination of many locally-based broadcasting efforts at all five stations. Needless to say, the numerous individuals deemed incompatible with the network's updated purposes would not take their pink slips gratefully or gracefully. Quite the contrary, they would resist their removal with picket lines, web sites, and lawyers.

As tensions throughout Pacifica heightened in the 1990s, the foundation's management gradually lost patience with the environment in which they worked. They came to see the organization's grassroots base as their enemy, and outside governmental and semi-governmental agencies such as the Corporation for Public Broadcasting as allies. They developed a collective managerial thick skin designed to protect them emotionally while they pursued their impossible institutional crusade. Conversely, the network's core base of active listeners and volunteers increasingly perceived Pacifica leadership as "hijackers," brought in by the corporate state to take the network away from them.

It was in this context that high noon arrived in Berkeley on March 31, 1999. Displaced programmers – casualties of Pacifica radio's attempt to restructure itself through the 1990s – and their supporters joined forces with KPFA's professional staff, who were anticipating their own displacement. Together they rose up against the firing of one general manager. Pacifica's latest leaders, committed to a long-agreed-upon, albeit unworkable, trajectory, responded rigidly to the crisis, provoking a social explosion that began in the city of Berkeley and spread throughout the network. As leftists across the country struggled to understand the chaos sweeping through their beloved organization, partisans within Pacifica and the Left offered the public two competing interpretations of the crisis. One argued that Pacifica was simply experiencing some growing pains on the road to becoming a more relevant and effective organization. The other contended that the very market forces that had corrupted broadcasting elsewhere had sunk their teeth into the last citadel of noncommercial, alternative radio. Liberals and progressives, increasingly preoccupied with the extent to which the nation's mass media had left them behind, easily read Pacifica's troubles as a metaphor for the larger crisis of the media.

The second narrative triumphed. After a long and bitter internecine struggle, the progressive public supported a legal democratization of the Pacifica network.

Scope and Structure

Most of this study focuses on a single decade of Pacifica history, the ten years following the end of the Cold War. But it also functions as a general history of the Pacifica organization from the late 1970s onward. Several important books contain chapters that look at Pacifica history from the 1970s through the early 1990s. Jeff Land's *Active Radio: Pacifica's Brash Experiment* (1999) thoughtfully explores the culture of Pacifica station WBAI in New York City in the late 1960s and 1970s. Ralph Engelman's comprehensive *Public Broadcasting: A Political History* (1996) places Pacifica circa 1980 within the broad context of public broadcasting's evolution. Jesse Walker's exuberant *Rebels on the Air: An Alternative History of Radio in America* (2000) describes the network's history as part of a libertarian narrative of broadcasting from the Progressive Era to the present. I wrote

17

a history of Pacifica as well. My *Pacifica Radio: The Rise of an Alternative Network* (1999, 2000) narrates the foundation's ideological development from the 1940s through the early 1970s. But no major study thus far has devoted its pages entirely to the Pacifica network's progress from the 1970s onward. This book attempts to begin to fill that gap.

The work of media historians Susan J. Douglas and Robert W. McChesney informs my understanding of the regulatory environment in which Pacifica functions. Douglas's masterpiece, *Inventing American Broadcasting*, traces the social construction of broadcasting in the United States from the development of wireless to the state controls over radio established before, during, and after the First World War, culminating with government approval of the Radio Corporation of America in 1919. She argues that the essential assumptions about government regulation of the airwaves were already in place by the 1920s. Key decisions would be made privately, in favor of corporate interests. Government and the corporate sector shunted the nonentrepreneurial public – especially the nation's enormous amateur broadcasting movement – out of the process. Even before the birth of what we understand as radio today, Douglas writes, a nonprofit vision of broadcasting had been passed over in favor of a highly centralized strategy to "promote cultural homogeneity, to mute or screen out diversity and idiosyncrasy, and to advance values consonant with consumer capitalism."[31]

This background informed the first comprehensive regulations of broadcast radio, instituted in the late 1920s and early 1930s. Robert McChesney's *Rich Media, Poor Democracy* describes the battle nonprofit broadcasters fought in both the United States and Canada to establish bandwidth space for noncommercial radio. Canadian reformers succeeded in this crusade, largely because of legitimate fears that without publicly controlled Canadian radio, the United States would dominate Canada's media life. U.S. reformers, fragmented, elitist, and hopelessly outspent and outmaneuvered by the corporate broadcasting lobby, fared far worse than their northern colleagues. Congress rejected their plea to reserve bandwidth space for nonprofit broadcasters. The Communications Act of 1934 codified what was to be touted by the corporate sector as the "American" system of broadcasting – bought and paid for by commercials. This placed radio's nonprofit sector in a no-win situation, McChesney writes. While Canadian and British broadcasters saw their task as speaking to entire nations, U.S. noncommercial radio producers enjoyed no such opportunity. "The function of the [U.S.] public or educational broadcasters," McChesney argues, "was to provide that programming that was unprofitable for the commercial broadcasters to produce."[32]

This meta-analysis of noncommercial radio in the United States glosses over the specific context in which Pacifica came into being. Lewis Hill and his associates did not create KPFA to supplement commercial radio, but, rather, to foment a worldwide anarcho-pacifist revolution. They did not succeed, obviously, but that was their plan. However, McChesney's historical narrative very accurately characterizes the general situation of nonprofit radio in the United States, constantly scrambling at the margins for scarce resources and the relatively small audiences such resources summon. An appreciation of this condition is absolutely essential to understanding Pacifica's ongoing crisis, which in the future may not play out as dramatically as it did in the recent past (one hopes), but will not end until the fundamental structure of broadcasting in the U.S. changes.

These are the assumptions with which this volume on Pacifica history works. *Uneasy Listening* begins by dropping the reader right into the trenches. Chapter 1, "The Battle of Berkeley," offers a blow-by-blow narration of KPFA's revolt against its parent, the Pacifica Foundation. The chapter concludes with a single question: How did it come to this? Chapter 2, "Foundation and Empire," looks to Pacifica's earliest years for the internal roots of the crisis. Why did Hill and his associates create a framework that excluded the economic bedrock of the foundation – KPFA's listener-sponsors – from any formal say in governance? What impact was that to have on the subsequent history of the organization? Chapter 3,

"Inventing Community Radio," describes the growth of Pacifica from the early 1960s through the late 1970s. During this period Pacifica integrated many new groups into its three older stations, without the benefit of additional air space to accommodate them. Pacifica also inaugurated two more radio stations, whose signals broadcast to environments that presented challenges the institution had not faced before. Overwhelmed by new voices and new ideologies, the organization settled into a *de facto* system of governance that I describe as "anarcho-feudalism."

Chapter 4, "LA Confidential," describes the first serious attempts to find a unifying mission in the light of the triumph of Reaganism for what was now a five-station foundation. It explains why that effort failed, and how the fallout augured the pattern of Pacifica dissidence for the next fifteen years. The chapter also examines how, beginning with the later years of the Carter administration, the regulatory environment around Pacifica changed dramatically, limiting the possibilities for personal and creative noncommercial radio beyond Pacifica's five stations and setting the stage for the institution's troubles in the 1990s. Chapter 5, "Strategic Plans," narrates Pacifica's continuing efforts to rationalize and centralize its programming and governance, and the critique that developed on a governance/managerial level of the organization's "community"-based culture. By the mid-1990s, grassroots opposition to these plans had solidified at WBAI, KPFA, and KPFK. While Pacifica officials and others dismissed these forces as marginal, their leaders showed considerable sophistication about the Internet and public broadcasting law. The chapter also introduces the reader to the most controversial person ever to serve as chair of Pacifica's board, Mary Frances Berry of the U.S. Civil Rights Commission.

Under Berry's leadership, in 1999 the organization exploded into total internecine chaos. Chapter 6, "In Defense of the Realm," examines the attempts to defuse the crisis in Berkeley made by a small coalition of writers associated with KPFK in Los Angeles and *The Nation* magazine. It contrasts their ideas about the network's future with those of the Free Pacifica movement. Chapter 7,

"Revolution," describes the so-called Christmas Coup of December 2000 – Pacifica's calamitous attempt to reorganize WBAI in New York City, leading to the "Pacifica Campaign." It was this well-funded, carefully organized dissident onslaught that framed the crisis in a manner that finally forced the Pacifica National Board to sue for peace. Chapter 8, "Frequently Asked Questions," overviews the causes and implications of the Pacifica crisis and outlines how the struggle fits into the larger battle for media democracy.

* * *

For the most part, this history will be narrated conventionally, in the third person. To do so entirely, however, would conceal the fact that I was a very active participant in Pacifica from the 1980s onward. I began my association with Pacifica radio as a very young listener to WBAI in New York City. After relocating to the Bay Area of northern California in 1982 I immediately subscribed to KPFA-FM in Berkeley and soon enrolled in the station's training course for radio news reporters. There I remained for eight happy years, covering Bay Area politics for the KPFA *Six O'Clock News* and occasionally hosting a classical music concert. In 1989 I made the decision to pursue a career as an academic historian, taking a master's degree at the University of California at Davis, then a Ph.D. at the Claremont Graduate School.[33] When the matter of my doctoral dissertation came up, I decided to write a thesis on the early years of the Pacifica Foundation. Two years later Temple University Press published my study as *Pacifica Radio: The Rise of an Alternative Network*, just in time for the organization's meltdown.

Up until 1999 I had been skeptical of Pacifica's critics. They appeared unwilling to engage in a frank discussion of the failures of community radio in the 1970s and 1980s. Many had personal axes to grind. Others seemed far more interested in fighting with each other over the Internet than in working toward constructive change. But when in February of 1999 Pacifica turned its national board into a self-appointing body, I began to harbor fears about the capacity of the leadership to move into the future while preserving the best elements of its past. Pacifica's governors confirmed these fears during the summer of 1999, with its lockout of the KPFA staff. They subsequently acted in ways that indicated to me that they had learned nothing from the experience.

Thus I became a Pacifica dissident, joining the opposition to the organization's board of directors. Because I had published a university press book on the history of Pacifica, newspapers constantly called on me for background information and opinion.[34] Within the "community of community radio," as radio pioneer Lorenzo Milam calls it, I became a familiar name, appearing regularly on noncommercial radio stations across the country.[35]

Thus, while I was hardly one of the key players in this story, I was no detached bystander either. I shared all the passion, anger, confusion, and hope that thousands of Pacificans displayed as their beloved organization went through its time of trouble. I therefore occasionally pop up in this narrative, in the manner of a historical fly on the wall. Many, many people helped me write this book in some way. Their generous efforts are mentioned in the acknowledgments. Doubtless they will be grateful for my assurance that none of them bear any responsibility for the words you are about to read.

June 2005

Notes

1   Federal Communications Commission document, "Broadcast Station Totals as of September 30, 2002" (Washington, D.C.: FCC, 2002).

2   Peter M. Lewis and Jerry Booth, *The Invisible Medium: Public, Commercial and Community Radio* (Washington, D.C.: Howard University Press, 1990), p.115.

3   Lorenzo Wilson Milam, *Sex and Broadcasting: A Handbook for Starting a Radio Station for the Community* (San Diego: MHO & MHO Works, 1988), pp.19-20.

4   Matthew Lasar, *Pacifica Radio: The Rise of an Alternative Network* (Philadelphia: Temple University Press, 1999), pp.3-26.

5   Susan Smulyan, *Selling Radio: The Commercialization of American Broadcasting, 1920-1934* (Washington: Smithsonian Institution Press, 1994), p.67.

6   Robert W. McChesney, *Telecommunications, Mass Media, & Democracy: The Battle for the Control of U.S. Broadcasting, 1928-1935* (New York: Oxford

University Press, 1994), pp.66-67; Nathan Gotfried, *WCFL: Chicago's Voice of Labor, 1926-78* (Urbana: University of Illinois Press, 1997), p.149.

7   Charles Fairchild, *Community Radio and Public Culture: Being an Examination of Media Access and Equity in the Nations of North America*, (Cresskill, New Jersey: Hampton Press, Inc., 2001), p.138.

8   Office of the Secretary of State of California, "Articles of Incorporation of Pacifica Foundation (a Non-profit Organization)," (August 24, 1946), pp.1-4.

9   Lewis Hill, "Commentary," in Eleanor McKinney, ed., *The Exacting Ear: The Story of Listener-Sponsored Radio, and an Anthology of Programs from KPFA, KPFK & WBAI* (New York: Pantheon, 1966), p.250; Lewis Hill, "Report to the Listeners" (July 25, 1950), Lewis Hill Papers (henceforth *LHP*), Folder 5; Lewis Hill, "Report to the Listeners" (August 1, 1950), *LHP*, Folder 5.

10 Lewis Hill, *Voluntary Listener-Sponsorship: A Report to Educational Broadcasters on the Experimental KPFA, Berkeley, California* (Berkeley: Pacifica Foundation, 1958), pp.45-50.

11 "Marijuana," Radio Program, 1954, Pacifica Radio Archives, Los Angeles.

12 *The Homosexual in Our Society: Transcript of a Radio Program in Two Parts* (San Francisco: Pan Graphic Press, 1959); Minutes, Executive Membership, Pacifica Foundation, May 14, 1953, pp.2-3.

13 Hill, *Voluntary Listener-Sponsorship*, p.5.

14 Hill, *Voluntary Listener-Sponsorship*, p.5.

15 Vera Hopkins, "Growing Pains-with Special Reference to KPFA" (unpublished manuscript, 1987), p.19.

16 Gene Marine, interview with author (April 22, 1996), pp.6-7.

17 "The Report of Special Agent Jack Levine: A Documentary Broadcast by WBAI," transcript, 1962; "COMMUNIST INFILTRATION OF PACIFICA FOUNDATION INTERNAL SECURITY; From: Director, FBI" (November 2, 1962), pp.1-3, *Pacifica National Office Papers* (henceforth PNOP), Box 3, Folder 2.

18 "The House Un-American Activities Committee," in McKinney, *The Exacting Ear*, pp.78-79; "Is Freedom Academic? The Berkeley Student Demonstrations," radio broadcast on KPFA in 1964 (Los Angeles: Pacifica Radio Archive).

19 John Dingus, "What's Going On at Pacifica?" *The Nation* (May 1, 2000): www.thenation.com/doc.mhtml?i=20000501&c=1&s=dinges.

20 Lasar, *Pacifica Radio*, pp.163-64.

21 Alan Snitow, quoted in "Pacifica Radio: Purpose and Goals, 1946 – September 1977," in Vera Hopkins, ed., *The Pacifica Radio Sampler* (Los Angeles: Pacifica Foundation, 1984).

22 Matthew Lasar, "Hybrid-Highbrow: KPFA's Reconstruction of Elite Culture, 1946-1963," *Journal of Radio Studies*, vol. 5, no. 1 (Winter 1998): 49-66; Jeff Land, *Active Radio: Pacifica's Brash Experiment* (Minneapolis: University of

Minnesota Press, 1999), pp.113-32.

23 Jesse Walker, *Rebels in the Air: An Alternative History of Radio in America* (New York: New York University Press, 2001), p.112.

24 James Andrew Lumpp, "The Pacifica Experience-1946-1975: Alternative Radio in Four United States Metropolitan Areas" (Ph.D. dissertation, University of Missouri, 1977), p.262.

25 Jon Arquette Degraff, "Radio, Money, and Politics: The Struggle to Establish WPFW-FM, the Pacifica Foundation's Black-Oriented Washington Station" (Ph.D. dissertation, University of Maryland, 1995); William Barlow, "Fly in the Buttermilk: WPFW-Pacifica and the Future of Community Radio," paper given at the *Public Broadcasting and the Public Interest* conference, University of Maine, June 15-17, 2000: www.umaine.edu/pbconference/partic.htm.

26 Minutes, National Board of Directors, Pacifica Foundation, September 11-12, 1971, p.7; Ralph Engelman, *Public Radio and Television in America: A Political History* (Thousand Oaks: SAGE Publications, 1996), p.220.

27 "Highlights of Pacifica Radio's 50 Year History of Radio Broadcasting," Pacifica Foundation: http://www.pacificaarchives.org/learn/history.php.

28 "Pacifica Lofts an Alternative Satellite Schedule," *Current* (December 15, 1997): www.current.org/rad/rad723s.html; "Pacifica Radio Network-Satellite Schedule for February 1999."

29 David Giovanoni, "To: The Pacifica Foundation Board of Directors" (February 25, 2000), p.1.

30 *Pacifica: Radio with Vision Since 1949* (Pacifica Foundation brochure, 1996), pp.13-23.

31 Susan J. Douglas, *Inventing American Broadcasting* (Baltimore: John Hopkins University Press, 1987), p.320.

32 Robert W. McChesney, *Rich Media, Poor Democracy: Communications Politics in Dubious Times* (Urbana: University of Illinois Press, 1999), p.247.

33 It is now called the Claremont Graduate University, but I like the old name better.

34 Steve Lopez, "This Just In, We're Fired," *Time* (January 29, 2001), p.6; Evelyn Nieves, "Ever a Voice of Protest, Radio KPFA Is at It Again, but with a Twist," *The New York Times* (June 30, 1999), p.12; Bharati Sadasiviam, "Morning Sedition": http://www.villagevoice.com/issues/0103/sadasivam.php.

35 Lorenzo Milam, *Sex and Broadcasting*, p.348.

CHAPTER 1

The Battle of Berkeley, 1999

> Radio B92 condemns in the strictest terms the repression and
> exertion of force against the staff of Radio KPFA and Radio
> WBAI and their listeners. Long live freedom of speech! And
> down with media repression which knows no ideological or
> national boundaries, in either Berkeley or Belgrade.
>
> STATEMENT OF SOLIDARITY FROM BANNED RADIO
> STATION B92 OF SERBIA, 1999

L ynn Chadwick had reached the height of her career when she
took the job of executive director for the Pacifica Foundation in
1998. A short, bustling persona, brimming with energy, over two
decades Chadwick had climbed from community radio station
volunteer in the Washington, D.C., area to president of the National
Federation of Community Broadcasters, a consortium of over one
hundred community radio frequencies across the United States. In
the course of this journey she had developed a close working
relationship with the Corporation for Public Broadcasting (CPB), a
semi-governmental agency which gave Pacifica millions of dollars in
the 1990s. It also gave Chadwick its Edward R. Murrow Award in
1995 for "transforming the [NFCB] into an industry leader." At least
on resume paper, Lynn Chadwick in charge of Pacifica made sense.
As executive director, she would enjoy more formal authority than
any in the history of the organization. Her national office would
manage a budget that had, since the 1970s, grown to almost six

times its original size as a percentage of the organization's wealth. It employed more personnel than ever before, including communications, development, and human resources directors and supporting staff.[1]

Equally important, Chadwick could count on the backing of a new, streamlined Pacifica board of directors, whose principals had recently changed the foundation's bylaws to become a self-selecting body, eliminating mandatory appointments from the network's five station local advisory boards (LABS). To top it all off, now chairing the Pacifica board was one of the most prominent progressives in American life, Dr. Mary Frances Berry of the United States Civil Rights Commission. Chadwick's remarks to the network at the foundation's board meeting in February of 1999 reflected her confidence and her determination to move forward. "The Strategic Plan directs us to take Pacifica to a different place." she concluded. "The culture of the organization must change as well. Clarity on the mission will provide the stability to support the organization through the changes to come. Everyone is aware of the changing communications environment. Our challenge is to fulfill the mission of Pacifica better than ever in a world where our programming will become increasingly precious."[2]

By all conventional measures of institutional power, Lynn Chadwick and Mary Frances Berry should have been able to take Pacifica to that different place. They should have been able to review personnel, hire and fire as they saw fit, and lead the organization toward the vision outlined in its recently issued Strategic Plan: a centralized, integrated network generating original and diverse national programming for the country's community radio system and beyond.

But Pacifica did not operate according to such measures. Although the network had grown over the years and the formal governance structure of the organization had centralized, the essential political economy of the network remained the same. The Pacifica Foundation did not, like other foundations, bestow money upon others. Instead it took money from the organization's five radio stations, which raised funds by selling noncommercial radio to their respective listener-subscribers. While legal power rested in the hands of a newly centralized board, the actual economic basis of the organization remained the listener-subscribers and station staff, the former constantly hearing from the latter during fund-raising marathons that Pacifica radio belonged to them. Indeed, the Strategic Plan's introduction referred to the organization as "democratic communications."[3]

Chadwick and Berry had another problem. By the mid-1990s a new wave of dissidents had tapped into this democratic rhetoric to justify resistance to the gradual centralization of the organization. They pointed to the distance between Pacifica's constant paeans to free speech and its refusal to allow discussion over the radio about the dramatic transformations taking place throughout the network, as well as the contrast between the network's frequent on-air praise of democracy and its increasingly undemocratic internal practices. These critics, however, had limited success in reaching the progressive community, in part because of their unwillingness to grapple with real problems in the community radio system that had evolved at Pacifica in the 1970s and 1980s.

What would happen, however, if Pacifica took actions that alarmed and threatened central participants in the system and their allies, rather than those speaking from the margins? That is exactly what took place at KPFA in Berkeley during the summer of 1999. Pacifica made a personnel decision that alienated many of its former allies, revealing to them that although they did the work and paid the money, their voices did not count when it came to a crucial question: the choice of general manager for Pacifica's first radio station. Faced with the resultant uproar, the formal governors of the foundation acted rigidly, continuing with their plans as if they had encountered some momentary bad weather. They stubbornly refused to acknowledge that whoever legally controlled the institution, actual power was broadly dispersed. In the crisis that ensued, they exposed stark contradictions within the network and convinced thousands of Pacificans who had not been involved in earlier struggles that radical steps would have to be taken to resolve them.

Best Wishes

Nicole Sawaya went through a six-month probationary period when she was first hired as KPFA's general manager (GM). A bright, gregarious, second-generation Lebanese-American in her mid-40s, Sawaya had made a splash as general manager of community radio station KZYX in Mendocino, had worked for National Public Radio, and had been recruited as KPFA's general manager before Chadwick came on board. Sawaya's next employment contract took her to the end of October 1998. Shortly before that deadline, Mary Frances Berry met with her and explained that all five Pacifica station managers would receive new contracts, but only for six months. A new executive director had not been hired, and Berry wanted the next director to be able to negotiate his or her own agreements. "Well," Sawaya told Berry, "I'm a little reluctant to sign it because, you know, what guarantee do I have that there's a job after this?" According to Sawaya, Berry told her not to worry. "I remember her words distinctly," Sawaya later explained. "'It's just pro forma. Everybody's at the same level.'"[4]

And so the months went by, Sawaya managed KPFA, and she and the staff quickly developed a good rapport with each other. Sawaya became intricately involved in the daily coming and goings of the station. "She was good on the air," news director Aileen Alfandary later recalled. "She was really involved. You know, on fund drives she was everywhere-on the air, in the phone room." Sawaya even helped the news department broadcast its live election-night coverage, something no manager had done for decades. Charming and articulate, she won over listeners . Unlike the station's last two general managers, Sawaya seemed to enjoy KPFA for what it was at least as much as for what it could be turned into. For that she won the staff's undying gratitude. "The morale around the station had been pretty low before Nicole came on board," Alfandary remembered. "It instantly went way up."[5]

But Pacifica did not approve of this new era of good feelings. According to Sawaya, the previous executive director, Pat Scott, had told her to clean house, to fire three senior staff at the station, Jim Bennett and Michael Yoshida of engineering, and development director Amina Hassan – the first two most likely because they had quarreled with the national office over Pacifica's satellite distribution system. Sawaya refused to sack anyone. "I said, I'm not a hatchet woman," she told Scott. "I'll come to my own conclusions."[6] Sawaya also fought with Pacifica over the station's budget. During a 1998 national board meeting she outraged the national office and much of the governing board by suggesting that if station budget cuts were necessary, KPFA could tighten its belt by reducing its annual tithe to the Pacifica national office, perhaps even by declining national programming. By Scott's final days in office, she wanted to fire Sawaya, who had been her own choice for KPFA's general manager. "I thought [Sawaya] really went in and stirred up what was already stirrable within KPFA staff and said, 'I'm one of you guys,'" Scott explained.[7] These tensions were obvious to KPFA staff. Although Scott later denied that she wanted more firings[8], the perception at the time that Sawaya stood between them and a personnel blood bath quickly spread.

Then Scott stepped down and Chadwick took over as executive director. Sawaya's next contract expiration date, March 31, 1999, neared. She started calling the other managers to find out whether they had heard anything about their agreements. They told her that none of them had, from which she summoned some optimism. "It's just Pacifica," she told herself, referring to the organization's famous inertia.

Sawaya's staff at KPFA, however, became increasingly nervous. Key personnel at the station had sent Pacifica a statement urging Sawaya's renewal, but had not received a response.[9] They knew that Chadwick and Sawaya had a long history of conflict going back to the days of the Healthy Station Project, a Corporation for Public Broadcasting initiative to refurbish community radio stations. Second-tier management at KPFA – assistant manager Phil Osegueda, business manager Meigan Devlin, the news department's Mark Mericle and Aileen Alfandary – constantly checked in with their boss to see whether anyone at Pacifica had mentioned Sawaya's contract. She bravely assured them that everything would be fine, and busied herself with preparations for KPFA's fiftieth anniversary celebration on April 15.[10]

March 31 found Sawaya in her office talking with KPFA producer Cheryl Flowers about upcoming events. Around 4 p.m. she noticed Chadwick and assistant Cheryl Garner-Shaw hanging around the KPFA office kitchen. "Well, maybe I'd better go," Flowers suggested. As soon as Flowers departed, Chadwick appeared at Sawaya's door. "May we come in?" she asked. As Sawaya tells the story, the pair sat down in front of Sawaya's desk and, after a brief pause, explained their purpose.

"We've decided not to renew your contract," Chadwick said, avoiding eye contact. "Here," she continued, and handed Sawaya a form that offered a month's severance pay in exchange for her forfeiting the right to sue the organization. "We wish you success in your future endeavors," it concluded.[11]

Sawaya stared at the document in that moment of shock that comes before disappointment and then shame. "Can I ask why?" she asked Chadwick.

"Because you are not a good fit for the organization," Chadwick said, then looked at Garner-Shaw.

KPFA's now ex-general manager returned the form to Chadwick. "I'm not going to sign this."

That apparently did not please the executive director. "You have an hour to get your stuff out," Chadwick declared. "I'm going to come back in an hour, and I want you out."

"Thank you," Sawaya snarled. "Now *you* can get out."

And with that Chadwick and her factotum left the building. In need of a friend, Sawaya staggered into the newsroom to give news co-director Alfandary the bad tidings. Alfandary saw the expression on Sawaya's face and immediately suspected the worst. "My contract wasn't renewed," Sawaya said. "I was let go."

Alfandary's eyes flared, as they always did when something displeased her. She stood up. "The hell you are," she said. "The *hell* you are! You are not leaving!" Her voice, that of someone who rarely shouted, functioned as a fire bell throughout the station. KPFA staff rushed to the second floor to hear Sawaya's story. Alfandary had already heard enough. She began telling her volunteers to make phone calls to station allies.

"Somebody get a tape recorder," Alfandary instructed. "This is going on the evening news."[12]

Things Fall Apart

Everyone at some point winds up in the wrong place at the wrong time. It was the fate of Lynn Chadwick to wind up there for a very long time. "We have to stop the rudeness, the bullying, the you-can't-tell-me-what-to-do attitude," she had lectured the Pacifica board at its last meeting.[13] For the next year Chadwick would apply all the lessons she had learned in public and community radio to Pacifica – stick to your guns, don't let people intimidate you, show resolve – and none of them would work. Quite the contrary, they would backfire with the most spectacular results, starting on March 31, 1999.

Chadwick returned in an hour, as she promised she would, to make sure Sawaya had packed her bags. By then notices had appeared around the station announcing a union meeting to discuss Sawaya's dismissal. Witnesses saw Garner-Shaw ripping down the signs, and staff angrily warned that she violated union rules by so doing. Meanwhile Chadwick marched up to Sawaya's office. "Are you getting your stuff out?" she demanded. "Yes," Sawaya replied, fighting back tears. "Just leave me alone."[14]

But as the executive director turned away, the station descended upon her. A news department staff person thrust a microphone in her face, asking for a statement. Susan Stone of the drama and literature department began following her about. "We've got to talk," she pleaded. Station engineer Jim Bennett and music department director Chuy Varela approached her. "So who is going to be the KPFA manager?" Varela asked. "I guess I will be now," Chadwick replied, according to Bennett. That was not what the KPFA staff wanted to hear. Between the departure of the previous manager and the hiring of Sawaya, Chadwick had served as interim general manager. In that brief time she dismissed no fewer than four people, including Bari Scott, head of the Third World department.[15] A bigger crowd gathered, demanding an explanation. Chadwick would have none of it. A decision had been made, and that was that. "No, I'm going back into the offi-", she declared, and unable to finish her sentence, fled the KPFA building.[16]

Aileen Alfandary and a few other staff members, however, followed her down the block and knocked on the door of the Pacifica national office. Chadwick's assistants cracked open the entrance. Then Chadwick herself peeped through the opening, refusing to let anyone in. Was it true, KPFA staff asked, that Sawaya had been dismissed? Yes, Chadwick replied. Would Pacifica consider rescinding the decision? No, she insisted.

"You know," Alfandary then said, "I may have to cover this as a news story."[17]

With that, she returned to her office and called several national board members to tell them what had happened, among them June Makela and Berkeley Congressmember Ron Dellums's assistant Roberta Brooks. According to Alfandary, neither of them knew of the decision not to renew Sawaya's contract. Brooks seemed sympathetic to the dismissal. Makela just wanted to get off the telephone. "I did tell Roberta that this was a very bad decision and it really needed to be reversed and there was going to be trouble," Alfandary recalled later.[18]

Hanging up the phone, Alfandary then returned to Chadwick's office for another attempt at an interview. Chadwick asked her why she thought this would not be a violation of the network's dirty-laundry rule. The phone rang and the executive director turned to answer it. Alfandary gave up and went back to KPFA.

Shortly after she returned, someone handed her a fresh memorandum from the Pacifica national office. "I am directing you not to air a story about Nicole's termination," Chadwick wrote. "This is not a news story. Airing this story would be a violation of Pacifica policy."[19] The communiqué intimidated some staff. Several approached the news department and urged caution. Bennett feared that the move would displease Pacifica and make subsequent negotiations more difficult.[20] But Chadwick's memo only made Alfandary angrier. "After a 20-year career at KPFA, I was not going to let the likes of Lynn Chadwick tell us what to broadcast or not to broadcast," she later explained.[21] She quickly convinced her colleagues to support the disclosure. What if the *San Francisco Chronicle* ran a piece about the firing the next day? she worried. "I knew it was going to be a big story, although I didn't know how big. We had to do it."[22]

And so, shortly after 6 p.m., the *KPFA Evening News* broadcast a feature about the dismissal. A glum Nicole Sawaya drove across the Bay Bridge and tuned in to the station. "In a move that sent shock waves through KPFA," Alfandary told listeners, "the Executive Director of Pacifica today fired general manager Nicole Sawaya. Sawaya says she was shocked and dismayed." The item mentioned that the news department had been warned not to run the story.[23]

Thousands of people heard the news that night. "Jaws dropped all over northern California," as one journalist later put it.[24] And when they stopped dropping, their owners started phoning. This act of protest had not come from some disgruntled ex-programmer. It had come from the senior staff of the station. More specifically, it had come from the news department, whose training program had hundreds of graduates throughout the Bay Area, many now working elsewhere as reporters, or, as in the case of KPFA local advisory board chair Sherry Gendelman, as an attorney. During her tenure as head of the advisory board, Gendelman had become a fan of Sawaya's. Gendelman began calling practically every progressive lawyer she knew, looking for someone who could handle a lawsuit.[25] Then she rushed to KPFA, as did dozens of local activists. Within an hour of the KPFA news story, I had received a flurry of messages on my answering machine. "[BEEP] Matthew, they've fired Nicole. Please call me. [BEEP] Matt, are you there? I can't believe they could be this stupid. Did you hear about Sawaya? [BEEP] Hi Matt. They've canned Nicole. Call out the troops!"[26]

Once the news department had broken the story, KPFA hosts declared the matter open season for on-air discussion and editorial comment. Feature reporter Wendell Harper devoted part of his 7 p.m. public affairs show to the controversy, as did Grateful Dead aficionado David Gans, whose 8 p.m. *Dead to the World* easily counted as one of KPFA's most popular music shows. Gans quickly brushed aside Chadwick's warning about airing the matter. "I don't see that there's much of a point in protecting these sons of bitches anymore," he declared.[27] With that the matter went to bed for the evening, at least as far as the station on-air staff were concerned. The Pacifica national office closed shop. KPFA personnel and activists scurried off to nearby restaurants for long meetings.

Unfortunately, someone with a gun decided to drop by. At 11 p.m. that night he or she fired into Pacifica's storefront windows. Shards of glass splayed into the office. A large window frame collapsed onto a desk. The office was empty; no one was hurt.[28] The police never found the shooter. But the assault suggested to everyone that the controversy could easily spin out of control.

As Alfandary had anticipated, the press quickly picked up on this social-explosion-in-progress. *San Francisco Chronicle* investigative reporter Phillip Matier, a dedicated Deadhead, listened to David Gans regularly. On Friday, April 2, the subject of Gans's diatribe found its way into Matier's regular column, shared with colleague Andrew Ross. "Big Ruckus at Free-Speech Radio Station After Boss' Ouster," ran the headline. Like many reporters, Matier and Ross sympathized with the news department's defiance of the gag order. "Not a smart thing to say to free speechers," they commented. "No sooner than you could say 'Birkenstock,' the news department bucked the bosses and went on the air with the story." The article obviously sided with KPFA. "[S]taffers and volunteers have felt they've been getting squeezed as more and more money and resources are siphoned off to support the foundation's growing bureaucracy." As for the shooting, the team sympathized with Pacifica – sort of. "Although Pacifica spokeswoman Elan Fabbri declined to discuss Sawaya's removal, she was eager to talk about the gunshots. 'It's hard to believe that it was just a coincidence,' Fabbri said, adding that the shooting 'was the real story here.'" Matier and Ross obviously thought otherwise. Their piece ended with a public service announcement: "Next up in the saga: A noon rally today at the station to protest the manager's firing."[29]

KPFA's staff had already issued a statement protesting Sawaya's dismissal, demanding her rehiring, and calling for mediation. "How high is the cost that national management is willing to pay" for autocratic control of the network? their petition asked. "The fund-raising capabilities, the goodwill, and favorable publicity from KPFA's 50th anniversary celebration lie in ruins." With that, about 150 people gathered in front of Pacifica for the rally the *San Francisco Chronicle* had so kindly publicized. Pacifica's national affairs correspondent, Larry Bensky, had already read the writing on the wall. A big, shaggy haired man in his 60s who had been associated with KPFA for many years, Bensky was one of the first speakers. "If, in the coming days, you should miss the voices you're used to hearing," he told his supporters, "know that it's not voluntary."[30]

By now Chadwick realized that she had to come up with some kind of response to the upheaval her decision had provoked. For the most part, she faced the problem alone. In the early days of the crisis, Mary Frances Berry made little effort to help her beyond a comment to a reporter defending the removal of Sawaya. "As executive director, [Chadwick] has a right to have staff there that she is comfortable with," Berry told the *Oakland Tribune* on April 2. "She didn't feel that Nicole was helping her make the administrative and staffing changes. And if Lynn doesn't achieve these goals, she'll be out the door. It's that simple."[31]

Unfortunately, things were now anything but simple for Pacifica's executive director. Without risking a lawsuit, she could not candidly explain over the airwaves exactly why she had dismissed Sawaya. Her assistant Fabbri even conceded this to reporters. "The problem [is] we're so limited in what we can say, by our own lawyers," she told Jacqueline Conciatore of *Current*, the magazine about public broadcasting.[32] In addition, Chadwick's own policy regarding the airing of dirty laundry put her in a bind. The most effective way to counter KPFA staff's on-air pronouncements would have been to go on the air herself. But by doing so, she would be violating the very rule she had warned Alfandary against ignoring. Nonetheless, Chadwick ordered KPFA staff to repeatedly broadcast her prerecorded statement about the controversy. "We have made decisions that reflect the best management practices for the organization, regardless of their popularity," she declared over KPFA's airwaves, adding that "internal Pacifica issues and management decisions are not news." It is not appropriate, she insisted, "for KPFA to use airtime to voice internal grievances, nor should a parent organization such as Pacifica use airtime to counter such grievances."[33] Thus Chadwick broke her own policy-and paid the price. "That's when we said to ourselves, well, she has now justified us talking about it, because she's doing it herself," Jim Bennett later explained.[34]

But it was the executive director's often legalistic approach to the crisis that did the most damage to her case. Chadwick and Fabbri, for example, repeatedly insisted to reporters and protestors that Nicole Sawaya had not been fired. "Ms. Sawaya was not fired," a standard email reply from Fabbri explained; "her one-year contract expired on March 31st and it was not renewed."[35] Doubtless the few management lawyers who paid attention to Pacifica politics heartily approved of this correction, but it missed the point. The KPFA community had not hit the streets over a matter of lexicon; whether Sawaya had been "fired" or "not renewed," they wanted her back. That, as Fabrri and Chadwick surely understood, was the real issue, even as they prepared to make matters worse.

The weekend arrived, bringing Larry Bensky's recently inaugurated two-hour show, *Sunday Salon* – broadcast on that day from 9 a.m. to 11 a.m. Bensky spent most of it on the crisis in Yugoslavia, then reserved the last nineteen minutes for the crisis unfolding around him at his radio station. He started out by rebroadcasting Chadwick's canned communiqué of April 2, and he read the staff's petition demanding the reinstatement of Sawaya.[36]

Pacifica responded quickly to this commentary. The following Friday Bensky received notice that *Sunday Salon* had been cancelled. Pacifica's press release cited "Mr. Bensky's April 4th on-air attack of Pacifica Radio Foundation and members of its management" as cause for dismissal, denouncing it as "a direct violation of Pacifica policy, as well as his AFTRA union contract, both of which prohibit airing personal grievances on the air." It is difficult to imagine what Chadwick thought this would accomplish. With Bensky sacked, KPFA's staff completely circled the wagons; every half-hour, whoever ran the station studio board read a one-page statement denouncing Pacifica and calling for the rehiring of both Bensky and Sawaya. The entire staff now refused to honor what they dubbed "the gag rule." Bensky sued Pacifica for wrongful dismissal.[37]

A Half-Century of Gagging

With the firing of Larry Bensky for violating the "gag rule," many questions emerged. Who invented this policy? Was it Pacifica founder Lewis Hill? Had it always been in effect? The stakes regarding the controversy became clear. If the rule had a past at Pacifica, why had KPFA staffers ignored it now? Not surprisingly, KPFA's public institutional memory regarding the policy suddenly headed for the hills. Programmers now represented the dictum as an autocratic whim unexpectedly inflicted upon the station staff. "They claim it's a 30-year-old policy," news department co-director Mark Mericle told a reporter. "It's barely a rumor to me. It's not in the Pacifica employee handbook, it's not in our union contract." Other programmers questionably asserted their First Amendment right to say whatever they wished over the airwaves, when, in fact, the First Amendment only enjoins the government, not the supervisors of non-government-owned radio stations, from interfering with speech.[38]

Privately, however, most senior staff at KPFA knew the truth. The soundness of the gag rule had been self-evident to them and to others throughout the organization for decades. "At KPFK it is tantamount to dismissal to go on the air and bad-mouth the station or personnel," read the Pacifica governing board minutes of June 22, 1974. "Free speech does not mean you surrender your judgment about what is good radio. WBAI also has a firm policy about air attacks – the offender is subject to dismissal."[39] Throughout the 1990s, most KPFA staff had faithfully enforced the gag rule, infuriating station dissidents. But there were good reasons for the dictum.

Past Pacificans feared allowing unchecked on-air discussion of Pacifica policies, for three reasons. First, the network invited private lawsuits if programmers engaged in slander or publicly disclosed why other programmers had been fired, suspended, or demoted. Second, without restraint, some hosts would inevitably urge their listeners to write to station management demanding that the programmer in question receive more air time, or better equipment, or some other benefit. Zen writer Alan Watts inaugurated this brazen practice in the 1950s on KPFA, concluding a lecture by asking his devoted fans to send money to the station for a better tape recorder for the spiritualist's personal use.[40] Finally, such talk could spread across a station like a virus – the critical on-air comments of one programmer provoking counter-responses from colleagues, leading to endless on-air chatter about controversies that were, after all, far less important than the course of local, national, or world events.

Ironically, no story better illustrated the organization's long-standing fealty to the gag rule than one from the days when Larry Bensky himself served as KPFA's general manager. On January 8, 1977, programmer Jeff Echeverria and two others walked into the station's control room and began broadcasting what Bensky later described as "a series of personal commentary concerning KPFA, personal histories of the station, and a series of demands concerning KPFA." In quick response, Bensky sent a directive to all KPFA staff, the local advisory board, and the Pacifica national office. He called the broadcast "completely contrary to the general interest" of the station. "At no point was an offer made to express contrary views nor was a disclaimer made indicating that the viewpoint expressed was that of disappointed job seekers." Echeverria and his fellow broadcasters were banned from KPFA, Bensky's memo declared, except with explicit permission from the general manager to enter the premises – in other words, from himself. Not only that, but henceforth the scheduling of all station board operators would be centralized under the authority of the production director and the station manager.

And to any who still doubted that Bensky meant business, he disclosed that Pacifica's attorneys were pursuing criminal and civil charges against the alleged malefactors, for "slander and contempt of court."[41] Pacifica official Peter Franck backed these actions up two days later, instructing Bensky in a memorandum to "see to it that the Station Control Board is operated, at all times, by persons who will not divert from scheduled programming and who will not cooperate with any attempt at unauthorized activity." In the event that anyone tried something like Echeverria's offense again, Franck's letter continued, "you are instructed to take all necessary steps to maintain control of the air including, if necessary, termination of broadcasting." A Federal Communications Commission rule hovered over these instructions, requiring the owners of radio licenses to demonstrate consistent control over their air sound, although no outburst of a cranky station programmer had ever resulted in the loss or suspension of a Pacifica license.[42]

But with Chadwick's dismissal of Bensky and her threats to the news department, all this history suddenly went up in smoke. Why?

The answer is that the gag rule functioned, like every rule, as a covenant between those who made it and those who obeyed it. All parties knew that, whatever the organization's bylaws said about governance, whoever controlled the airwaves truly controlled the fate of the network. Depending on how much and what kinds of information they meted out about the institution's affairs, Pacifica senior staff could either induce the listeners to accept the status quo or incite them to revolt. Most of the time, Pacifica on-air hosts abstained from the second choice, because the organization formally or informally dealt them and the communities they served into the decision-making process. But, as we shall see in subsequent chapters, over the past half-decade governance had pretty much been taken out of the hands of everyone save the national office and the national board. The local advisory boards had been neutralized. The volunteer staff – a majority of the programmers at most of the stations – had been removed from station collective-bargaining agreements. Forums for discussing controversial questions about Pacifica policy, such as the station *Folio*, had been discontinued. And now Pacifica asserted its right to remove the station general manager against the wishes of almost everyone else involved.

The covenant had been broken, so the old rules no longer applied. In that context, KPFA's staff acted logically in abandoning past arrangements and reaching for their most potent weapon. "There was the feeling that we were powerless," Jim Bennett recalled. "That all we had were our voices and that we were going to make people aware of what was going on." Outside the KPFA building, listeners had no knowledge of the gag rule's history. They simply wanted to hear discussion over the airwaves about the changes taking place at their station.[43] With the dismissal of Sawaya and Bensky, Pacifica had inaugurated a free-for-all power struggle, a fight that KPFA's senior staff gradually realized they could not win alone.

The Indispensable Woman

Although often seen by Pacifica's top brass during this period as institutional rascals, KPFA's twenty-odd salaried programmers and administrators were, in truth, reluctant troublemakers. They had, for the most part, supported the centralizing direction in which Pacifica's leaders had taken the organization over the last decade. After a brief flurry of outrage in the first week of April, they became increasingly anxious to settle their dispute with Pacifica with as few words, meetings, and pyrotechnics as possible. But as Chadwick's stance hardened, it became clear to them that they needed to reach out to the larger community for help. Unfortunately, the activist listeners whose assistance they now sought deeply resented what they saw as their collaborations with Pacifica over the previous five years. KPFA's paid staff had removed volunteer staff from their collective bargaining agreements, accepted the purging of many collective programs in the mid-1990s, and even helped Pacifica write parts of its Strategic Plan. Most important, throughout this period they had supported the gag rule, steadfastly refusing to open KPFA's airwaves to discussions that might have publicly revealed the extent to which Pacifica had centralized the organization and dealt other groups out of governance.

Within the station, however, a few programmers now pushed for a strategy of outreach, particularly Sunday folk-music host Robbie Osman, who had opposed the direction the station had taken in recent years. But in their initial meetings with activist listeners, the paid staff found negotiations slow going and tense. "They [the listeners] kept fearing or thinking that the union would sell them out," KPFA news co-director and union steward Mark Mericle later recalled.[44] Few of these non-staff players, however, possessed the organizing skills and resources necessary to reframe the fight as something bigger than a labor/management dispute. Into this void stepped one of the Bay Area's most formidable radical organizers.

If the city of Berkeley cultivated a love/hate relationship with any single resident, it had to have been with Barbara Lubin. Born in 1941 to a conservative German-Jewish family, Lubin's accent still hinted at the solid middle-class Philadelphia roots she had dedicated her life to repudiating. As a teenager she couldn't wait for the '60s, so she dropped out of high school at age 15 and had two children. Outraged by the Vietnam war, she took up draft counseling. Frustrated by her lack of progress in convincing young men to refuse the draft, she persuaded one of her inductees to let her go to his physical as him. Lubin showed up for the exam in drag with the man's papers. "I actually crammed a whole lot of flyers into my pants," she recalled, "and when they told us to strip down in the draft board – there were about seventy-five young men and myself – we all stripped, and I started leafletting and counseling the young guys there." The boys laughed. The enraged draft board summoned a gaggle of GIs, who literally fixed bayonets and dragged the half-undressed Lubin out of the room. One draftee followed them and refused to enlist. From this victory the young anti-war activist drew her first and last principle of organizing – anything is possible; just try it and see what happens.[45]

In 1973 the Lubin family switched coasts and settled in a Berkeley neighborhood called Elmwood. By then she had four children, her boy Charlie born with Down's syndrome. "I was unhappy to be at home, and yet I hadn't gone to school, and I felt like I didn't know what I wanted to do with my life." Like all overworked mothers, she sought and cherished comfortable routines. Every day Charlie spent the late afternoon in a nearby soda fountain named Ozzie's. He would order a tuna sandwich, chips, and a Coke and converse happily with Ozzie, the proprietor. A simple pleasure for Charlie, two hours off for his mom.[46]

But on a July afternoon in 1981, Charlie came home with bad news. "Ozzie's has been sold!" he said. Lubin ran around the corner and to her horror discovered the news was true. Speculators had bought the building and planned to raise the rent by 400 percent. Panicked at the prospect of losing her impromptu day-care center, she ran home and called the buyer. "You don't know me, my name's Barbara Lubin," she began. "I have a son who's retarded, he's just a little boy, and he eats at Ozzie's every day. I need this soda fountain to stay there." Without the vaguest idea of how to follow through, she offered to buy back the pharmacy at a profit for the buyer. He laughed. "You must think I'm crazy, that I would give up a deal like this for some crazy woman and her retarded son."

Lubin became furious. "[Y]ou have just made the biggest mistake of your life," she declared. "You will *never* develop that property, ever."[47]

And he never did. Within two weeks, under the banner of "Save Ozzie," she organized 400 people into the Elmwood Preservation Alliance. The Alliance raised $8,000, hired legal consultants, and launched an initiative drive for the first commercial rent-control ordinance in the United States since World War II. Berkeley speculators and landlords overwhelmed the city with propaganda against the proposal. *The Wall Street Journal* published a feature story about the controversy. The statute won 73 percent of the vote.[48]

From then on, Lubin's political career functioned as an extension of her parental life. After years of fighting for special education for Charlie, she ran for and won a seat on the Berkeley school board, just in time to learn that the district owed millions of dollars. To the horror of the city's upper class, Lubin closed four schools in the affluent Berkeley hills. She further enraged voters by serving on a commission that pushed for low-income housing units in middle-class neighborhoods. She had an affair with the mayor of Berkeley, who also happened to be a member of the Communist Party. She organized a Jewish committee for Jesse Jackson's 1984 presidential campaign, just before the disclosure of his infamous "hymie-town" remark. Not satisfied with these assorted transgressions, in the late 1980s Barbara Lubin turned her attentions to the Middle East.[49]

As a public official in Berkeley, Lubin was constantly being asked to sign statements on behalf of anti-imperialist movements, especially those in Nicaragua, El Salvador, and South Africa. However, having grown up in a staunch Zionist household, she had always avoided the Palestinian question. "Our first allegiance was to the state of Israel – because I was told all my life that when they came for us here, like they came for the Jews in Nazi Germany, if we kept Israel strong and secure, we would all have a safe place to go."[50] Lubin's political work, however, brought her into frequent contact with activists who bombarded her with news of the Israeli occupation. After the first Intifada, with some skepticism she agreed to join a delegation of Americans visiting the West Bank as guests of the Palestinians. What she saw there horrified her. "We were shot at, we were tear-gassed, we were body searched," she remembered; "anything that could have happened, happened."[51] With the conclusion of her stint on the school board, she threw herself into the Free Palestine movement.

Not surprisingly, Lubin focused her concerns on the fate of Palestinian children. In 1988 she and her husband, Howard Levine, founded the Middle East Children's Alliance (MECA), a humanitarian organization dedicated to helping families on the West Bank and the Gaza Strip. Over the next decade the group's delegations delivered over five million dollars in food, medicine, and toys to Occupied Palestine. MECA volunteers built dozens of playgrounds, sports fields, and recreation centers for Palestinian schools. Most important, MECA activists took upon themselves the difficult task of educating the American public – and especially American Jewry – about the realities of life for Palestinian families.[52] As with everything she did, Lubin went all the way. "I don't walk the line," she later explained. "I believe the only way to peace is to end the occupation and for Palestinians to have a state within the '67 borders and East Jerusalem is their capital and all settlements out of the West Bank and Gaza and the right of return. However that is worked out."[53]

In the course of building this philanthropic movement, Lubin found herself increasingly dependent upon a nearby listener-supported radio station. "My connection with KPFA was that it was the only place where I could go and speak about what's happening to Palestinians," she said. "And KPFA took a lot of heat for it, for many years."[54] KPFA announced MECA fund-raising events and often co-sponsored them; its programmers interviewed members of MECA delegations when they returned from the Middle East. Its drive-time programmers, especially Dennis Bernstein, host of KPFA's 5 p.m. show *Flashpoints*, gave consistently sympathetic coverage to pro-Palestinian activists. And its just-deposed general manager, Nicole Sawaya, was a Lebanese-American sympathetic to the Palestinian cause. Robbie Osman sat on MECA's board and played a prominent role in its activities. By March 31, 1999, KPFA had become an indispensable resource for the Middle East Children's Alliance. It was in that context that Lubin, listening to the KPFA news that evening, learned of Sawaya's dismissal. "Something snapped in me," she recalled, "and I realized that this is a battle that I was going to fight."[55]

For Barbara Lubin, here was Ozzie's soda fountain all over again-something she felt she urgently needed to make her life work. For the next three years this parallel played itself out on a daily basis.

The Pacifica national office and board would see Lubin much as did Ozzie's landlord, that is, as a crazy woman to whom they had no obligations. They did not understand that she was one of the most powerful people in Berkeley, that she ran a nonprofit with influential friends around the world, or that in order to support her work she also ran a graphics and direct mailing company which would repeatedly raise tens of thousands of dollars and put the money into posters, t-shirts, concert benefits, strike funds, and just about anything else the KPFA community needed.

But Lubin exacted a price for this support. She forced the senior staff at KPFA to open up the fight to precisely those forces inside and outside the building that they had for years held at arm's length: the unpaid staff and the dissident groups, now recruiting dozens of new members every day. In their protest statement following Sawaya's dismissal, KPFA's staff had demanded mediation "by a respected independent outside group or individual subject to the mutual approval of KPFA *paid* staff and the Pacifica national board [italics added]."[56] Lubin immediately recognized this for what it was, a shortsighted attempt to narrowly define authority at the station – a blunder that would allow Pacifica to frame the fight as nothing more than a labor dispute.

"The way I see it," Lubin later explained, "this is a community radio station, and this belongs to all of us. Not to the union and the people in the union, or anybody in the station, to tell you the truth."[57] She insisted that any negotiating committee organized to deal with Pacifica include not only paid staff and management, but representatives from the station volunteers, the major donors, and the listener-subscribers. Long-standing KPFA dissidents like Jeff Blankfort, who had played a key role in Pacifica struggles in the mid-1990s, respected Lubin, largely because of her activism concerning the Middle East. Invariably serving as emcee at the frequent demonstrations held in front of KPFA's doors, Barbara Lubin was to function as a bridge between the station's now de-facto management and the social movement exploding around them.

Happy Birthday, KPFA

If ever a natural organizing opportunity presented itself to the KPFA community, it occurred on April 15, 1999: the station's fiftieth anniversary on the air. Intended as a day of fund-raising and celebration for Pacifica, it became instead an afternoon of cheerful mobilization against the license owner. By then all of the station's major donors had withdrawn from Pacifica's Fiftieth Anniversary Committee, most significantly Bay Area philanthropist Alice Hamburg.[58] Many of them instead began writing checks for Lubin and Osman's newly formed group, Friends of Free Speech Radio. By the time I arrived at the station that day, about 1,500 people had gathered around a flatbed truck was parked in front of the building, supporting a huge PA system. Demonstrators carried signs: "REHIRE SAWAYA AND BENSKY," read one large placard. "SAVE PACIFICA FOR THE PEOPLE NOT THE CPB ELITE."[59]

The speechifying had begun, broadcast live over KPFA. Programmer Dennis Bernstein, always ready to perform, arrived with a blue neckerchief tied over his mouth to symbolize the gag rule. He took it off to make his remarks. "A couple of weeks ago," he began, "[t]hey fired Nicole Sawaya, a manager who came into this station and unified us, brought us together, cared about our needs, took us seriously. " The audience applauded warmly.

"To describe the limits of free speech," he continued, "they always use that example of [yelling] fire in a crowded theater. Right? But if there is a fire in that theater and you do not speak up, you must bear the responsibility. Are we going to speak up?"

"Yes!" the crowd responded.

"We believe in free speech radio," Bernstein declared.

"FREE SPEECH RADIO! FREE SPEECH RADIO!" they chanted in response.

Maudelle Shirek, the 87-year-old African-American vice mayor of Berkeley and close political ally of Lubin, stood prominently in the audience, waiting her turn to speak.

"Good afternoon," she told the crowd, sounding like a third grade teacher.

"Good afternoon," the audience chanted back, suddenly sounding like third grade students.

"My name is Maudelle Shirek," she declared, then waited for the cheering to stop. "And for almost fifty years I have been waking up and going to sleep with KPFA on my radio.... Instead of celebrating 50 years of community radio, we are here to stop the takeover of KPFA!"

Next came the station's music director, Chuy Varela, who pointed emphatically at the demonstrators. "You are the lifeblood of KPFA!" he cried out. "Give yourselves a big, big 'Viva!'"

After they did, he continued, "Today it is important for us to recognize that we work for you!" and the crowd chanted "Si, se puede!" [60]

But not everyone came with unequivocal praise for KPFA and condemnation for Pacifica. Ex-Soviet affairs program host William Mandel, dismissed from his program four years earlier for discussing station policy over the air, took the mike. "I would like you to remember," Mandel admonished the suddenly quieter audience, "that the first person to be canned for violating the gag rule was myself. At this moment you are suffering from that in a very concrete form.... While the job at this moment is for all of us to back the staff totally without reservation, without conditions, in putting this station back in our hands, there are other things that we have to look into and all stay active about so it does not take only an atrocity like this to bring out this stupendous crowd."[61]

With that said, the parameters of the struggle were made clear. In order to preserve its institutional autonomy, KPFA would reopen itself to the community and plead for support. Its paid staff and volunteers would nail "free speech" to the masthead and insist that they worked for the people whom they now encouraged to mobilize. But the community to which they appealed had a long memory, its participants anxious to look into the "other things" to which Mandel referred: the closing down of the station *Folio*, the general downgrading of volunteer programmers, and the purging, four years earlier, of a dozen collective shows without listener-subscriber input. In a very real sense, KPFA's senior staff would now find themselves negotiating with two groups: one, their legal employers, the Pacifica national office and board; the other, the people whom they publicly insisted represented the "lifeblood" of the network, the listener-subscribers. For whom did they really work? That became the central question.

Meanwhile, Lynn Chadwick continued to take actions suggesting that she had little sense of the gravity and complexity of the situation unfolding around her, continuously offering legalistic explanations for actions that shocked the KPFA community. The next day she appeared on Pacifica's flagship show, Amy Goodman's Democracy Now! Goodman's other guests were communications historian Ralph Engelman, who had chaired WBAI's local advisory board in the 1970s, and me. The formal purpose of the show was to celebrate Pacifica's fiftieth anniversary on the air. The real purpose was to deal with the crisis at KPFA. During the conversation Goodman popped the obvious question, What do you think of the gag rule? Chadwick ignored the fact that we were all breaking it at the moment and explained that Pacifica's airwaves were not open to the "personal issues" of its staff:

> This gag rule – so-called gag rule – has been in place for some thirty years, and I'm sure it came about after long discussions. . . . But it's important that at Pacifica we do not allow free speech. We don't allow anti-Semitic speech. We don't allow sexist speech. We don't allow racist speech. That's important to us. And those values we want to convey to our listeners. So, there's reasons behind that, and I think they are core to the value of what we're talking about, in terms of what Pacifica's goal is in presenting the progressive agenda to the country.[62]

This response was technically correct. The Pacifica radio network did set limits to the extent to which its programmers could speak freely. But for tens of thousands of Pacifica listeners and supporters, "free speech" represented, not a set of violations against the rules of some bureaucrat, but a hallowed, decades-old tradition of dissent against government and corporate power. And to many of the activist listener-subscribers of the network, Chadwick's statement raised more questions than it answered. Who made these decisions? they wondered. Who put these people in charge? Chadwick did not appear to understand that practically every time she spoke in public, she further exposed and inflamed the contradictions of the organization and empowered the network's most radical elements.

The same went for Mary Frances Berry. At first she attempted to negotiate with key players via long-distance phone calls. She spoke with Alice Hamburg and the other major donors associated with the now dissolved KPFA Fiftieth Anniversary committee. But Pacifica's chairperson consistently refused to consider KPFA's key demand, the rehiring of Nicole Sawaya and Larry Bensky, and she played lawyer's hardball with everyone. Berry called me, for example, and before I could utter a word, raised the issue of the lack of diversity in KPFA's audience. "Do you realize that KPFA's audience is overwhelmingly white?" I recall her declaring. She seemed far more interested in putting me on the defensive than in figuring out how to resolve the situation at the station.[63]

Finally, on May 5, Pacifica's chairwoman gave a live on-air report to KPFA's listeners. More moderate elements at the station hoped that somehow her intervention would lead to a resolution of the crisis. Instead they received a painful audio experience. Chadwick tried to supervise the program from KPFA's studios, but despite her prior radio experience, she somehow neglected to identify herself to the listeners. All they heard from the executive director was, "Wait 'til fadeout. OK, you're on." Then Berry, who probably phoned in from somewhere around Washington, D.C., opened in a decidedly unfriendly tone. "Thanks for tuning in to KPFA tonight. I'm Mary Frances Berry, chair of the board of directors of the Pacifica Foundation. Board members serve as unpaid volunteers. I only point that out because I've been getting emails from people telling me they're paying my salary and why am I not in Berkeley going to work every day."[64]

Having set everyone straight, Berry got to the heart of the matter. You regular listeners, she began, have doubtless heard about a recent "labor dispute" at KPFA – "How could you not have heard?" she added caustically – and then began reading from a script: "On March 31st, the one-year contract of KPFA's former station manager expired, and she was told it would not be renewed. Personnel and labor laws do not allow us to share how we came to our decision not to renew the contract, but please be assured that there was a great deal of care, deliberation, and exploration of options put into the decision. And we sincerely wish her [Sawaya] the very best."[65]

That settled, at least to Berry's satisfaction, the chair launched into what was to become the party line, the larger purpose behind Pacifica's recent course: "Taken as a whole, our programmers, local advisory board members, and listeners do not reflect the rich cultural and age diversity of our country, which our mission clearly requires us to do," she explained. "We must include more people of color as programmers and on local advisory boards, and we must expand our listener base while keeping the listeners we have now, if we can, by attracting a younger and more diverse audience."[66]

Berry's tone came across as arrogant, but she was right. Every survey available suggested that older white people dominated KPFA's audience. The station's share of non-white listeners was miserable. A 1998 Arbitron-based analysis of the five Pacifica stations revealed that during the weekday hours from five a.m. through midnight, the percentage of black and Hispanic listeners could scarcely be represented on a bar graph. At some times in the day, black listeners constituted less than 1 percent of the station's drive-time audience. And the median age of those who tuned in at 9 a.m. was 43; at 5 p.m. it shot up to 50. In other words, many listeners who tuned in at those times were far older than the median.[67] Pacifica activists scoffed at Arbitron surveys, pointing out, correctly, that they had been designed for commercial rather than noncommercial stations. But even if these findings missed the mark by a factor of 200 or even 300 percent, they still indicated that KPFA had miles to go if it wanted to build a younger, more diverse listener base.

Taking Berry's lead, a small group of local documentary filmmakers and public-radio people-most of them friends of Lynn

Chadwick-organized themselves into the Diversity Coalition for Public Broadcasting. Members included Jim Yee, executive director of the Independent Television Service; Karolyn van Putten, head of Western Public Radio; independent filmmaker Rick Tejada-Flores: and former KPFA staff member Peggy Berryhill. The social composition of KPFA and its audience, they insisted in a June press release, represented the real issue:

> There is a short list of the People of Color who have attempted to bring about change from inside KPFA. Those who did were given positions, either as volunteers or with $1/4$ or $1/2$ time pay. They were often relegated to "ghettoized" departments that reflected ethnicity or gender. A few have been Training Directors or Program Directors and fewer were General Managers and Business Managers. One true thing is that all were met with overwhelming opposition when they tried to make substantive programming changes that reflected the broader culture of communities of color, women and lesbians and gays.

As a result, they argued, although KPFA reached the entire Bay Area, its broadcast style reflected the city of Berkeley:

> [T]he air sound usually reflects the Berkeley character and philosophy. As we move into the next decade we must ask ourselves the following questions: does Berkeley represent the local and regional description of diversity in appearance and philosophy? Does Berkeley represent the changing face of our national diversity?[68]

While the Diversity Coalition's basic criticism remained sound, its racially coded rhetoric drastically overstated the case. The statement falsely stereotyped Berkeley, whose populace the 1990 census had determined to be 45 percent nonwhite. It also distorted the history of diversity struggles at KPFA in the 1970s, the true nature of which some of these Diversity Coalition members knew well. As we shall see in Chapter 3, white people at KPFA had not relegated people of color to "ghettoized" departments that reflected ethnicity and gender. The latter had, for better or worse, demanded such places for themselves as zones of institutional autonomy.

In the 1990s Pacifica itself encouraged the abolition of these departments, sponsoring purges throughout the network which, as foundation insiders privately admitted to me, made these stations less diverse and undercut the foundation's credibility on the diversity question. The head of KPFA's Third World department had recently been laid off – by Lynn Chadwick, who, the Diversity Coalition conveniently forgot, had also just removed the station's first Arab-American general manager, Nicole Sawaya. Many of the purged at KPFA in 1995 had been people of color with late night, evening, or weekend shows. Pacifica encouraged these purges because of the perception that the network's air sound had become fragmented, broken down into many disconnected programs. But now those people of color who had just been dropped from the network could hardly take seriously Pacifica's renewed calls for more people of color-nor could those who had survived. "KPFA's African-American programmers will not be complicit in any Pacifica-driven purge of KPFA staffers under the guise of 'diversity,'" declared a statement by thirteen of the station's black programmers, from African studies scholar Walter Turner to hip-hop deejay David "Davy D" Cook.[69] Probably the most popular reading in Berkeley during the summer of 1999 was former KPFT programmer Rafael Renteria's online essay, "Race and Power at Pacifica Radio," in which he described in painful detail the elimination of minority activist shows at KPFA's sister station in Houston throughout the 1990s:

* There is no longer a single public affairs program rooted in the Latino community – a community that makes up fully a third of Houston's population.
* The Persian Program – founded by anti-Shah/ anti-Khomeni activists – was eliminated at a time when there was imminent danger of war between Iran and US imperialism, as the US had warships in the Persian gulf.
* The Arabic Hour – one of the most intellectually respectable programs on KPFT, was eliminated during Desert Shield – as the US prepared to go to war against Arab Iraq to seize strategic control of the world's oil supply.

* Gay programming has been significantly cut – it[']s been depoliticized – it is no longer the force – or the threat – it was when KPFT volunteer programmer Fred Paez, a high profile gay activist, was murdered by Houston Police.
* Lesbian programming has been driven off the air – including Breakthrough – a hugely popular program that was one of the station[']s highest revenue generators.
* There is now one hour of feminist programming each week.
* *Peace, Pipes and Visions*, the Native American program, is gone.
* The Atheist program is gone.
* The Viet Namese program is gone.
* The Chinese program is gone.
* The Pakistani program – gone.
* Only one Black program remains today at KPFT and an African music program.[70]

The KPFA listener community had been, for the most part, oblivious to these changes elsewhere in the network. But the firing of Sawaya and Bensky now made them receptive to a more critical look at the transformations of the last four years. Berry seemed to understand none of this. I sat at my car radio and gasped as she suggested that Pacifica must keep its current listeners, "if we can." Speaking of the listeners, Berry's audience, in the third person implied that they were superfluous to the future of the station – this at a time when hundreds of them were demonstrating outside the building every week. To these dissidents Berry represented a disembodied voice informing them that they were part of the problem. Pacifica's legal governors, mesmerized by their Strategic Plan, titles, positions, and professional experience, simply could not comprehend that these noisy, scruffy, supposedly irrelevant white people actually had power – the power to demonstrate, fill meeting halls, flood email readers and voicemail accounts, throng to local advisory board and national board meetings, call politicians and journalists, and, as their generational comrade, Berkeley Free Speech Movement leader Mario Savio, put it, place their "bodies upon the gears and upon the wheels, upon the levers, upon all the apparatus," and make it stop.[71]

And that is just what they would do. Four days after the Fiftieth Anniversary rally, the uprising forced its first exit from the Pacifica national board. East Bay Congressmember Ron Dellums's assistant Roberta Brooks resigned on April 19. Having received no fewer than 400 faxes, telephone calls, and emails within 24 hours, all demanding Bensky and Sawaya's restoration, she decided that she was in way over her head. "I regret that so many of the messages I have received have been so personalized and so full of vitriol," Brooks wrote in her public resignation statement. "It is interesting to me to note how so many people act according to directives from certain individuals or with very limited or one-sided information. I understand that the Pacifica Board's and Pacifica executive director's position has not been readily available. Suffice it to say that the executive director was waiting for a response to her offer of April 7 to sit down face to face with KPFA staff. She was waiting to be able to report something."[72] Both KPFA and Pacifica claimed that the other side refused to sit down and negotiate seriously. Whether or not Chadwick and Berry really wanted to bargain, it took a while for the KPFA community to figure out who exactly they were, and who would do the talking for them.

Things Fall Further Apart

KPFA's staff also agonized over whether to honor their scheduled May fund drive. How could they denounce the Pacifica Foundation over KPFA's airwaves, some staff members asked, and then ask the listeners for funds – over 17 percent of which would be kept by the Pacifica national office? Their solution was to sponsor a marathon in which listener-subscribers could pledge money as always, but in this instance "under protest" – or, if they wished, make their contribution conditional upon the rehiring of Sawaya and Bensky. To their amazement, the subscribers responded beyond anyone's expectations. A marathon with a fund-raising goal of $410,000 raised over $600,000 – 6,200 of the listener-sponsors checking off the "under protest" box on their pledge cards and a smaller number stipulating that their money could not be spent until the two in question were returned to their jobs. "The listeners have spoken," crowed one sympathetic reporter for the *East Bay Express.* "Now it's Pacifica's turn."[73]

Pacifica responded with a remarkable press release claiming that the foundation did not take conditional funds. "While the staff at KPFA hopes to use such conditional pledges as leverage to have their demands met," Elan Fabbri explained in a press release, "longstanding Pacifica policy prohibits such fundraising activity and we will not accept donations made with conditions attached."[74] This announcement came from governors who, three months earlier, had completely reorganized the network's legal structure – in order, they explained, to meet the Corporation for Public Broadcasting's alleged conditions for funding.

Meanwhile the national office kept trying to keep its head above water at KPFA – without success. A week after Berry's talk, Chadwick began hiring security guards. In the wake of the shooting, almost anyone could sympathize with such personnel being placed in front of Pacifica's headquarters. But instead she stationed them next door, at KPFA – both around the entrance to the building and inside the main hall. The initial impetus for the guards seems to have been paranoia. "Many unknown people are coming and going from the station during the Fund Drive," read a confidential chronology of events at KPFA that summer later written by Pacifica for Mary Frances Berry. "As a precaution, security guards are placed at the station on a 24-hour basis."[75] These people may have been "unknown" to Chadwick, but to the KPFA staff they were just the usual volunteers answering phones during Pledge Week. At first, staff and activists expressed indignation at the guards, as well as at the requirement that all visitors and staff sign in and out of the station. Some charged that the guards drank on the job and sexually harassed employees.[76] But most came to regard them as harmless – "basic cheapo rent-a-cops," as Aileen Alfandary put it – mostly middle-aged men, the kind of people hired by supermarkets and department stores. "They were schleps," Barbara Lubin later recalled. Some of the dissidents who now regularly picketed in front of KPFA provided beach chairs for the guards and began sharing their lunches. One day I dropped by KPFA to find guards and picketers, the latter mostly elderly women, sitting in such chairs around a Save Pacifica food/information table and chatting. The scene resembled a weekend picnic. It was difficult to tell who staffed the information table, the dissidents or the guards.

But such moments of rapprochement rarely surfaced that summer, even when Chadwick sought them. She had every reason to reach some kind of truce; the national board was scheduled to meet in Washington, D.C., in two weeks, and they would doubtless be anxious to hear her report on the situation in Berkeley. According to one volunteer, shortly after the marathon Chadwick congratulated the staff on their restraint in breaking the gag rule, announced that she would return to manage KPFA (as opposed to working at Pacifica next door), and expressed her hope that things might calm down.[77]

That was precisely what others feared – that things might come to stasis, the firings accepted as facts of life. And so on June 13, 1999, Robbie Osman, Barbara Lubin's closest ally at the station, used seventeen minutes of his own Sunday morning show to push the envelope. "There was a meeting at my house last week," he explained to his audience:

> Several lawyers, including a past president of Pacifica, a past director of KQED, people very much in the know about entertainment and nonprofit law; a handful of private investigators who have sought us out to donate their services to the effort to protect KPFA. The convening group, who were Friends of Free Speech Radio, who called the meeting and invited everybody: people who have, up until recently[,] worked for and around Pacifica, who know where the bodies are buried. And we had a long and fruitful brainstorming session about what to do in legal approaches. Stuff is in the works.[78]

As for Osman's position on the gag rule, it came almost as an afterthought: "You can come and get me now," he concluded. "I am conscience bound. . . . By my sense of conscience, by my sense of morality, I understand the gag rule. I think it's illegitimate. I will not abide by it."[79]

As everyone expected, Chadwick came and got him. "[Y]ou have forfeited your access to the KPFA/Pacifica airwaves due to your prolonged statement on the air during your broadcast last Sunday, June 13th," she wrote to Osman the following Friday. "As you acknowledged, your statement last Sunday is in direct violation of Pacifica policy, and thereby grounds for your removal."[80] The executive director took the bait and created a third martyr. That evening, the KPFA news department broadcast an indignant story about his firing. Staff added his program's restoration to their list of demands. The following Sunday, the station broadcast two hours of silence in lieu of Osman's show. Demonstrators outside KPFA and Pacifica upped the ante. "We are bringing sleeping bags and tents," dissident Jeff Blankfort told the *San Francisco Examiner*. "This is going to be more than a picket. We are going to sleep in."[81]

And they did just that. "Station Chief Blocked from Building," ran a front-page story in the *San Francisco Examiner* the following Monday afternoon. In the early morning hours, Berkeley police patrolling the area discovered a host of demonstrators, housed in five tents, camping out around the Pacifica national office's front door. A 6-by-10-foot oil painting of a blonde angel crying "Help! KPFA is under attack!" stood over them, produced by mask and puppet artist Annie Hallatt.[82] At 5 a.m. they approached one of the tents and found none other than Barbara Lubin inside, wearing a Palestinian neckerchief. They ordered Lubin and her troops to clear the sidewalk, which they did, but only until Chadwick and her employees showed up for duty. Then they blocked the entrance again.

Chadwick arrived to find a small team of protestors, including one elderly woman in a wheelchair, standing and sitting in front of Pacifica's door, which they had covered with anti-Pacifica posters. Radio, TV, and newspaper reporters already surrounded the scene. "I can't go to work!" witnesses heard Chadwick exclaim. Lubin immediately went into press-conference mode. "If Larry Bensky can't go to his work, if Nicole Sawaya can't go to her work, if Robbie Osman can't go to his work, you're not going to work," she declared. "You hire Nicole back, you can go to work. But we're not having business as usual here."

Pacifica's executive director then called the Berkeley police, who came back to the scene. Chadwick immediately asked them to arrest Lubin and her crew. Officers nervously surveyed all the microphones and cameras. Recognizing the politically sensitive nature of this fight, they wanted to avoid arrests. "Can we negotiate this out?" one of them asked Lubin. "Yes," Lubin answered. "It can be negotiated immediately if *she*" – pointing to Chadwick – "picks up the phone and calls Nicole Sawaya and rehires her. Then everything's back to normal."

Chadwick once again demanded arrests, to which the police demurred. Exasperated, she told the police she wanted to make citizen's arrests. "Are you sure you want to do that?" one asked. "I'm positive," she replied. The police explained the proper procedure, which Chadwick began to execute. "Barbara Lubin, I'm asking you to leave from my office," she declared, while pointing at her opponent. "No," Lubin replied. "I can't leave until you rehire Nicole Sawaya."

"Then I'm making a citizen's arrest," Chadwick replied, and the police began taking Lubin, Blankfort, and their associates away.

The next day Friends of Free Speech Radio placarded posters all over the area. "Free Speech Radio?" the poster declared in giant red type. "Fire Lynn Chadwick. SAVE KPFA. REHIRE NICOLE SAWAYA, LARRY BENSKY, ROBBIE OSMAN." The poster showed a very dour Chadwick, accompanied by two police officers, pointing to Barbara Lubin and demanding her arrest.[83]

If any chance of stasis had still existed, it had now slipped down the toilet. Hundreds of people were joining new and extant KPFA solidarity groups daily. Disgruntled major donors such as Alice Hamburg and former KPFA news director Alan Snitow formed the Ad Hoc Committee of Concerned Friends of KPFA, which I joined. Listener-subscribers as far north as Sacramento and Mendocino and as far south as Santa Cruz organized local solidarity groups. I would guess that by late June a teach-in on the controversy was being held somewhere in the San Francisco Bay Area almost every other day, at Unitarian churches, progressive Catholic churches, synagogues, union halls, retirement homes, day-care centers, high schools, and colleges: any institution that had KPFA listeners opened its doors to a panel discussion on the Pacifica crisis, a presentation that invariably ended with a sign-up sheet and a hat passed around for money. Email discussion lists exploded with members. Larry Bensky inaugurated a new Web site, www.savepacifica.net, which provided daily, and sometimes hourly, email updates on Pacifica-related news, teach-ins, and demonstrations.

All the while, the fight to restore Sawaya, Bensky, and Osman played itself out in the press. When KPFA dissidents weren't calling up national board members and demanding that they either do something or resign, they faxed, emailed and telephoned every journalist they knew personally or knew of, demanding that they cover the story. These volunteers quickly outnumbered Pacifica's public relations department – Elan Fabbri – by about a thousand to one. Media Alliance, the Bay Area's resource center for progressive journalists, sent out a steady stream of press releases on behalf of KPFA, complete with contact information for dozens of station activists. By mid-June, some story about KPFA made its way into the *San Francisco Chronicle* or the *San Francisco Examiner*, or both, every day – often on the front page. Most local reporters, not surprisingly, empathized with KPFA's staff. Some, like Matier and Ross, bristled at management interference with the editorial decision-making process. Others could not understand why Chadwick did not see what they saw – that her rigid enforcement of the gag rule had turned KPFA into a circus. "There may be worse administrators than Lynn Chadwick," *San Francisco Examiner* columnist Jon Carroll confided to his readers, "but it would be hard to come up with their names. The late King Zog of Albania springs to mind."[84] Examiner cartoonist Brian Kelly depicted Chadwick as a deranged general, plotting her next move over a war-room strategy table. "Sorry," she declares in the cartoon, slamming her fist on the table. "There's no such thing as free speech." Meanwhile a pint-sized messenger wearing a white tuxedo and a fez arrives with a dispatch. "IT'S FROM THE FRONT! of the building," he says. "[E]veryone wants to know . . . *why?*"[85]

Paul Rauber of the weekly *East Bay Express* sympathized with KPFA for the same reasons as Matier, Ross, and Carroll. He also had another. Like hundreds of local Bay Area journalists and writers, Rauber had gone through the KPFA news department training program and had served as a volunteer or part-time staffer at the station for years. With the possible exception of the *San Francisco Bay Guardian*, his "Sticks and Stones" column provided more coverage of the KPFA story than any other Bay Area journalism. Up until now, Rauber had been skeptical of Pacifica's critics. But after Pacifica's attack on the news department, he rushed to defend his alma mater. On May 7, 1999, the *Express* published his lengthy feature story "War at KPFA." "Is the Pacifica Foundation going to destroy KPFA in order to save it?" he asked rhetorically. Unlike most other reporters, Rauber quickly realized that this was going to be a long fight. "The war between KPFA and Pacifica is like the Cold War, in that both sides have the power of mutually assured destruction," he wrote. "Many KPFA old-timers are working overtime trying to defuse the crisis, but as the pacifists know, that is more easily done before hostilities have begun."[86] Rauber's reporting set the tone for most subsequent Bay Area coverage of the story: sympathetic toward KPFA and extremely skeptical of Pacifica. "The Pacifica Foundation concedes," wrote another journalist, "that in the public relations battle it is getting flattened."[87]

Please Do Not Use Deadly Force

But Berry and Chadwick appeared immune to and even uninterested in this overwhelming expression of dissatisfaction. Control seemed to be their only concern – over a situation that obviously defied control. On Monday, June 21, a group of Berkeley city mothers and fathers attempted to speak with Chadwick at KPFA.

They numbered about a dozen, according to Father Bill O'Donnell, parish priest of Saint Joseph the Worker Church, who accompanied the delegation. The very elderly Alice Hamburg and Maudelle Shirek led the group. Seeing these oldsters, Chadwick responded by fleeing, with the assistance of a police officer. Two days later Elan Fabbri informed the *San Francisco Chronicle* that beefed-up security at the station would be necessary because thirty people had "stormed" into her office, unannounced, that afternoon. At the next Pacifica national board meeting Berry added a zero to the number, claiming that three hundred protestors had assailed the executive director. Privately, the national office estimated the number at 20.[88]

Now frantic, Chadwick directed Pacifica's new human resource director, Gene Edwards, to contact IPSA International, a management security firm run by former Drug Enforcement Administration (DEA) and FBI agents.[89] "During hostile terminations, our protection specialists provide a virtual safety net," read IPSA's Web site. "They can help defuse an emotionally charged environment and bring about a sense of calm."[90] On Friday, June 25, IPSA forwarded a memorandum of understanding to Edwards regarding the occupation of KPFA. "It is recommended that Pacifica Radio management should be prepared to close down portions of or all of the station and its operations at the Berkeley location as deemed necessary," the memo stipulated. "As discussed with Gene Edwards, IPSA International will reserve the right to increase the coverage (number of personnel) based on a fluid and dynamic review of ongoing threat assessments," it continued. "Should IPSA International be requested to provide armed coverage for the client at other locations, the site evaluations will be conducted by one or more of our regional offices and personnel assigned will be under the direction of those offices."[91]

That Saturday night, Jim Bennett and Chuy Varela were taping a concert at Yoshi's, Oakland's popular jazz club, when they received a telephone call from Victoria Fernandez, one of KPFA's studio board operators. Fernandez was very upset. New guards had arrived at the building, she explained. They had kicked out the old guards and told her that they were putting the building into "lock-down." What did that mean? she asked Bennett. KPFA's chief engineer didn't know, so he and Varela rushed back to the station. When they arrived, the new guards, dressed in business suits, refused to allow them inside the building.

"What are you here for?" the guards asked.

"We work here. Who are you?" Bennett and Varela replied.

"We're the new guards," they responded. "What's that you've got in your hands?"

"It's station equipment," Bennett explained. "Who hired you?"

"We can't tell you that," the guards replied.[92]

The next day the new guards laid down the ground rules. They explained to KPFA's staff that they had guns but would never take them out unless someone exposed a gun to them.[93] Then the staff received a memorandum from Lynn Chadwick. "Due to the present disregard for facility security, effective immediately the following procedures will be enforced in order to maintain security of the KPFA staff, volunteers and property." First, the guards would keep an authorized personnel list; staff on the list would be permitted entry into the building only after they had shown a picture ID. Staff members could bring only one guest into the building at any time. The new "security professionals" would be stationed at the main entrance and the parking garage around the clock. "Thank you for your cooperation during this time of conflict," Chadwick's memo concluded.[94]

The executive director obviously expected the worst. "We've heard from two different sources that there may be an attempted take-over of KPFA surrounding tonight's protest," she wrote in a confidential memo to Edwards on June 28. Change the locks on all the doors, Chadwick instructed. Get a list of all security access codes. Get the Operations Manual from Jim Bennett and tell Cheryl Garner-Shaw to keep it in her car. "Tell Jim I've asked you to review it for general information purposes," she added. Finally, "Please instruct the security firm NOT to use deadly force under any circumstances."[95]

Chadwick's imagined takeover attempts never happened, but the presence of armed guards horrified key personnel at the station. In addition to everything else, the IPSA men removed all station door codes; staff had to check in with them in order to enter the building. "It was miserable to come into the building every day," Aileen Alfandary recalls. "I always come in through the side door, let myself in with the code, and I would so many times lock my bike up, go to start to do the door code, and remember, 'Oh fuck! I can't even let myself in the door. I have to go all the way around and let some asshole with a gun let me into my workplace.'"[96] Alfandary and her colleagues walked among the guards outraged, even stunned. "It made me feel like I was a prisoner in my own home," Jim Bennett later said. "That I was being arrested for something that I didn't do."[97] It provided little consolation that IPSA's rigid security measures consistently gave Pacifica more bad press. The *Express* reported that, on the following Sunday, classical music host Mary Berg invited an a cappella duo into the studio for a live broadcast. The sentries only permitted one vocalist into the building.[98]

Circumstances now forced unity upon KPFA's disparate forces. By late June, a "Committee of Eleven" regularly met at Robbie Osman's house in Oakland, preparing for mediation with Chadwick and Berry. The committee consisted of representatives from station management (Jim Bennett and development director Amina Hassan), the staff union, the volunteer staff, the local advisory board, and delegates from Friends of Free Speech Radio, the Coalition for a Democratic Pacifica, and the Ad Hoc Committee.[99]

By the end of the month Chadwick and this consortium had agreed to talk, but since Pacifica refused to budge on the firings, there wasn't much to talk about.[100] Mary Frances Berry finally flew to the Bay Area on June 12. She met with the station's union stewards, who informed her that she could not negotiate alone with the collective bargaining unit.[101] Then Berry unexpectedly showed up that afternoon at the Oakland Marriott Hotel for a press conference. When, at the last minute, staff at the station got wind of the press conference, they rushed reporters and community activists to the twenty-first floor of the hotel, where Pacifica's chairperson had set up camp. There more security guards stopped them, explaining that it was an invitation-only appearance. Unfortunately for Berry, the sentries also began blocking journalists from some of the region's biggest newspapers. *San Jose Mercury News* columnist Brad Kava described his initial encounter at the conference in a front-page story for his newspaper. "You're not on the list," a guard told him. "Go away." When frustrated reporters demanded an explanation, Elan Fabbri tried to help. "It wasn't to exclude anyone," the *Berkeley Daily Planet* quoted her as saying. "It was to try to keep the protestors away."[102]

As the bickering continued, Berry saw that her strategy had backfired. "Let them in. Let them all in," she told one of her sentinels. At first, the guard refused. "This is my meeting," she declared. "And if I say to let them in, let them in."[103] Berry collected herself and began the conference. "I know it's a story when you exclude people," she told the reporters. "To heck with it. I'm a big girl."[104] She had come to the Bay Area, Berry explained, "to make clear that the board supports the work of Lynn Chadwick." Bensky and Sawaya would not be rehired, she declared. The mission of the organization was to become more diverse. "I want the network to look like the face of America." As for the chaos Chadwick's firings had caused, Berry struck a note of conciliation. "We miscalculated how people would react to management change," she acknowledged. But she had good news. KPFA would now open its airwaves to frank discussion about the network's policies – for one hour a month (which, ironically, had been Nicole Sawaya's practice as general manager of the station).

But when it came to the guards, Berry remained steadfast. They would have to stay, she added, almost as an afterthought, in case a false rumor that the station was being sold set off a new wave of protests.[105]

Sell the Unit

The next morning, July 13, a staff member at Media Alliance opened her email to discover a remarkable message. It came from Pacifica national board member Michael Palmer in Houston and had been intended for Mary Frances Berry. The substantive portions of the document read as follows:

> From: Palmer, Michael@Houston Galleria
> To: Mary Frances Berry
> Hello Dr. Berry,

> I salute your fortitude in scheduling a news conference opportunity in the beloved Bay Area regarding one of the most pressing issues of our time.

> But seriously, I was under the impression there was support in the proper quarters, and a definite majority, for shutting down that unit and re-programming immediately. Has that changed? Is there consensus among the national staff that anything other than that is acceptable/bearable? I recall Cheryl saying that the national staff wanted to know with certitude that they supported 100% by the Board in whatever direction was taken; what direction is being taken?

> As an update for you and Lynn I spoke with the only radio broker I know last week.... The primary signal [KPFA-Berkeley] would lend itself to a quiet marketing scenario of discreet presentation to logical and qualified buyers. This is the best radio market in history and while public companies may see a dilutive effect from a sale (due to the approximate 12 month repositioning effort needed), they would still be aggressive for such a signal. Private media companies would be the most aggressive in terms of price, which he thinks could be in the $65-75m range depending on various aspects of a deal. It would be possible to acquire other signals in the area, possibly more than one, to re-establish operations, but it could take a few years to complete if we want to maximize proceeds....

> Mary I think any such transfer we would ever consider requires significant analysis, not so much regarding a decision to go forward,

but how to best undertake the effort and to deploy the resulting capital with the least amount of tax, legal and social disruption. I believe the Finance Committee will undertake a close review of the Audigraphics data provided recently to determine what it is costing us per listener, per subscriber, per market, per hour of programming . . . in order [to] give the Executive Director and the General Managers benchmarks for improvement. . . . My feeling is that a more beneficial disposition would be of the New York signal [WBAI-New York] as there is a smaller subscriber base without the long and emotional history as the Bay Area, far more associated value, a similarly dysfunctional staff though far less effective and an overall better opportunity to redefine Pacifica going forward. It is simply the more strategic asset. . . .

My feeling is that we are experiencing a slow financial death which is having the normal emotional outbursts commensurate with such a disease. We will continually experience similar events, in fact we have been experiencing similar events over the past several years, primarily because we are not self supporting through subscriber contributions and have a self imposed constraint on asset redeployment that leaves us cash starved at a time when our industry is being propelled in new directions, each requiring capital outlays of consequence. We're boxed in at our own will. This board needs to be educated, quickly, and to take action that will be far more controversial that [sic] the KPFA situation. How can we get there?

So, now I've exhaled more than I should, but you know where I'm at. Let's do something.[106]

It is easy to conjecture how Media Alliance might have received this message. Mary Frances Berry's email address at the University of Pennsylvania was mfberry@sas.upenn.edu. Media Alliance's was ma@igc.org. Any email browser that automatically suggested an address on the basis of the first letter input would choose the latter rather than the former, and a careless click of the mouse might send it off.

However Palmer's prose arrived, Media Alliance did something first. They had a computer specialist check it. He pronounced the missive authentic. The Alliance then distributed the misdirected memo across the Internet that same day. Thousands of Pacificans read the text within minutes. Some reacted with instant horror. Others couldn't believe their eyes. KPFA news director Aileen Alfandary didn't want to put it on the news that day. "I actually doubted its veracity," she later admitted. "I did not want to go on the air with something that couldn't be proved. It just seemed a little too unbelievable."[107] Bay Area Pacifica National Board member Pete Bramson frantically called Palmer three times in an hour for verification. "I cannot even begin to fathom the capacity of the damage this communication has and will bring to Pacifica should this be found to be (truly) from Michael," he wrote to the rest of the board.[108]

But Palmer did write the message, as both he and Pacifica would publicly acknowledge. Having established its authenticity, many readers found the document's chummy tone just as disturbing as its advocacy of a station sale. In August, Mary Frances Berry appeared on Pacifica station WBAI in New York City and took listener phone calls, the first from an irate woman. "There's that famous email that has been all over the Internet," she asked, "in which it is clear that Dr. Berry had initiated selling some or all of the stations. How in the world does she have the gall to deny it?"

"Your question has a great deal of gall in it, if I may be permitted to say so," Berry replied. She categorically denied that the email said "anything about me being committed to selling anything. That is a patent falsehood."[109] Indeed it was. But the memo's warm, informal language suggested to many listeners that Palmer considered Berry and Chadwick at least sympathetic to the idea of selling a station. Chadwick herself betrayed a similar tone when *Current* magazine reporter Jacquelyn Conciatore raised the question several months earlier. Is a station sale possible? she asked. "Things could happen," Chadwick replied, "but that is not at all on the agenda here. These stations are what we are all about, they're our most valuable asset. There have been conversations at odd times . . . but the organization is financially stable right now . . . That's not what it's all about."[110]

KPFA supporters also puzzled at Palmer's opening comments.

"Shutting down that unit and re-programming immediately": What did he mean by that?

What Words Did I Say?

By that afternoon, everyone at KPFA knew that something very bad was about to happen; they just did not know what. Five days earlier Chadwick had ordered all KPFA mail forwarded and held at the Berkeley Post Office.[111] Boxes of programs from the Pacifica Archives began appearing at the station.[112] "These shipments of tapes kept arriving," Alfandary remembered. "Why on earth would you need all these shipments of tape?"[113] Then Garland Ganter showed up.

Chadwick introduced Pacifica Houston station KPFT's beefy general manager that day at an early-afternoon meeting of KPFA staff. She had also summoned from Los Angeles a very uncomfortable Mark Torres of the Pacifica Archives. According to witnesses, Chadwick and Ganter explained that the latter would be taking over for a while, "and that we needed to really start behaving as radio professionals," Jim Bennett recalled. "In other words, they were going to enforce the gag rule and we better not break it."[114]

Dennis Bernstein, host of *Flashpoints*, asked a question. "Does that mean that we're not allowed to talk about that which is being regularly talked about and discussed in the mainstream media?" According to three people who had been present at the meeting, Ganter gave the staff permission to broadcast events covered by other news providers. The news department's Mark Mericle looked grimly at KPFA's new acting general manager. "Garland," he said, "I don't think this is a good career move for you." Chadwick abruptly closed the meeting. The staff went back to work.[115]

Shortly afterward, Ganter approached Bennett. "We want to know if you will help us if we need to reroute the air signal to another room," Ganter said, according to Bennett.

Bennett refused to help. "They said, 'Well, we need to have a contingency plan,'" he later recalled. "And I said, 'isn't that what you have Mark here for?' And they said 'yes'. And I said, 'he's your answer then.'"[116]

Bernstein's query to Ganter had been pertinent, because about a dozen KPFA activists had called a press conference at the nearby Berkeley Municipal Courthouse for that afternoon. They stood around the front entrance and spoke to reporters, including the *San Francisco Examiner*, about Palmer's memorandum and the upcoming trial of protestors arrested for blocking Pacifica's front doors. *Flashpoints* staff taped the event, returned to the station, and broadcast it around 5:30 p.m., along with a prerecorded expression of solidarity for KPFA from novelist Alice Walker and death row inmate Mumia Abu-Jamal.

When the program finished, Bernstein emerged from the studio to discover Garland Ganter waiting for him. Ganter told Bernstein that he had been suspended for breaking the gag rule and should leave the station immediately. Bernstein became indignant. The press conference had been a legitimate news story, he protested. The Mumia Abu-Jamal statement had not disclosed any "dirty laundry" – it had simply expressed support for KPFA's staff. Ganter remained unmoved.

"I don't have my car keys," Bernstein declared. "They're up in my office."

"I'll bring your car keys out to you," Ganter replied, according to Bernstein.

"Well, I don't want you going into my office," Bernstein responded. "And I think I'm going to go upstairs because actually I have another news story now, that I've been suspended. I better go tell the news department."[117]

With that, Bernstein rushed to the news offices on the second floor of the building. Ganter and three IPSA men followed close on his heels. As Bernstein ran up, Alfandary came down – "basically to see what was going on with Dennis," she explained. "If anything was going to happen. Because it seemed like a distinct possibility something would." Something was definitely happening, she concluded, so she scrambled back to explain the situation and help Mark Mericle, who was already anchoring the *Six O'Clock News* and reading news headlines.[118]

"Good evening, it's Tuesday, July 13th," Mericle told listeners, and read through the evening's national and international headlines. Last came a local story: "Thirteen protestors who staged civil disobedience in front of the Pacifica offices in support of the KPFA staff three weeks ago are arraigned in court today. Meanwhile Pacifica executive director Lynn Chadwick issues a new memo to KPFA staff not to discuss internal matters on the air. Chadwick threatens offending staff with termination."[119]

Bernstein, now followed by five people, slipped into the news department suite, then into the console room just outside the news department's on-air studio, where Mericle read copy introducing a *Pacifica Network News* piece on a new universal health care initiative unveiled that day in Washington, D.C. Two guards quickly cornered Bernstein against the tape machine playing the feature. Frightened, he began yelling at the men. "Keep your weapons in your holsters! Don't you know where you are? This is a free speech radio station. You don't have the *right* to be in here." *Flashpoints* staff member Leslie Kean grabbed a video camera and began taping the scene.

During this confrontation, Bernstein bumped against the tape console. The health care story stopped playing. Listeners heard dead air. Mericle came out of his studio and threaded the tape back on, and the story continued. Now Bernstein, blocked by two football-player-sized men standing an inch from his face, saw only one way out. He disturbed the console yet again, stopping the story for the second time. For another minute listeners heard dead air. Mericle rushed out once more to fix the tape, but this time Amy Pomerlow, the studio's exasperated board operator, switched more microphones on. For a few seconds KPFA listeners heard the health care story and Bernstein's protests simultaneously: *I'm a news reporter! . . .* the majority of the uninsured are white. . . . *I reported on a press conference! . . .* also professionals . . . *What words did I say? . . .* African-Americans . . . *I'm afraid you are going to hurt me."*

Ganter saw what had happened and switched the mikes off, indicating to Pomerlow with a swipe of his hand to stay away. One of the guards turned his head, noticed this, and moved on Bernstein, either to grab him or to grab a notepad from his hand. Bernstein responded by pulling back and sitting on the console. Then he dropped to the floor next to the tape machine. The taped program died. Ganter rushed out of the room. By now Mericle had had enough. "I came to the conclusion that I was not going to be doing my newscast if this was going to be happening," he later explained.[120] So he went back to his microphone and told his audience what had just taken place. Mericle's voice trembled as he spoke:

> We interrupt the story by Mark Bevis on HMOs because Dennis Bernstein of Flashpoints has been put on administrative leave for his playing of a press conference concerning the crisis here at KPFA on Flashpoints just within the last half an hour. The guards placed in KPFA are trying to drag him out of the studio. The . . .

Listeners could hear Bernstein continue to object-loudly. "*I broadcast a press conference! And here you are . . . what is Pacifica coming to?*" "and you can hear that in the background," Mericle continued. "Garland Ganter, who is the general manager of the Pacifica station in Houston, was brought in by Pacifica Executive Director . . ."

And with that Ganter opted for his contingency plan, shutting down the news studio and routing broadcasting to another room. After one minute and twenty seconds of silence, KPFA listeners heard an archival tape of Los Angeles activist Eric Mann offering a Marxist analysis of the 1960s.[121]

Having listened to the news, about fifty KPFA supporters in the immediate neighborhood rushed to the front vestibule of the station, only to be blocked by four Berkeley police already positioned inside. Barbara Lubin and Robbie Osman managed to get in before the cops. They stood next to Bernstein and tried to reason with the guards, who patiently explained that they were only following orders. For the rest of the evening, Bernstein would sit on the floor, two guards stationed by his side. Mericle and Alfandary dropped any effort to revive the evening news. Instead, they began calling other reporters to explain what was happening at KPFA. "We called everybody that was on our contact list," Alfandary remembered. "Lots of local media people."[122]

Now hundreds of listeners gathered outside the station, chanting in support of Bernstein. Berkeley's chief of police, Dash Butler, and police captain Bobby Miller arrived and made their way up to the newsroom. Butler listened to Bernstein's explanation of what had happened and patiently conveyed what would happen next. "We've got a pretty serious problem here," Butler began. "I'll tell you what the problem is right now. We probably have 100 to 200 people outside. At some point in time we're going to be asked to do something about this. We don't have the bodies to do this. We don't want to do this." Butler explained that he had on duty at the moment about 26 people at most. If Pacifica insisted on clearing the building, he would be forced to call out his entire force and leave the rest of the city without police protection.[123] Miller made a suggestion to Lubin and Bernstein. If Pacifica could be convinced to restore KPFA to regular programming – or at least to broadcast a dialogue with Bernstein about what had happened – would that suffice to alleviate this immediate crisis? All three agreed that the idea was worth pursuing, and Miller left the newsroom.[124]

The captain then found Ganter and told him how much it would cost the City of Berkeley to clear the area: $16,000 minimum. But KPFT's general manager refused to budge. "Garland explained that he understood the Chiefs [sic] concerns," a Pacifica internal report disclosed, "but that the police had been called to protect the property of the Pacifica Foundation located in Berkeley." Miller suggested that Ganter reinstate Bernstein. "Garland explained that KPFA's FCC license was at stake and that we had to demonstrate that we had control of the situation." At Miller's insistence, Ganter did meet briefly with the host he had just suspended. "Bernstein said he was ready to talk to end the situation," the narrative continued. "Garland asked Bernstein if he was willing to leave peacefully." Bernstein refused. "Garland thanked Capt. Miller for trying to arrange the dialogue but cited this as yet another example of Bernstein's intransigence."[125]

The evening turned to night. Staff, reporters, lawyers, activists, and guards wandered through the building. By now a throng of angry KPFA supporters were demonstrating outside, more arriving by the minute. The police told Ganter that if he wanted arrests, he would have to order them himself. Ganter picked up a bullhorn and announced that he was making citizen's arrests of all "trespassers."[126] The cops then began putting plastic handcuffs on the station's defiant staff. Cuffed programmers sat despondently on stairwells or hallway benches or lay on the ground. Those not yet arrested busily collected papers and possessions and waited their turn. Eventually Bernstein and 51 more would be taken away in police vans and booked.[127]

Upon hearing the news, I drove to the scene as quickly as I could. KPFA programmer Mary Berg gestured to me from one of the ground-floor front windows. She passed some books through an open pane and asked me to hold them for a day or two. To our right, tactical police dressed in riot gear trotted in military formation toward the building. They snaked through our ranks, positioned themselves on the sidewalk, fixed batons, and methodically shoved us back – 2,000 furious KPFA fans, chanting, shouting, jeering, crying, or just standing on the street in stunned, outraged silence.

Siege

Pacifica took six days to produce a one-sentence-long press release explaining its shutdown of KPFA to the public. "Regular programming was replaced by tapes from our fifty-year archives and music," read Elan Fabbri's statement of July 19, "after regular programming was disrupted by an unauthorized takeover on the air by some members of KPFA's staff on Tuesday night, July 13th."[128] It took the KPFA community no time at all to tell the world who in this drama acted without authority.

The next morning – Bastille Day – San Francisco public radio station KQED's Michael Krasny gave an hour of his morning forum program over to Nicole Sawaya, local advisory board members Jay Imani and Sherry Gendelman, and myself. The program broadcast segments of the previous evening's newsroom drama, and its participants announced a late-afternoon rally on behalf of the station, whose staff, Pacifica told the *San Francisco Examiner*, had been put on administrative leave, "until we're able to cool things off."[129]

Nothing cooled off that afternoon. The streets in front of KPFA's now bolted and chained entrance overflowed with demonstrators against Pacifica. "They are hoping for this to fizzle out," a 20-year-old college student told the *San Francisco Examiner*. "Our only hope is to keep this presence alive."[130] Some of the most important progressives in the United States joined them. Daniel Ellsberg, famed leaker of the Pentagon Papers, spoke to the crowd. Ellsberg admitted that he could barely believe what he had read in the newspaper that morning. "What this story claims," he declared, holding a paper in his hands, "is that there is a person they call Mary Frances Berry. Obviously there's no Mary Frances Berry. I mean, where is she? If she's here, let her identify herself right now."

The audience laughed and went along with Ellsberg's rhetorical ploy. "This is a person, the Chairman of a listener sponsored radio station . . . who . . . has snuck into town for an invitation-only press conference, to which they're not invited. A closed press conference to a closed press."

The crowd hissed and booed.

"Well," Ellsberg concluded, "if there is such a person as Mary Frances Berry and Lynn Chadwick, these are obviously people who should have nothing to do with press, media, free speech, democracy. It shouldn't be allowed near them!"[131]

Waves of applause accompanied Ellsberg's conclusion. They turned into an ovation as novelist Alice Walker took the podium. "Freedom is such a constant struggle," she told her supporters. "But I have to say that I never expected to be standing here in front of KPFA talking about trying to save KPFA. This is the place that we consider ours. This is our radio station."[132]

Thus spoke two of the most significant figures in American arts and letters on the subject of America's first listener-supported radio station. By putting KPFA's staff on administrative leave, Pacifica gave their opponents unlimited free time to call in debts from every kind of celebrity associated with the Left: writers, musicians, artists, academics, and performers. All would come to KPFA's aid in its moment of peril. Cynics observed this phenomenon and scratched their heads. "Stupid management tricks" at KPFA, wrote Anthony York for *Salon* magazine, "make people care about free speech there even if they don't listen to it anymore."[133]

But this irony missed the immediate point. Whether they listened to the station on a regular basis or even at all, practically every prominent or obscure person who would join the barricades had been served by KPFA at some point in their lives. They had fought in a cause in which KPFA had given coverage when no one else would, or they had organized an event, or many events, which KPFA had publicized, usually alone among radio stations. They had once been volunteers at KPFA, as had many activists who now worked as legislative aides for Bay Area mayors and state representatives. They had been on KPFA *before* they had become famous, as had Alice Walker. With the station suddenly shut down, multitudes of Bay Area residents, and many outside the area as well, remembered KPFA's numerous good deeds. They read the newspaper, tore up their schedules, and rushed to the defense of the frequency.

Barbara Lubin and Robbie Osman cheerfully enrolled them in the cause. Lubin sent out direct mail appeals that would gradually raise hundreds of thousands of dollars for Friends of Free Speech Radio. The money would be spent on everything necessary to keep the movement afloat: from newspaper ads, posters, and t-shirts to airplane tickets for public speakers and, ultimately, three lawsuits. Osman seized the moment to organize a massive "Save KPFA" concert – Lubin convincing Shirley Dean, Berkeley's conservative (at least for Berkeley) mayor, to lend them the Berkeley Community Theater on a moment's notice ("Here I've tortured that woman for years," Lubin guiltily confided to me later, "and she comes through like this."). On July 16, Joan Baez, Michael Franti, Dr. Loco and His Rockin' Jalapeño Band, and Utah Phillips drew a capacity audience to the theater. "We are going to use the people's airwaves as we see fit and to suit our needs," Phillips declared, "and not as they are defined for us by a bunch of capitalist swine."[134] The audience growled their approval. Baez performed last, made no introductory speech, but brought down the house with a rendition of "Joe Hill." The benefit raised eighty thousand dollars in four hours.[135]

Meanwhile the crisis at KPFA had become a national and international news story. *The New York Times, The Los Angeles Times, The Village Voice, The Washington Post,* and *USA Today* ran articles within days of the shutdown.[136] *The Economist, The Guardian* (UK), and *Le Monde* quickly followed.[137] The drama received so much coverage that the Internet portal *Yahoo* created its own special Web news page for Pacifica.[138] Bay Area television news stations now provided nightly updates on the controversy; during the months of July and August camera crews could invariably be found wandering around KPFA's immediate neighborhood looking for picket lines, demonstrations, dissidents, or, with occasional luck, someone from Pacifica willing to talk to the media.

But Berry and Chadwick now had bigger problems than TV reporters. They were operating, with few allies, in a city utterly hostile to their presence and intentions. If they thought that voices of moderation would come to their aid now, they were mistaken. Even the *San Francisco Chronicle's* editorial page, hardly sympathetic to KPFA's politics, described the events of July 13 as "a ham-handed takeover." Pacifica, an unsigned opinion penned two days later concluded, "should not forget that KPFA is a Berkeley institution with a unique voice in an industry grown bland seeking ratings at any cost."[139] As for local journalism to the left of the *Chronicle,* both the *San Francisco Bay Guardian* and the *East Bay Express* quickly assured their already imaginative readers that High Noon had arrived. "The Pacifica Foundation is likely deciding on one of two options for KPFA: selling the frequency for tens of millions on the open market or drastically reformatting the station," wrote the *Guardian's* A. Clay Thompson. "Will Pacifica Sell KPFA, or Just 'Re-Program' It?" wondered the *Express's* headline.[140]

No one was going to stay home and wait to find out. Within hours of the shutdown, the streets surrounding KPFA became host to an endless, fluid, 24-hour demonstration, sit-in, sleep-in, teach-in, tent city, jam session, prayer vigil, picket line, and homeless shelter. On the night after Pacifica's expulsion of the staff, Van Jones, attorney for the local Ella Baker Center for Human Rights, led over 100 protestors wearing white gags in a nonviolent sit-in on University Avenue, a demonstration that made the pages of *The New York Times*. "I haven't been arrested before," one participant told *Times* reporter Ellen Nieves, "but for this it's worth it." The next day, Friday, 400 listeners defied 50 police in riot gear, creating a human buffer around 9 demonstrators who climbed to the station's second-floor balcony on a ladder. The cops swept the streets, rushed into the building, and arrested "the Ladder Eleven," as they came to be called.[141]

Within hours the protestors returned and established "Camp KPFA," a phalanx of half a dozen tents parked in front of the station. Activists took stacks of cardboard left out by grocery stores and set up makeshift barricades on both ends of the block leading to KPFA. No sooner did police tear them down than they were replaced. Supporters donated furniture and food. An ensemble of six women percussionists endlessly beat drums on the corner of University Avenue while demonstrators held signs that read "HONK IF YOU LOVE FREE SPEECH." Low-power-FM activists claimed a piece of the street and built a 40-watt version of KPFA that broadcast at 87.9 FM and over the Internet. Thousands of desperate KPFA supporters listened to it for updates on the struggle.[142]

Hundreds of listeners milled about the tents during the day, twenty or thirty sleeping in them by night. Lubin and Andrea Buffa of Media Alliance spent most nights there, functioning as camp managers and constantly negotiating with the police. Not surprisingly, homeless men and women quickly thronged to the scene. Tensions sometimes arose between Save KPFA organizers and the homeless, who, understandably, resented directions on how to be conspicuous and annoying. "What do you yuppies know about sleeping on the street?" one homeless man angrily demanded of an activist. "We've been sleeping on the street for years!"[143]

In the late afternoons and evenings this throng enjoyed a constant stream of entertainment. A concise accounting of the music ensembles, theater troupes, and individual performers who passed through this social phenomenon is lost to history, but I personally witnessed three hip-hop rallies, two extended conga sessions, and what was described to me as a Native Central American evil spirit exorcism dance accomplished by 20 performers in full Mayan regalia.[144] Anything that happened in front of KPFA during those weeks turned into news, including nothing. "Quiet Day at Camp KPFA," ran the front page story for the *Berkeley Daily Planet* on Friday, July 23.[145]

It was in this context that Chadwick, Ganter, and their guards occupied KPFA and tried to figure out what to do next. While Pacifica publicly declared that they had expelled the staff in order to demonstrate to the FCC that they retained control over the frequency, Jim Bennett feared that their lack of familiarity with the station's equipment and technical procedures would prove the opposite. He asked them to let him stay in the building, to check levels, fill out FCC-required programming logs, and keep tabs on the all-important KU satellite system, which transmitted the *Pacifica Network News* and *Democracy Now!* Another staff member brought Bennett a sleeping bag, and he set an alarm to wake himself up every two hours in order to read the station's transmitter power meter. "And while I was in the office I was making lots of phone calls to the outside," Bennett recalled, "trying to let people know what was going on." He also briefed an already dismayed Mark Torres on what had happened over the preceding weeks. Appalled, Torres walked out and returned to Los Angeles.[146]

Then, to his alarm, Bennett got wind of a plan to reroute KPFA's transmitter to the signal of another Pacifica station, using ISDN equipment that had been ordered fifteen days before the shutdown. Steve Hawes, KPFA's transmitter supervisor, found a packing slip indicating that the Zephyr 9200 ISDN unit had been shipped to "Pacifica . . . PO# Garland G" at a Federal Express office in Oakland on June 29, weeks before the shutdown.[147] He leaked the information to Bennett. "They're going to try to broadcast from someplace else," Hawes warned, probably, he feared, from KPFK in Los Angeles.

On July 16, KPFA staff called reporters and rushed a union informational picket line up to the station's transmitter tower on Grizzly Peak Road, high in the Oakland hills. Elan Fabbri insisted to newspapers that the reports weren't true. "We have absolutely no plans to do that," the *Berkeley Daily Planet* quoted her as saying. "We won't be reprogramming KPFA with KPFK programming."[148]

Technically, Fabbri told the truth. Pacifica eventually replaced their steady stream of archival broadcasts at KPFA with fare from KPFT in Houston rather than KPFK.[149] But not without a struggle. At first Pacific Bell technicians wouldn't cross KPFA's picket line, since the Communications Workers of America represented both Pac Bell and KPFA staff.[150] As late as Monday, July 26, Chadwick still told newspapers that "we do not have any remote studio right now" – until they did, to the chagrin of reporters who had been told something else. "The way that it's come out and has been viewed by a lot of the critics," one delicately explained to Chadwick, "is that Pacifica says 'We're not doing this, we're not going to be using alternate means for using KPFA's transmitter,' and then the announcement comes out that 'Yes, we are installing an ISDN line.' What some people are saying is that it's hard to believe Pacifica's word."[151]

Pacifica's credibility gap on the transmitter question, however, paled in comparison to the national office and governing board's inability to get its story straight on the matter of a station sale. "Contrary to rumors and reports," a July 19 Pacifica press release declared, "neither KPFA nor any of Pacifica Foundation's four other radio stations are for sale." The release included a public apology from Michael Palmer. "I'm just sorry that a wrong keystroke on my part has created such an uproar," he said. "I still think we should look at selling one of our frequencies, but it's evident that the board and national organization don't agree with me."[152]

By the second week of the shutdown, Pacifica had fallen into a pattern that would continue for years: public declarations of no sale accompanied by a steady stream of evidence that, privately, key members of the board, furious at the station's staff, wanted to sell KPFA's license. "A proposal to sell Berkeley station KPFA is expected to come today before the policy-making body of KPFA's governing Pacifica Foundation," Charles Burress of the *San Francisco Chronicle* reported on July 28. Burress cited three anonymous sources close to the board who told him that its seven-member executive committee would vote on a sale, and that a majority of the committee appeared ready to approve the idea. "Unconfirmed reports said options could include re-establishing KPFA at a less-desirable spot on the FM dial with a non-union staff," the article continued.[153]

These reports would have remained unconfirmed had not one national board member decided to blow the whistle. On the afternoon of July 28, Pete Bramson, surrounded by reporters and KPFA supporters, held a press conference in Berkeley about the meeting. "Pacifica Board Chair Mary Frances Berry has repeatedly said during these past several weeks that she has no intention of selling KPFA," Bramson declared.

> That's not true. . . . During a telephone conference call yesterday, Pacifica Board Vice Chair David Acosta put forward the following proposal. I want to emphasize there was no vote. But the executive committee of the board was to continue discussing this issue today. I do not serve on that committee. There are several parts to this plan, which is somewhat complicated and was floated in an incomplete fashion yesterday. So I'll give you the highlights.

> Acosta proposed taking out a five million dollar loan against the value of the KPFA license. That could happen quickly. He proposed selling the KPFA frequency, which has an estimated value of 65 to 75 million dollars.

> That would take longer to accomplish. With a small portion of the proceeds of the sale of KPFA, Acosta proposed that Pacifica set up another northern California station-perhaps in Palo Alto, which, Mary Berry said, might be a friendlier city than Berkeley. A possible Palo Alto station would have only a fraction of the potential

audience that KPFA currently could reach.

As part of the discussions of selling KPFA, questions were raised about the financial costs of the current dispute – the armed guards and the new public relations firm. While Mary Frances Berry did not provide specific figures on the cost, she did say there may only be enough money left to continue paying the staff for two or three weeks. . . .

There was no hint that Mary Frances Berry has any intention of trying to reopen KPFA, put the staff back to work and resume broadcasting the wonderful local programs, which have been produced here for 50 years.

We do need our radio station back. I call publicly on my fellow board members to do the right thing and give KPFA back to its community.[154]

Reporters who called Elan Fabbri for a response to this statement discovered that she had been abruptly fired and replaced by a crisis-management public relations firm, Michael Fineman and Associates, whose principal quickly repeated the official mantra. Mary Frances Berry, Fineman assured the *Chronicle's* Charles Burress, "emphatically denied" that a sale was "an option being considered." But the board was incapable of sticking to this line. Later Jacqueline Conciatore of *Current* magazine reported Berry as insisting that Bramson misheard the Acosta conversation. "But [Berry] also said the board would listen to offers for KPFA," Conciatore continued, "such as a reported bid from the Berkeley city council that at least now appears to be little more than a rumor."[155]

As for the Berkeley City Council, at an emergency meeting it passed a resolution calling for the resignation of Lynn Chadwick and the reopening of the station, as did Oakland's City Council.[156] Berkeley's Mayor Dean, furious that police protection had already cost the city $150,000, called on the force to cut back its presence at the station and to install portable bathrooms nearby, "so that protesters can really settle in and feel comfortable."[157] Fairness and Accuracy in Reporting (FAIR), the progressive media watchdog group, called for the resignation of the foundation's leadership.[158] The state's top Democratic Assembly leaders demanded, and eventually received, a formal legislative hearing into whether Pacifica had violated its state tax-exempt charter by shutting down KPFA.[159] The National Writers Union, the Central Labor Councils of Alameda, San Francisco, and Contra Costa County, and the American Federation of State, County and Municipal Employees (AFSCME) asked Pacifica to reopen the station.[160] The Working Assets telephone credit card firm announced that it would pull Pacifica from the list of nonprofit groups to which it gave money.[161] And a coalition of groups supporting KPFA announced a Bay Area-wide demonstration scheduled for that coming Saturday, July 31. The protestors would rally at UC Berkeley's Sproul Plaza – where the Berkeley Free Speech movement had been born 25 years earlier- and march to nearby Martin Luther King, Jr., Park.[162]

And so Berry and the executive committee of the Pacifica board met, as planned, and tabled their alleged discussions on a station sale. Instead they concluded, at last, that the time had come for tactical retreat. The Committee of Eleven and Pacifica had committed to federal mediation by now, negotiating at a suite of offices near the Oakland airport. Suddenly both sides learned from newspaper reporters that Berry had made an announcement – at least to the reporters. The station would be reopened, she declared. "KPFA's Staff Gets Call to Return to Work," ran the *San Francisco Chronicle's* front page headline the next day. "I persuaded my colleagues" on the board, Berry explained to the *Chronicle's* Charles Burress, "that we should take a risk and make a good faith effort to invite the staff to come back."[163]

Thought for the Day

At first, hardly anyone at KPFA believed that Berry's offer was true. "Why wasn't it brought to the mediation table?" asked Mark Mericle. Two days later, the station's staff still hadn't received anything in writing. "We're not going in the doors until Pacifica comes clean," KPFA news staffer Wendell Harper told reporters. "We don't know what their intentions are. They're not seriously negotiating with us."[164]

That decision was just as well. By now, mobilization and public outrage against Pacifica had reached fever pitch and would have to zenith before both sides could clean up the mess. The apex came the next day, Saturday, as thousands of people gathered at Sproul for their demonstration. By the time I got there at about 11 a.m., it was already obvious that the event would be enormous. The plaza had become a forest of placards – "FREE FREE-SPEECH RADIO" and "Free Speech SAVE KPFA." Dozens of organizations that depended on the station for outreach – Physicians for Social Responsibility, Global Exchange, Berkeley's La Peña Cultural Center, Earth First! – came with their own banners. "We've got no SAY without KPFA," read one. Dozens of activists came to the Sproul steps to speak. "I will protect KPFA until the day I'm done," declared Dolores Huerta of the United Farm Workers Union.[165]

Then Larry Bensky introduced attorney Dan Siegel. Thirty years earlier Siegel, as president of UC Berkeley's student body, had spoken at a noon rally urging students to take back People's Park, a piece of land cordoned off by the university administration. Berkeley officials rewarded him with an inciting-to-riot charge, which he beat in court. Now Siegel represented a group Pacifica station local advisory board members who on June 16 filed suit in Alameda County Superior Court, charging that Pacifica had created "a self-perpetuating [National] Board without any accountability to the members and subscribers of the Foundation." Unless restrained, the complaint continued, "the Board now threatens to utilize its newly created powers to abandon the mission and historic role of the Pacifica radio network and threatens to sell one or more of the Foundation's five radio stations."[166]

"Look around," Siegel told the crowd. "There's something wrong with this demonstration this morning. And it's not a lack of diversity. It's not a lack of commitment. What's wrong with this demonstration is that it's not being carried live on KPFA."

The audience roared its approval.

"So here's my thought for the day," Siegel concluded. "Let's go down and take our radio station back!"

And with that the throng, led by a dance/percussion ensemble and veterans of the Berkeley Free Speech movement, marched down Telegraph Avenue. Marching bands played "Keep Your Eyes on the Prize." One delegation brought a float depicting a cheerful Lynn Chadwick wielding an axe over handcuffed KPFA listeners. Others manipulated giant puppets – gagged, of course – who hovered above the walkers. A demonstrator in pink tights rode on a unicycle around banners urging justice for Leonard Peletier and Mumia Abu Jamal. Behind them union locals – especially the service unions – carried banners and American flags.

After five blocks, they turned right on a side street corner to the accompaniment of drums, crying, "Shout it out loud . . . free speech now!" and marched down to KPFA. The police were gone. Pacifica had boarded up the station's front door and windows. Although some suggested occupying the building, it would have been a point-less act of defiance, since Pacifica controlled the transmitter on Grizzly Peak. Demonstrators raised their fists and uttered war whoops as they passed the structure. Others just gazed sadly at their building and wondered how things had gotten this far. A band played "We Shall Overcome" and "We Shall Not Be Moved" as the protestors slowly made their way toward the park. Bensky, Alfandary, Bernstein, Dolores Huerta, and a dozen other staff now led the charge with a huge banner: "FREE SPEECH 1964-1999 . . .? SAVE KPFA!"

At Martin Luther King, Jr., Park, Shirley Dean greeted the demonstrators. "Thank you for being strong," she declared. "Thank you for being there. Save KPFA!" She was followed by a procession of Bay Area politicians whose offices had been overwhelmed over the previous three weeks by email, voice mail, snail mail, and faxes – among them, San Francisco supervisor Tom Ammiano and San Francisco's Mayor Willie Brown. Brown called for the resignation of the Pacifica board as some protestors, irate at his housing and homeless policies, stupidly booed him. It was, in fact, a testimony to the strength of this movement that so many political figures ambivalent about the station's politics came to pay homage. Equally remarkable declarations of solidarity came from afar, one from an alternative radio station banned in Serbia. Larry Bensky read its communiqué at the rally. "Radio B92 condemns in the strictest terms the repression and exertion of force against the staff of Radio KPFA and Radio WBAI and their listeners," its staff declared. "Long live freedom of speech! And down with media repression which knows no ideological or national boundaries, in either Berkeley or Belgrade."[167]

The park was packed; the streets beyond overflowed with people. Police estimated that ten thousand demonstrators had come to defend KPFA, the biggest East Bay crowd since the Vietnam antiwar protests, and surely the largest demonstration in American history on behalf of a radio station.[168]

Eye of the Hurricane

Several days later, Pacifica opened KPFA up to its community and staff, but not without a tussle. Human resources manager Gene Edwards called Jim Bennett and told him that it was time to return. Members of KPFA staff arrived and were told by Edwards to meet them at the back entrance of the building. There, Edwards dangled the keys to the building before Bennett. Pacifica management lawyer Larry Drapkin waited inside the building.

"Before I let you back in," Edwards said. "I need to ask you a question. Are you coming back to work?"

"Well, we're all here," Bennett replied. "We would like to come back to the building, but we're not sure if the building is safe, and we need to determine whether the working conditions are safe, whether there's electricity, whether there are any hazards before we come back to work."

The question seemed to throw Edwards. He made a phone call, then asked again, "Are you coming to work?"

Bennett insisted, "We need to be able to inspect the building to see what its conditions are before I would recommend that any of us come back to work."

Edwards repeated the question. Bennett repeated his answer. Edwards paused and made another call; Bennett suspected it was to Drapkin. "Who do you have to do the inspection?" Edwards finally asked.

Bennett pointed to the people around him. Mayor Dean, the city manager, and the chief of Berkeley's fire department, among other city officials, stood by his side. "It was kind of like a Mickey Rooney/Judy Garland moment," Bennett later recalled, "like we had the whole city behind us."

Edwards abandoned whatever legal maneuver he had planned. "OK," he exhaled. "Come on in."

The guards walked out; the staff walked into the building. There they found broken glass scattered all over the floor near where the windows had been boarded up. Much of the station's studio equipment had sustained damage. "The alarm panel that we had in terms of the security system," Bennett explained, "they had cut the wires to the system, they had torn open the fuse box for all the alarm stuff and had unattached it, because evidently they didn't know how to disarm it, so they just ripped it out of the wall. That kind of stuff."[169] Over the next few weeks the cost of Pacifica's expulsion of the staff would be revealed: $390,000 for security guards, $58,317 for public relations, $9,000 for transmitter equipment, and $10,000 to board up KPFA's windows. "What did they use," asked a dumbfounded Brenda Payton, columnist for the *Oakland Tribune*, "bronze nails?"[170]

It took days for KPFA supporters to clean up the mess and get the transmitter rerouted back to KPFA. Finally, on August 5, a Thursday, studio engineer Barbara Fisher approached a microphone and spoke to the station's anxious listeners. "This is live. There ain't nothing like the real thing," she joyfully declared. "Welcome to the Morning Show." Media jammed the station's studios. "You might be hearing a lot of background noise, maybe a little echo," *Morning Show* host Philip Maldari explained. "We've got two TV cameras here with us and reporters are all over the place, so bear with us."[171]

From 3,000 miles away, Mary Frances Berry explained to newspapers that she was willing to bear with the situation, up to a point. She decreed the gag rule lifted but warned that KPFA had six months to demonstrate that its staff could increase diversity at the station and build audience. Back at Berkeley, nobody could think about anything but picking up the pieces. "I think the staff feels brutalized," Maldari told KPFA's audience. "This was a horrible thing to do to KPFA." Although Berry told reporters that she and other foundation officials "would not involve themselves in KPFA management decisions in the future," Pacifica still refused to rehire Sawaya and Bensky.[172] Bensky returned to the station as a volunteer. Robbie Osman, who had always been a volunteer, returned to his regularly scheduled Sunday program. On a programmatic level, nothing had changed since July 13, except that the KPFA community had retaken the building.

In a much more fundamental sense, however, everything had changed. The people who resumed broadcasting at KPFA that day may have looked the same, but within the context of their own organization they were socially and politically transformed. A huge grassroots solidarity movement now surrounded KPFA, its principals discovering each other and building alliances over the Internet. Inside KPFA, even the most institutionally conservative members of the paid staff now spoke of expelling the present governing board and "democratizing" Pacifica. "When Nicole was fired, a lot of us felt like we could reach out, we could resolve this, and reason could prevail by reasoning with the board," Alfandary later reflected. "By the time we got to July 13th, I thought that that was no longer a possibility."[173] And the greater progressive community, whose stars once regarded Pacifica politics as an obsession of the terminally marginal, now began to sign on to the cause, or at least to wonder whether warnings they had dismissed should have been heeded.

The *East Bay Express's* post-KPFA shutdown issue revealed the extent to which the Bay Area progressive community had been shaken by the events of the past four months. "THE EYE OF THE HURRICANE," ran its 200-point boldface headline, correctly implying that the worst was yet to come. Two articles, Chris Thompson's "What Happened?" and Paul Rauber's "What Lies Ahead?" took up most of the space in the August 6 edition, released a day after KPFA's staff resumed broadcasting. Both essays all but called Pacifica a pack of scoundrels. Rauber expressed satisfaction at the extent to which the press had refrained from caricaturing the KPFA community as hippies living in the past. "There probably would have been a lot more of this coverage had Berry and Chadwick been able to contain their authoritarian impulses," he wrote. "Instead, through most of the crisis, the foundation's officers and spokespeople refused to talk to the press or, when they did comment, lied to them." They lied about the transmitter, Rauber charged, and they "widely lied" about a possible station sale.[174] On these points he could expect little dissent among *East Bay Express* readers or the KPFA community. Pacifica's "treachery knows no bounds," declared local advisory board member Jay Imani over KPFA's airwaves after the shutdown. "We won't allow Pacifica to be run by LIARS!" a demonstrator's sign proclaimed at the July 31 demonstration.[175]

But lies, while painful, are hardly the most devastating blow an institution can sustain. Berry and Chadwick certainly shocked the KPFA community by their rigidity and ruthlessness. Although the organization had a well-deserved reputation for infighting, no administration had ever pushed matters this far before. Many of their public statements were arrogant, contradictory, or suspicious, to put it mildly. In the final analysis, however, Berry and Chadwick jolted the organization beyond immediate repair not because of their lack of candor, but because of their plain, simple honesty. During these months they disclosed the legal realities of the organization with an arrogance that in retrospect appears almost guileless. On May 22, before the shutdown, Elan Fabbri gave governing board members, now besieged with protest mail, a set of recommended responses to questions. "Don't community radio stations belong to the community?" ran hypothetical question 2. "In fact, they do not," Fabbri's recommended reply began. "The Federal Communications

Commission (FCC) is the only entity that may grant permission to use the airwaves." Question 5 asked "Why are you trying to gag free-speech radio?" Here is why, Fabbri would have board members explain. "In most broadcast settings and by all broadcast professionals, it is clearly understood that disclosure of internal issues is cause for immediate dismissal."[176] Shortly after KPFA reopened, a *Chronicle* reporter asked Berry to respond to the accusation that Pacifica had, like a thief, stolen KPFA from its community. Pacifica's chairperson reversed the charge. "Berry said [that] 'a better analogy' would be that thieves broke into Pacifica's house and then were allowed to keep part of what they took."[177]

KPFA's staff, the local advisory board, the listener community – all thieves. These were the very public answers that Pacifica's leaders gave to tens of thousands of Bay Area working people who had until now stayed away from KPFA politics. For decades they had faithfully paid their pledges and been told that KPFA was their radio station, that if something important happened KPFA would tell them about it. But no, they were wrong. Pacifica was not owned by the community, Fabbri explained. It did not permit free speech, Chadwick declared. KPFA was Pacifica's, not theirs, Berry insisted, and not only that, but the people who thought it was theirs were the wrong kind of people. By September of 1999, Pacifica had starkly exposed each and every one of the organization's contradictions – the deep chasm between its moral understanding of itself and its actual legal power structure and rules. During the summer of 1999, Chadwick, Berry, and Fabbri did the worst thing they could possibly do for their cause. They told the plain truth about the Pacifica Foundation. Whereas previous administrations had carefully veiled these realities, Pacifica's new governors shone a bright spotlight on them, apparently mindless of the consequences. Earlier Pacifica leaders "never would have said the things that Mary [Berry] said on the air," later observed KPFK local advisory board member David Adelson. "Mary did not understand the way a Pacifica audience would hear what it was she was saying."[178]

The KPFA community listened and asked the first obvious

question. If the foundation has never really been ours, they wondered, how do we make it so now? The rest of the network and the American Left asked the second obvious question. How on earth had it come to this? To answer question number two, we must go back to the dawn of Pacifica radio.

Endnotes

1   "Chadwick Praised as NFCB Enters New Era," *Public Broadcasting Report* (March 27, 1998), p.1; Jacqueline Conciatore, "NFCB Veteran Lynn Chadwick Promoted to Head Pacifica Radio," Current (October 26, 1998); in 1973 Pacifica's member stations paid a tithe of 3 percent of their annual income to the foundation. By 1999 that figure had grown to 17.2 percent: see Minutes of the Pacifica National Board, March 31 and April 1, 1973, p.9; Minutes of the Pacifica National Board, February 28, 1999, pp.76-77.

2   Lynn Chadwick, "My First Hundred Days," *Pacifica Foundation National Governing Board Meeting Booklet* (Berkeley, California: Pacifica Foundation, 1999), p.2.

3   Dick Bunce, "The Crisis of Democratic Communications," in *A Vision for Pacifica Radio: Creating a Network for the 21st Century* (Berkeley: Pacifica Foundation, 1997), pp.4-8.

4   Nicole Sawaya, interview with author (August 13, 2002), p.41.

5   Aileen Alfandary, interview with author (September 10, 2002), p.6.

6   Nicole Sawaya, interview with author (August 13, 2002), p.24.

7   Pat Scott, interview with author (January 31, 2003), p.20.

8   Jim Bennett, interview with author (September 19, 2002), p.2.

9   Aileen Alfandary, interview with author (September 10, 2002), p.5.

10 Sawaya, interview with author (August 13, 2002), p.41.

11 Paul Rauber, "War at KPFA: Is the Pacifica Foundation Going to Destroy KPFA in Order to Save It?" *East Bay Express* (May 7, 1999), p.1.

12 Sawaya, interview with author (August 13, 2002), pp.41-43.

13 Chadwick, "My First Hundred Days," p.2.

14 Sawaya, interview with author (August 13, 2002), p.44.

15 Ibid., p.24.

16 Ibid., p.45; Jim Bennet, interview with author (September 19, 2002), p.3.

17 Alfandary, interview with author (September 10, 2002), p.5.

18 Ibid., p.6.

19 Paul Rauber, "War at KPFA," p. 9.

20 Jim Bennett, interview with author (September 19, 2002), p.3.

21 Alfandary, interview with author (September 10, 2002), p.6.

22 Ibid., p.7.
23 Alfandary, quoted in Veronica Selver and Sharon Wood, *KPFA on the Air* (video documentary, 1999).
24 Rauber, "War at KPFA," p.9.
25 Sherry Gendelman, interview with author (March 6, 2002), p.7.
26 Recollection of author.
27 Rauber, "War at KPFA," p.11.
28 Jacqueline Conciatore, "Pacifica's Heated Conflict Boils Over at KPFA," *Current* (April 22, 1999): www.current.org/rad/rad907p.html.
29 David Matier and Andrew Ross, "Big Ruckus at Free-Speech Radio Station After Boss' Ouster," *San Francisco Chronicle* (April 2, 1999), p.A17.
30 Rauber, "War at KPFA," p.11.
31 Cecily Burt, "Firing of KPFA Manager Leads to Assault Attempt," *The Oakland Tribune* (April 2, 1999), p.Local-3.
32 "Pacifica Heated Conflict Boils Over at KPFA": www.current.org/rad/rad907p.html.
33 Rauber, "War at KPFA," p.11.
34 Bennett, interview with author, (September 19, 2002), p.8.
35 Elan Fabbri, "Sent to the GB from: Elan Fabbri" (May 22, 1999), email message. *Webster's Ninth New Collegiate Dictionary* defines *fire* as "to dismiss from a position."
36 Rauber, "War at KPFA," p.13.
37 Ibid.
38 Ibid.
39 Minutes of the Pacifica National Board, June 22, 1974, p.6.
40 Phil Elwood, interview with author (February 17, 1995), p.6.
41 Larry Bensky, "To: All KPFA Staff. Local Advisory Board, National Pacifica Office. From: Larry Bensky" (10 January, 1977), p.1.
42 Peter Franck, letter to Bensky, 10 January 1977, p.1.
43 Bennett, interview with author (September 19, 2002), p.3.
44 Mark Mericle, interview with author (November 19, 2002), p.4
45 Penny Rosenwasser, *Visionary Voices: Women on Power* (San Francisco: Aunt Lute Books, 1992), pp.148, 151.
46 Ibid., p.153.
47 Ibid., pp.153-54.
48 Ibid., p.154.
49 Ibid., p.156.
50 Ibid., p.149.
51 Ibid., p.150.
52 "About the Middle East Children's Alliance:" http://www.mecaforpeace.org/meca.html; "Playgrounds for Peace:" http://www.mecaforpeace.org/playgrounds.html.

53   Barbara Lubin, interview with author (March 28, 2002), p.1.
54   Ibid.
55   Ibid., p.2.
56   "Statement of KPFA Staff re the Termination of Nicole Sawaya" (April 1, 1999) (italics added).
57   Barbara Lubin, interview with author (March 28, 2002), p.9.
58   Alice Sachs Hamburg, *Grass Roots: From Prairie to Politics: The Autobiography of Alice Sachs Hamburg* (Berkeley: Creative Arts Books Company, 2001), p.214.
59   Video of KPFA demonstration (April 15, 1999).
60   Ibid; Spanish for "Yes, we can."
61   Ibid.
62   Lynn Chadwick, quoted on *Democracy Now!* (April 16, 1999), transcribed by John Sommers: www.radio4all.org/f/04-16dem_now-transcript.htm.
63   Recollection of author.
64   Mary Frances Berry, "KPFA Report to the Listeners w/Mary Frances Berry and Lynn Chadwick," audio cassette (May 5, 1999).
65   Ibid.
66   Ibid.
67   Leslie Peters, ed., *Audience 98: Public Service, Public Support* (Audience Research analysis, no date), p.10.
68   Peggy Berryhill, Rick Tejada-Flores, et al., "Open Letter from the Diversity Coalition in Public Broadcasting to the Pacifica Board of Directors, the Staff and Volunteers of KPFA, and the General public," press release, June 26, 1999 (italics added).
69   1990 Census U.S. Data for the City of Berkeley: www.pacunion.com/demographics/berkeley.htm (percentage calculated by the author); "Open Letter to Dr. Mary Frances Berry, From: The African-American Programmers at KPFA" (May 21, 1999).
70   Rafael Renteria, "Race and Power at Pacifica Radio" (July 2, 1999): www.savepacifica.net/0702_race.html.
71   Mario Savio quoted in Todd Gitlin, *The Sixties: Years of Hope, Days of Rage* (Toronto: Bantam Books, 1987), p.291.
72   Robert Brooks, "Statement of Resignation" (April 19, 1999): www.radio4all.org/fp/brooks_resigns.htm. Berry eventually convinced Brooks to stay until the conclusion of her term.
73   Paul Rauber, "What Part of 6,200 Don't You Understand?" *East Bay Express* (June 4, 1999): www.savepacifica.net/0604rauber.html.
74   Elan Fabbri, "Pacifica Foundation Fundraising Policies (rev)," press release (May 26, 1999).
75   Vanessa [no last name], "Chronology of Events, March 31, 1999-Present; To: Dr. Berry" (September 21, 1999), p.2, PNOP, Box 181.
76   Ibid.

77 "Robbie Osman Statement On-Air" (June 13, 1999): http://www.savepaci-fica.net/0613AGD.html.
78 Ibid.
79 Ibid.
80 Chuck Finnie, "KPFA Feud Costs Another DJ His Job," *San Francisco Examiner* (June 20, 1999), p.C-5.
81 Ibid.; Stacy Finz, "Firing of DJ Stirs Protest in Berkeley," *San Francisco Chronicle* (June 21, 1999), p.A13.
82 Julie Chao, "Pacifica Chief Blocked from Entering Building," *San Francisco Examiner* (June 21, 1999), p.1.
83 Barbara Lubin, interview with author (March 28, 2002), pp.3-5.
84 Jon Carroll, "A Little Static on the Radio," *San Francisco Chronicle* (June 23, 1999), p.B-8.
85 Brian Kelly, cartoon, *San Francisco Examiner* (July 7, 1999), p.A-23.
86 Rauber, "War at KPFA," p.14.
87 Evelyn Nieves, "The Battle for the Berkeley Airwaves Rages On," *The New York Times* (July 23, 1999), p.A10.
88 Father Bill O'Donnell, parish priest, St. Joseph the Worker Church, Berkeley, interview with author (September 11, 1999); Charles Burress, "125 Protesters Rally at KPFA, Demand Ouster of Director," *San Francisco Chronicle*, p.A16; Vanessa, "Chronology of Events, March 31, 1999-Present; To: Dr. Berry," p.3; Mary Frances Berry, quoted in "Pacifica Foundation National Board Meeting, June 27, 1999," p.27.
89 For IPSA management background, see www.ipsaintl.com/about/our_team.cfm.
90 Chris Thompson, "KPFA Lockout: Spontaneous Reaction or Planned Management Coup," *East Bay Express* (July 23, 1999), p.3.
91 Unsigned letter from IPSA International to Gene Edwards, June 25, 1999, p.2, PNOP, Box 181.
92 Bennett, interview with author (September 19, 2002), p.13.
93 Ibid.
94 Lynn Chadwick, "MEMORANDUM, All KPFA Staff, Volunteers and Guests" (June 26, 1999), PNOP, Box 181.
95 Lynn Chadwick, "Confidential Memorandum, To: Gene Edwards" (June 28, 1999).
96 Alfandary, interview with author (September 9, 1999), p.7.
97 Bennett, interview with author (September 19, 2002), p.13.
98 Paul Rauber, "Pacifica's Big Guns," *East Bay Express* (July 2, 1999), p.5.
99 "The Committee of 11" (July 13?, 1999): http://home.pon.net/wildrose/comm11.htm.
100 Jeff St. John, "Interference on the Airwaves," *San Francisco Bay Guardian* (June 30, 1999), p.12.

101 Mark Mericle, interview with author (November 19, 2002), pp.1-2.
102 Ali Berzon, "Mixed Signals," *San Francisco Bay Guardian* (July 14, 1999), pp.12, 14; Brad Kava, "Political Fight Endangers Radio Station's Freedom," *San Jose Mercury News* (July 15, 1999), p.1; Rob Cunningham, "KPFA Showdown," *Berkeley Daily Planet* (July 13, 1999), p.1.
103 Kava, "Political Fight," *San Jose Mercury News*, p.1.
104 Berzon, "Mixed Signals," *San Francisco Bay Guardian*, p.12.
105 Ibid.
106 Michael Palmer, quoted in "Freedom's Just Another Word," *The Texas Observer* (August 6, 1999): www.texasobserver.org/showArticle.asp?ArticleID=316.
107 Alfandary, interview with author (September 10, 2002), p.7.
108 Pete Bramson, "Text of Alleged E-mail from Michael Palmer to Dr. Berry" (July 14, 1999), p.1.
109 Mary Frances Berry, radio appearance on WBAI in New York City, audio tape (August 25, 1999); the caller was my mother, Rita Lasar.
110 Jacqueline Conciatore, "Tempers Rise as Pacifica Decides to Select Its Own Members," *Current* (March 8, 1999): www.current.org/rad/rad906p.html (ellipses in original).
111 Lynn Chadwick, "Re: Release of Mail," memorandum (August 4, 1999), p.1, PNOP, Box 181.
112 Jim Bennett, interview with author (September 19, 2002), p.5.
113 Alfandary, interview with author (September 10, 2002), p.5.
114 Ibid., p.6.
115 Dennis Bernstein, interview with author (September 9, 2002), p.2; Jim Bennett, interview with author (September 19, 2002), p.6; Aileen Alfandary, interview with author (September 10, 2002), p.7.
116 Bennett, interview with author (September 19, 2002), p.6.
117 Dennis Bernstein, interview with author (September 9, 2002), p.4.
118 Alfandary, interview with author (September 10, 2002), p.7.
119 *KPFA Six O'Clock News* (July 13, 1999), quoted in Leslie Kean, "Lockout! KPFA Under Siege," videotape (no date).
120 Mericle, interview with author (November 19, 2002), p.3.
121 Ibid.
122 Alfandary, interview with author (September 10, 2002), p.3.
123 Kean, "Lockout!"
124 Ibid.
125 Vanessa, "Chronology of Events, March 31, 1999-Present; To: Dr. Berry," p.2.
126 Ibid., pp. 5-7.
127 Kean, "Lockout!"; Ilene Letchuk, "New KPFA Firing Sparks 52 Arrests" (July 14, 2002), p.A1.

128 Elan Fabbri, "Programming at KPFA," press release (July 19, 1999).
129 Michael Krasny, *KQED Forum* (July 14, 1999); Letchuk, "New KPFA Firing Sparks 52 Arrests," p.A2.
130 Ilene Letchuk and Marianne Constantinou, "Fans Rally Through the Night for Station," *San Francisco Examiner* (July 17, 2002), p.A-7.
131 Daniel Ellsberg, speech at KPFA rally (July 14, 1999): www.metalab.unc.edu/pub/multimedia/radio4all/fp/ellsberg7.14.99.mpg.
132 Ray Delgado and Matthew Yi, "500 Rally to Support Locked-out KPFA Staff," *San Francisco Examiner* (July 15, 1999), p.A-2.
133 Anthony York, "The War over KPFA," *Salon* (July 17, 1999): www.salon.com/news/feature/1999/07/17/kpfa/index.html.
134 Utah Phillips, Save KPFA concert at Berkeley Community Theater (July 20, 1999), videotape.
135 Phil Elwood, "Baez Blasts from Past for KPFA," *San Francisco Examiner* (July 21, 1999), pp.C-1, C-7; William Brand, "KPFA Protesters Sweep over Pacifica Site" (July 21, 1999), p.2.
136 Mary Curtis, "Listeners Besiege Berkeley Station After Staff Arrests," *Los Angeles Times* (July 15, 1999); Nieves, "The Battle for the Berkeley Airwaves Rages On," p.A10; Carol Morello, "Radical Radio Station Riled Up over Power Struggle," *USA Today* (July 21, 1999), p.7A; Cynthia Cotts, "Is Free Speech for Sale?" *The Village Voice* (July 21, 1999); Frank Ahrens, "Station of the Cross at KPFA in Berkeley," *The Washington Post* (July 26, 1999).
137 Duncan Campbell, "Radio Battle Played Out on Airwaves," *The Guardian* (July 16, 1999); Barbara Epstein, "Radical Radio Fights to Be Heard," *Le Monde Diplomatique* (October 10, 1999); "The Left's Last Gasp," *The Economist* (July 17, 1999).
138 This page once thrived at www.dir.yahoo.com/News_and_Media/Radio/Networks/Pacifica_Radio/Consumer_Opinion/.
139 Editorial, "The Battle for KPFA," *San Francisco Chronicle* (July 15, 1999), editorial page.
140 A. Clay Thompson, "Pacifica's Endgame?" *San Francisco Bay Guardian* (July 21, 1999), p.15; Chris Thompson, "Will Pacifica Sell KPFA, or Just 'Re-Program' It?" *East Bay Express* (July 16, 1999).
141 Charles Burress and Janine DeFao, "Legislators Step into KPFA Clamor," *San Francisco Chronicle* (July 16, 1999), p.1; John Paige, *Remembering Camp KPFA: Scenes, Voices* (self-published manuscript: Berkeley? 2002?), pp. 2-4; Barbara Lubin, interview with author (March 28, 2002), p.12; Nieves, "The Battle for the Berkeley Airwaves Rages On," p.A10.
142 Michael Albert, "Tense KPFA Standoff Continues" (July 22, 1999), p.A9.
143 Paige, *Remembering Camp KPFA: Scenes, Voices*, pp.2-4; Barbara Lubin, interview with author (March 28, 2002), p.14.
144 Recollections of author.

145 Judith Scherr, "Quiet Day at Camp KPFA," *Berkeley Daily Planet* (July 23, 1999), p.1.
146 Jim Bennett, interview with author (September 19, 2002), p.9.
147 Telos Systems packing list (June 29, 1999), "Ship to: Pacifica HOLD @ FEDERAL EXPRESS 1221 Broadway PO# Garland G Oakland, CA 94612.," document in possession of author.
148 Jim Bennett, interview with author (September 19, 2002), p.9; Judith Scherr, "Transmitter for KPFA 'defended'," *Berkeley Daily Planet* (July 17-18, 1999), p.1.
149 Robert Selna, "KFPA Transmitter Still Off-Limits to Staff," *San Francisco Examiner* (August 3, 1999), p.A-3.
150 Malcolm Glover, "KPFA Protesters Fold Their Tents," *San Francisco Examiner* (July 21, 1999), p.A-4.
151 "Pacifica Is Not Using a Remote Studio for KPFA, Chadwick Says," *Berkeley Daily Planet* (July 26, 1999), p.4; "No Sudden Shift in Mission or Goals, Top Pacifica Official Says," Berkeley Daily Planet (July 27, 1999), p.4.
152 Elan Fabbri, "KPFA Is Not for Sale," Pacifica press release (July 19, 1999).
153 Charles Burress, "Foundation Denies KPFA to Be Sold," *San Francisco Chronicle* (July 28, 1999), p.A15.
154 Pete Bramson, "Pacifica National Board Member Pete Bramson's Statement at a 7/28/99 Berkeley Press Conference," press release: www.radio4all.org/freepacifica/bramson.htm.
155 Jacqueline Conciatore, "Pacifica Opens KPFA's Doors, Staffers Continue Protest" (August 2, 1999): www.current.org/rad/rad914p.html; Charles Burress, "KPFA Parent Company Turns to PR Firm for Help," *San Francisco Chronicle* (July 23, 1999), p.A20.
156 Burress, "Foundation Denies KPFA to Be Sold," p.A15.
157 Anita Wadhwani, "Berkeley Mayor Moves to Cut Cordon of Cops Around KPFA," *San Francisco Examiner* (July 27, 1999), p.A-4.
158 Charles Burress, "Media Critics Urge KPFA Radio Leaders to Resign," *San Francisco Chronicle* (July 17, 1999), p.A13.
159 Robert Salladay, "Legislators Question KPFA Use of Funds," *San Francisco Examiner* (July 16, 1999), p.A-8.
160 "Unions Ask Pacifica to End KPFA Lockout," *San Francisco Chronicle* (July 26, 1999), p.D10.
161 Charles Burress, "Berkeley Council Measure Demands KPFA Be Reopened," *San Francisco Chronicle* (July 27, 1999), p.A-14.
162 Wadhwani, "Berkeley Mayor Moves to Cut Cordon of Cops Around KPFA," *San Francisco Examiner* (July 27, 1999), p.A-4.
163 Charles Burress, "KPFA Staff Gets Call to Return to Work," *San Francisco Chronicle* (July 29, 1999), p.A1.
164 Ibid.; Jim Herron Zamora, Larry D. Hatfield, and Julie Chao, "KPFA

Workers Reject Offer to Return to Work," *San Francisco Examiner* (July 30, 1999), p.A1.

165 This description of the July 31 rally is derived from a videotape taken of the event.

166 Adelson et al., "Verified Complaint for Injunctive and Declaratory Relief for Violations of Corporations Code and Unfair Business Practices," Alameda County Superior Court (July 16, 1999).

167 This statement was located at www.helpkpfa.rtmark.com/.

168 Venise Wagner, "Huge Berkeley Rally Calls for Local Autonomy at KPFA," *San Francisco Examiner* (August 1, 1999), p.D-8.

169 Bennett, interview with author (September 19, 2002), p.11.

170 Brenda Payton, "Pacifica Runs Up $428,315 Tab," *Oakland Tribune* (September 14, 1999).

171 Larry D. Hatfield and Robert Selna, "KPFA Back on the Air with Live Programs," *San Francisco Examiner* (August 5, 1999), p.A-6; William Brand, "KPFA Returns to Air After 23-Day Absence," *Oakland Tribune* (August 6, 1999), p.1.

172 Maria Benko, "Pacifica Offers to Remove Guards, Reopen KPFA," *The Daily Californian* (July 30, 1999), p.1; Charles Burress, "KPFA's Air Attack," *San Francisco Chronicle* (August 6, 1999), pp.A1-A29; "Live from Berkeley, KPFA," editorial, *San Francisco Chronicle* (July 30, 1999), p.A24.

173 Alfandary, interview with author (September 10, 2002), p.7.

174 Paul Rauber, "What Lies Ahead?" *East Bay Express* (August 6, 1999), p.7; also see Chris Thompson, "What Happened," same edition.

175 Burress, "KPFA's Air Attack," p.A19.

176 Elan Fabbri, email, "Sent to the GB by Elan Fabbri" (May 22, 1999).

177 Burress, "KPFA's Air Attack," p.A19.

178 David Adelson, interview with author (December 27, 2002), p.31.

CHAPTER 2

Foundation and Empire, 1946-1968

It matters whether the man who writes, or works in the
shipyard, is a pacifist; but as to the man who is first, last and
only a pacifist – it doesn't matter at all that he is a pacifist.

LEWIS HILL, 1951

So What?

It was November of 1947. The Cold War had begun. In June the
United States gave millions of dollars to help Greece and Italy
resist insurgent Communist movements, then initiated the Marshall
Plan – massive economic aid to speed Western Europe's recovery. In
July a prominent analyst for the U.S. State Department called for
the "containment" of the Soviet Union. At the end of the month
Congress created the National Security Council, the Joint Chiefs of
Staff, and the Central Intelligence Agency (CIA).[1]

Lewis Hill sat at his desk in a San Francisco office and wrote to a
friend about his project, a noncommercial radio station to be established in the San Francisco Bay Area. His mind raced. He had just
returned from Washington, D.C., where during the Second World
War he had worked as a lobbyist with the American Civil Liberties
Union on behalf of conscientious objectors. Hill had been one of
those COs. So had his friend Roy Finch, to whom he wrote. "In the
last day I've had this letter on at least three typewriters," Hill

98

confessed, and it had "almost reached a point where it could be wrapped up and mailed, but by that time it had lost intelligibility. I'll start again, guaranteeing nothing."

Finch had shown Hill's formal proposal for what would become KPFA to Charles Siepmann, a Federal Communications Commission consultant who advocated FM radio as an alternative to the hyper-commercialized AM system of broadcasting prevalent throughout the country. Siepmann worried that Hill's broadcasting plans might "alienate" listeners, Finch reported back to his comrade. Hill had to admit that Siepmann had a point. "One could hardly deny that the controversial part of our programming will alienate all kinds of people," Hill wrote to Finch.

> So what? I think the rest of the planned program will support the enterprise, and beyond that it is high time that all kinds of people were alienated by things said over the radio. Even here, though, I am not sure at all about the total effect of our "educational" programming. We won't have many, if any, one-man commentaries, lectures on how to think. My own experience has long ago convinced me that the most effective propaganda can be achieved not by exclusiveness, but by its opposite. An argument is a thousand times more convincing if it succeeds in the context of its opposite. For this reason most if not all of our ideological programming will be centered in forums and roundtables of the very liveliest and most explosive sort. We will have everybody on these forums all the time-including the American Legion, etc. What we will depend on is our ability to get participants with the right point of view on the subject in question who can also out-parry the others. If we follow this program consistently, we will go places.[2]

This paragraph illuminates the two impulses that have been in conflict with each other to varying degrees at Pacifica radio since the earliest days of the organization. If we highlight the first three sentences of the statement, concluding with "it is high time that all kinds of people were alienated by things said over the radio," we have the dissenting, insurgent voice. Insistent, indignant, and self-righteous, this sensibility cares little about how it is received. It demands its democratic right to speak, and having spoken, it is satisfied. It speaks, therefore it is. The rest of the paragraph, however, reveals the other side of Pacifica's divided self. Here we have the persona that longs for relevance and legitimacy. Acutely conscious of how it looks to the rest of society, it thinks not only about what it is going to say, but about how it will be heard. It is willing to meet the larger culture halfway if it believes that the compromise will enable it to "go places."

Lewis Hill embodied both of these impulses because he was more than a pacifist dissenter, he was a critic of pacifism and of the dissenting style in American life. Indeed, his inspiration to create KPFA derived as much from his disillusionment with pacifism in his time as it did from his desire to promote it. Hill understood far better than most of his associates that the Second World War had marginalized organized pacifism. By 1945 Hill saw his comrades for what they were – angry outsiders taking what appeared to most patriotic Americans to be an incomprehensible political stance. Pacifists, Hill wrote to a friend, needed to abandon "the puerile notion of creating an awareness of crisis by entering the community from the outside at the top of one's lungs, with a crummy propaganda sheet."[3] They needed to get beyond a rarified discourse designed for consumption by other pacifists, usually pacifist intellectuals.

The first public Pacifica document, a prospectus for KPFA written by Hill in 1946, made it clear what audience Hill wanted to reach. The opening text explained that while pacifists published many newsletters and magazines, such organs usually served an inner circle. "There is little doubt that war cannot be prevented through primarily intellectual appeals," Hill wrote. "The major job for those determined to see a pacific world in our time is, therefore, to enter the region close to home, to speak through the newspapers on the street and over the radio stations – in short, to identify principles of world understanding where they have direct import in familiar situations."[4] In private Hill put the matter even more succinctly. "It matters whether the man who writes, or works in the shipyard, is a pacifist," he wrote to a friend in 1951; "but as to the man who is first,

100

last and only a pacifist – it doesn't matter at all that he is a pacifist."[5] After years of working with COs, Hill understood what full-time radicals constantly forget, that the majority of people in the United States do not live for ideology and politics and cannot be reached through the self-absorbed style of those who do.

Finally, Hill charged that pacifists often assume that a program focused solely on alerting people to the wrongs of the world will spur people to action. In 1945 a friend of Hill's suggested that they initiate a new postwar pacifist magazine. Hill rejected the idea. "It would be easy to make a weekly digest of all the domestic and international shenanigans which are inimical to a world of brotherhood," Hill wrote, and went on to suggest that pacifism needed "a new organ which can place all these events in the perspective of a dynamic, conscious and completely premised program of its own." By the year of Pacifica's founding, Hill had come to the same conclusion as the writer Dwight Macdonald – that decent people were perfectly capable of doing nothing in the face of overwhelming evidence of injustice. "That extreme Evils are committed today, with no large-scale opposition, by the agents of great nations – this leads me to conclude not, with the liberals and the Marxists, that the peoples of those nations are horrified by these Evils," Macdonald wrote in 1946, "but rather that, on the contrary, these Evils are rejected only on a superficial, conventional, public-oration and copy-book-maxim plane, while they are accepted or at least temporized with on more fundamental, private-levels." Radicals, Hill wrote, had become accustomed to "imposing a specific fiat upon the ethical without having awakened its necessity."[6]

To awaken people, Hill concluded, required radical institutions that did not interrupt them but functioned as an intricate part of their lives, primarily by entertaining them. The first Pacificans hoped that KPFA would function as a "war-resistance" project that would avoid the errors Hill had outlined in his writings. KPFA was definitely intended to promote a "pacific world in our time," as the station's literature put it, but to do so as a member of the community, not as an angry stranger preaching to the converted.

And so early Pacifica programming sought an air sound that reached a larger audience than the explicitly political. Music and dramatic reading pervaded the early schedule of KPFA, much of it live. The station devoted no less than one out of every six hours of programming to children. Many early KPFA shows dealt with politics by creating a dialogue-oriented public-affairs programming schedule in which various members of the community would appear on the station's regular programs as commentators, debaters, or panelists.

The first Pacificans wanted to convince their listeners that pacifism and war resistance were good things, but they knew from experience that if KPFA aired only the viewpoints of pacifists, the station's credibility would be called into question. Therefore KPFA allowed persons of any viewpoint to appear on the station as panelists or commentators, but simply steered discussions toward pacifist/anarchist questions. Early KPFA's pacifist politics often emanated from the critical questions the station's staff posed, not from the answers provided. For example, a panel assigned to debate the question "Is the Atomic Age Destroying Our Civil Liberties?" featured a UC Berkeley physicist, a member of the San Francisco Lawyer's Guild, and a member of a local chapter of the Veterans of Foreign Wars. KPFA's pacifists sought to define the center of public debate, not the margins. Conservative-minded people could listen to these discussions, because they included actual conservative voices, not subjects spoken of derogatorily in absentia. In addition, these panels fulfilled a fundamental Pacifica goal: to demonstrate that people with disparate political ideas could resolve their differences peaceably, or at least come to a "lasting understanding" leading to "a pacific world in our time," as early Pacifica literature put it.[7]

Shouting Fire

In the long run, however, KPFA failed to implement the original vision of Pacifica. The station single-handedly inaugurated a golden age of radio, brilliantly representing the San Francisco art, music, and literature scene, but it fell far short of reaching the "average" person with a credible message of peace and social justice. Instead, by the middle 1950s, KPFA functioned as a culture of refuge from the suffocating atmosphere of the times, rather than a culture of resistance or significant challenge to the "establishment." A variety of reasons contributed to this shift. Turned down by the FCC for an AM license in the ethnically diverse, working-class city of Richmond, California, Pacifica opted to launch its first radio station in Berkeley, a racially segregated university town. This redefined KPFA's audience even before the station went on the air. FM was in its infancy at the time. Most FM receivers in the area were owned by a minority of exceptionally educated people in the upper income brackets, centered on the University of California. "It was agreed that it will be necessary at first to aim at a smaller[,] more exclusive audience than originally envisioned," read the Pacifica Foundation Radio Committee minutes of March 5, 1948.[8]

In addition, lack of funds required KPFA's first staff to solicit contributions from the wealthy and to represent the station publicly as a haven for the elite. This proved particularly obvious in a report written by Lewis Hill for the Ford Foundation, which in 1951 gave Pacifica $150,000. "As a general rule, it is persons of education, mental ability, or cultural heritage equating roughly with the sources of intellectual leadership in the community who tend to become voluntary listener sponsors," Hill explained. "Obviously, to earn systematic support from the community's intellectual leadership, the listener-sponsored station must give the values and concerns of that leadership an accurate reflection at their highest level."[9]

But the most important reason for the weakness of the dialogue model was the onset of McCarthyism. Years later, early KPFA programmer Gene Marine recalled the impact of the Cold War on the station's policy. "One of the problems was ... you had this station that was determined, and it was determined from the beginning, to present every possible point of view," he recalled. "But because every possible point of view included points of view on the Left, it became almost impossible to represent the points of view on the Right, because they [the Right] thought that this is a communist station because those Left wing or communist people were on it."[10]

Not only did the repressive atmosphere of the 1950s make it difficult for Pacifica staff to find people on the Left and the Right to debate each other on the air, it gradually encouraged Pacificans to see their dialogue-oriented project as futile, or at least as secondary to a more immediate goal: open political combat with McCarthyism and Cold War foreign policy. Even Lewis Hill, who insisted before KPFA's inauguration that the station would not broadcast lectures to people on "how to think," wound up offering many himself, usually on Friday nights during his regular manager reports. Many of these talks showed remarkable courage, including a 1950 statement against U.S. intervention in the Korean civil war, which Hill described as the beginning of "World War III" and merged into a statement against loyalty oaths in city and state government: "I am going to oppose World War III, and the Oakland loyalty oath, and the government purges, at every place where they touch upon my life and provide a tangible opportunity to oppose them," he declared over KPFA's airwaves. "Whether I speak against them is not important. What I do is important. I am going to refuse to fight the war."[11]

But these declarations set the stage at Pacifica for the dominance of precisely the romantic persona Hill had hoped to transcend: the Angry Outsider defiantly offering the dissenting point of view in isolation from the larger American community. No one symbolized the rejection of dialogue more than Hill's successor, KPFA's late 1950s program director, Elsa Knight Thompson. "You see," Knight Thompson later commented to several KPFA producers, "most liberals think that if you can find the middle of anything and you can squat there, that somehow or another virtue had been achieved." Liberals, she continued, "are never prepared to admit that there is such a thing as right and such a thing as wrong and that if it's wrong, you say so."[12]

When the government subpoenaed a dozen Pacifica officials to testify before the anti-Communist Senate Internal Security Subcommittee in 1963, the organization's leadership needed to come up with a formulation of the network's mission that satisfied both its own priorities and those of the state. KPFK programmer and future Pacifica president Hallock Hoffman perfectly summarized what was to become the organization's relationship with American society for the next three decades. "Pacifica should lean toward programs that present either opinions or information not available elsewhere," he explained. "Just as I feel little obligation to spend time on my broadcasts saying what is wrong with communist governments, since everyone hears what is wrong with communist governments from every side, I think Pacifica serves the ideal of balance if it spends little time reinforcing popular beliefs."[13]

Hoffman's comments represented an adaptation of Lewis Hill's original mission which enabled the organization both to justify itself to the liberal anti-Communist state and to maintain the loyalty of its radical base. Leaning "towards programs that present either opinions or information not available elsewhere" satisfied the Federal Communications Commission's requirement for balance. Pacifica would provide such balance by presenting, not all points of view, but only the viewpoints excluded elsewhere, thus allowing Pacifica's leftist programmers to pursue their sympathies for radical movements at home and for socialist and anti-colonialist movements abroad.

This compromise represented the essence of what would come to be called "alternative media" or "shit-kicking radio," as community radio pioneer Lorenzo Milam described it with both admiration and ambivalence. The doctrine became the Pacifica Foundation's raison d'être, its self-defined relationship with American society. For the next two decades Pacifica Foundation officers, directors, and managers would reiterate Hallock Hoffman's original "question of balance" statement, each time as if it had just been constructed. "We especially welcome those voices which are denied access to other media by those inside and outside of Government who confuse 'free speech' with 'safe speech,' " explained a Pacifica Foundation president in 1970. "Pacifica is high-risk radio," concluded a 1975 brochure, borrowing rhetoric from a crucial Supreme Court decision. "When the theater is burning, our microphones are available to shout fire."[14]

This praxis of unabashed dissent won Pacifica a loyal, passionate audience in three crucial metropolitan regions: the San Francisco Bay Area, where KPFA broadcast; Greater New York, home to WBAI; and KPFK in Los Angeles. In 1967 KPFA enjoyed a roster of 8,398 paying subscribers and had the previous year reported an income of over $212,000. A little more than 13,000 subscribers supported WBAI in 1967, its income in 1966 listed at $232,031. KPFK reported 7,567 paying customers in 1967 and the previous year had collected $236,312 in cash from them.[15] As opposition to the Vietnam war heated up during the Nixon years, support for WBAI in particular would explode, one historian estimating the audience at approximately 600,000 listeners.[16]

From the McCarthy era through the early Reagan years, Pacifica radio's self-defined relationship with American society would serve it well. But the organization's departure from Hill's original vision of a dialogue-oriented network would constantly come back to haunt it. Hints of this tension surfaced from time to time, as in 1965 when WBAI's Chris Koch became the first American to cover the Vietnam war from Hanoi. Infuriated that Koch had not forewarned Pacifica of his illegal trip, board members forced him to submit his scripts to them for review. They demanded over 100 changes in the narrative. Had 4,000 listeners not threatened to cancel their subscriptions in protest over this interference, it is unclear whether Koch's reports would have broadcast over WBAI.[17]

Over the decades, programmers and governors of the organization would grapple with the same question: how could Pacifica influence American discourse if it did not provide programming that reached the Left's "opposites," as Hill put it, as well as its base? These concerns were often expressed by Pacifica activists following their departure from the organization. "Acting on the dubious assumption that conservatives are always part of the mainstream Establishment, with its pervasive economic and political power, Pacifica program planners elected to concentrate their limited resources in promoting leftist perspectives," commented KPFA local advisory board member Charles Brouse in 1974. "This inevitably made Pacifica sound more ideological, rhetorical, and repetitive than it had before."[18] With the ascendance of Reaganism in the 1980s, the concern that Pacifica had become a choir-preaching institution resurfaced with a vengeance. But before then, the network had a far more immediate source of instability to reckon with: its system of governance.

The People's Plutocracy

In mapping out a governance structure for Pacifica, Lewis Hill and his associates had to confront a difficult question: how democratic would they make their foundation? They approached this problem with almost a split personality: they favored democracy within the pacifist movement, but they distrusted it just about everywhere else. And so Hill included a formal role for the foundation's workers, who were mostly fellow COs he had recruited to the project. He also dealt in the project's major financial supporters, wealthy Quakers and liberals, many of whom would wind up on KPFA's advisory board. But he drew the line at sharing governance with whoever happened to subscribe to the station. After all, in 1946 he had no idea who those people would be, since KPFA had yet to become functional. More important, he and his friends had simply learned to distrust popular democracy.

The ideas for Pacifica were mapped out by pacifists during a war overwhelmingly supported by the American public following Japan's attack on Pearl Harbor. The first Pacificans had little confidence in the average citizen's ability to think critically. They feared what Eleanor McKinney, an early KPFA programmer, called the "mass attitudes" of the public.[19] For KPFA publicity director Roy Kepler, to cite just one example, the "average" person had become someone to keep at bay, rather than someone to dialogue with or attempt to influence. "The common man is now free; he has the vote, a job and can even get a college education," Kepler declared in a 1953 KPFA commentary entitled *The Vulgarian Revolution*. "So what does he do with it all? He buys a shiny car, a shiny refrigerator, a TV set, and indulges himself in the popular culture; that is, soap operas, Bob Hope, Mickey Spillane, and Marilyn Monroe."[20]

Hill, Kepler, and their associates also distrusted the nonpacifist Left, especially the Communist Party, which in 1941, when Nazi Germany attacked the Soviet Union, suddenly abandoned its stance against intervention in Europe. Since then the Party had become infamous for its efforts to infiltrate other groups. "Our greatest difficulty in those days," recalled Lewis Hill's wife Joy, "was the risk that the Communist Party would take over. And we were constantly on guard against this."[21] Guarding against this meant not including the listener-subscribers in governance, a position Hill emphasized in a short book he wrote about KPFA in the mid-1950s entitled *Voluntary Listener Sponsorship*. The subscription, he insisted, functioned as "a direct payment to the station in consideration of services received by the listener at his loudspeaker. While various privileges or advantages from time to time were associated with a KPFA subscription, these arose entirely from the station's promotional activity, and bore no relations to the control of its policies. Pacifica Foundation, the non-profit educational corporation operating KPFA, had a controlling membership of community leaders separate from the subscribing audience developed by the experiment."[22]

And so Hill created a governance structure for the Pacifica Foundation – which was to own KPFA and oversee its activities – that shared power with the foundation's workers, but not with its paying customers – the listener-subscribers. He created an anarcho-syndicalist style "executive membership" which consisted of people who worked for the foundation or KPFA or exhibited "[k]een interest over a substantial period of time in the purposes and activities of the Foundation and an ability to aid in its development" (in other words, people who had not yet become involved with the foundation but whom Hill identified as potentially useful to the organization). These executive members periodically voted for a committee of directors, chosen from their own ranks. The members of the committee managed the "immediate" affairs of the foundation and reported back to the executive membership at regularly scheduled meetings. The directors also appointed a chairman, who, invariably, was Lewis Hill.[23]

After Hill died in 1957, and after Pacifica expanded from one to three listener-supported radio stations, the foundation's leaders came to regard the executive membership system as outdated and unwieldy. The foundation's "members" – the staffs of WBAI, KPFA, and KPFA – now worked thousands of miles from each other and could not review the committee of directors' immediate decisions as easily as when most of them lived in Berkeley. In 1961 the organization opted to replace the executive membership system with a traditional board of directors. Pacifica president Harold Winkler created a sixteen-member board, five of whose members also sat on the executive committee. Within six months the new board had delegated to itself extremely broad powers, authorizing its executives "to act for this Board in all respects except that the Executive Committee shall have no authority to amend the By-Laws of the Corporation." In 1968 the board clarified its governmental relationship to Pacifica's three regional communities. Each station area would be represented on the "national board," as it was now called, by at least three members. These three members from each region would each appoint three additional members as a local advisory board for their own radio station, their station manager functioning as an ex-officio member of the local board.[24]

In theory this gave the national board enormous authority. But in practice Pacifica's newly reorganized governing body, which legally owned all three Pacifica station licenses, had little actual power over the stations. Hill had never figured out how to structure a key component into his foundation: money. The boards of powerful foundations often draw their strength from their control over a financial endowment, but not Pacifica. The foundation attempted to compensate for this in its early years by placing millionaires on its boards of directors, but even so, KPFA probably would not have survived through the 1950s had it not been for that grant to Pacifica from the Ford Foundation in 1951 – a windfall the organization spent quickly. Thus the governors of Pacifica enjoyed legal authority, but none of the string-pulling power that comes with control of a big wad of cash to be distributed to others. That power resided with the one sector of the organization that had been formally disenfranchised: the listener-subscribers, who donated money on a regular basis. The closest semblance to democratic legitimacy the national board enjoyed was its connection to its three local boards. But the national board made the functions of these lesser boards completely advisory, stipulating that they could take no actions that "preempt the authority or responsibility of the national board of directors."[25] Occasionally the local boards did take such actions, but never without the approval of the national board – and in any case Pacifica's listener-subscribers did not elect the local boards either.

In short, the people at the top of the Pacifica network had legal authority, but no money or real legitimacy; the people at the bottom the foundation's actual philanthropists – provided money, but enjoyed no legal power. By the mid-1960s, this glaring contradiction within the political economy of the organization would be resolved, as well as it could be, by the staffs of Pacifica's three radio stations.

It's "Your" Radio Station

The small programming and managerial staffs of KPFA, WBAI, and KPFK faced a daunting task. To them fell most of the work of soliciting money from audiences whose individual members knew they could listen to these stations without donating funds. Indeed, audience research specialists estimate that about 90 percent of those who regularly listen to public and community radio stations do not pay for the privilege. In order to get that remaining 10 percent to open their checkbooks, Pacifica staffs had by the 1960s developed a ritual that remains central to Pacifica and the rest of public broadcasting: the fund-raising marathon. Programmers abandoned their regular scheduling and engaged in round-the-clock on-air appeals for money, while listener volunteers sat in telephone rooms and took pledges from subscribers who had heard the number to call on the air.

To generate enthusiasm among listeners for this philanthropic task, Pacifica staffs broadcast the most popular shows of the past few months, usually musical performances, documentaries, and rousing speeches by prominent civil rights or anti-war leaders. But they also cultivated what could be called a rhetoric of moral ownership – a set of on-air assurances designed to give the impression to the audience that their donations went to an institution that was, in essence, theirs. As a listener to Pacifica radio, I long ago lost track of how many times I heard examples of this rhetoric over the organization's airwaves: "Give to [KPFA, WBAI, KPFK], your radio station," along with appeals to "join the Pacifica family." "JOIN US," a KPFA automobile bumper sticker from the 1980s proudly declared, without explaining what exactly the station meant by "join," or, even more ambiguously, "us." Longtime KPFA listener Curtis Gray, who played a role in democratizing Pacifica in the 1990s, also recalled the ubiquity of such rhetoric. "It was sort of a selling point," Gray later reflected. "'Give us money. We depend on you. Without your money we wouldn't be here. We really are your station. You are us and we are you.'" Statements often included meditations on staff "accountability" to listeners, assurances that obscured a fundamental reality – at Pacifica radio the listeners, or accounters, had no formal role in mapping how accountability would be defined for the station staff.[26] In other words, the accountable defined their accountability for themselves – the essence of non-accountability in any modern organization.

This contradictory rhetoric did accomplish two essential tasks. First, it helped convince listeners to give money to Pacifica. Second, it created a sort of vague general impression that the organization ran on democratic principles. "Whatever the legal technicalities under which Pacifica is governed," historian and KPFA listener Theodore Roszac wrote in 1968, "I think I speak for thousands of KPFA subscribers when I say we regard the station as ours, that it defines the community to which we belong." KPFA "*sounded* democratic," later recalled John Whiting, an early station staff member.[27] So persuasive was this "sound" that in the early 1950s the founders of San Francisco's public television station KQED created a listener-subscriber-elected board in part under the mistaken impression that Lewis Hill had done the same at KPFA. "I later learned that this was not true," a chagrined former KQED program director commented in 1996.[28]

By the 1960s, then, the essential parameters of Pacifica radio were in place: a public mission, a system of governance, and a funding base. Both the mission and the system of governance, however, had been constructed out of compromises with forces above and below the organization's leadership: Pacifica told the United States government that its plainly one-sided leftist programming somehow balanced the skewed center-to right-wing bias of most American media, and it convinced its listener-subscribers that somehow, even though the listeners had been excluded from the organization's governance, they owned the network. As flimsy as these mystifications were, they provided the Pacifica governing board with the only legitimacy it would enjoy for four decades. They allowed an institution that excoriated the national security state to represent itself as a contributor to that state's civic health. They also allowed Pacifica's unelected, penniless board to represent itself as the proper leadership of the organization. As we shall see in the next chapter, Pacifica's listeners and staff generally accepted the latter claim, as long as the claimants did not try to accomplish anything.

Endnotes

1   Martin Walker, *The Cold War: A History* (New York: Henry Holt, 1993), pp.4855.

2   Lewis Hill, letter to Roy Finch (November 14, 1947), *Lewis Hill Papers* (herein abbreviated *LHP*), Folder 7.

3   Lewis Hill, letter to Henry Roy Finch, Jr., February 18, 1951, p.2, *LHP*, Folder 2.

4   Pacifica Foundation, *Radio Prospectus* (November, 1949), p.vi.

5   Lewis Hill, letter to Roy Finch (April 16, 1951), p.4, *LHP*, Folder 2.

6   Lewis Hill, letter to Jay Tuck, March 15, 1945, p.1; Dwight Macdonald, "The Root Is Man, Part II," *Politics* (July 1946); 195; Lewis Hill, letter to

Henry Roy Finch, Jr., February 18, 1951, p.2, *LHP*, Folder 2.

7   "Report to the Executive and Advisory Members of Pacifica Foundation on the Experience of Radio Station KPFA in Its First Five Months" (Berkeley: Pacifica Foundation, 1949), pp.37-39.

8   Pacifica Foundation Radio Committee Meeting, March 5, 1948, in Vera Hopkins, "Excerpts from Minutes of the Pacifica Foundation," p.11.

9   Lewis Hill, *Voluntary Listener-Sponsorship: A Report to Educational Broadcasters on the Experimental KPFA*, Berkeley, California (Berkeley: Pacifica Foundation, 1958), pp.13-14.

10   Gene Marine, interview with author (April 22, 1996), p.3.

11   Lewis Hill, "Report to the Listeners" (August 1, 1950), p.2, *LHP*, Folder 5.

12   Ibid., p.173; Elsa Knight Thompson, quoted in *Elsa Knight Thompson: A Remembrance*.

13   Hallock Hoffman, "The Problem of Balance," in Eleanor McKinney, ed., *The Exacting Ear: The Story of Listener-Sponsored Radio, and an Anthology of Programs from KPFA, KPFK & WBAI* (New York: Random House, 1966), p.33.

14   Quotes from "Pacifica Radio: Purposes and Goals, 1946-September 1977," pp.8-10, in Vera Hopkins, ed., *The Pacifica Sampler* (Pacifica Foundation, 1984).

15   Robert Schutz, "The Senate Investigation of Pacifica" (unpublished manuscript, 1963), p.36; "Pacifica Foundation, Income and Subscriptions Through 9/30/67," no page number, in Hopkins, *Pacifica Sampler*.

16   Jeff Land, *Active Radio: Pacifica's Brash Experiment* (Minneapolis: University of Minnesota Press, 1999), p.115.

17   Chris Koch, email to author, July 17, 2003; Brett Harvey, "Radio Impossible: Permanent Revolution at WBAI" *The Village Voice* (September 23, 1986), p.20.

18   Charles Brouse, "Pacifica – A Note About Future Directions" (April 26, 1974), quoted in Gene R. Stebbins, "Listener-Sponsored Radio: The Pacifica Stations" (doctoral dissertation, Ohio State University, 1969), p.301.

19   Eleanor McKinney, interview with author (July 8, 1995), p.5.

20   Roy Kepler, "The Vulgarian Revolution" (unpublished manuscript, October 25, 1953), p.3, possession of author.

21   "Pacifica Is 25: A Documentary by Larry Josephson," WBAI radio program, 1974.

22   Lewis Hill, *Voluntary Listener-Sponsorship: A Report to Educational Broadcasters on the Experiment at KPFA, Berkeley, California* (Berkeley: Pacifica Foundation, 1958), p.5 (emphasis added).

23   "Pacifica Foundation By-Laws, 1955," esp. Article II, section 2(a)ii; Article III, section 1; Article V "officers": www.pacifica.org/governance/551031_PacificaBylawsRevision.html.

24 Pacifica Foundation, "Organization and Procedure" (adopted by Board of Directors March 9 and amended June 1, 1968), Section 1, quoted in Stebbins, "Listener-Sponsored Radio," p.199.

25 Stebbins, "Listener-Sponsored Radio," p.200.

26 Recollections of the author, a Pacifica listener-subscriber since the late 1960s; Curtis Gray, interview with author (July 28, 2004), p.2.

27 John Whiting, "*Review of Pacifica Radio: The Rise of an Alternative Network,*" Diatribal Press (July 14, 1999): http://groups.google.com/groups?selm =7mtrle%24hv7%241%40clavin.efn.org&oe=UTF8&output=gplain.

28 Jon Rice, interview with author (February 14, 1996), p.1.

CHAPTER 3

Inventing Community Radio, 1968-1979

> I didn't know what the fuck I was doing.
>
> RAY HILL, FORMER MANAGER OF KPFT

The success – and notoriety – Pacifica radio enjoyed in its formative years had, like all successes, unforeseen consequences. The most notable of these was an enormous influx of people who did not fit into the organization's predominantly white, middle-class radical/liberal culture, but constantly heard on Pacifica frequencies sentiments suggesting that the network valued openness and inclusivity. In truth, many of the advocates of these fine statements did cherish such things far away, say, at Arkansas's Little Rock High School, site of a heroic integration struggle. Closer to home, older Pacifica programmers tended to see the matter as more complicated, particularly when it came to protecting their own air slots dedicated to classical music, books, or radical political ideas. But the outsiders who would gradually make themselves insiders at Pacifica in the late 1960s and 1970s had no choice but to fight their way in. "The fact that there was no PBS," recalled Chris Koch, "the fact that there was no NPR, meant that if you wanted to turn to anything different than network news, your only place to go was Pacifica."[1]

By the early 1970s a wave of newcomers had arrived at Pacifica because it was the only place where they could become noncommercial broadcasters themselves at stations which enjoyed powerful broadcasting signals. Suddenly the subjects of race and gender emerged as both journalistic topics and questions confronting the internal life of the organization. KPFA, KPFK, WBAI, and soon two more Pacifica radio stations would have to accommodate people who came from very different backgrounds from those of the network's first and second generations.

In the course of this tense process Pacifica once again redefined itself. By the early 1980s it had gone from dialogue, free speech, and dissent radio to "community radio." Looked at carefully, this latest term suffered from the same wobbliness as the monikers Pacifica had previously used for self-definition. At the moment, however, it made immediate institutional sense. The idea that a Pacifica station broadcast to a wide variety of "communities" – African-Americans, Latinos, gay men, lesbians, and various kinds of activists – enabled it to absorb a whole new generation of personnel while at least trying to maintain some overarching philosophical purpose.

But Pacifica's new credo created as many problems as it solved. The inherently decentralizing assumptions of "community radio" made Pacifica more ungovernable. Older programmers, invariably derided within the network as white liberals (which they usually were), gradually built up a series of standard observations about Pacifica's community radio system. Individual programmers regarded themselves as unaccountable to anyone except people they regarded as part of their group. The need to accommodate many more people into the station broadcast sound resulted in increasingly atomized and fragmented on-air schedules. The new programs – often representing some ethnic nationalist or identity-based perspective – tended to focus on delivering a message without giving much thought to how the message was being delivered.

Eventually many of those who arrived at Pacifica during the community radio period would come to agree with these criticisms. But first their revolution would have to run its course.

KPFA on Strike

In 1972, despite the upheavals of the 1960s, from the perspective of on-air content KPFA still bore a strong resemblance to the station of its founders. As in the beginning, the frequency's daily programming embraced news, public affairs, readings of literature, and a flexible interpretation of classical music – first the European masters, then American jazz, then Asian traditions such as Chinese opera, Javanese gamelan, Japanese koto, and Indian raga. Folk music played fifth fiddle in this ensemble, even though the Bay Area had been swept up by the folk music revival just as violently as most other urban regions in the United States. A good deal of KPFA's live talk focused not on the major news stories of the day but on literary matters, served up in the form of lectures by prominent critics. And when the station did not broadcast classical music, it broadcast people talking about classical music. "NICOLAS SLONIMSKY MEETS THE PRESS," began KPFA's folio listing for 7 p.m. on Sunday, December 24, 1972. "The dean of musical lexicography visited KPFA to talk with Robert Commanday and Charles Amirkhanian. Slonimsky plays the piano with his back to the keyboard in an unbelievable demonstration of his dexterity at age 76."[2]

Programmers who had seen the earliest days of the station still showed up for their regularly scheduled shows. Kenneth Rexroth, renowned anarchist poet, essayist, and mentor to the Beat writers, still reviewed nonfiction books on Sundays.[3] Gertrude Chiarito, who had run KPFA's live studio board on April 15, 1949, the station's first day on the air, still arrived every Friday night for her live folk music extravaganza, *Midnight Special*, where radio listeners first heard a young performer named Jerry Garcia.[4] William Mandel, who had first been interviewed on KPFA in 1950, continued to broadcast his show entitled *Soviet Press and Periodicals*, as he would for years to come.[5]

The station's *Folio* guide, though typeset and larger now than the sometimes mimeographed affair of the 1950s, still resembled the early days in tone: bohemian, intellectual, and suspicious of formal

117

education. Its December 1972 cover featured aphorisms by Archibald MacLeish and Walter Lippman, and an abbreviated passage by Buckminster Fuller: "The true business of people should be to . . . think about whatever it was they were thinking about before somebody came along and told them they had to make a living," the inventor of the geodesic dome was quoted as saying. The ellipsis concealed the words "go back to school and."[6]

But between the cracks of the schedule, especially during the late hours, one could discern evidence of a different future for KPFA. *Reflecciones de la Raza*, for example, broadcast in English and Spanish. A feminist program titled *On Unlearning Not to Speak* had also recently appeared on the roster, as had *Chinese Media*. These shows all had one thing in common: they appeared during the later hours of the weekday schedule or on weekends.[7] This would soon become an issue, as would many other matters related to the gender and ethnic composition of the station.

From Third Programme to Third World

By the early 1970s the region surrounding KPFA had gone through a series of highly visible upheavals over diversity in admissions and hiring at its two major public colleges, the University of California at Berkeley and San Francisco State. The San Francisco State strike of 1968 and 1969 certainly generated the most fireworks. Although the school served the area that had given birth to the Black Panther Party, only 700 of SF State's 18,000 students were black, a mere 4 percent at a time when they represented 20 percent of San Francisco's populace.[8] And so State's Black Student Union demanded that the school hire twelve African-American faculty to establish a Black Studies Department and that all black students who applied to State be admitted, tuition free. Negotiations between students and administration broke down after one student leader suggested that black students bring guns to campus, and the Panthers staged a demonstration, famously chanting, "Revolution has come. Off the pig! Time to pick up the gun! Off the pig!"[9] The state chancellor then appointed a new president for the campus, the conservative semanticist S.I. Hawakawa, who responded to these sparks with generous doses of gasoline. Faculty firings, student suspensions, and police raids became the norm, leading to a season of strikes, violence, and the arrest of 700 activists.[10] At UC Berkeley, a coalition of students calling themselves the "Third World Liberation Front" also struck the campus, demanding a separate college for minorities. In the end both confrontations resulted in ethnic studies departments on their respective campuses.[11]

Eventually the Bay Area minority activist community turned their attention to KPFA, which was, after all, still run by an overwhelmingly white staff. It would have been difficult to penetrate KPFA's internal structure in 1969. Strict union rules excluded all but a chosen few from the station's production studio. "The engineers sort of controlled everything," one minority activist later recalled. "The way of governing people was just by denying them access to production."[12] A small cadre of staff tightly controlled the schedule, and most of them still took their journalistic standards from the British Broadcasting Company's Third Programme, a prejudice that won them points with senior Pacifica national board members. Very "BBC-ish," one former Pacifica general manager described them. "First of all," he recalls, "you couldn't use the word 'show' in Pacifica. You had to call it a 'program.' I always thought that kind of implicit in their pronunciation was that it had two 'm's' and an 'e.'"[13] So before outsiders could make any claim to KPFA's resources, insiders would have to loosen the place up a bit. By the early 1970s they had set their sights on the ruling matriarch of the station, former BBC employee Elsa Knight Thompson.

Younger white Pacifica programmers both admired and resented Knight Thompson. They loved her path-breaking interviews, especially her sympathetic conversation with Black Panther Party leader Huey Newton and her remarkable 1958 panel discussion, "The Homosexual in Our Society," the first gay-rights radio documentary in U.S. history. But they chafed under her strict rules and almost fanatical supervision of the life of the station. No one detested her more than Lorenzo Milam, a KPFA programmer who fled Pacifica to pioneer a network of community stations across the United States. Years later, long after Knight Thompson's death, Milam would still rail against her "shallow, box like" vision of programming, all but explicitly comparing her to Josef Stalin. "She and her fellow-travellers used every guile to steal the frequency from the gentle anarchists [who founded Pacifica]," he wrote, "utilizing the extended coup, back-stabbing as a high art form, and unyielding bleakness. Under her aegis, the often happy-go-lucky, intellectually galvanizing radio station fell into a Slough of Despond, and became a voice-box of the tendentious left."[14]

Less bitter but also critical of her was a young KPFA newcomer named Larry Bensky, who questioned her strict rules for radio production, especially her insistence that interviews for broadcast be prerecorded and cleared with her a week in advance. "She not only wanted to do her thing," he explained, "she wanted to be sure that anybody who did anything like her thing did it in her manner."[15] In the early 1970s, neighboring free-form underground rock stations such as KSAN in San Francisco championed a spontaneous music and interview style that Knight Thompson had essentially declared verboten at KPFA. Many young radicals in the Bay Area experienced KSAN as far more receptive to their ideas. "KPFA was thought to be very stuffy and sort of old-fashioned and didactic and boring and not with-it culturally," Bensky later recalled.[16]

Women programmers also deeply resented Knight Thompson, largely because she consistently chose men to train and mentor: "Elsa's boys," they were called.[17] Like many strong, talented women of that time, Knight Thompson knew, consciously or instinctively, that the male-dominated institution in which she thrived could tolerate no more than one prominent female presence. Hence she discouraged others. A telling moment occurred when a woman schoolteacher approached Knight Thompson, politely asking if she could volunteer at the station. KPFA's public affairs director told her that she would see what she could do and walked into Gertrude Chiarito's office to discuss the matter. "There's a lady out there," Knight Thompson began, within earshot of the woman. "She seems terribly stupid, she says she wants to help, but I think she's too stupid."[18] Confident of her stature well beyond the point of arrogance, Knight Thompson lost sight of the network's central reality: no one person or faction embodied its mission.

And so her enemies laid a set of traps for the self-proclaimed heir to Lewis Hill's legacy, and she fell into them. In 1971 Al Silbowitz, the latest general manager of KPFA, convinced her to accept the managerial position of program director, a promotion that denuded Knight Thompson of her union seniority rights. Then Pacifica asked her to serve temporarily as general manager at KPFK in Los Angeles. In her absence, Silbowitz declared publicly that she had retired. A KPFA programmer disputed this over KPFA's airwaves, insisting that Knight Thompson had been fired. The controversy caused uproar in the station community. Finally, on Thanksgiving Day, the programmer interviewed Knight Thompson for an hour. Her replacement, Larry Lee, one of the founders of KPFT in Houston, ran the control board at the time. He concluded the interview with a selection from the soundtrack to *The Wizard of Oz* – "Ding Dong the Witch Is Dead" – and then added his own remarks, to the station's everlasting shame: "We finally got rid of that male chauvinist pig in drag," listeners heard Lee declare.[19] Seven years earlier, Knight Thompson's dismissal had provoked a staff strike that won her job back. Now 62-years-old, surrounded by personnel four decades younger, she and her followers found themselves isolated at the station. Soon she was gone.[20]

Her departure opened a leadership void at KPFA. Into it would step programmers roughly divided into two categories – younger white producers inspired by the free-form radio movement of the late 1960s, and minority producers who sought to open the station to a more multicultural sound. Larry Bensky and Roland Young, denizens of the Bay Area underground radio scene, represented the best of both these tendencies. Bensky appeared on his own show, as well as with sociologist Todd Gitlin and economist Doug Dowd in a late-night public affairs forum whose title, *The Surplus Prophets*, played to the Marxist insomniac crowd.

A talented black musician, Roland Young treated KPFA listeners to exquisite evenings of world music and jazz.[21] He represented the vanguard of a critical mass of minority activists anxious to transform the social and demographic base of the station. Among their principals was Emeliano "Jeff" Escheverria, a passionate twenty-two-year-old who had been volunteering at KPFA since his sixteenth birthday. The son of a family fled from the 1954 U.S.-backed coup in Guatemala, Escheverria had risen through the ranks at KPFA, from teenage errand boy to trusted production studio engineer. Ironically, he admired Knight Thompson and regretted her ouster. But now he sought more space for minority voices, especially those of Latinos.[22] Escheverria hooked up with another programmer, Raoul Torres, and the two began producing a regular Saturday morning segment on Latino/Chicano politics, *Reflecciones de la Raza*. During *Reflectiones's* tenure, Torres and Escheverria interviewed just about every important Latino leader in the country. The program could not have been more timely. The United Farm Workers verged on winning their national grape boycott. Twenty thousand Los Angeles Latinos had just staged their Chicano Moratorium, a march and protest against the Vietnam war.[23] Their show attracted listeners, and, not surprisingly, people who wanted to get in on the action.

Prominent among the latter group was twenty-year-old Isabel Allegria, who worked for an experimental school for Chicano children in Berkeley. One day Torres invited her to bring her students to the KPFA studio. Placed before the microphone, Allegria's toddlers read their poetry and sang songs to guitar accompaniment. It went so well that Torres asked her back again, and then once more. When Torres invited Isabel and her brother Andres to help KPFA cover the first La Raza Unida convention in El Paso – a venture into third-party politics for Chicano activists – she leapt at the chance. There she interviewed a young woman whose husband had just been shot to death by the police. Allegria was struck by how similar she and her interviewee were in age and appearance. "I had to think a lot about what it meant to hear her, and then turn around and tell other people what she had to say. It was the beginning of my sense of what journalism was." The young reporter returned to the station "bitten by the bug," she later confessed.[24]

But producers who came from very different journalistic backgrounds also sought a presence at KPFA, and initially they stole the show. Bill Schechner, a future NBC News correspondent, arrived from his public affairs director post at WBAI in New York City to host KPFA's morning slot, which began at 7 a.m. The *Folio* rarely listed the specifics of his program, *The Ungodly Hours*, preferring to tease the audience. "Bill Schechner constructs a brave new world with his brand new tinker toys," ran the Friday, December 1, listing. "With Bill Schechner, whose cat got his tongue, so he'll whistle instead," read Wednesday the 13th.[25] Schechner lasted about two years, to be replaced by another WBAI veteran. The wry Larry Josephson titled his version *The Colgate Human Comedy Hour*, perhaps an early poke at enhanced underwriting. *Folio* descriptions for his stint were equally vague. "Larry Josephson buys five bananas, some cream, bakes a pie and throws it in the face of the morning blahs," declared the mailing on Friday, December 14, 1973. "Larry rejoins the gypsies," a subsequent listing confided.[26]

These two funny men delighted many KPFA listeners. "I liked Larry," longtime KPFA listener Sharon Wood later reflected (Wood would later co-produce a documentary about KPFA). "He would play something like 'The Bluebird of Happiness,' and then spend the rest of the morning complaining. I related to it."[27] But Schechner and Josephson inspired resentment among others, especially indigenous West Coast progressives and minority activists seeking to transform the station. Josephson in particular struck some as contemptuous of the region. "They were New Yorkers," Escheverria later explained. "And you can call this regional chauvinism, or you can call it whatever you want, [but] the Bay Area has a very proud and very consistent sense of history all its own and does not need people from another part of the country to tell them how to do their struggles."[28] For many it came down to a question of to whom and how the station would allocate its scarce resources.

Most of the minority collectives producing individual programs at that point shared one small closet that had been converted into a studio. "We didn't see ourselves . . . as integrated into the station," Allegria said. "We used to have a joke that we were like the cockroaches – the 'cuccaraches' – that would go and work at night, you know, and sort of run all over the station doing everything we needed to do, and then disappear in the morning."[29]

Thus the question of KPFA's future sans Knight Thompson came to a head – the first of many heads – in the summer of 1972, when a coalition of these groups met with Lee, who had replaced Silbowitz as station manager, to discuss the matter of station access. A young woman named Yolande de Freitas spoke for the insurgents, her mixed ethnicity uniquely qualifying her for the task. She was "everything," an admiring Escheverria later explained, "black, Chinese, white, Portuguese, from Trinidad."[30] To the table de Freitas brought the following demands: a Third World department with a full-time paid staff member equipped with keys to all important station doors, to be consulted before the hiring of any Third World people at the station, and to train all Third World people at the station; a requirement that all Third World programs come through the aforesaid department; and ten hours of Third World air time per week guaranteed. Hovering over these negotiations were the threats of an activist group, the Community Coalition for Media Change (CCMC), whose attorneys warned Pacifica that they would challenge KPFA's FCC license renewal if Lee did not accede to the proposal.[31]

Lee sympathized with the essence of what de Freitas wanted. He conceded that KPFA's local advisory board had no African-American members and that the station employed only two half-time black producers. But both federal law and his own sense of Pacifica's mission prevented him from creating something uncomfortably close to a racially segregated departmental structure. At first Lee and de Freitas compromised on a "Third World Communications Project." But this simply delayed the inevitable. By early 1973 the Project members declared themselves the Third World department and began to press for more resources.

Perhaps sensing the waterfall ahead, Larry Lee resigned. A small congress of Latinos campaigned for Raoul Torres to replace him, but to no avail. After a stormy candidates' meeting in November of 1972, KPFA's local board picked an affable but obstinate Englishman named Roger Pritchard for the job of general manager. Pritchard made his situation worse by passing over various minority candidates and hiring yet another WBAI staffer, Paul Fischer, to head KPFA's news department.[32] Then management warned Isabel Alegria's brother Andres to stop taking the Third World department's grievances to the airwaves, lest the faction lose its air time. In response, they piled into Pritchard's office, unannounced, on a hot July evening. For over two hours his captors regaled him with non-negotiable demands galore: three full-time paid positions for the Third World department, to be expanded to five in a year; a $25,000 departmental budget; autonomy in hiring of department staff; two pages reserved in the *Folio* for Third World programming; and the immediate hiring of Escheverria to head the operation.[33] The meeting went nowhere. Then one week later a very nasty incident occurred, about which, not surprisingly, Pacificans offer conflicting accounts.

According to Pacifica's first institutional historian, Vera Hopkins, no friend to Third World departments anywhere, a score of "Third World people" entered the station and tried to get into the control room – "one drunk," she recounted, "one with a cinder block, threatening to kill someone and destroy the station."[34] Escheverria's version is more complex. According to him, after their meeting, Pritchard cancelled further Third World programming until negotiations regarding the department had been settled. Unfortunately, he didn't tell the Third Worldians. They showed up for their regular 10 p.m. news show to find the station's program director, Fran Watkins, and several other white staff members locked inside the control room, cueing up classical records for the hour. "So I had a key to the door," Escheverria recalled. "I had a key to every door in the station. I had been a trusted volunteer at KPFA for years by that time, and I open the door and say, 'Look, it's time for us to do our program.'"

The white staff refused to budge, and the two groups exchanged angry words. Finally the program director threatened to switch off the station transmitter. At that point Escheverria lost his patience completely. "Well, you do that, you ain't leaving here alive," he replied. Later Escheverria acknowledged his bad judgment. "I didn't have the means [or] ability to deal with that, to back that up. It was cute, it sounded rhetorically funny, a kind of polemic-of-the-times kind of thing. But it wasn't the right thing to say. And they used that opportunity as a pretext to claim that the station and its people were under threat."[35]

Indeed they did. KPFA management banned Escheverria and the entire Third World staff from the station.[36] First Escheverria took the ban to court and lost. Then he just ignored it and continued to produce programs at the station anyway. The CCMC went ahead with their FCC complaint, accusing the station and Pacifica of racial discrimination.[37]

The rest of the network followed these tribulations nervously, debating the organization's future. Prominent on the Pacifica national governing board were women and men who had been involved with the organization for decades and had known its founder, Lewis Hill. In the mid-1970s R. Gordon Agnew still served on the national board in various capacities. Agnew had written Hill's epitaph in the *KPFA Folio* in 1957. Now he told other members of the board that Hill had never wanted KPFA to become a "cause station," as he put it. "Hill wanted to change the situation in which people were propagandized," a witness to Agnew's comments later recounted, "and give the thoughtful citizen a total picture."[38] This represented a half-truth. In reality KPFA had always been a cause station of some kind or other. The pressing question now – seven years after the passage of the 1964 Civil Rights Act – was whether white people would remain the primary caretakers of the cause.

But those presently banging on the doors to the castle could not have offered a vision less palatable to Pacifica's predominantly liberal keepers of the flame. When Third World activists at KPFA made demands, they often made them for separate institutions within the station structure and for separate resources and programming. Even their politest statements all but disqualified white people from dealing with the question of race and race relations. "Third World people have been historically relegated to less than first class status, not to mention the way in which the cultures and histories of Third World people have been slandered and generally misrepresented," a *KPFA Folio* essay in December of 1974 declared. "We see ourselves as the *only* people responsible and capable of adequately dealing with general issues affecting the lives of Third World people."[39]

Thus the Third Worldians would not have gotten very far at KPFA on the merits of their own rhetoric. But they had allies, white programmers who continued to chafe at the vision of the organization's national board, summarized by 1970s WBAI general manager Frank Millspaugh as "discussions by the leading minds of our time with the listeners privileged to listen in, to overhear, as if they were a fly on the wall at these great, momentous, intellectual occasions."[40] Roger Pritchard's hiring reflected this conservatism. His plan for a marathon special, as proposed to a 1974 national board meeting, consisted of interviews with ex-KPFA staff who had gone on to mainstream journalistic careers, mostly notably John Rockwell, John Leonard, and Alan Rich. Clueless as to how bitter KPFA's minority programmers felt about station governance, he hired a white program director, Craig Pyes.[41] Pyes posed for a five-inch glamour photograph of himself on the fold-out page of the July/August 1974 edition of the *KPFA Folio*, then settled in for what quickly degenerated into a six-week staff strike that shut the station down during the last days of the Nixon administration.[42]

The 1974 KPFA strike was formally a revolt against impending layoffs and the refusal of management to recognize the Third World department. Eventually the strikers won national board recognition of a program council, a sort of collective-of-the-whole, which met regularly to make station programming policy. In the early days of this institution, sometimes as many as 80 people showed up for a council meeting, including those previously called volunteers and now formally defined as "unpaid staff" (another victory of the strike). This classification initially included everyone at the station, since the walkout had left KPFA completely broke. "We went back on the air just a few hours at first a day," Larry Bensky recalled. "We weren't able to pay anyone, so we had free lunches catered every day, and dozens of people ate free lunch there. It was the only perk you got." Bensky and now acting station manager Warren Van Orden set themselves the task of reconstructing the station's books. The program council, impressed with Bensky's initiative, elected him permanent station manager.[43]

More fundamentally, the strike represented recognition that a new generation of younger KPFA programmers had come into their own and needed the authority to work out their own vision for the station. "Ironically, after the strike, which was such a supposedly revolutionary event in the history of the station, we returned to programming that was not very, not hardly at all different from what we had gone out on," recalled KPFA news director Alan Snitow. "There was not a transformation of programming. That's partially because everyone went out on the strike, so that all of the constituencies that had programs when they came back in were still represented."[44] Interestingly, the KPFA strike of 1974 probably had as much impact on a frequency 3,000 miles away as it did on itself.

To Dream a Station

While the KPFA staff returned to their jobs, Pacifica attorneys were locked in a battle to win a license for what was to become the foundation's fifth radio station, WPFW in Washington, D.C. Since 1968, when they first filed an application, the struggle had not been going very well. Pacifica had competition for the frequency from Howard University and the National Education Foundation. The NEF embarked on an aggressive campaign to knock Pacifica out of the race, charging that the network provided air time to Communists and promoted "genocidal race hatred."[45] Howard's attorneys played their strong suit. As a university they could more appropriately lay claim to what the FCC defined as an "educational" radio license. But, miraculously, in 1970 the FCC denied Howard's application. Then NEF found a radio station elsewhere. Now Pacifica could focus entirely on convincing the government that it had a coherent, unified vision for a D.C. listener-supported frequency.[46]

Unfortunately, it didn't. Privately, foundation staff knew that they had no serious financial backing from the D.C. community, no seed-money commitments from local organizations, and no sense of who might constitute the station's first local advisory board. In addition, different elements within the network had different expectations for what WPFW would ultimately become. For the national governing board, one participant recalled, "the idea was that it would be a Washington version of what Pacifica was at that time," in order to wield some influence in Congress and at the White House.[47] But D.C. was in a state of rapid transformation. In 1968 the city endured riots over the assassination of Martin Luther King, Jr. Since then its black community had been in a state of continuous political mobilization, ultimately resulting in the election of civil rights activist Marion Barry as mayor in 1978. Washington, D.C., was now "chocolate city" to its culturally and politically conscious black residents. Constituting nearly 80 percent of the population, they joined an increasingly integrated workforce while continuing to live in segregated sections of the D.C. region. But by dint of sheer numbers, they dominated the city's political life.[48]

The leadership of the Pacifica foundation, however, had little sense of this change. When video producer Denise Oliver, former member of the Black Panthers and Young Lords, got wind of Pacifica's campaign for a local license, she called a member of the governing board for details. "It was a pretty amorphous concept. I mean, it was vague," she later remembered. "It was going to be Pacifica. It was going to be in D.C." And to her alarm as well as to the discomfiture of others, it had not occurred to the board to recruit a black station manager for a listener-supported license broadcasting to a predominantly black city, despite the fact that the man who had been supervising the license application process, local broadcaster Phil Watson, was himself black.[49]

By 1974, news of Pacifica's plans or lack thereof for WPFW had reached the insurgent staff at KPFA. They, especially the station's now formally recognized Third World department, reacted with alarm. KPFA went so far as to bring a "jumping and screaming" delegation, as one observer described it, to the next national board meeting, demanding that Pacifica hire an African-American general manager for WPFW. The delegates impressed Oliver tremendously, among other reasons because "a lot of the people that were doing the jumping and screaming were white," she recalled.[50]

The national board and the network's more radical elements managed to develop a compromise. They hired as WPFW's general manager a Harvard law school graduate named Greg Millard, a young African-American native of Houston, Texas. Unfortunately, they gave Millard no money to get the station started. To a suspicious Oliver it looked liked they'd set him up to fail "so [they could say]: 'Yes, we made the attempt, look what happens, it didn't get on the air, we've made a mistake and now let's get our nice person who's going to put our classical music/news bureau on.'" Concerned, Oliver contacted Millard, who appointed her the station's program director.[51] She then assembled a group of volunteers, who produced pilot programs for WPFW.

"What we actually did was to dream a station," Oliver explained. Then she took her dream on the road. First she flew west to KPFA, where volunteer programmers played her pilot shows during the next station marathon. "And then we would just talk – talk about the opportunity for the first time in the nation's capital to have a Pacifica station that would also be black and it wouldn't be racist. And the money poured in from KPFA listeners." From there Oliver took her show south to KPFK, where legendary science-fiction-show host Mike Hodel helped her raise money. She finished her tour at WBAI in New York City with enough cash to get the station up and running. By then, 1977, Pacifica had won a temporary license for WPFW. On February 28, the Pacifica Foundation's fifth radio station finally went live, broadcasting what was to become its signature tune,

Duke Ellington and Billy Strayhorn's "Take the A Train." *The Washington Post* took note: "Not with bang nor whimper but with something of a lurch, radio station WPFW-FM ended a nine-year marathon of bureaucratic rigamarole and frantic fund-raising and actually went on the air, at precisely 8 o'clock last night. Or approximately 8 o'clock last night."[52]

The Ellington song was a key component of Oliver's search for a workable format for WPFW. "D.C. has a strong middle-class or working-class community that are devotees of that music," she explained. "And I thought that that would be a way to bring both the suburban population, where there are also big jazz fans, together within the context of Pacifica." Although classical music was still the rage at Pacifica's East and West Coast stations, broadcasting it in the nation's capital made little sense, since WPFW would have to compete with three long-established classical stations in the area. Oliver's music director, Sigidi Braudy, called the format "jazz and jazz extensions" to keep the vision flexible enough to include blues and Latin music. "Black folk, White folk, Latino folk, women folk men folk, rich and poor folk all appreciate jazz," he explained in a programmers manual. "Because of this jazz and jazz extensions are ideal for gluing our audience together, giving them a common bond."[53] A bit of luck fell to the station when Georgetown University's WGTB exploded in controversy. Georgetown's Jesuit administration put up with WGTB's anti-war programming but raised a fuss when its feminist show, *Sophie's Parlor,* began talking about abortion and gay rights. When students refused to purge the program, the university shut the station down. At least four radical public-affairs shows, including *Sophie's Parlor,* moved to WPFW, as did one of its hosts, a young woman named Lynn Chadwick who was later to become Pacifica's executive director and a key figure in the crisis of the late 1990s.[54]

Not surprisingly, once live over the airwaves, this compelling format began luring recruits to the station. Nap Turner was 46 years old when he first heard WPFW. Born and raised in rural West Virginia, he now made his living as a professional jazz musician and staff member at the city's drug treatment facility, having once suffered from heroin addiction himself. One afternoon he turned on his FM receiver, stumbled onto WPFW's signal, and listened in a state of silent astonishment. "I thought something was wrong with my radio," he later remembered. "They kept playing all these Charlie Parker tunes." But it wasn't just the quality of the music that impressed Turner, it was the devotion to the music. "They were playing these Charlie Parker tunes and nobody was saying anything. And finally this guy comes on and says, 'This is WPFW, your listener-funded radio.'" Turner immediately went to the station and became a volunteer.[55] There he met one of the great unsung geniuses of radio history.

From the early 1980s onward, a portly middle-aged man named Jerry Washington would arrive at WPFW at 11 a.m. on Saturdays and spin a remarkable ongoing tale. It involved the fictitious life and times of an African-American man in his fifties whom Washington referred to as "the Bama" – slang for a black man from the rural South and a play on the name of the state of Alabama. This particular Bama had a complex set of relationships to maintain, at the forefront his Japanese wife, their two college-bound daughters, and Brandy, their collie. Had this been the sum of the Bama's life, it would not have attracted many listeners. But then there were three past families to support, and Denise, a gorgeous young woman with whom he was sexually and romantically involved. This exquisite mess constituted the storytelling subject matter of the *Bama Hours*, which occupied 180 minutes of WPFW's schedule from late Saturday morning to 2 p.m. A "trickster's soap opera," broadcasting historian William Barlow has aptly described Washington's production, "a parody in a parody . . . downhome radio street theater in the black oral tradition."[56]

Underneath Washington's tales of daily life and intrigue he laid a bed of strategically timed R&B tunes, from B.B. King's "The Thrill Is Gone" to Otis Redding's "You Don't Miss Your Water 'Till Your Well Are Undried." To listeners who received the Bama's relationship with Denise skeptically, Washington offered wry candor. "The

132

people ask me, they say, 'How can a tired old dude like you have a pretty girl like that?'" he mused one Saturday afternoon. "She just don't look like she belong with me, but that's all right. We can get through that as long as she don't change her mind." Like a novelist, Washington often borrowed his characters from real life. "Denise" was, in fact, a secretary at his day job, for whose name he scrupulously asked permission before using it on the radio.[57]

In reality, Jerry Washington was anything but the ladies' man he portrayed over the airwaves. Stricken with diabetes and recovering from a stroke, by the end of his days he came to the station in a wheelchair, one leg amputated, and nearly blind. Moreover, Washington was no country bumpkin. He was an educated man who posed as a hick, like his friend Marion Barry, mayor of D.C. and an occasional guest on his program. Before Barry's entrance into politics, the young man had studied for an advanced degree in chemistry. Similarly, Washington attended Atlanta's Morehouse College with Martin Luther King, Jr., then joined the Air Force. Barry, whose personal life did resemble the Bama's, often cultivated a "street affectation . . . that was more political than personal," as two journalists who wrote a book about his reign over the city put it.[58] The mayor did so to win support from poor D.C. blacks who had been marginalized not only by Jim Crow segregation but by the city's African-American middle class. Compared to Barry, Washington had modest goals, seeking listeners rather than votes.

At this he succeeded magnificently. Not only did his program raise more money for WPFW than any other show, the *Bama Hours* scored higher audience ratings than any other weekend radio program in the city. Washington's fans included prizefighter Sugar Ray Leonard and Republican political strategist Lee Atwater.[59] Traditional Pacifica listeners sometimes found Washington's coziness with Atwater a bit disturbing. But to D.C. journalist Askia Muhammad, a longtime WPFW commentator, Washington's friends in high places only added to his charm. "He would talk about Lee Atwater on the air," Muhammad recalled. "It's like you couldn't believe it, you know, 'This nigger can't be talking about, really talking about Lee Atwater!'"[60]

Even people who didn't like the show checked in from time to time, especially those who accused Washington of being a bad role model for black youth. "Particularly at work I would find people listening," Nap Turner recalled. "They would say things like, 'I hate him. I don't like that guy. The things he is talking about on the radio. That's not appropriate!' So I would ask, 'Why do you keep listening?'"[61]

But while WPFW quickly developed a loyal coterie of listeners, the station had a more difficult time achieving financial stability. Quickly incurring a $30,000 debt by 1978, it took Pacifica's D.C. outlet three and a half years to conduct a successful listener pledge drive.[62] Oliver kept the frequency going by aggressively pursuing foundation and church money, including support from a group of Long Island Unitarians who never actually heard WPFW's programming. By the early 1980s she and her associates had stabilized the station's books. "And we developed a really strong base of listener support of regular people. I'm talking about average working-class folks in Washington, D.C."[63] Indeed, Arbitron surveys indicated that by 1982 WPFW had 155,400 listeners. But it also now had a new competitor. That year the University of the District of Columbia inaugurated WDCU, which also adopted a jazz format.[64] While from time to time WPFW would surface for financial air, it often treaded water in a sea of red numbers, and on more than one occasion it came close to drowning.

The reason for this persistent problem is a delicate matter within the Pacifica organization, although it should not be. By the early 1980s WPFW had pioneered an extraordinary radio sound, especially on the weekends, mixing jazz, blues, African and Caribbean popular music, storytelling, and commentary into a unique new schedule. But the station was working with a new public broadcasting audience. Most of its black listeners had grown up with black commercial radio, "an immediate culture," as Askia Muhammad described it, "where radio stations will give you money if you're the 5,010th caller. They'll give you money. They offer to give you money to listen. So why should people give money to listen to this station . . . ?"[65] In his doctoral dissertation on WPFW, communications scholar Jon Arquette Degraff grappled with the basic structural challenge facing the station: its principled decision to reach a black audience meant that it depended on a subscriber pool with less money than a white audience. "Securing finances for the station through the practice of listener-sponsorship placed a burden on station management," Degraff concluded. "This was the one factor that overshadowed the material styles and personalities of WPFW. Many pledges to the station were promises that awaited to be honored. The percentage of listeners that did not fulfill their pledges constituted an uncontrolled variable."[66]

And so this bastion of extraordinary creativity struggled in an atmosphere of frustrating limitations. By the mid-1980s WPFW was so cash-poor that its talented news announcer, Don Foster, resorted to desperate measures to bring his audience the day's events. "I would have to run down from the station, go over to the Martin Luther King Library that had a wire service, and steal the wire service copy off there and then run back to the station," he recalled. "This was like guerrilla radio, right? It was a trip."[67] The lack of understanding and even the level of suspicion with which the rest of the network sometimes viewed WPFW only compounded this dilemma. Charges of technical incompetence and paucity of public affairs programming wafted across the organization's information byways, often lobbed by individuals who had little knowledge of WPFW's history or the challenges it faced.[68] Doubtless the staff of one other Pacifica frequency could empathize with this dilemma: KPFT in Houston, Texas.

Houston, We Have a Problem

There is only one radio station in the United States whose staff can boast that the Ku Klux Klan dynamited its transmitter. Not once, in the case of KPFT in Houston, but two times. Practically all literature about Pacifica mentions these attacks, and today KPFT proudly displays the wrecked device in a special shrine built into its studio headquarters. But the context in which this violence took place and its implications for Pacifica's southernmost station have never been fully explored.

When KPFT began broadcasting on March 1, 1970, it did so to one of the most volatile regions in the country. The population of Houston had almost doubled in two decades. It now stood at 1,232,802 people. The Chamber of Commerce estimated in 1974 that the city was taking in new residents at an average of 55,000 a year. They rushed to work at Shell Oil, the LBJ Manned Spacecraft Center in Clear Lake, or the port, which annually handled over 100 million tons of cargo by the end of the decade. Downtown, the rate of office space construction tripled. At its margins the city exploded, constructing suburban neighborhoods far faster than its demographers could keep track of them.[69]

Yet this metropolis on the Gulf Coast still hadn't decided whether it was an old Western town or something new. An "odd mix between a big cow paddy and an international city," one KPFT programmer called it.[70] Politically, Houston roughly divided into two camps. Older, conservative, white residents, alarmed at the rate of change taking place around them, forged political alliances with recent suburban migrants anxious to stabilize their lives. Meanwhile African-American and Latino activists and their student allies sought the integration of the city's public education system. When Houston's school board voted to adopt voluntary integration plans in 1970, the city split down the middle, the two sides charging in opposite directions. Furious white parents organized two different groups to stop even these mild reforms. Civil rights activists sued the board in federal district court and got a mandatory system that included faculty as well as student integration. Mexican-Americans declared a boycott of Houston's schools and organized a new political party, La Raza Unida.

Social violence, pointed and random, accompanied this turmoil. On July 26 of that same year, students and black activists engaged in a gun battle with police after a political rally. A prominent black organizer died in the fight. Four others were wounded, three of them black. A grand jury cleared the police of any wrongdoing. Around the same time a prominent conservationist was shot to death. Unidentified terrorists bombed one of Houston's alternative newspapers and the headquarters of the Socialist Workers Party. The Ku Klux Klan had never been shy in Houston. During the integration sit-ins of the early 1960s, three white Houstonians caught a protestor, beat him, slashed the letters "KKK" on his body, and tried to lynch him. Now a coalition of progressive organizations accused the police department of shielding members of the Klan who had committed acts of terror. In response, the Grand Dragon of the city's Klan proudly announced that Houston had the biggest chapter of the Invisible Empire in the country. "The strength of the Klan lies in the secrecy of the Klan," he boasted to a reporter. "You may be working with a Klansman." The Houston Police Department recorded 287 murders in 1970. Two years later its detectives caught three men who eventually confessed to the murder of nearly 30 teenage boys.[71]

It was in this atmosphere that KPFT began broadcasting to the city of Houston. Journalist Larry Lee, who later joined KPFA, got the station started largely because he feared for the survival of *The Texas Observer*, a local progressive newspaper, and wanted to see some venue for leftist ideas remain in town (fortunately, the *Observer* got through its troubles and continues to publish). Lee admired Pacifica, but it isn't clear whether he wanted to affiliate with the network at first. He settled on the relationship when he saw that it would smooth out the FCC license application process to have the backing of an established noncommercial broadcaster.[72]

Once the news got around that a Pacifica station was coming to Houston, local hostiles laid siege to KPFT. Even before the station started transmitting, someone fired shots at its office in downtown Houston, followed by a barrage of stink bombs. The staff received threatening telephone calls. Then, two months and twelve days after its first broadcast, a Klansman laid 15 sticks of dynamite at KPFT's transmitter building outside Houston. A huge explosion took place at 11 p.m .on May 12. Had the station's engineer not arrived a few minutes late for his regularly scheduled maintenance check, he surely would have perished in the blast.[73]

Fortunately, none of this surprised the KPFT staff, seasoned activists who had plenty of firsthand experience with racist thugs. The assault generated a wave of national sympathy for the station. Contributions from all over the country augmented the insurance payment to cover the cost of a new transmitter, now constructed inside a concrete-block fortress. This did not discourage the Klan, however, whose operatives in October sneaked into the new transmitter's one vulnerable spot, the roof vent. There they laid dynamite underneath a pile of sandbags, so that the force of the explosion would radiate downward. The second bombing did less physical damage to the transmitter but more financial damage to the station. KPFT lost its insurance coverage, and despite another crest of national outrage and goodwill, had a difficult time raising the $50,000 needed to get back on the air. When it returned in October, a subscriber marathon fell far short of its anticipated goal.[74]

These assaults on KPFT placed in stark relief the dilemma the station would face for the foreseeable future. Unlike KPFA, KPFK, and WBAI, Pacifica's Houston frequency operated in an atmosphere of intense local social and political hostility. To put it simply, the outlet was surrounded by hard-core reactionaries and even terrorists who hated its politics and literally wanted it destroyed. To shield KPFT from the hostile environment into which it had been born, its staff would eventually embed their creation within a layer of social concrete. In a few years they would place it deep in the city's underground subculture, situated at the time in the Montrose District of Houston.

Degentrification

Located about two miles southwest of Houston's center, Montrose, a big patch of stately mansions going back to the Victorian era, had originally been one of the city's silk stocking neighborhoods. The great suburban exodus of the 1950s ended this golden age. Montrose parents died; their children moved away. Suddenly the district became "a place with a lot of big old houses that were not taken well care of," as one resident politely put it. Rents plummeted, to the delight of the city's beleaguered counterculture. They rushed to the section and quickly made it their own. Artists moved in. Gay couples moved in. Hippies migrated in droves. "It was, like, the only neighborhood you could walk around in with long hair without being threatened by rednecks," one migrant recalled.[75]

KPFT's founders first situated its studios in downtown Houston and, when the smoke from the bombings cleared, hired Larry Yurdin as its new general manager. Yurdin had by then drifted through at least a dozen commercial and noncommercial radio jobs, including as producer at WBAI in New York City and as program director of a rock station in Austin, Texas.[76] Upon his arrival at KPFT he quickly assessed the immediate problem: the station's staff were trying to produce a very bad copy of KPFA. That wouldn't do for Houston, he told a reporter in 1973: "Instead of a bunch of freaks programming radio for older liberals, which is generally what other Pacifica stations do, [KPFT is] gonna be a bunch of creative radio maniacs, programming exciting alternative listening for whoever is excited and awed by what's on the air." With that said, Yurdin organized a ten-hour "Cosmic Cowboy" benefit that brought the "outlaw" Austin sound – Waylon Jennings and Asleep at the Wheel – to KPFT. Eight thousand people, including the mayor of Houston and his family, came to the event, which netted the station a desperately needed $22,000.[77]

Then Yurdin purged about half the station's staff and replaced them with a small battalion of unofficial experts on every kind of rock, blues, country, and Cajun music known to the Southwest. Perhaps some of these people fit into the "creative maniac" category a bit too comfortably. At the top of that list proudly stood *Crazy Cajun Show* host Huey Purvis Meaux, whose sideline as a child pornographer would eventually surface after the police caught up with him in 1996.[78] On the other hand, Yurdin gave the late night hours to a blues-loving, wheelchair-bound Vietnam veteran with a speech impediment, who, to everyone's delight, became so proficient that he moved on to commercial radio.[79] The rest of the crew were just maniacs in the usual Pacifica sense – passionate above all else about various sounds piped through a radio transmitter. They turned KPFT into itself, not just into a bad copy of what somebody thought Lewis Hill might approve.

But while Yurdin's efforts gave KPFT its identity, they fell far short of bringing in a subscription base that could keep the station going. By 1974, a year before Yurdin moved on and the frequency relocated to the Montrose district, KPFT had recruited a total of 4,900 subscribers. That represented more than a 200 percent increase over a year earlier, but hardly the number needed to keep the station financially stable, and less than a third of the estimated number of subscribers at KPFK in Los Angeles.[80] A year later an audience survey indicated that KPFT had only 14,700 listeners.[81] And admiring accounts of Yurdin's creative iconoclasm rarely mention his campaign to bring National Public Radio (NPR) to KPFT after Pacifica had decided not to affiliate with the service. Having dismissed the rest of the network as freaks pandering to liberals, KPFT's manager claimed that his staff could not produce public affairs shows of quality comparable to that of other Pacifica outlets. The national board reluctantly acceded to his request in 1974, over the strong objections of WBAI's station manager, Larry Josephson, who warned that "it would tend to blur the distinction between Pacifica and a well-run city or education station."[82]

Any way you looked at it, Pacifica station KPFT faced a big problem: it broadcast to Houston, Texas. Even with all of Yurdin's innovations, one anonymous staffer wrote in the newsletter Alternative Radio Exchange, KPFT operated in an atmosphere of "tension due to the hostile regressive nature of the Houston community, which not only fails to listen or support, but also fails to volunteer." The lack of pay and proper equipment caused people to become "aggressive, so the conditions become worse, so you get even sicker. Your sickness is symptomized by shortness of temper, foresight, and insight."[83] By 1975 Larry Yurdin had moved on and KPFT had relocated to Montrose, "a small, subcultural city within a city, or little town within a city," as one KPFT staff member put it.[84] Five years after that, a remarkable man who had only recently been released from the Texas state prison system became station manager.

The Other Hill

Less noted than the Ku Klux Klan bombings is the fact that in the early years of its operation KPFT received not insubstantial financial support from the earnings of a professional commercial burglar. The Robin Hood in question was born in Houston in the 1940s. Ray Hill grew up and went to school in the Galena Park district, an industrial slum east of Houston proper. His parents were union organizers, father in the shipyards, mother in hospitals. By the time Hill celebrated his eighteenth birthday he was serving as secretary for the local NAACP (he is white) and had come out as a homosexual – no minor act of bravery in 1958.

Over the next decade Hill established himself as a Houston activist in the field of civil rights. In 1968, a year before the historic Stonewall Riot in Greenwich Village was to put gay liberation on the map, he asked a local late-night TV interview show host if he could come on to talk about homosexual issues. The host agreed, but only under strict conditions. "So I wound up going on the air with a preacher that thought I was a sinner," he explained, "a cop that thought I was a criminal, and a psychologist who thought I was sick." Hill held his own throughout the ambush, and found a suitably impressed Larry Lee – a gay man himself – waiting for him on the studio set. "He was cute," Hill remembered, "a good-looking little blond, fresh out of University of Texas, and I thought, well, you know, I wouldn't mind hanging around with a guy like this."[85]

And so Hill helped Lee and his associate Don Gardner raise money for the station. Hill seemed to have a talent for the task. What Lee and Gardner did not know was that by 1968 Ray Hill was making his living by breaking into business establishments and stealing from them. "I had a lot of money that I couldn't report," Hill later explained, perhaps trying not to appear too altruistic. "You get into trouble if you try to pay taxes on more money than you

141

can justify. And so I made some nice anonymous contributions to KPFT, but about that Larry Lee and Don Gardner . . . had no idea until the newspaper articles started coming out." In 1970 the police caught up with Hill, a bemused chief of police confronting KPFT staff. "And we all thought you were getting your money from the Soviet Communists," he confided. The station went on the air in March. Hill went to prison in November. He didn't get out until 1975.[86]

During the years Hill languished in the slammer he listened, passionately, to KPFT. "I credited KPFT for saving what little sanity I managed to preserve during the prison experience," Hill explained. The station went through Larry Yurdin's tenure, then chewed up and spat out several more station managers. Upon his release, the state of Texas gave Hill a check for $200, which he promptly donated to KPFT's latest manager, Bob Rogers. Soon Hill was hosting a gay rights program on KPFT titled *The Wilde and Stein Show*, named after Oscar Wilde and Gertrude Stein.

Meanwhile, the frequency continued to devour senior staff. By 1979 it had purged and counter-purged two more managers. The latest boss hadn't been seen in weeks. Volunteers continued to do their shows, but some noticed that the boss's office door was locked and began to fear the worst. Being the only burglar on the staff, Ray Hill picked the lock. To everyone's relief, the room was empty. A note had been left behind. "Fuck you," it read. "I'm getting tired of all this goddamn work, putting up with all these fucking prima donna programmer volunteers and not getting paid for it. Screw this shit. I'm out of here."[87]

Grateful to Hill for his initiative in solving the mystery, the KPFT staff appointed him its latest general manager. Hill reviewed the station's financial ledger. KPFT had $157 incoming and $12,000 in bills. Desperate for ways to increase subscription income, Hill opted for a technological fix. He summoned the station's engineer and commanded him to jack up the transmitter power from 49,000 to 100,000 watts. This immediately provoked a call from the regional Federal Communications Commission. "What are you doing?" a

142

furious FCC compliance engineer demanded. Hill was defiant. "The license says a hundred thousand watts, and we've been broadcasting at 49,000. I want my wattage back." The FCC conceded the point, and Hill set himself the task of building audience.

A consummate outsider, Hill found himself a kindred spirit to serve as the station's program director. Rafael Renteria grew up in Houston's predominantly African-American South Park neighborhood, his father Latino, his mother white. By the age of 15 Renteria had become an avid KPFT listener. His favorite show was SDS activist Jeff "Nightbird" Shero's midnight mix of radical discussion and psychedelic rock. "I thought that I had hit the center of the cultural universe," he recalled. By 1979 Renteria had joined the news department with a Corporation for Public Broadcasting grant. He was then 24 years old.[88]

Hill and Renteria differed in age and style. The former was an easygoing raconteur and pragmatist, the latter a flamboyant, self-styled Third World revolutionary. In their different ways they were open to whatever it took to build a paying audience for a 100,000-watt radical radio station in a city full of Klansmen and indifferent-at-best white suburbanites. That meant pursuing what could be described as the other Houston, a fragmented array of subcultures and marginalized ethnic groups. At first Hill approached the Houston Harpsichord Society, who asked if they could purchase time on KPFT. "No," Hill replied. "But I'll tell you what we can do. We can broadcast your harpsichord concerts and let me pitch your people for support." From there he and Renteria managed to find a local Iranian who, in the middle of the Iran-hostage crisis, would broadcast to all factions of the Houston Iranian community in Farsi. Then came a show in Arabic, a Hungarian music program in Roma dialect, breaks during drive time for Muslim morning prayers, and an hour of discussion in Vietnamese. By the time Renteria left KPFT after a dispute with Hill, the station broadcast to the Texas Gulf Coast in over a dozen languages.[89] KPFT had become both Larry Yurdin's Cosmic Cowboy experience and the link to a hodgepodge of Houston communities that had no other voice on the radio.

For Renteria, these dramatic programming changes linked Houston to insurgent revolutionary movements around the world, particularly in Iran, Nicaragua, and El Salvador. "Rebellion was very much in the air, and there was this sense of possibility. This was right before Reagan, right before the clamps came down, you know, in such a heavy way," he recalled. "But at that point that door was wide open, and we seized the moment, we seized the day, and just went straight forth."[90] For Ray Hill it was less about ideology and more a moment of experimentation, an attempt to find allies who would keep KPFT alive in Houston. "I didn't know what the fuck I was doing," he later confided. "I had no idea [about] of all the theories that come from the National Federation of Community Broadcasters. So my mind was not polluted with that particular brand of bullshit. I saw radio from a Marshall McLuhan standpoint, that is, that media can very usefully and successfully serve the needs of real people."[91]

For the latest generation of Houston radical youth, KPFT functioned as an almost indescribable revelation, a shrine within the Mecca that was Montrose. "We just kind of muddled through without any money," recalled Torry Mercer, then a young volunteer at the station.

> There were no cartridges on the turntables, and the tape decks didn't work, and the DJs with the nice record collections would have to bring their own cartridges for their turntables when they came down to the show so they wouldn't plow up their records. And the front door was just open twenty-four hours a day. It never closed. And people off the street would just wander in, and you get some real colorful folks in that neighborhood just dropping by, and the DJs would put them on air and have some wonderful late-night talk shows. It was a lot of weirdness, but a good kind of weirdness. It was in touch with that community. It was the community radio station of Montrose.[92]

And what did the Pacifica governing board think of all this? "You know, it was my impression, you know, like, they didn't even know we existed," Mercer said.[93] Indeed, Pacifica's legal guardians seemed far more interested in affairs elsewhere, particularly at KPFK in Los Angeles.

The "Southern Project"

The most important historical fact about Pacifica's second radio frequency is that its founders did not want the station to be governed by the Pacifica Foundation. Paradoxically, the people who organized KPFK were ideologically far closer to the founders of Pacifica than were the progenitors of the network's other three stations. William Webb, KPFK's guiding spirit during the station's planning years, had been a conscientious objector during the Second World War. As vice president of the foundation, he and a small group of followers moved the project through its various complex stages. By 1958 he had convinced Pomona College's radio station to relocate its frequency down a few notches so that KPFK could apply – successfully, as it turned out – for its 90.7 spot on the educational band, he had recruited a staff for the station, he had raised enough money to pay them, and, amazingly, he had enrolled 800 subscribers before KPFK ever went on the air.[94]

But this relatively smooth voyage hit an iceberg when the question of KPFK's formal relationship to Pacifica had to be resolved. Webb committed himself to this work with a crucial understanding: KPFK would be governed by an autonomous body. He outlined his own vision of KPFK's relationship to Pacifica in early 1959. The "southern project," as Webb called it, would for the moment remain under the foundation's legal umbrella, but would "ultimately be organized under a separate corporation from Pacifica Foundation, using the name Pacifica Foundation of Southern California. This new corporation would embrace the same purposes as Pacifica Foundation and would operate a station in the same general manner as KPFA." The two separate entities would maintain ties through a "joint council," whose purposes would include exchanging programs and fund-raising in common.[95]

Harold Winkler, who inherited Pacifica's presidency after the death of Lewis Hill, rejected this plan. To the dismay of Webb's followers, Pacifica's lawyers insisted that a separation could not ensue without FCC permission, although they did not explain why the FCC would not grant such permission if all parties requested it.[96] Furious, Webb resigned. Not surprisingly, a period of chaos ensued. Webb's followers, prominent pacifists in and around the Los Angeles region, expected to function as the station's legal board. "The Southern California Project for subscription radio finds itself at a crossroads of decision," they now wrote in a public statement. "Its Development Committee no longer has any substantial connection with Pacifica Foundation of Berkeley – or will have no connection very soon."[97] Some of its principals drifted into other projects; others eventually joined the Pacifica governing board.[98] Pacifica recruited new staff, most notably future CBS correspondent Terry Drinkwater, as its general manager. The station went live on July 26, 1959.[99]

Thus commenced KPFK's endlessly uneasy relationship with the national Pacifica organization. This tension came to a head most famously in the spring of 1967, when KPFK's headstrong general manager, Paul Dallas, and his followers led an open rebellion against the Pacifica board. Dallas had feuded with the organizers of the summer Renaissance Pleasure Faire, an entrepreneurial couple who, in exchange for publicity over KPFK's airwaves, shared a portion of the annual event's profits with the station. Ignoring the old adage to be careful what you ask for, Dallas demanded more control over the festival. When he got it, the celebration fell apart. The wife of television actor Walter Brennan led a coalition of conservative activists in filing an appeal to the board of supervisors of Ventura County demanding the cancellation of the Faire. To everyone's horror, they succeeded.

Taken completely by surprise, KPFK's demoralized staff began fighting about the debacle over the station's airwaves. The first few programs about the lost Renaissance could be regarded as constructive. They gave the principals involved in the debacle an opportunity to make full disclosure to the listener-subscribers and the many disappointed volunteers involved in the Faire. But one show led to another. They sometimes lasted as long as three hours.[100] Finally Pacifica's president, Lloyd Smith, ran out of patience with what had become something close to an obsessive-compulsive pattern. He sent Dallas a communiqué that he requested be read repeatedly over KPFK's airwaves. It essentially told the staff to shut up about the Renaissance controversy, invoking "a limitation which is somewhat vaguely and inadequately described as 'responsibility.'" By now everyone knew what everyone thought about this unfortunate episode in the station's history, Lloyd declared. "So I conclude with what may be an old Renaissance benediction – may peace be with us all."

Dallas, infuriated at this intervention, defied Smith's order. Despite being stricken with pneumonia, he went on the air to deliver another long and rambling sermon on the Renaissance that wasn't. Within two weeks he was fired. His supporters organized demonstrations at the station's headquarters in North Hollywood. KPFK's deposed manager went so far as to self-publish a book, amusingly titled *Dallas in Wonderland*, essentially calling for the overthrow of Pacifica's leadership and the establishment of a subscriber-elected national board. But Pacifica's president stuck to his guns, and once again the KPFK community's rebellious spirit rose and fell within a few months.[101]

Within this stormy context, KPFK drew to itself the creativity of the Los Angeles cultural and political Left. From the get-go, the station's staff bristled at what they saw as KPFA's commitment to political marginality. Situated as they were close to Hollywood and CBS Television City, their prospect of career opportunities inconceivable in the San Francisco Bay Area made KPFK personnel more open to alliances with the mainstream. "We were able to call on the RAND Corporation – something that would be unthinkable at KPFA – and ask them to check out some facts for us," recalled KPFK staffer Gene Marine, who had worked at both Pacifica stations. "Most of the people at KPFA would not call up the RAND Corporation on principle. And in the second place they would never believe that they would be willing to help us. It's that sort of hopeless 'I'm out in the cold, little match girl' feeling. We just refused to do it. We insisted on behaving like any other professional outfit."[102]

Terry Drinkwater came to KPFK with many plans – first and foremost, to get a job with CBS. While at KPFK he sought to make a name for himself by interviewing the notorious right-wing anti-Semite Gerald L.K. Smith. By the early 1950s Smith had joined forces with McCarthyite California state senator Jack Tenney of Los Angeles. When Tenney lost the Democratic primary for mayor of Los Angeles in 1952, he ditched conventional politics altogether and accepted the vice presidential slot in Smith's fascist and anti-Semitic Christian Nationalist Party, Smith campaigning for the top seat.[103]

Needless to say, the publicity-hungry opportunist accepted Drinkwater's invitation for an interview in the autumn of 1959. Seated in the studio, he immediately began talking about his favorite subject: Jews. "I have to tell you in advance that you will never broadcast this tape," Smith warned Drinkwater, "because organized Jewry will not allow it. They will come down on you like gangbusters." In fact, Smith was half right. When the *KPFK Folio* came out, listing the interview with Smith, the United Jewish Appeal and several other Jewish organizations besieged the fledgling station with protests. "We started getting phone calls," Marine recalled. "All the support we were not going to get; all the public attacks that were going to happen. They were going to kill us; they were going to run us out of town; and nobody had heard this tape outside the station!" In fairness to all those hypersensitive Jews, six million of whose European relatives had been slaughtered 15 years earlier, the listed *Folio* title of Drinkwater's program, "Crusader, Traitor, or Neither," offered a decent chance that this self-proclaimed bigot might not be so bad after all. But Drinkwater wisely responded to the deluge by inviting three prominent Jewish leaders down to the studio to audit the tape. To their own amazement, they approved what they heard. "What happened on tape was that Smith made a total idiot of himself," Marine later explained. "Terry just made him look like a fool, because he was a fool." The interview ran as scheduled. KPFK began building an audience.[104]

The audience grew in the mid-1960s with the inauguration of *Radio Free Oz*, a late-night KPFK comedy show whose masters of free association – Phil Proctor, Peter Bergman, David Ossman, and Phil Austin – began improvising movies over the radio, complete with characters and scripts. Holes in the plot were sometimes filled in with listener call-ins.[105] Soon the quartet morphed into *Firesign Theater*, whose faux public-service-announcement skits took wicked delight in lampooning small-town American patriotism:

> "What's it all about, Mr. and Mrs. John Q. Smith from Anytown U.S.A.?
> Well, it's about this long . . .
> And about that wide . . .
> And it's about this country, about which we're singing about! . . .
> Yes we've got a lot of everything in this land of ours.
> And a lot of places to put it in.
> And maybe that's where you fit in, Mr. and Mrs. John Q. Smith from Anytown U.S.A.!"[106]

The station's listener-subscriber base continued growing into the early 1970s, with the hiring of Ruth Hirschman as the station's new program director and Will Lewis as its general manager. Hirschman had a "showman's eye," in the words of one admirer, and a knack for the bold stroke. The station's former drama and literature director, she supplemented Pacifica's live coverage of the Watergate Hearings with live readings of the Nixon tapes. "Her coverage probably brought in the most money and the highest ratings ever," conceded a subsequent KPFK general manager.[107]

Hirschman and Lewis even knew how to turn KPFK's internal dramas into political theater. On June 7, 1974, KPFK broadcast a tape sent to the station with the voices of Patricia Hearst and Symbionese Liberation Army members Emily and William Harris (KPFA would also broadcast SLA communiqués). The station then sent a copy to the police, who promptly demanded the original along with information about an earlier incendiary communiqué received by KPFK management. When Lewis refused to cooperate,

a judge ordered him jailed indefinitely at the Federal Detention
Center on Terminal Island. He spent 16 days in prison before the
Supreme Court ordered his release. Soon KPFK received another
message from the New World Liberation Front, which it broadcast
as a news item. When police demanded the original, Lewis refused
again. Exasperated, on October 10 the cops arrived at KPFK's front
door with a no-notice search warrant. KPFK reporters armed with
microphones followed the police around the station's halls, broadcasting the search live throughout the day (the staff had hidden the
cassette underneath a mattress in an alley behind KPFK).[108]

Not everyone at KPFK approved of this live guerrilla theater. "I
believe Ruth and Will got caught up in the excitement and, frankly,
lost their judgment," recalled former station engineer Rachel Kreisel.
"To me the SLA had their politics confused with their Oedipal issues
and couldn't distinguish between a psychopath and a true radical. I
was sitting in the [KPFK] control room when the station got the first
bomb threat. Will Lewis meandered in and calmly said that if I chose
to I could leave my post. I was out like a shot."[109]

But if Hirschman and her staff discarded the caution of early
KPFA, she shared the managerial style of her equivalent up north,
Elsa Knight Thompson. Staff at KPFK called her "The Iron Whim,"
and it was a nickname well earned. She purged people and eliminated shows on a regular basis. "It was all very calculated," veteran
KPFK programmer Mario Cassetta later recalled. "No one got a
hearing – they were just gone. And Ruth could be a cobra if you
challenged her. It was terribly stressful." Like Knight Thompson,
Hirschman eventually provoked a staff revolt that forced her resignation in 1976. She fled to KCRW-FM in Santa Monica and, in the
words of one journalist, "made it the hot place on the dial for all
those '60s hippies turned '80s yuppies to tune in to as they cruised
down the 405 in their shiny new Volvos."[110] Hirschman's disappearance at KPFK created the same destabilizing void that Knight
Thompson's absence provoked at KPFA. But at the moment all eyes
turned to WBAI in New York City, which was beginning to go
through one of its periodic meltdowns.

Radio Uncontrollable

By the late 1960s commercial FM had been swept up by a movement that briefly transformed broadcasting throughout the country: free-form radio. Taking advantage of FM's vastly superior tone and its increasingly sophisticated audience, celebrated free-formers such as Tom Donahue and Jim Ladd and "Rosko" at WNEW in New York abandoned the crude advertising tunes, silly jingles, and staccato delivery of AM deejays for unpredictable play lists, long sets, and radical monologues, often set on a bed of psychedelic music. "We didn't think of ourselves as radio announcers or deejays," Boston FM host Charles Laquidara insisted. "We were ourselves, guys who communicated as individuals, not radio personas. Deejays were those fucking hype-heads on AM top 40."[111] As noted earlier, KSAN represented the dominant free-form presence in San Francisco and quickly stole the limelight from KPFA. Its principals reveled in a spontaneity hitherto unknown to commercial radio. "I'd sit there while a record was playing and say, 'What's gonna sound good after this, what's gonna take this feeling further or embellish this or change it in a way that I want it to change?'" recalled KSAN in San Francisco programmer Tony Pigg.

Unfortunately, KSAN's spontaneous fervor hit a snag when Larry Bensky, its news director in 1970, interviewed some workers who had been dismissed from Jeans West, a major KSAN advertiser, for refusing to answer lie detector tests about their sexual orientation. Not only did management fire Bensky, it ordered staff to read an on-air apology to the clothing manufacturer. Bensky moved on to KPFA, where the free-form spirit rarely infected Elsa Knight Thompson's daytime schedule. Similarly, with the exception of *Radio Free Oz*, whose bite-sized skits eventually became a staple at free-form stations, much of KPFK's cultural programming remained decidedly old-school Pacifica.[112]

WBAI, however, did not merely embrace free-form, it pioneered the genre. Although some of Knight Thompson's acolytes had relocated there, most notably Chris Koch and Dale Minor, no single figure dominated the frequency's talk and music stream. Following the flap over Koch's tour of North Vietnam in July of 1965, WBAI's general manager fled the station, as did some of his supporters. The station's new chief, Frank Millspaugh, had a programming void to fill.[113] Three men helped him fill it with something very new.

Bob Fass came to WBAI in the early 1960s and quickly staked out the earliest morning hours for himself (until he arrived, the station had signed off at midnight). A theater actor and singer with a deep baritone voice, Fass began his nightly broadcasts, *Radio Unnameable*, by establishing an intimate, almost conspiratorial tone with his audience. "Good morning, cabal," he whispered to his listeners at the outset. After that, listeners could expect almost anything. Fass's typical spontaneity was aptly described by his biographer, Jay Sand:

> Fass could begin one night's program with several songs from the Library of Congress blues collection, then speak for a while about a War Resistance demonstration while Dylan's "Chimes of Freedom" would fill the background, then talk with a woman whose friends had been arrested at a march and try to collect the $500 to bail them out, then take a phone call from Abbie and Anita Hoffman who just want[ed] to say hello, then play Arlo Guthrie's "Alice's Restaurant" and sing along, then talk with a woman who has lost her cat about how his cat is also named "Mao," then play *Sergeant Pepper's Lonely Heart's Club Band* over and over because he loves the album, then talk with a hippie named Quasimodo about a "shindig" being thrown for volunteers of Liberty House. Fass could open another night with a discussion with a hippie about her seeing a woman let her child run wild at the Be-In ("It was just sort of a sad commentary," the hippie says. "Her little daughter is just left there so that she can go spread her love around to other people. It was just sad, that's all." "Do you draw a larger truth from that?" asks Fass. "No," she replies. "It's just that I was wondering if in the middle of this institutionalized love there's a little of this sad aspect. . . . It bothered me, that's all.")[114]

Listeners knew that their host's exposition had concluded when he breathlessly whispered his perennial signoff, "Bye-bye."

With that, sunrise programming began, often with his free-form colleague Larry Josephson. A former computer programmer, Josephson's morning show *In the Beginning* took a stance toward WBAI's listeners that was obvious from the outset. "He hated them," one of his colleagues fondly recalled, and reveled in a "wretched hostile attitude" that made fun of the phony cheer of the commercial AM drive-time deejay.[115] A brilliant junior-college dropout named Steve Post completed WBAI's free-form trio. He named his Saturday night show *The Outside* and specialized in turning the world upside down. Post exhorted his fans to organize a "fat-in," celebrating the bodies of those labeled less-than-beautiful. Five hundred responded to his call with a Central Park gathering – "in the flesh," as Post put it. For about 12 months he encouraged an on-air relationship with a mysterious caller who referred to herself as "The Enema Lady," phoning in with songs and poems about her favorite bathroom activity. No taboos seemed to inhibit the broadcasts of these three men. Indeed, they sometimes wondered what, if any, limits could possibly exist, Josephson speculating, according to Post, that "if we presented several hours a week of nothing but farting, the program would soon have a large and dedicated following." They played the same song over and over or let the needle repeat over damaged grooves while talking over the repeating pattern. They made fun of listeners. They fought with each other over the air. Most significantly, they reached far beyond Greater New York's counterculture ghettos of Greenwich Village and the Upper West Side of Manhattan. "[Bob Fass] was my friend, my reality for years, long before I met him," one listener from conservative Staten Island later explained. "I never heard anyone come out and say that the Vietnam war was wrong. It didn't even occur to me. You couldn't have that kind of a thing. And they made it sound like a party! There was a party every night. And my life was pretty drab and miserable then, but there were these guys on at night." Listeners adored them. College radio deejays launched careers imitating them. Richard Avedon took their photograph for *The New Yorker*.[116]

Bolstering the station's free-form schedule was its uncompromising coverage of the Vietnam war. WBAI's news department used foreign wire services to bring a completely different take on the war. A twenty-year-old news programmer named Paul Schaffer would scour the New Jersey press for obits of Vietnam war veterans, bringing the impact of the war home to listeners well beyond Greenwich Village.[117] They tuned into the station in unprecedented numbers. "Everyone was against the war by 1970," Larry Josephson remembered. "All these people from Westchester and Great Neck didn't just listen, they subscribed to WBAI. This wasn't your hard-core New Left or counter-culture types from the Village, but thousands of middle-class lawyers and teachers who liked to get high. They were the ones giving us all our money." By most accounts WBAI had about 600,000 listeners by the late 1960s, 30,000 of whom subscribed to the station.[118]

Standing at the margins of this remarkable success were the same people who sought access to KPFA in Berkeley: blacks, Latinos, radical feminists, and gay liberation activists. These outsiders listened to WBAI and heard a rhetoric that could not have been better crafted to suggest that they deserved a presence at the station. Post and Fass in particular constantly hailed WBAI as the home of the outcast and the marginal. By 1971 a critical mass of non-white-male outsiders took power at the station. Following an article in the *WBAI Folio* charging that a "male power elite" dominated the frequency, a majority of the staff elected radical feminist programmer Nanette Rainone to be program director.

Two scholars provide what has become the master narrative of the conflict between WBAI's countercultural establishment and its newcomers: Jeff Land in his excellent study *Active Radio: Pacifica's Brash Experiment* and Jay Sand in his fine online thesis *The Radio Waves Unnameable: BAI, Bob Fass and Listener-Sponsored Yippie*. According to Sand, by the late 1960s WBAI had begun "falling through fragmentation." Feminists and gay activists demanded and received air time for shows that specifically addressed the concerns of their constituencies, rarely tailoring their shows to the station's general audience. WBAI's staff gradually split into "pro-movement" and "anti-movement" factions. "The former group believed that each minority had the right to be represented in a program sculpted to solely fit its own needs," Sand wrote. "The latter maintained that while a minority member certainly had a right to have his or her own program, the programming schedule should not be apportioned due to minority membership." Land put the dichotomy somewhat differently. "Throughout the sixties and into the early seventies, WBAI opened its microphone to political agitators who were generally less concerned with the formal elements of broadcasting than with the righteousness of their message," he explained in *Active Radio*. "Although these agitators often had important insights into the dynamics of American society, in their idealism (or dogmatism), they simply lacked the patience to master the skills of 'good' radio."[119]

But both of these studies relied heavily on the perspective of Larry Josephson for their overall picture of WBAI's decline in the 1970s. Josephson, who would become general manager of the station after a brief stint at KPFA, functioned as WBAI's most outspoken defender of what he called "good radio" and critic of the fragmentation allegedly caused by the onset of identity politics on the Left. "Radical lesbian ayatollahs," he famously derided his opponents at the station.[120] "The difference between the '60s and the '70's," Josephson told Jay Sand, "is the '60s included everybody on the Left, every alternative, everything was under one big tent, and then the women and the gays and the blacks and the Latinos all split off into their own separate little enclaves and said, 'We don't give a fuck about the rest of them. We're gonna just do our thing.'"[121]

Putting this debatable historical analysis aside (ask early second-wave feminists, often cursed at by men during political conferences, whether they experienced themselves as part of the Left's "big tent" during the late 1960s), as a listener to the station during that period, I did not experience WBAI's air sound as categorically split between quality programming and mediocre ideological ravings. Post, Fass, and Josephson often created compelling radio during the 1960s. They also broadcast their fair share of mediocrity. By the 1970s

Post's morning show had gotten very tired. He often fell back on a stock array of predictable rants, endlessly repeated records, and boring on-air quarrels with listener callers. His less talented imitators at the station sometimes took delight in provoking listeners to telephone in with opinions, only to cut them off and insult them. To cite only one example, I recall one of WBAI's apprentice free-formers taking an on-air listener comment. "I agree with you about this, but," the caller began. "You know," interrupted the host, "there's an old saying that everything after 'but' is bullshit." "Uh, OK," the intimidated listener replied, then got off the line.

The advocates of free-form radio at WBAI sometimes criticized older Pacifica public affairs programming – conventional interviews with writers and public figures – as elitist and stodgy, treating the listener, to revisit Frank Millspaugh's comment, as if he or she were a "fly on the wall at these great, momentous, intellectual occasions." But listeners often remained flies during the free-form era, now either to be swatted or to buzz admiringly around the host, who had replaced the interview guest as the central focus of the program. WBAI's free-form gods found themselves surrounded by special-interest shows in part because their own programs neglected large sectors of Greater New York's Left, focusing primarily on the white male counterculture. Josephson justly criticized WBAI's feminist shows for refusing to take calls from male listeners. But the opposite problem received far less attention: the majority of call-ins to WBAI's free-form segments came from men. As for the charge that the station's newer identity-oriented programmers often did "their own thing," WBAI's free-form old guard less often acknowledged that their self-centered, individualistic style served as the model for subsequent programming. By the early 1970s free-form, more than anything else, had helped turn WBAI into an extremely balkanized station. In a *Folio* article, Post viewed the situation "with particular personal despair," as he confessed, "since I have supported, to a large extent, the current direction and management of the station . . . We have all become captives of the rhetoric of this deplorably fragmented culture, though as an institution of innovation we should have exercised greater restraint."[122]

A significant decline in subscriptions by the mid-1970s compounded this tension. It probably had less to do with station management and more with the conclusion of America's military intervention in Vietnam. As WBAI programmer Margot Adler later observed, by the late 1960s a huge portion of the station's audience tuned in for its news department's unique coverage both of the war and of New York's enormous anti-war movement. "The Vietnam War ended, and we lost half our audience," she explained. "It was as simple as that. WBAI grew from the blood of the Vietnamese."[123] Jay Sand provided the statistics. Between 1971 and 1976 the station lost 7,000 subscribers. By May of 1976 its estimated listener base had dwindled to 87,000 people.[124]

Concerned that free-form had mutated into free-fall, WBAI's local advisory board intervened. In any conventional setting their decisions would have made good sense. They passed over Steve Post as the station's next general manager and instead hired Anna Kosov, an experienced community organizer and affirmative action advocate. Kosov then appointed WBAI programmer and Puerto Rican community activist Pablo Yoruba Guzman to the position of program director. Apparently Kosov and Guzman were under the impression that they had a mandate to make change at WBAI. But they had been appointed by people who had little to do with the daily life of the station and who had no perceivable mandate themselves.

Staff tolerated Kosov, despite her admonitions not to smoke pot in the employee lounge and not to discuss station politics over the air. But Guzman's tenure quickly came to an end when, on February 9, 1977, he proposed a drastic reorganization of WBAI's schedule, including the introduction of a three-hour daytime program called El Nuevo Barrio – Latino music and talk – and the replacement of Bob Fass's show with popular music. WBAI's programming was "so white-oriented it was shocking," Guzman declared, "a disgrace."[125]

WBAI's scattered army of poorly paid programmers and volunteers now had something upon which they could agree. They announced their intention to form a union and told listeners over the airwaves that they refused to accept the changes. Kosov in response told Pacifica officials that she no longer had control over the radio station. On February 12, WBAI's local advisory board voted to shut the station down, not, they insisted, because they opposed unionization, but because the net result of staff demands "would be to wrest from the manager and program director – that is, management – their ultimate responsibility to manage the station and determine program content"[126] In other words, they wanted to head off the kind of political victory won by KPFA's staff in 1974.

In the ensuing power struggle WBAI staff outwitted their opponents at every turn. A few rushed to the station's transmitter site in the Empire State Building and locked themselves in the room. When power was finally cut, silencing the frequency, other staff locked themselves in WBAI's headquarters on 62nd Street. There they remained for 35 days, until the police forced them out.[127]

What could Pacifica's governors do? They did not really pay WBAI's staff. WBAI's staff essentially paid themselves by collecting money from the station's listener-subscribers. They could not take over the station themselves and resume programming. And, unelected by listener-subscribers, they had no real democratic mandate to govern. Not surprisingly, most active listeners supported the staff during the strike. WBAI's audience knew the on-air personnel – Bob Fass in particular – far better than they knew anyone on the local or national board. Although Pacifica had legal authority over WBAI, its principals had no real power over the station. Realizing this, the board recognized WBAI's union. In exchange the union conceded the board's legal authority, at least in theory. The staff returned to work on April 1, 1977, April Fool's Day. The question of who actually controlled WBAI had been resolved, at least for the moment. The question of WBAI's future had not. "We saved the station from the board," one programmer later reflected, "but we could not save it from ourselves."[128]

Thinking Big

In the midst of all this chaotic innovation, conflict and growth, a critical mass of grassroots radio activists began organizing across the country. At last in 1974 they arrived in Madison, Wisconsin, for the National Alternative Radio Konvention (NARK), the representatives of a host of small, mostly noncommercial radio outlets – college stations, the Pacifica stations, and mangers from Lorenzo Milam's so-called KRAB radio network. They came to build some kind of national alliance but couldn't agree on a phrase that described what they did. Finally they agreed on a core word, "community," a signifier picked by "a huge committee," one participant later explained. "[It] was a compromise between political ideologues, radio experimentalists, media-philosophers, and total greenhorns – all of whom could feel that the rubric 'community broadcaster' would suit their image of themselves."[129] A year later they regathered and established the National Federation of Community Broadcasters (NFCB), which would lobby in Washington, D.C., on behalf of about 50 to 100 radio stations through the rest of the twentieth century. Soon NFCB released a pamphlet fleshing out the concept of "community," or at least giving it a try:

> Since the mid-1970s, there has been a rapid nationwide growth of community radio. This movement has not only brought countless new voices to the air across the country, but has set an example of creative programming, community participation and listener support that's changed the whole nature of public radio in this country. Despite their diversity, these stations are united by a philosophical political and aesthetic approach to radio that emphasizes localism and community needs; radio as an activist resource for community development and social justice; experimentation and diversity in music, cultural and informational programming; involvement of people traditionally excluded from the mass media; and community participation through accessible governance and extensive opportunities for public participation in all aspects of operations and programming.[130]

In other words, the NFCB defined "community radio" as whatever people were doing at the moment at community radio stations. At Pacifica, the term functioned less as a coherent philosophy than as an attempt to bring ideological order to institutional chaos, a tacit recognition that by the late 1970s the network had filled to the brim with a host of people who had only vague connections to one another and equally vague inclinations to collaborate.

While the "community" concept met the need of the organization to represent itself to the public, it dissatisfied older Pacificans. "[I]n my bones I think the 'community radio' aspect of KPFA is counter to what early KPFA sounded like and what the staff thought was the purpose of KPFA," Vera Hopkins wrote to Larry Bensky in 1983.[131] And as general manager of KPFA in the late 1970s, Bensky found himself overwhelmed by community radio's primary task: getting people to get along. "I mean we had three different radical-lesbian collectives at the station at the time," he remembered, "each of which was ready to shred the others to pieces. I'm not just singling out lesbians. It's just an example. We had people on both sides of the radical struggle in Chile . . . . We had people who were black nationalists, and people who were into black progressive culture . . . . [N]ot to mention conflicts between those groups and the whole other dominant group. And it was just an incredible task to try to even get these people to figure out what the commonality of what we were doing was."[132]

And the regions to which Pacifica stations broadcast could hardly be characterized as communities. KPFA's frequency, for example, could be heard as far south as San Jose and as far north as Sacramento. And in 1975 a non-profit foundation in Fresno created KFCF, allowing KPFA to broadcast to much of the Central Valley.[133] Listeners could tune in to KPFK from San Diego, Fontana, or Santa Barbara. Both signals transmitted to areas comparable in size to nation-states. In truth, in 1978 words like "network" and "community" functioned at Pacifica more as public relations signifiers than anything else. The organization could more accurately be described as an independent confederation of regional noncommercial radio stations, operated by five bureaucracies that had little to do with one another. On the regional level, each of these bureaucracies broke down into an array of sub-bureaucracies-collectives, cliques, and factions that did the day-to-day work of each station. Lewis Hill originally structured KPFA as an anarcho-syndicalist workers' collective. Anarcho-feudalism best characterized the "network" thirty years later. Chastened by their lack of success in managing the upheavals of the 1970s, Pacifica's governing board began allowing the organization's five local advisory boards to appoint members to the national body.[134]

One of the few moments during the 1970s when Pacifica spoke with one voice on the national scene was when the Federal Communications Commission cited WBAI for "indecency" after the station broadcast comedian George Carlin's famous "seven dirty words" monologue over its airwaves. Pacifica appealed the action, won in Washington, D.C., Circuit Court, and lost in the United States Supreme Court. In 1978 five justices sided with the FCC because, as Justice John Paul Stevens claimed, broadcasting is "uniquely accessible to children, even those too young to read." Ever since Pacifica vs. FCC, the FCC has wielded what one scholar calls a "freewheeling" definition of indecency that has driven a generation of broadcasting lawyers to distraction.[135] This case probably represented Pacifica radio's most important moment in national American life during the Nixon, Ford, and Carter years.

Regionally, by the late 1970s the five Pacifica stations retained a core of passionately loyal listeners but had fallen behind their more conventional noncommercial neighbors. In 1980 Pacifica commissioned a comparative Arbitron survey of KPFA, KPFK, WPFW, and WBAI and their competitors. This limited statistical tool indicated that KQED in San Francisco claimed 2.7 percent of the Bay Area listening population, while KPFA took 2.0 percent. In Los Angeles KUSC came in with 2 percent, while KPFK in Los Angeles commanded 1 percent. WPFW retained the loyalty of 2.2 percent of D.C. listeners, but its competitor, WETA, easily held a 6-percent share of the nation's capital. WBAI came in last, with 0.7 percent of

Greater New York's radio listeners, not surprising since it had recently spent a month off the air. Its competition, WNYC, attracted 2.2 percent of New York listeners.[136] Then there was KPFT, whose audience was so small in 1979 (16,800 listeners, according to Arbitron) that Pacifica didn't even bother comparing it with the performance of the University of Houston's KUHF.[137] How, wondered Pacifica's leaders, could they turn this boisterous organization into something greater than the sum of its parts? And how could they do it when, as was made evident time after time, the Pacifica governing board had no effective authority over the operations of the organization?

Gradually Pacifica's community-radio generation conceded that while the network had become more diverse, the criticisms of older Pacificans made sense. In April of 1981 Pacifica's five program directors met to discuss the future. "It was agreed that Pacifica's 'mission' was all but lost," they concluded, "and that the charter required affirmation and reinterpretation to establish a basis for unity within the organization."[138] Pacifica's first attempt at reinterpretation would take place in the early 1980s at KPFK in Los Angeles.

Endnotes

1   Chris Koch, quoted in Veronica Selver and Sharon Wood, *KPFA on the Air*, videotape (California Newsreel: 1999).
2   *KPFA Folio* (December 1972), p.12.
3   Ibid., p.9.
4   Ibid., p.7; Sandy Troy, *Captain Trips: A Biography of Jerry Garcia* (New York: Thunders Mouth Press, 1994), pp.36-37.
5   *KPFA Folio* (December1972), p.5.
6   Ibid., p.1; full Fuller quote in Eric Britton, *Rethinking Work* (Paris: EcoPlan, 1996), p.19.
7   *KPFA Folio* (December 1972), pp.5, 10.
8   Terry Anderson, *The Movement and the Sixties: Protest in America from Queensboro to Wounded Knee* (Oxford: Oxford University Press, 1995), p.294.
9   Ibid., pp.295-96.
10 Ibid., pp.298-99.
11 Anon., "The Third World Liberation Front Strike Circa 1969":

www.ibiblio.org/twf/page6feb2003.pdf.
12 Don Foster, interview with author (July 6, 2002), p.4.
13 Frank Millspaugh, quoted in Jay Sand, "The Radio Waves Unnameable: BAI, Bob Fass, and Listener-Sponsored Yippie!" (November 26, 1995), chapter 4: www.wbaifree.org/fass/fasschp4.html#top.
14 Lorenzo Milam, "*Review of Pacifica Radio: The Rise of an Alternative Network,*" in Ralph: The Review of the Arts, Literature, Philosophy and the Humanities, vol. XVI, no. 2 (Mid-Spring 1999): www.ralphmag.org/pacifica-2S.html.
15 Larry Bensky, "Pre-Camera Interview with Veronica Selver," p.5; Larry Bensky, "On Camera Interview with Veronica Selver" [Video tape, no date], p.5.
16 Larry Bensky, "Pre-Camera Interview with Veronica Selver," p.2.
17 Ibid.
18 Gertrude Chiarito, "Interview with Veronica Selver" (June 1993), p.8.
19 Emiliano Eschevarria, interview with author (April 2, 1996), p.10; Milam, "*Review of Pacifica Radio.*"
20 Minutes, National Board of Pacifica Foundation, 9/11/1971, p.5; Minutes, National Board of Pacifica Foundation, 3/31/1973, p.10; Vera Hopkins, "Growing Pains-with Special Reference to KPFA" (unpublished manuscript, 1987?), p.31.
21 William Barlow, "Pacifica Radio: A Cultural History" (unpublished manuscript, 1992), pp.49-50.
22 Eschevarria, interview with author (April 2, 1996), pp.1, 6.
23 Anderson, *The Movement and the Sixties*, pp.364-65.
24 Isabel Allegria, "Interview with Veronica Selver" (video tape, no date), pp.1-3, 6.
25 *KPFA Folio* (December 1972), pp.5, 8.
26 *KPFA Folio* (December 1973), pp.9, 11.
27 Sharon Wood, interview with author (August 28, 2002); even after Schechner's departure, station management paid homage to him with a weekend show titled "The Bill Schechner Memorial Amateur Hour." See *KPFA Folio* (December 1973), pp.9, 11.
28 Eschevarria, interview with author (April 2, 1996), pp.1, 6.
29 Allegria, "Interview with Veronica Selver," p.9.
30 Eschevarria, interview with author (April 2, 1996), p.10.
31 Larry Lee, "Memoranda [sic]to KPFA Staff and Board" (June 26 and August 4, 1972), quoted in James Andrew Lumpp, "The Pacifica Experience-1946-1975: Alternative Radio in Four United States Metropolitan Areas" (Columbia: University of Missouri, 1977), pp.271-72.
32 Ibid., p.274.
33 "National Board" (September 15, 1973), quoted in Lumpp, pp.273-74.

34 Hopkins, "Growing Pains-with Special Reference to KPFA," p.32.
35 Eschevarria, interview with author (April 2, 1996), p.7.
36 David Salniker, interview with author (May 30, 2002), p.2.
37 Lumpp, "The Pacifica Experience," p.275.
38 Hopkins, "Growing Pains," p.32.
39 "The New Third World Department," *KPFA Folio* (December 1974), p.3 (italics added).
40 Frank Millspaugh, quoted in Sands, "The Radio Waves Unnameable," chapter 4: www.wbaifree.org/fass/fasschp4.html#top.
41 Minutes, Pacifica National Board Meeting, March 9, 1974, p.3.
42 Craig Pyes, "Program Notes," *KPFA Folio*, (July/August, 1974), pp.1-2.
43 Larry Bensky, interview with author (September 14, 2002), p.10.
44 Alan Snitow, interview with author (March 29, 2003), p.8.
45 Robert Levy, "Another Station for Pacifica?" *Washington Post* (January 10, 1972), p.B1, quoted in Jon Arquette Degraff, "Radio, Money, and Politics: The Struggle to Establish WPFW-FM, the Pacifica Foundation's Black-Oriented Washington Station" (doctoral dissertation, University of Maryland, College Park, 1995), p.84.
46 Degraff, "Radio, Money, and Politics," p.89.
47 Quote from ibid., pp.88-89; also see Peter Franck, "Interview with Veronica Selver" (July 12, 1992), p.33.
48 William Barlow, "Pacifica Radio: A Cultural History" (unpublished manuscript, 1992), p.55.
49 Denise Oliver, interview with author (March 8, 2003), p.16.
50 Ibid.
51 Ibid., 6.
52 Ibid., pp.5-7; Tom Shales, "After a Lot of Static, Pacifica Is on the Air," *Washington Post* (March 1, 1977), p.C1, quoted in Degraff, "Radio, Money, and Politics," p.97.
53 Sigidi Braudy, "WPFW Music Programmers Handbook" (WPFW: Washington, D.C., 1977), p.2, quoted in Barlow, "Pacifica Radio," p.57.
54 Ibid., p.59; Oliver, interview with author (March 8, 2003), p.16.
55 Nap Turner, interview with author (October 4, 2002), p.3.
56 Barlow, "Pacifica Radio," pp.61-63.
57 "The 'Bama: Talking and Living the Blues on Radio," *The New York Times* (April 5, 1992), p.18; Barlow, "Pacifica Radio," p.64.
58 Harry S. Jaffe and Tom Sherwood, *Dream City: Race, Power, and the Decline of Washington, D.C.* (New York: Simon and Schuster, 1994), p.34.
59 Barlow, "Pacifica Radio," p.62; "The 'Bama," *The New York Times*, p.18.
60 Askia Muhammad, interview with author (October 22, 2002), p.9.
61 Nap Turner, interview with author (October 4, 2002), p.3.
62 Degraff, "Radio, Money, and Politics," p.155; Barlow, "Pacifica Radio," p.60.

63   Oliver, interview with author (March 8, 2003), p.13.
64   Degraff, "Radio, Money, and Politics," p.108.
65   Askia Muhammad, interview with author (October 22, 2002), p.9.
66   Degraff, "Radio, Money, and Politics," p.155.
67   Don Foster, interview with author (July 6, 2002), p.26.
68   Askia Muhammad, interview with author (October 22, 2002), p.7.
69   Ray Miller, *Ray Miller's Houston* (Houston: Ray Miller, 1982), pp.198-200.
70   Rafael Renteria, interview with author (September 22, 2003), p.7.
71   Gary Thiher, "A Conversation with the Grand Dragon of Texas," audio
     recorded at KPFT in Houston in March 1971 (Los Angeles: Pacifica
     Archives, 1971); Ray Miller, "Booming Economy," *Houston Heritage*:
     www.gomainst.com/houston/historic/history5q.htm; Terry Anderson, *The
     Movement and the Sixties: Protest in America from Greensboro to Wounded Knee*
     (New York: Oxford, 1995), p.46.
72   Lorenzo Milam, interview with author (June 19, 2003), p.1.
73   Ray Hill, interview with author (January 5, 2003), p.3; James A. Lumpp,
     "The Pacifica Experience-1946-1975: Alternative Radio in Four United
     States Metropolitan Areas" (doctoral dissertation, University of Missouri,
     1977), p. 260; Jesse Walker, *Rebels in the Air: An Alternative History of Radio in
     America* (New York: New York University, 2001), p. 112. KPFT's official
     history of the event claims that in 1981 Houston's Grand Wizard publicly
     stated that his greatest achievement was "engineering the bombing of a left
     wing radio station." By then the statute of limitations on prosecution for
     the incident had expired. See "The Early History of KPFT":
     www.kpft.org/aboutkpft/history.htm.
74   Lumpp, "The Pacifica Experience," pp.26063.
75   Torry Mercer, interview with author (September 21, 2002), p.5.
76   Walker, *Rebels in the Air*, p.110.
77   Lumpp, "The Pacifica Experience," pp.264-67; Barlow, "Pacifica Radio,"
     p.54.
78   S.K. Bardwell, "Meaux's Probation Is Revoked," *Houston Chronicle*
     (February 2, 2003), p. A25; Walker, *Rebels in the Air*, pp.114-15.
79   Ibid., pp.113-14.
80   Minutes, Pacifica Foundation National Board, Houston, Texas, September
     21, 1974, p.5.
81   Rob Stone, "Data from Survey January/February 1980 for Pacifica Stations,"
     Arbitron Radio (May 9, 1980), p.6.
82   Minutes, Pacifica Foundation National Board, December 8-9, 1973, El
     Cerrito, California, p.8; Minutes of the Meeting, Pacifica Foundation
     National Board, June 22-23, 1974, Lafayette, California, p.7.
83   Anonymous staff member "Marie," quoted in Lumpp, "The Pacifica
     Experience," p.267.

84   Rafael Renteria, interview with author (September 22, 2003), p.7.
85   Ray Hill, interview with author (January 5, 2003), p.3.
86   Ibid., p.4.
87   Ibid., p.7.
88   Renteria, interview with author (September 22, 2003), p.2.
89   Ibid., p. 9; Ray Hill, interview with author (January 5, 2003), p.9.
90   Renteria, interview with author (September 22, 2003), p.10.
91   Hill, interview with author (January 5, 2003), p.10.
92   Torry Mercer, interview with author (September 21, 2002), p.16.
93   Ibid.
94   William Webb, "Progress Report" (July 1, 1958), pp.2-3; possession of
      author.
95   William Webb, "Statement of Resignation of William Webb," (January 19,
      1959), p.2; possession of author.
96   Harry Plotkin, Pacifica attorney, quoted in Lumpp, "The Pacifica
      Experience," p.177.
97   Conrad Moss, Henry Geiger, et al., "To the Supporters of Listener-
      Sponsored Radio for Southern California," (flyer).
98   Israel Feuer, interview with author (March 9, 2002), p.2.
99   Lumpp, "The Pacifica Experience," p.179.
100   Matthew Lasar, Pacifica Radio: The Rise of An Alternative Network
      (Philadelphia: Temple University Press, 2000), p.223.
101   Paul Dallas, Dallas in Wonderland (Los Angeles: Paul V. Dallas, 1967),
      pp.169-73, 177-85, 205-8.
102   Gene Marine, interview with author (April 22, 1996), p.8.
103   David Caute, The Great Fear: The Anti-Communist Purge Under Truman and
      Eisenhower (New York: Simon and Schuster, 1979), pp.77-78.
104   Marine, interview with author (April 22, 1996), p.7; Terry Drinkwater,
      "Crusader, Traitor, or Neither: Gerald Smith interviewed by Terry
      Drinkwater," audio tape (KPFK, Los Angeles, September 28, 1959).
105   Walker, Rebels in the Air, pp.78-80.
106   Firesign Theater, How Can You Be in Two Places at Once? audio recording
      (1968).
107   Jim Berland, quoted in Joe Domanick, "Left for Dead: How KPFK Missed
      the Revolution," LA Weekly (October 4-10, 1996), p.24.
108   Lumpp, "The Pacifica Experience," pp. 290-94; Clark Spark, "Interview
      with Veronica Selver" (December 1993, video tape), p.1.
109   Rachel Kreisel, interview with author (December 8, 2003), p.3.
110   Domanick, "Left for Dead," pp.24, 26.
111   Quoted in Susan Douglas, Listening In: Radio and the American Imagination
      from Amos 'n' Andy and Edward R. Murrow to Wolfman Jack and Howard Stern
      (New York: Random House, 1999), pp.270-71.

112 Larry Bensky, interview with author (September 14, 2002), p.2.

113 "Freeform Timeline," *lcd* 21 (no date): www.wfmu.org/LCD/21/timeline.html

114 Jay Sand, *The Radio Waves Unnameable* (November 26, 1995): www.wbaifree.org/fass/fasschp5.html#chp5.

115 Steve Post, *Playing in the FM Band: A Personal Account of Free Radio* (New York: Viking Press, 1974), pp.71, 80-81.

116 Ibid., pp.28-29, 36, 84-86, 105-7; the Avedon photo appears in an unnumbered page in Post's book; Staten Island listener quoted in Sand, *The Radio Waves Unnameable*: www.wbaifree.org/fass/fasschp5.html#chp5; Avedon photograph on unnumbered page.

117 Walker, *Rebels on the Air*, p.76.

118 Josephson quoted in Jeff Land, *Active Radio: Pacifica's Brash Experiment* (Minneapolis: University of Minnesota Press, 1999), p.122.

119 Jay Sand, *Radio Unnameable*: www.wbaifree.org/fass/fasschp8.html#top; Land, *Active Radio*, p.125.

120 Land, *Active Radio*, p.126.

121 Sand, *Radio Unnameable*: www.wbaifree.org/fass/fasschp8.html#top.

122 Post, *Playing in the FM Band*, pp.xxii; "restraint" comment on page 226.

123 Margot Adler, quoted in Land, *Active Radio*, p.122.

124 Sand, *Radio Unnameable*: http://www.wbaifree.org/fass/fasschp8.html#top.

125 Ibid.; Land, *Active Radio*, p.129.

126 "WBAI Local Board Statement" (February 12, 1977), p.2.

127 Sand, *Radio Unameable*: www.wbaifree.org/fass/fasschp8.html#top.

128 Land, *Active Radio*, p.132.

129 Walker, *Rebels in the Air*, p.140.

130 National Federation of Community Broadcasters, "We Make Community Radio: Community Radio in the United States" (Washington, D.C., 1982), p.18, quoted in William Barlow, "Community Radio in the US: The Struggle for a Democratic Medium," *Media, Culture and Society*, vol. 10 (SAGE: London, 1988), pp.81-105.

131 Vera Hopkins, quoted in Land, *Active Radio*, p.114.

132 Larry Bensky, interview with Veronica Selver (April 1993, video tape transcript), pp.17-18.

133 "KFCF, 88.1 – Thirty Years of Community Radio," www.kfcf.org/Mambo/index.php?option=com_content&task=view&id=2&Itemid=2

134 Peter Franck, "Interview with Veronica Selver" (July 12, 1992, video tape transcript), pp.75-76.

135 Marjorie Heins, *Not in Front of the Children: "Indecency," Censorship, and the Innocence of Youth* (New York: Hill and Wang, 2001), pp.101-5; John Crigler and William J. Byrnes, "Decency Redux: The Curious History of the New FCC Broadcast Indecency Policy," *Catholic University Law Review* 38 (1989): 330-63.

136 Rob Stone, "Data from Survey January/February 1980 for Pacifica Stations," pp.2-3; possession of author.
137 Ibid., p.6.
138 Clare Spark, "Pacifica Radio and the Politics of Culture," *American Media and Mass Culture* (Berkeley: University of California Press, 1987), p.577.

CHAPTER 4

L.A. Confidential, 1979–1984

I think we made a mistake. I think we jumped into something
we didn't hear all sides of and I think we ought to back off.

PAT SCOTT, 1984

In November of 1979, as the Pacifica network celebrated its thirty-
first anniversary, the American people elected Ronald Reagan as
president of the United States. He defeated the incumbent president, Jimmy Carter, by eight million votes, capturing popular
majorities in all but two states. Reagan entered the White House
prepared to inaugurate a far more aggressive military policy abroad
and to attack the established Great Society/New Deal order at home.
"Government is not the solution to our problem," Reagan declared
in his inaugural address. "Government is the problem."[1]

Reagan's triumph stunned the American Left. It forced activists
and intellectuals around the country to rethink their understanding
of the political moment, as well as their strategies and tactics. It also
prompted a season of soul-searching at Pacifica radio. Just before
Reagan's election, KPFA news director Alan Snitow attended
California's Republican State Convention. "I was knocked back on
my heels," he later explained. "I saw this incredibly powerful right-
wing movement developing, with people who were completely self-
confident, who had extremely well-developed arguments. I realized
that we on the Left were really unprepared to engage this."[2]

169

Central to this re-evaluation was a heightened awareness of the power of media in American life and over American politics. A year before Reagan's election, sociologist and occasional KPFA programmer Todd Gitlin's germinal study *The Whole World Is Watching: Mass Media in the Making and Unmaking of the New Left* was published. Gitlin's book outlined in painstaking detail how CBS television and *The New York Times's* coverage of Students for a Democratic Society (SDS) literally changed the politics and direction of the organization. Both media outfits constantly redefined SDS's purposes. Their reporters made and broke leaders simply by deciding which to interview and which to ignore.[3] Following Gitlin's study came Edward Herman and Noam Chomsky's widely read analysis of journalism and foreign policy, *Manufacturing Consent: The Political Economy of the Mass Media*. Using statistical data, the authors showed how the country's major newspapers and television networks legitimized the "free world" in their skewed coverage of international events. Charts revealed how American newspapers focused on single human-rights abuses behind the Iron Curtain while systematically ignoring the murder and disappearance of hundreds of human rights activists by U.S.-backed military governments in Central America.[4] "In sum," Herman and Chomsky concluded, "the mass media in the United States are effective and powerful ideological institutions that carry out a system-supportive propaganda function by reliance on market forces, internalized assumptions, and self-censorship, without significant coercion."[5]

But nobody on the Left had to read these books to know how powerful media had become. They had only to look at the nation's new president, a former Hollywood actor and television spokesperson for General Electric. The question facing the Pacifica organization was whether it could provide a coherent national broadcasting response to the conservative onslaught. The advent of Reaganism forced the organization to revisit the question with which Lewis Hill had grappled in the 1940s: How could radicals build a media that reached beyond the faithful? In 1981, as already noted, Pacifica remained an extremely decentralized institution. All of its stations had recently gone through upheavals as the result of efforts by management to exert some kind of authority over them. Most of these interventions had failed. But the perceived potential of the network as a force able to counteract corporate media guaranteed that successive administrations would continue to try to turn Pacifica into something more than the sum of its parts. "There is a battle going on for the minds and understanding of the people of the world," declared Peter Franck, the foundation's president, in a 1983 essay titled "A Plan for Pacifica," "and Pacifica can do no less than work very hard to position itself to be a strong warrior in this battle."[6]

The work to accomplish this, however, would entail unifying an organization whose disparate sectors either strongly disagreed about what kind of institution they wanted or were reluctant to meet the expectations suddenly thrust upon them. It would also take place within an organization whose principals had, as radio broadcasting became increasingly corporate elsewhere, few better places to go if they wanted to do big-signal, noncommercial community radio. To borrow an old Cold War term, Pacifica radio was well on the way to becoming a contained network.

The first serious debates about Pacifica's future as a nationally oriented five-station network centered on the strong personalities who gravitated to KPFK in Los Angeles in the early 1980s. The conflicts that emanated from KPFK would augur both the structure and the content of Pacifica struggles for the next two decades: What were the most important subjects for Pacifica to talk about and report? Should Pacifica focus on general community access, or advocate for a predetermined and coherent program for change? How should Pacifica fund its ambitious new plans? Between 1979 and 1984, the conflicts over these questions generated a set of winners and losers within the organization. The actions of the losers – ousted from their positions and faced with few other broadcast mass-media venues – would prove paradigmatic of future Pacifica fights. In retrospect, the events that transpired during this five-year period should have raised questions for the institution's leaders about the practicality of attempting to restructure Pacifica drastically in a contained broadcasting environment and without a clear democratic mandate.

Beyond the Newsletter

In the late 1970s the Pacifica Foundation's treasurer, Oscar Hanigsberg, warned that the regulatory environment surrounding the organization had become more hostile. Government agencies paid more attention to charitable organizations than they had in the past. Indeed, during this period the New York Department of Charities almost denied WBAI the right to fund-raise over the air, so disorganized were its finances.[7] Fearing that Pacifica might fail a system-wide audit, Hanigsberg attempted one on his own. $11,000 later, he knew what he needed to know: Pacifica was incapable of passing an internal CPA audit, let alone surviving a government inspection.[8]

And so in the late 1970s the organization hired its first executive director in nearly a decade, Joel Kugelmass, whose main task was to establish an auditable fiscal system for the network. This meant the appointment of financial controllers and the elimination of the station practice of making a favored on-air host bookkeeper because he or she needed a job.[9] In the early 1980s Sharon Maeda took Kugelmass's place. She helped KPFT and WPFW achieve fiscal solvency. By 1982 the WPFW audience had shot up to 155,000 listeners, making it the second most popular noncommercial station in Washington, D.C. The network reduced its debt load from almost a quarter of a million dollars to a far more manageable $47,582.[10]

In 1980 Pacifica chose a new president for the organization. Peter Franck's involvement with Pacifica began in the late 1950s, when Elsa Knight Thompson interviewed him on KPFA in his capacity as a student activist at UC Berkeley. After he graduated from law school, KPFA's station manager, Roger Pritchard, asked Franck to join the local advisory board. "I thought, well, nice liberal station, might be good for my law practice to be on the board," Franck later recalled. "No intention of getting seriously involved."

Then in 1972 the Symbionese Liberation Army began sending communiqués to KPFA to be broadcast, and the police came with search warrants demanding them. Pritchard went to Franck and asked him what to do. Don't give them to the police; give them to your lawyer, he counseled, then asked who Pacifica's lawyer was. With that, Pritchard handed Franck the tapes.[11]

Franck served as the organization's attorney through the difficult years of the 1970s, then, when a vacancy emerged, he fell into the position of president. In this capacity he initiated a discussion that, two decades later, still preoccupied the organization: How could Pacifica, as a unified national network, further the interests of the Left? "I felt that you can't organize a movement for social change on a mass basis," he later explained, "if you haven't got media that helps people see the connections of things, empowers them, [and] pushes values of working together rather than individualism." Franck emphasized that it was important, but not sufficient, for Pacifica to promote the activities of this or that activist group. The question, he asked, was whether Pacifica would function as "the newsletter of the Left or the newspaper of the Left." Would the network serve as a kind of "house organ among which the convinced activists communicate and know when to go to the next demonstration," or would it serve as "an instrument reaching out with the message of progressives to a broader constituency?"[12] He rejected Lewis Hill's 2 percent model, which regarded that share of listeners as adequate to supply the needs of a listener-supported station. At that level of audience participation, Franck wrote his 1983 position paper, "A Plan for Pacifica," the network reached only 0.4 percent of the populace." It is an elitist luxury to use our precious transmitters and the talents and skills of our hundreds of programmers and staff to reach such a tiny part of the American people." He suggested that Pacifica target about 5 percent of the population as its direct audience.[13]

Unlike the millionaires and trust fund radicals who had dominated previous Pacifica boards, Franck was a working lawyer. He argued that, to achieve his vision, the organization had to move beyond its time-honored plutocratic model of governance. For twenty-five years Pacifica's national governing board had been dominated by the wealthy – the only people with the time and resources to perform essential administrative functions without pay. At the station level, management and programming also often fell to the affluent – the only individuals able to live on Pacifica's meager salaries.[14] These people did not necessarily have the skills to help the organization grow. After years of service to the network, they often had an investment in the status quo rather than in constructive change. Now, Franck wrote, Pacifica needed to hire professional staff to take on key tasks. They especially required a development director and someone to take on the difficult job of building a true organization-wide consensus on the future. "[T]his kind of process will be essential if Pacifica is to remain a democratic institution," he wrote. "Pacifica is too big and too important to allow either elitist top-down decision making, or *de facto* control room decision making."[15]

Pacifica's new president also argued that in order to expand the network's reach, it would have to create a fund for development. That meant venturing beyond the organization's reliance on listener-subscriber support. "Listener support has rarely, if ever, capitalized Pacifica," Franck explained, and cited the obvious and pertinent examples. In order to keep KPFA afloat in the early 1950s, Lewis Hill obtained a Ford Foundation grant. Philanthropists provided the seed money to put KPFK on the air. A millionaire donated WBAI to Pacifica as a functioning radio station. All of Pacifica's frequencies operated with powerful transmitters paid for by the federal government's equipment facilities program. Campaigns to build the foundation's audience would obviously have to pursue similar venues. "It is essential and very possible for us to develop an on-going set of relationships with the network of organizations and funding sources which represent our natural constituencies and which share our communities." To facilitate such ties, Franck recommended that the Pacifica National Office move to Washington, D.C., by May of 1984.[16] Finally, Franck encouraged the streamlining of governance.[17] Under his leadership, station local advisory boards sent two rather than four members to the national governing board. "I thought that each station should have two people who don't do anything else for [their] station," he explained. They "still stay on their local board, but their thing is the national board, so there would be a more involved national."[18]

In the early 1980s Peter Franck outlined a vision for the organization that his successors would for the most part adopt as their master plan for the next two decades: professionalize, streamline, and try to create a truly national organization. But while most of his colleagues agreed with Franck's basic structural goals, disagreements over the larger political objectives of the organization loomed. By 1981, KPFK in Los Angeles had once again become the network's hot spot. This time its explosion would prove paradigmatic of Pacifica fights for the foreseeable future.

A City Divided, a Station Isolated

After Ruth Hirschman and Will Lewis fled from KPFK, Pacifica hired as general manager the programmer who had led the revolt against the station in response to a series of particularly arbitrary firings. Activist Jim Berland came from a union-organizing background. He took the position in 1978 with a mandate to do something or other for KPFK, depending on which account you read. One quotes him pledging to "build a multi cultural and multi racial organization and program schedule." Another has Berland recalling that he "wanted to move Pacifica away from preaching to the already converted," to "open up the dialogue to representatives of the center and right, and engage them in political debate."[19] The chances are that he had a mandate to do both, and so hired Clare Spark to combine the two programs. A former L.A. high school teacher with an education degree from Harvard, she came to the job having hosted a feminist show titled *Sour Apple Tree* at KPFK for almost a decade.[20] As was mentioned in Chapter 3, Spark saw the challenge as being to provide multiracial community access while developing the station's character as an instrument of social change

– a newspaper of the Left, to use Franck's shorthand.[21] She probably picked the toughest big city in the United States in which to implement this agenda.

By 1980 no U.S. region had as fragmented a Left as Los Angeles. It had not always been so. The historian Gerald Horne describes L.A. as a city polarized by the twin blows of McCarthyism and the 1965 Watts race riots. Prior to the post-World War II anti-Communist onslaught, L.A. boasted the highest concentration of Communists in the country – perhaps as many as 4,000 members. L.A.'s considerable black community flocked to the Party largely because of its courageous defense in the early 1930s of the Scottsboro Boys, nine black southern lads falsely accused of raping two white women. The Party and its front organizations brought together Angeleños who came from starkly different backgrounds. Screenwriter and Hollywood Communist Party chair John Howard Lawson sat on the board of directors of African-American journalist Charlotta Bass's *California Eagle*. Lawson often worked with Pettis Perry, African-American trade unionist and the Party's most prominent voice in Los Angeles.[22] In 1946 the Party and its allies organized a multiracial Civil Rights Congress to fight police harassment and housing discrimination in the city. Lena Horne and Frank Sinatra signed on as sponsors.[23]

McCarthyism devastated this alliance. The House Committee on Un-American Activities marauded through Hollywood in the late 1940s. It met with only the futile resistance of a small group of subpoenaed writers known as the Hollywood Ten, who refused to testify and quickly received prison sentences for their courage. The vast majority of actors, producers, directors, and screenwriters queued up to make patriotic statements, name names, or plead the Fifth Amendment. Far more vulnerable than white activists, much of the Los Angeles black community fled from the organized Left. In 1952 black actors Hattie McDaniels and Louise Beavers both declared that they would "disavow and repudiate" an upcoming conference on equal rights. Four years later the Marxist scholar W.E.B. DuBois announced that he planned to tour Los Angeles.

Officials from the local NAACP, an organization DuBois had helped found, publicly objected to his visit.[24] L.A.'s multiracial coalition had been scattered.

But a void had been created in the African-American community, and it was quickly filled by black cultural nationalism. By 1965 Bass's left-wing *Eagle* had been driven out of business and replaced by the *Los Angeles Herald-Dispatch*, described by Horne as "a militant right-wing nationalist organ that engaged in baiting of the Jewish community, especially the black Jewish celebrity Sammy Davis, Jr., and provided an initial forum for the Nation of Islam."[25] The Nation emphasized separatism, patriarchy, entrepreneurship, racial purity, and endless suspicion of white people, Jews, and the Left. It found fertile ground in the predominantly black Watts section of Los Angeles, whose residents were so poor that even middle-class blacks avoided the area.[26]

On Wednesday, August 11, 1965, a California Highway Patrol official pulled over one Marquette Fry of Watts. The two men exchanged angry words. A crowd gathered. Violence broke out. The police rushed to the scene with 80 helmeted men, and a full-fledged insurrection ensued. It lasted for seven days, during which 34 people died, 1,000 were injured, and an estimated 35,000 adults rioted. A U.S. military force larger than that used to invade Santo Domingo that year put down the civil disturbance. They did the Nation of Islam an enormous political favor by targeting its mosque on South Broadway, mindlessly firing 1,000 rounds into the structure and arresting almost 60 of its members. The Nation's leadership came out of the ordeal as heroes. Marquette Fry pronounced himself a member. "On all sides," Horne concludes, "there was a recognition of a heightened prestige for the Nation of Islam and, inevitably, for its beliefs."[27]

For the next three decades white radicals in Los Angeles would constantly have to ask the question: How closely did they want to ally themselves with African-American nationalists whose views, save for the separatist racial angle, often resembled those of the L.A. Chamber of Commerce? Nowhere in Los Angeles did that dilemma present itself more starkly than at KPFK. Spark invited all of Pacifica's program directors for a meeting there in 1981. Out of that meeting came a draft resolution reinterpreting the network's articles of incorporation as a mandate to fight "racism, sexism and imperialism" throughout the world, including within Pacifica. The resolution also called for all programming to include a "race, class and gender analysis."[28] But Spark found that while many of the new programmers she and Berland recruited were delighted to critique U.S. imperialism, they offered a host of homegrown chauvinisms to replace them. "I was particularly concerned with the divisiveness of the cultural nationalists and separatists," she later wrote, "who tended to dominate programming about women and blacks, and who resisted debate with or airing of integrationists."[29] Spark had no easy time with older white programmers either. One afternoon KFPK host Bobb Lynes began his *Old Time Radio Hour* with an excerpt from *The Amos and Andy Show*. The previous program had been a teach-in on apartheid South Africa. Spark was appalled. Lyons obstinately objected to her interference.[30]

Meanwhile, Berland hired as the station's news director a young man who was to play a crucial role in the Pacifica crisis of the late 1990s. A talented and compelling writer, in the late 1960s Marc Cooper served as translator for Chile's Marxist president, Salvadore Allende. He barely escaped the country after the CIA-backed coup of Augusto Pinochet, then built a career as an independent correspondent on Latin American affairs. Cooper came to KPFK with the requisite personality traits of an alternative media star: quick wit, combative spirit, and few visible signs of modesty (he would subsequently author two books demurely titled *Roll Over Che Guevara: Travels of a Radical Reporter* and *Pinochet and Me: A Chilean Anti-Memoir*).[31]

Cooper took over the news at KPFK, and he shone. The station's listeners, alarmed at Reagan's victory, showered the station with money. He and Spark hired more staff, inaugurated a new morning show, and beefed up the afternoon drive-time hours with quality programming on El Salvador and Central America. Spark put dozens of new programmers on the air in a relatively short time. They assembled exciting live audience teach-ins on Northern Ireland and South Africa. Cooper won no fewer than five journalism awards in a few scant years.

But the new staff at KPFK were also arrogant – almost swaggeringly so. "We thought that our competition was CBS, not NPR," Cooper later bragged. "That's the way we wrote our newscasts. We were trying to hold both local station management and network management accountable. We were saying 'Okay, we got our shit together. How about you? When are you going to go out and raise that money you promised you'd raise? When are you going to ensure that the national news is actually played nationally and not be afraid that the people at the Washington, D.C., station will accuse you of telling black people what to do?'"[32] Apparently it occurred to neither of them to tread a little more lightly. Certainly Spark had no such plan: her *KPFK Folio* essays contained sensible ideas but read like *Pravda* editorials seasoned with New Age rhetoric:

> 1. The Vanguard. The Pacifica agenda – our legal mandate – is the most humane, most highly evolved project that I know. It is unambiguous in its language and intent: the study of the causes of conflict, with the goal of a lasting understanding among all peoples. Pacifica programs and programmers, therefore, are mandated to create programs and social processes that show what people must do to heal conflicts. People whose agenda it is to exacerbate conflict in order to perpetuate structures of domination are, it seems to us, not to be in control of our air (i.e., present themselves as representing Pacifica or as exempt from critical dialogue). Rather, such people are to be the subjects and objects of our collective inquiry."[33]

Spark's prose signaled an awareness among Pacifica managers of the extent to which the Pacifica stations, especially KPFK, had become captive to a collectively incoherent array of individual voices who not only often conflicted with each other but sometimes spoke in opposition to one other. But not surprisingly, many KPFK programmers took a dislike to their new ministers of information and culture. "Clare Spark is trying to remake KPFK in her own image," one station staff member anonymously told the *Los Angeles Times*. "If you disagree with her politics, if you express an alternative point of view, you run the risk of getting tossed off the air." Some programmers saw in Spark's personnel decisions a purge of centrist and conservative viewpoints. Respected Chilean commentator Carlos Hagen, whose views often stood to the right of his new supervisors, found his show curtailed and issued a statement denouncing station management. The program of his even more conservative colleague Lowell Ponte was eliminated, prompting Ponte's fans to charge censorship. "[T]his was not an overnight decision made by Clare Spark alone," Spark told the *Times* in defense of her policies. "Nothing happens at KPFK without a consensus."[34]

But however KPFK made personnel decisions, Spark, Berland, and Cooper faced an even bigger problem than the deep cultural divisions facing the city they served. They worked in a broadcasting environment that offered a shrinking range of opportunities for programmers who wanted to provide locally or regionally based, public service-oriented radio. While Pacifica had grown considerably in population, its respective stations could not expand into available space. In 1980, WBAI, KPFK, and KPFA still offered the same amount of aggregate air time to their constituencies as they had in 1968: a maximum of 24 hours of broadcasting time a day, 168 hours a week. The government's collaboration with powerful broadcasting corporations greatly worsened this situation. In the late 1970s the Federal Communications Commission (FCC) began deregulating the airwaves in ways that would exclude from mainstream broadcasting the very populations that Pacifica accepted with relatively open arms.

Pacifica's leaders sometimes acknowledged this external trend, but they rarely took into account its internal implications. As they prepared to restructure the institution in the 1980s and 1990s in pursuit of a more coherent network, they did not apprehend what in retrospect seems quite obvious – those programmers they deemed incompatible with a stronger mission had few better places to go and would not take their walking papers cheerfully. The dramatic shifts in the broadcasting environment that took place from the late 1970s through the early 1990s had unforeseen and unconsidered consequences for Pacifica radio.

Enclosing the Public

The earliest sign that something akin to an enclosure of the airwaves was about to take place – a wholesale expulsion of locally based programming deemed not properly attuned to the market – manifested itself in the destruction of free-form radio in the early 1970s. What happened to Jim Ladd at radio station KASH-FM in Los Angeles is typical of the fate of the genre. Through the mid-1960s, he and his co-deejays pretty much decided for themselves which rock and roll songs they would play, and what they would say between the sets. Ladd often commented on current events or invited his listeners to call in to check on his availability for romantic weekends. "I cannot tell you how many times over the years Mick Jagger helped me get laid," he bragged in his autobiography *Radio Waves*.[35]

That freedom ended one afternoon in 1969 when the station's program director introduced the staff to an innovation called "The Format." At the start of each shift, deejays would now receive a sheet dictating which songs they would play for the duration of their shift. After each tune the deejay had to initial an index card indicating that the selection had been broadcast. Ladd walked out of the meeting in a state of shock. "Now I knew what those animals on 'Wild Kingdom' felt like," he later wrote. "One minute you're running along free as a lion on the African plain, when suddenly, some two-legged bastard hits you with a dart gun." Worst of all, the system guaranteed that the sounds of the obscure, aspiring bands Ladd took delight in introducing to his audience would no longer reach the transmitter.[36]

In the 1950s and early 1960s FM radio flourished as a bastion of creativity, largely because AM remained the dominant form of transmission. But once FM found its way into cars and stereo sets, corporations rushed to quash uncertainty and maximize profits. "FM Rockers Are Taming Their Free Formats," reported

Broadcasting magazine in November of 1974. "To put it simply, the assembly line had come to FM," writes radio historian Susan J. Douglas, "breaking down free form programming into its component parts, robbing the disc jockey of autonomy, and making the final product – the show – more predictable."[37]

By the late 1970s the broadcasting industry had seized upon a strategy more ambitious than simply automating their own FM stations. Executives would continuously lobby the FCC to relax the public service requirements that had been established during the New Deal era for radio licensees. The first big campaign for deregulation took place just before the arrival of Ronald Reagan's new appointments to the FCC in 1981. The industry got agency staff to propose eliminating most public-service-content requirements for radio, especially rules mandating local and non-entertainment programming, such as the announcement of community events.[38]

If there were any doubts that President Jimmy Carter's FCC appointees would approve of these measures, his successor laid them to rest. Ronald Reagan named Mark Fowler to head the commission. Fowler quickly summarized his philosophical approach. "Television is just another appliance," Fowler declared. "It's just a toaster with pictures. . . . [It is] time to move away from thinking about broadcasters as trustees, [and to] treat them the way almost everyone else in society does-that is, as business."[39] And so the FCC did. Even content rules that specified a minimum of 5 percent local programming for each license went out the door. The agency extended broadcasting licenses to seven years and made renewal so simple that owners enjoyed a 99 percent chance of success. Broadcasters also found obnoxious the FCC's voluntary restraint rules regarding advertising, and so they were scotched as well, leaving, in the words of one analyst, "no constraints on either the number of [commercial] minutes per hour or the spillover of paid advertising into programming."[40] Then the agency retrenched many of its equal opportunity provisions for women and minority applicants in the competitive license-buying process.[41]

To complete the process, in 1987 the FCC's five commissioners voted unanimously to abandon the Fairness Doctrine. The rule, which dated back to the 1940s, required radio stations to broadcast opposing points of view on "controversial issues of public importance" and to provide citizens with "reasonable, although not necessarily equal," chances to respond over the airwaves of a radio station that had taken a partisan stand on some issue. Often the FCC enforced the rule at the behest of some listener concerned that a radio station editorial had been one-sided. "We have been informed that at approximately 7:30 a.m. on March 9, 1971, Station WGAY-FM broadcast an announcement advocating support for the SST super-sonic plane and implying that persons opposed to the SST project supported the Soviet Union and, by inference, were anti-American," read a typical FCC letter addressed to WGAY's station management. Did the station plan to offer anyone a chance to respond to this accusation of disloyalty?[42]

In the hands of Reagan appointees, the FCC simply announced that it would no longer enforce the nearly four-decades-old principle that the nation's citizens deserved fair access to the nation's airwaves. Congress passed a bill making the Fairness Doctrine law, but without enough votes to override Reagan's veto. A new generation of conservative, nationally syndicated talk-radio-show hosts hailed the course of events with enthusiasm. Right-wing talk show host Rush Limbaugh called the Fairness Doctrine the "Hush Rush" rule.[43] And he was right. If Congress had renewed the Fairness Doctrine, it would have required radio stations that broadcast Limbaugh's politically partisan program to provide access to the thousands of Americans seeking uninterrupted response time to his tendentious and frequently inaccurate remarks. The fall of the Fairness Doctrine facilitated the rise of a wave of national talk radio programs that shoved aside local programming and citizen perspectives, save those of the "dittoheads" who called in to praise Limbaugh's rants.

These developments marked the beginning of a process that denied radio access to a wide variety of groups and individuals who did not fit into a market-based formula. Every time a commercial radio station dropped its commitment to local news, on-air citizen commentary, local information, or local culture, it placed the burden on neighboring noncommercial stations, like Pacifica, or on more conventional public radio and television stations to pick up the slack. "Since deregulation there is no incentive for commercial stations to do public service spots," a Pacifica official noted at a 1981 national board meeting. "[P]ressure will increase on noncommercial stations to carry announcements, including worthy causes that don't necessarily fit our purposes."[44] But by the late 1980s, even public radio and TV were beginning to duck their commitment to local service.

National Public Radio

In 1968 Pacifica established a small bureau in Washington, D.C., which covered national and international events from the perspective of the nation's capital.[45] Soon it would begin sending feature stories by telephone to the news departments of the five Pacifica stations and other community radio stations around the country. But over the next five years a far more ambitious and better-funded project eclipsed what eventually would become the Pacifica Network News. National Public Radio was the brainchild of William Siemering, a rising star who, as general manager of a college radio station in Buffalo, New York, weaned the frequency from its dependence on "town and gown" listeners and built a broad regional audience. While Siemering's WBFO flourished, Congress established the Corporation for Public Broadcasting, a nonprofit, nongovernmental agency to provide funds for public radio and television. Sensing opportunity, in 1970 Siemering proposed the creation of "National Public Radio," a creative broadcasting service that would celebrate the nation's rich diversity: "National public radio will serve the individual; it will promote personal growth; it will regard the differences among men with respect and joy rather than derision and hate; it will celebrate the human experience as infinitely varied rather than vacuous and banal; it will encourage a sense of active constructive participation, rather than apathetic helplessness."[46]

On April 1, 1971, 90 radio stations in 32 states carried the premiere edition of *All Things Considered* (*ATC*), a mix of hard news, cultural reporting, and radio montage. Before long, 14 more radio stations had subscribed to the service. It won a Peabody award after 18 months in operation. By 1980, ATC's affiliate base had more than doubled, to 220 radio stations. By 1993 nearly 7 million people listened to National Public Radio every day. In some regions it had become the primary source of information.[47]

All Things Considered's first day on the air sounded very much like a 1960s Pacifica radio broadcast. It included coverage of a demonstration against the war in Vietnam, a reading of two anti-war poems circa World War I, and a conversation with poet Allen Ginsberg and his father about drugs and closing the generation gap.[48] But by the mid-1970s, it was obvious that the service's programmers had made a conscious decision to sound not only unlike commercial radio, but unlike Pacifica as well. "It's sane, not hyped," explained early *ATC* host Linda Wertheimer. "We don't talk down, we don't get freaked. Call it an island of calm discourse." Siemering quickly became defensive about descriptions of *ATC* as "alternative." "We did not regard NPR as 'an experimental alternative to commercial broadcasting'," he insisted years later. "We ceded nothing to commercial broadcasting . . . . We wanted to set new standards for broadcast journalism."[49]

When it came to the subject of National Public Radio, almost every Pacifican I interviewed for this book became uncomfortable, and some grew evasive. I must therefore emphasize the obvious myself. NPR represented a body blow to Pacifica radio. Prior to its inauguration, Pacifica offered the only network-like alternative to commercial broadcast news and information. By the mid-1970s millions of Americans across the country had an alternative to Pacifica. Vastly better funded – by 1986 receiving half its money from the federal government – NPR could focus on technical excellence, often offering its radio reporters traveling production engineers for extended feature-story projects. Unlike Pacifica managers, NPR administrators did not have to tend the complex affairs of five regional radio stations, but could focus solely on making a national news service work. As the sixties wound down, *ATC* offered, in the words of broadcasting historian Ralph Engelman, "a more polished and varied, less strident . . . approach to news and public affairs than Pacifica radio provided."[50] With the conclusion of Watergate and the Vietnam war, an exhausted liberal America gratefully switched their dials to National Public Radio.

Pacifica's national board responded to NPR with ambivalence. Pacifica affiliated at first, then, upon further reflection, decided to withdraw (although they did permit KPFT to use its services).[51] "Pacifica is something that a lot of people in this country could relate to as independent," declared KPFA's general manager at a 1971 national board meeting. "NPR has to satisfy the same kind of criteria that any of the government-funded agencies have to satisfy – that they are serving increasing numbers of people, and not making large waves." Hence the Pacifica national board sent NPR a disaffiliation statement while expressing a desire "to cooperate with [NPR] and support their activities."[52]

Unfortunately, much of that cooperation took a parasitical, not a symbiotic, character. By the late 1970s and early 1980s NPR had siphoned off dozens of Pacifica's most talented programmers and reporters, easily luring them into jobs with better pay, better conditions, and far better exposure. "We lost tons of people to NPR," former KPFA news director Alan Snitow later explained. "[I]t was a deluge out of the doors." The apocryphal story has it that in 1979 Pacifica's first executive director, Joel Kugelmass, met with NPR's CEO, Frank Mankiewicz, to propose greater cooperation between the two organizations. "Look, why don't you give us some money as a training ground, because you realize that we are a source of talent," Kugelmass suggested. Mankiewicz laughed. "You mean there are still talented reporters at Pacifica?" he replied. "I thought I'd hired them all."[53]

By the late 1980s even that sort of cooperation began to decline. While Pacificans may have believed that *ATC* and its partner, *Morning Edition*, didn't make waves, the organized American Right thought otherwise. The Heritage Foundation – President Reagan's unofficial think tank – led the charge, accusing *ATC* of inherent liberal bias. "There is little chance that NPR will run a negative story on Rep. John Dingell (D-MI, chairman of the House Energy and Commerce Committee) anytime soon, because Dingell's committee controls NPR funding," a mid-1980s Heritage report declared. The neo-conservative monthly *New Republic* weighed in with an article titled "All Things Distorted." Its author, Fred Barnes, suggested that the bias was particularly egregious given the amount of federal money NPR took. "Who complains about the small, left-wing Pacifica radio network?" Barnes asked. "It relies on listener-contributions and is unabashed about its political tilt."[54]

NPR managers began caving in to the pressure. NPR news director Robert Siegel allowed State Department officials to meet with NPR staff and complain about their coverage of the Nicaraguan Contras. During the 1984 invasion of Grenada, he refused to air the feeds of former WBAI producer Paul McIsaac, one of a handful of journalists who slipped past military efforts to squelch independent reporting of the action. "Are we describing the country that elected Ronald Reagan?" Siegel asked rhetorically of NPR's reporting.[55] Thinking about that question more meant hiring Pacifica reporters less.

As NPR became increasingly conservative, its vision narrowed. Siemering's original proposal had emphasized a nationwide matrix of audio laboratories sharing features on local issues and the arts, by the later 1980s a D.C. beltway mentality clearly dominated *ATC's* and *Morning Edition's* programming. "NPR has taken on some of the trappings of the establishment," wrote a professor for the *Columbia Journalism Review* in 1990, "most particularly the Washington establishment, into which several NPR correspondents, like their counterparts in the national press corps, are fairly well plugged."[56] As NPR became less local, so did the public radio stations that broadcast the service.

All Ratings Considered

The 1980s saw a new force descend upon the world of public radio and television: the audience marketing consultant. In 1977 consultants for the Corporation for Public Broadcasting began publishing national rankings of public radio stations based on Arbitron's quarterly cumulative audience statements. For the first time, public radio personnel could compare their performance to that of commercial radio stations. Next came CPB seminars for station managers on how to use Arbitron data. Those seminars helped convince NPR to use Arbitron methods to market *Morning Edition*. Armed with a clearly established method and a steady stream of money, a generation of audience consultants – most prominent among them one David Giovannoni – set out to change public broadcasting.[57]

"[H]e is quite possibly the most influential figure in shaping the sound of National Public Radio today," declared the *New York Times* of a man whom its feature writer described as "public radio's private guru." Born and raised in California's Central Valley, Giovannoni attributed his passion for radio to a single broadcast heard during his late teenage years. He tuned into KPFA-FM one day and "heard a man urgently incanting what sounded like his life story," according to the *Times*. "A whole world had revealed itself." It turned out to be Allen Ginsberg reading his famous poem *Howl*.[58]

Ironically, what Giovannoni's world revealed twenty years and a degree in communications statistics later was that public radio stations that broadcast long impromptu segments of poetry made less money than radio stations that consistently broadcast *All Things Considered* and *Morning Edition*. Indeed, Giovannoni's 1985 study, *Public Radio Listeners: Supporters and Non-Supporters*, functioned as an infomercial for those two programs. "While most listeners position public radio in terms of what the service provides for them," Giovannoni concluded, "those who consider its news and information programming (specifically *Morning Edition* and *All Things Considered*) to be high-quality programming services unique to

188

public radio are significantly more likely to support its operation."[59] By the 1980s Giovannoni's company, Audience Research Analysis, consulted for National Public Radio, the Corporation for Public Broadcasting, and Public Radio International. Giovannoni became the leader of a pack of self-proclaimed experts who had one message for public radio stations: no matter how much their activist audience clamored for locally based shows on bluegrass or symphonies or local culture, what the paying customers – the subscribers – really wanted was news and information. The response of one of Giovannoni's fellow consultants to a question asked at a CPB seminar spoke worlds about the philosophy of public-radio audience analysis. When was "the best time to schedule radio drama?" a station programmer asked. "1938," came the reply.[60]

Studies like Giovannoni's led station managers to three conclusions: high-production-value satellite shows like *ATC* brought in the most money, "niche" programming formulas that specialized in one format worked better than complex schedules that tried to satisfy a variety of constituencies, and local programming should be regarded with suspicion, to put it mildly.[61] Fans of old-style public radio railed against the audience research trend, largely because its definition of successful broadcasting tended to equate success with increased subscription income. "Guys in suits with charts and pages of numbers," *Prairie Home Companion's* Garrison Keilor worried out loud at a conference, "I think that this is a pretty dreadful development." Giovannoni received the lion's share of bile. A "numbers Nazi," WBAI's Larry Josephson, always good for a colorful quote, called him. When Giovannoni and another analyst won public broadcasting awards in 1994, KPFA's Larry Bensky reacted with astonishment. "Not since Henry Kissinger won the Nobel Peace Prize has there been a more inappropriate award," he told a scholar.[62]

These criticisms, however, were no substitute for an alternative system of audience measurement to counter Giovannoni's. Whatever anyone thought of the implications of his work, a Giovannoni study included precise definitions and conclusions that could not easily be ignored. His detractors offered no systematic method for answering two simple questions: How many people were listening, and who were they? Protests and outrageous remarks were not enough to keep inquisitive station general managers from reading Giovannoni and his associates' reports.[63]

Public broadcasting bureaucrats also found audience research attractive because it gave stations and satellite news services a way to sell their airtime to corporate underwriters. While Reagan's ideologues attacked NPR's politics, Reaganites in Congress attacked NPR's budget. It received a cut of one-third in 1984 – this after a massive financial crisis that the service just barely survived. By the late 1980s NPR was soliciting grants from corporations and corpo-rate-backed foundations for coverage of specific issues. Money for national security coverage came from the John D. and Catherine T. MacArthur Foundation; money for Japanese affairs from the United States-Japan Foundation. "The practice is unusual in American journalism," commented writer James Ledbetter. "[A]n individual reporter who accepted money for covering a story at a U.S. newspaper or radio station would likely be fired."[64]

All these trends made public radio stations less local and less connected to their regional communities. By the late 1990s public radio stations took the majority of their broadcast material from satellite services rather than local programmers.[65] Saddled with inherently more expensive production costs, public television fared far worse. In 1991 a Corporation for Public Broadcasting study concluded that most public television stations offered about 105 hours of local programming a year. Some stations, such as WQED in Philadelphia, produced only 60.5 hours of local programming a year and relied almost entirely on fare distributed by the Public Broadcasting System (PBS), itself heavily exposed to corporate underwriting. "By 1993," wrote sociologist Jerold M. Starr, "PBS on WQED had become little more than insects mating, British people talking, sauces simmering, beltway pundits barking, and corpora-tions hawking."[66]

Independent documentary producers found public broadcasting

a "hostile home," in the words of PBS historian B.J. Bullert, whose book *Public Television: Politics and the Battle over Documentary Film* chronicled the frustrating years it took for video documentarians of the gay rights movement, the anti-nuclear power movement, and the Palestinian struggle to jump over the institution's gatekeepers. "It is difficult to document the producers who ran out of funds, gave up before completing their projects," Bullert admitted in the conclusion, "or were able to complete their programs but were unable to secure an airdate on public television."[67] By the mid-1980s even PBS officials who advocated for or defended progressive documentaries came under attack. PBS news and public affairs director Gail Christian found her colleagues accusing her of being "out of step" with PBS.[68] In the early 1990s she found a new job as Pacifica's director of national programming.[69]

Healthy Stations?

The nation's matrix of community radio stations could not remain aloof from these trends. The federal grant dollars they took came with strict conditions attached, and those conditions shaped the nature of community radio in the 1980s. As already noted, from its earliest days the term "community radio" suffered from an almost purposeful vagueness that served to unify the often fragmented groups of people who governed and staffed noncommercial radio stations. Generally speaking, however, community stations shared three qualities. With the exception of the Pacifica frequencies, they operated on relatively low wattage signals; they all obtained the majority of their income from noncommercial sources (listeners, big donors, and grants); and they generated at least 70 to 80 percent of their programming locally.[70] Of the three qualities mentioned, the concept of localness remained most central to the philosophy of community radio. But by the late 1970s even these stations found themselves under pressure to conform to a standard model.

As early as 1972, lobbyists for the Corporation for Public Broadcasting and National Public Radio began asking the FCC to eliminate so-called Class D licenses, frequencies that broadcast at 10 watts. Both groups argued that these small stations took up positions on the dial that could otherwise be occupied by larger public and community radio stations. The CPB had set standards for qualifying for federal funds that were well beyond the capabilities of many educational stations at the time: an 8-hours, 6-days-a-week broadcasting schedule, and at least one full-time and four half-time paid personnel. CPB officials wanted to pressure community radio stations to expand their operations. NPR simply wanted more radio stations that were capable of raising the money to pay for and broadcast *All Things Considered*. Both groups saw the Class D licenses as an impediment to their plans.[71]

By 1979 the CPB's proposal had an unexpected ally, the NFCB, one of whose top officials sought a new location on the dial for his community station, a space that just happened to be occupied by a 10-watt high school frequency. "Were it not for existing Class D stations," an NFCB statement declared, "at least 40-45 new high-power noncommercial FM stations in the top 100 markets could be established." In response, the FCC eliminated Class D licenses. But the NFCB's prediction never came true: some of the 10-watt stations managed to upgrade themselves to the new minimum of 100 watts, but a portion of the spectrum tailor-made for low-income broadcasters and their communities had been squelched. The decision would come back to haunt the FCC in the 1990s with a renewed campaign for "micro-radio," as it came to be called.[72]

The CPB drive to redefine community radio continued in the early 1990s with the funding of a program that has become central to the demonology of community radio activists: the so-called Blueprint Project, wisely renamed the Healthy Station Project (HSP) several years later. David LePage, the project's administrator and husband of former WPFW programmer Lynn Chadwick, by then president of the NFCB, described the program as "a curriculum designed to support and create successful local stations" that "brings no hidden plan or agenda, no magic wands, no predetermined programming answers," but "evaluates a station's health based on its behavior and performance in relation to achieving its mission, not in relation to any particular program format or organizational structure."[73]

Community radio station volunteers and staff members often experienced the Project differently when it came to their neck of the woods. Much could be said for the HSP approach, especially at stations where programming decisions more often satisfied political than aesthetic concerns. But the program's consultants tended to give the same advice everywhere: professionalize and rationalize program flow. At WERU in East Orland, Maine, staff bristled at HSP insistence that planning meetings be held behind closed doors, out of earshot of volunteers and even of some paid staff. Volunteers panicked at proposals that the station drop its locally staffed morning show in favor of World Café, a daily music program produced at WXPN in Philadelphia.[74] At KZYX in Mendocino, California, the station's general manager, Nicole Sawaya, found exasperating HSP suggestions that her governance board refrain from raising money for the station – counsel that made sense in a big city, but not in a rural county where professional fund-raisers were scarce. "Where they were wrong was they just thought that they could come with a one-size-fits-all plan for every station," Sawaya later explained.[75]

In reality, the Healthy Station Project's philosophy bore a strong resemblance to David Giovannoni's, with his emphasis on consistency and predictability. But those who praised the Project revealed its politics far better than those who condemned it. In his 1996 essay "The Flaw in Community Radio: Captive Agent of the Left," media activist Brian Kearny praised David LePage's assistance in creating a mission for community radio station WFHB in Bloomington, Indiana, that avoided what he saw as the "flaws in the Lew Hill paradigm" – that is, noncommercial radio that tailored itself primarily for the Left. WFHB, the HSP-crafted mission statement read, "exists to provide a neutral forum for the discussion and exchange of ideas and issues; and to celebrate and increase the local cultural diversity." An obviously pleased Kearny elaborated on the significance of this sentence. "It also was important for what it didn't say as much as for what it did clearly state," he explained. "There was no mention whatsoever of trying to create justice in the world, nor to give a voice to groups or individuals who had been shut out of the media."[76] With praise like this, many community radio activists understandably read the HSP as a naked attempt to depoliticize community radio.

But if community radio stations refused to nibble on the Healthy Station Project's carrot, by the mid-1990s they had to jump to the CPB's stick. Faced with a Republican-dominated House of Representatives wielding a budget axe, between 1995 and 1997 the CPB began ratcheting up the audience and financial support requirements for its grantees. Using Arbitron ratings as the standard tool, if they wanted to keep receiving CPB money stations now had to demonstrate a CPB-determined minimum audience size or a compensatory level of financial support. Reflecting the Healthy Station Project's emphasis on professionalization, the level of volunteer support a public or community station received could not be factored into the equation. By 1997 the CPB had warned a dozen noncommercial radio stations across the country – from WYSO in Yellow Springs, Ohio, to KBOO in Portland, Oregon – that their funding could lapse unless they grew a bigger audience in a hurry. These policies had their intended effect. KPCC in Pasadena, California, replaced its locally based music programming with an all-information format. WFUV in Fordham, New York, cancelled specialty programming aimed at various ethnic groups. Many stations began soliciting corporate or business underwriting or sought to add to what they already had. The NFCB went so far as to launch a nationwide campaign for underwriting. "Community Radio . . . A Sound Business Alternative," their brochure package declared.[77] To make their programming more attractive to corporate underwriters, community stations broadcast more satellite material and less local fare.[78]

That suited the CPB just fine. Its officials now brought into question the validity of local-access programming. "With every Web-literate citizen [able to] craft their own local program service," one

CPB administrator asked at an NFCB conference, "what will be unique about public radio's broadcast-based definition of localism?" This rhetorical question ignored the facts that the majority of working- and middle-class Americans had no access to Internet radio, and that streaming audio itself was stumbling, thanks to copyright rules that made online radio programming too expensive for fledgling broadcasters. A few protested the CPB's new policies, most notably Mark Schubb, general manager of KPFK in Los Angeles. "These things seriously compromise democratic debate," he told *The New York Times*.[79] But a much more serious assault on public access to radio – easily the biggest in history – was in the making as he spoke.

Free at Last

While the CPB restructured community radio, Congress passed and President Clinton signed into law the Telecommunications Act of 1996. Among the many deregulatory provisions contained in the lengthy statute, Section 202(a) commanded the Federal Communications Commission to eliminate "any provisions limiting the number of AM or FM broadcast stations which may be owned or controlled by one entity nationally."[80] The result, notes communications historian Robert McChesney, was "the equivalent of an Oklahoma land rush." During the next three years half of the nation's eleven thousand radio stations were bought and sold.[81] One of the principal buyers, Clear Channel Corporation, quickly built an empire of 1,400 radio stations. By April of 2001 it owned radio stations in 247 of the nation's 250 markets. Having spent a fortune on acquisition, Clear Channel instituted a labor-saving practice known as "cyber-jocking" – sending out the digitally copied voice of one deejay to hundreds of radio stations. "Today, traveling across the country, radio listeners hear not only the same songs over and over but the same jocks from coast to coast," concluded investigative journalist Eric Bohlert in a series on Clear Channel for *Salon* magazine. He discovered that Clear Channel deejay Randi West broadcast simultaneously on stations in Cincinnati, Louisville, Des

Moines, Toledo, Charleston, and Rochester. "A Giant Radio Chain Is Perfecting the Art of Seeming Local," an admiring *Wall Street Journal* reporter titled her profile of the company.[82]

Across the country, the Telecommunications Act accelerated the trend: many local voices disappeared from the airwaves. In the San Francisco Bay Area, 21 radio stations almost immediately changed hands. The price of a radio station flew through the transmitter, and new owners, faced with mounting debts, quickly moved to simplify and automate their formats. Clear Channel acquired the "People's" hip-hop station KMEL and summarily dumped *Street Soldiers*, its award-winning talk show for troubled youth. Why cancel the program? Because KMEL's latest ratings had slipped from second to third, explained its general manager. Then CBS bought KITS, or "Live 105," San Francisco's alternative rock station. The frequency hosted a fast-paced morning program that showcased local comedians and musicians. CBS quickly replaced it with Howard Stern. Chancellor Media snapped up the Bay Area's only classical station, KDFC, and, to put it politely, lightened its format. *The San Francisco Examiner's* music critic put it less politely. A "classical pabulum station," he called KDFC, "which never met a mediocre 18th-century Italian piccolo concerto it didn't like."[83] Six years after passage of the Telecommunications Act, *The New York Times's* editorial page pronounced the death of audio broadcasting. A "flight to sameness and superficiality is narrowing the range of what Americans hear on the radio," declared Brent Staples, "and killing popular music."[84]

Much of this sad story unfolded long after Clare Spark and Jim Berland had left Pacifica radio, but they were the first Pacifica managers to try to reconstruct the network in the context of steadily declining opportunities for regionally based, noncommercial broadcasting elsewhere. "A major question we had to deal with was whether one medium can serve as both an instrument of social change – in our case representing a leftist viewpoint (albeit a broad, nonsectarian one) – and a community access open forum," Spark wrote shortly after leaving KPFK. "A system of communication more rational than the commercial American one, which leaves room for neither alternative, would allow for both in separate media, thus resolving the problems Pacifica faced in trying to combine the two."[85] The less rational system Spark worked with made personnel decisions at KPFK politically perilous, given that the programmers her management team dismissed often had nowhere better to go.

"We're Ready to Report!"

Meanwhile, news directors throughout the Pacifica organization struggled to reach consensus on how to upgrade the Washington Bureau's national newscast, directed by Marc Cooper's friend Tim Frasca. For several years, KPFA's Alan Snitow and Jill Hannum had been fund-raising for an expanded version of the *Pacifica National News Service*, which by 1981 provided 20 minutes of daily news features via telephone to 15 community radio stations around the country. Snitow and Hannum hoped to raise enough foundation money to expand the cast to 30 community radio stations via satellite, create a full half-hour presentation, and add a traveling reporter who would work with stations to build up their local news operations. The community stations, in turn, would contribute to the newscast.[86]

Substantial divisions existed, however, between KPFK and KPFA over the direction the newscast should take. By 1980 Snitow concluded that the nation's rightward drift warranted Pacifica providing close coverage of both Democratic and Republican party politics. Reluctantly the organization budgeted Snitow and a small news team $5,000 to cover the two conventions, while Pacifica staff elsewhere questioned the effort. Cooper and Frasca regarded international news as far more important; in 1983 Cooper characterized KPFA staff as "narrow about coverage that doesn't treat the regeneration of the Democratic Party as the most important issue."[87] Snitow regarded these criticisms as escapist. "They weren't willing to deal with the appeal of Reagan. They weren't willing to engage in debate [with] the Right," he later explained. "This was the period of time when you never got a right-wing voice except on the news. We tried to do this because we thought it was important to engage. You had to fight these people, you know."[88]

Snitow came back from his convention work exhausted, but determined to overcome staff differences in order to move the project forward. In May of 1981 he sent out a letter urging Pacifica executive director Sharon Maeda to authorize a satellite newscast out of KPFK. Cooper and Frasca ran with the proposal, but not before a nasty fight had broken out over Pacifica's decision to stop accepting news feeds from popular Israeli leftist reporter Peretz Kidron, one of the founders of *Yesh Givul*, an organization of Israeli soldiers who refused to serve in the Occupied Territories. In March of 1981 Cooper accused Kidron of standing in the way of finding Palestinian reporters for the service and of independently fund-raising from KPFK listeners. Writing a feature story on KPFK and Pacifica for *In These Times,* reporter Joan Walsh detected a less complicated reason for the dismissal, Kidron's allegedly "insufficiently anti-Israeli line." Whatever the motives, over the next few months Cooper resolutely tried to enforce the purge. In July he protested WBAI news director Robert Knight's decision to add a Kidron report to the network feed. "I am writing just to say that I think our [news service] and Pacifica in general would have so much more credibility as an organization if we stood together and showed some unity," Cooper wrote.[89]

Unfortunately, the organization had been anything but united over Kidron's ouster. Snitow regarded it as left-wing anti-Semitism. "I was livid," he later said. "I mean, here was the most important reporting that was coming out of the Middle East, and they fired this guy."[90] Not surprisingly, then, by May 1983 only KPFK ran the Cooper/Frasca Pacifica Report as a complete package. KPFA cut it up and used parts in their own broadcasts, not infrequently slicing off bylines. KPFT ran NPR news. WPFW ran their own locally produced news.[91]

In the midst of these tensions, serious divisions emerged on the national level between Pacifica's president, Peter Franck, and its executive director, Sharon Maeda, over the question of what kind of funding to seek. At one national board meeting from this period, Maeda presented the challenges for Pacifica as a set of either/or questions, most of them rhetorical. "Are we a social change organization or a business or both?" she asked. Should the organization continue to encourage "volunteerism as our backbone as an essentially middle-class concept[,] an activity not available to most working people[?]" Finally Maeda raised the binary opposition of "collectivism vs. efficiency as means of getting work done."[92]

Many people on the national board regarded these proposed binary oppositions as reasonable, but Maeda was willing to push the envelope a bit further than her colleagues. At the May 1983 national board meeting, participants discovered that Maeda had applied for grants from Gulf Oil and Toyota. This set off alarms throughout the organization. Frasca, Cooper, and WBAI's Robert Knight showed up for the gathering dressed in Mobil Oil caps. "We're ready to report!" they gleefully declared. All the news directors supported the protest. Maeda insisted that the applications were for equipment, not for programming, but Franck began to distrust his colleague. "[H]er world of reference was the world of public broadcasting ..." he later said, "whereas the constituency I wanted us to orient to was the world of political and social activism."[93]

It was in the context of these mounting tensions that Jim Berland fired Clare Spark. The dismissal came in August of 1982. Berland charged that Spark had shown herself unable to get along with much of the staff. By that point, two music directors had fled the station. Spark then got into a tussle with the latest interim replacement over, as she put it, "the producer of a Reggae special who refused to include any discussion of sexism or commercialism in reggae culture."[94] Programmers felt she was trying to put words in their mouths. Furious at her ouster, Spark publicly charged that Berland had settled for a "hippy dippy 60s" station. He wanted her to politicize KPFK, she told reporters, but refused to back up any of her decisions. Sparks's sister Barbara, volunteer chief of KPFK's popular film club, soon found herself purged as well.[95]

Meanwhile Maeda had grown considerably less entranced with

Cooper and Frasca, probably after their Mobil Oil cap stunt and a tirade at the May 1983 national board meeting over the lack of support their *Pacifica Report* received. "[W]e railed against this like you've never heard," Cooper later boasted. "We couldn't believe the organization couldn't find the decency and solidarity to air the only national program we have." The rant alienated not a few people in attendance – "contemptuous," one observer called it. Maeda, who had earlier supported Kirdron's ouster, gave Frasca a negative performance evaluation, calling his reporting "cynical." Indeed, KPFA news department staff experienced Frasca's coverage of domestic issues as so cynical that they sometimes took a razor blade and tape to his features to "de-snide" them.[96]

Then, in September of 1983, Cooper and Frasca decided to go to Chile. According to *In These Times's* Walsh, Maeda warned Frasca that leaving his post would result in his dismissal. Cooper told Walsh that he knew that Berland might retaliate as well, which is exactly what happened: Berland demoted Cooper, and Maeda fired Frasca. Franck went to KPFK to investigate the situation, but matters only got worse. He cranked out a 75-page summation of Berland's performance and fired him, concluding that Berland had "used up" his capital at KPFK. Three days later the Pacifica governing board hired Berland back. "Peter Franck conducted an investigation based on the Sparks [sisters] and people that the Sparks [sisters] got to write letters to Peter about mismanagement at the station," one board member told *The Los Angeles Times*. Within months Maeda filed a grievance against Franck, alleging that he had interfered with her work.[97]

Now It's My Radio Station?

Only one task now remained: blame assignment. Who would most cogently explain this mess to Pacifica's understandably confused audience and the general public? Spark, Cooper, Frasca, and their supporters energetically threw themselves into this task, and in so doing constructed the boilerplate logic and rhetoric for successive generations of Pacifica dissidents. The Spark sisters and "The

Committee to Save Free Speech Radio," which may have been one and the same, began organizing teach-ins, charging that KPFK management had expelled them in favor of a softer approach to international reporting. "KPFK IS IN DANGER!" read their leaflets. "TAKE BACK *YOUR* RADIO STATION."[98] Cooper/Sparks/Frasca supporters told Walsh that the expulsion of the three "anti-imperialists" marked an effort to make "Pacifica indistinguishable from National Public Radio." The trio accepted the label desaparecidos – "a rhetorical flourish," commented Walsh, "that for some symbolizes the ex-staffers' admirable solidarity with Third World struggles and for others their blend of political naiveté and arrogance." Spark accused Berland's KPFK of "pluralism" which "airs competing interest groups with no analysis of class or gender differences." Cooper added his own derision. Berland, KPFK's former news director confided to Walsh, "actually talks about the 'free marketplace of ideas," and compared KPFK union members who supported Berland to "Chilean shopkeepers who supported the fascists against Allende."[99] When WBAI management fired Robert Knight, allegedly for tardiness, his allies at WBAI, citing the loss of Frasca and Cooper, told the press that throughout the network a purge of programmers critical of Israel was taking place.[100]

Meanwhile Peter Franck and his supporters went on their own war path. On January 7 they marched off to San Luis Obispo, California, and issued a statement of protest:

> The Pacifica Network is in serious trouble. In a time of world-wide crisis, instead of responding with depth and passion, Pacifica is purging itself of its most radical elements. Careerism is replacing commitment. Power in Pacifica has become concentrated in the hands of a few. This power block, unaccountable to anyone, is bringing Cold War ideology to the airwaves. This is being accompanied by a politically selective process of firings and hirings. A process which has been obscured by a smoke-screen of personal attack.
>
> This situation could only come into being because of basic weaknesses in Pacifica's present structure and the lack of a sense of vision and purpose.[101]

To repair these weaknesses, the ten signers of what came to be known as the San Luis Obispo Statement called for "democratically constituted" local advisory boards, adding that "[f]inal programming decisions and judgments must be made by the listeners and the communities Pacifica seeks to serve."[102]

This declaration, which the then mayor of Berkeley, Gus Newport, signed, went over like a lead radio transmitter. Pacifica national board members responded to the statement with outrage. "We could not have planned a better attack on Pacifica than to have our President confuse, distort, and malign the work of stations, staff and board members," one declared.[103] I had just begun volunteering for KPFA's news department when copies of the statement appeared in everyone's mailboxes. It infuriated much of KPFA's low-paid staff, who did not appreciate being accused of "careerism" by a politician and an attorney. They also quickly associated the text with Cooper, Frasca, and Spark, although none of the trio had signed the document. David Salniker, KPFA's latest station manager, invited Franck to a staff discussion about the matter. The gathering quickly turned into "a total roast," as Franck later put it, but he toughed it out. "I was attacked viciously and unmercifully," he later said, "because the statement had said a lot of true things."[104] Soon Pacifica's governing board eliminated the office of president from the foundation's bylaws, putting Franck out of a job.[105]

As Peter Franck's governance career at Pacifica saw its last days, the controversy at KPFK took a substantial, but not fatal, toll. The controversy cost the station about 3,000 subscribers. An independent audit put its debt at a third of a million dollars. "If it survives through June," concluded a reporter for the *Los Angeles Times* in January 1984, "KPFK-FM (90.7) – Los Angeles' indisputable home of 'Huh?' programming – will celebrate its 25th anniversary." The celebration took place. Pacifica stations, like Hollywood cyborgs, have a remarkable talent for repairing themselves. Jim Berland quit by the end of the year.[106]

Will This Trip Be Necessary, Again?

The smoke cleared; the various antagonists dusted themselves off and went about their lives. Playing and replaying events over in their heads, Pacificans constructed their own versions of what had happened and who was to blame. The appropriate moment had come for a serious collective reassessment of Pacifica's grand plans, given the events of the past several years.

But no such assessment took place. Pacifica's national governing board doggedly marched toward their imagined future, summoning Tom Thomas of the National Federation of Community Broadcasters in 1984 for a long-range-planning workshop. Following the event, Thomas's summary remarks hinted at how desperately the organization sought to preserve a sense of unity. "Keep your assumptions on the table, things everyone accepts as a given," he counseled. "It is hard to think of anything about which there would not be some debate.... Today we identified one assumption, in radio broadcasting Pacifica will continue to be non-commercial. Another, over the next 3 years we will remain in radio, not get into TV."[107]

The attendees might have asked another question. Given the network's recent past, did Pacifica's aspiration to become a coherent national voice for the American Left make structural or political sense? By the early 1980s the leadership of the organization, now a five-station network, had reached some consensus on what a more streamlined Pacifica might look like. The institution had summoned a small group of talented and energetic individuals to rethink and expand its national newscast and to bring direction and purpose to its southern California radio station. Plans were made, visions outlined, and those given mandates put their shoulders to the wheel, only to see the machine they had set in motion explode again.

With the benefit of historical hindsight and with the recollections of the various antagonists, we can see why that happened. Whatever their strengths and shortcomings, Jim Berland, Clare Spark, and Marc Cooper came to KPFK with bright plans to remake a radio station full of people with few other places to go that compared to KPFK in location and reach. By the early 1980s the evisceration of community access broadcasting on the AM and FM bandwidths was already in full swing. Free-form FM had been destroyed. Class D FM had been banned. The FCC had abandoned any efforts to ensure local access, and soon it would scrap the Fairness Doctrine. Although the greater Los Angeles region enjoyed about half a dozen public radio stations, most of them now relied on small staffs and National Public Radio, whose politically besieged editors hastened to accommodate the Republican Right. It was in this context that the vanguard arrived at KPFK to turn the newsletter of the Left into the newspaper of the Left and to turn Pacifica's news service in what they saw as a more radical and effective direction.

Unfortunately the vanguard quickly discovered that while they had a mandate in their own minds, that was the only place it existed. They had no mandate from black nationalist programmers from Watts, or from Carlos Hagan and Lowell Ponte, or from the music hosts of whom Spark requested race, class, and gender context in their programming. As tensions rose, Spark and Cooper continued to push. Finally their supervisor, Jim Berland, lost confidence in the process and dismissed its germinators. "Such are the hazards," Spark later reflected, "to quote Trotsky, of trying to create socialism in one radio station!"[108]

But Spark did not take the Bolshevik leader's quote to its conclusion. Trotsky did not regard socialism in one country as a "hazard." He saw it as a dead end. Vanguard socialism, he warned, could not thrive as an island in a capitalist world.[109] Neither could a vanguard Pacifica. Situated in a corporately controlled, hyper-commercialized broadcasting environment, Pacifica had by the 1980s become the reservation for corporate media's outcasts, whoever they happened to be. Revolutionary internationalists, Democratic party reformers, ethnic nationalists: once expelled from Pacifica, they had little choice but to fight their way back in. There were few other places they could go to reach a mass radio audience.

And so the latest exiles abandoned vanguardism for a new

mandate: democracy. They borrowed from Pacifica's rhetoric of moral ownership, created to soften the contradiction in Lewis Hill's original system of governance. Spark urged KPFK listeners to take back "their" radio station. Franck and his followers demanded "democratically constituted" station boards. This rhetorical platform would become the mantra for Pacifica exiles for the next twenty years. Accompanying it would come a perennial warning, that Pacifica's principals "were moving," in Spark's words, "to seek corporate funding and a 'safer' kind of broadcasting similar to National Public Radio."[110] In the coming decades, these demands and alarums would consistently be raised by programmers who often had little in common save for the pink slip they had received from a Pacifica manager.

With the benefit of hindsight, we can ask the questions Pacifica officials could not ask then. Did the foundation's leadership-unelected by the listener-subscribers enjoy the legitimacy needed to dramatically remake a largely decentralized, community access-based network? Did Pacifica's board and national office possess the political and economic power necessary to countervail the inertia of the network's paid and unpaid staffs? Could the institution withstand the fallout that would come with a sizable shedding of unwanted personnel?

It is easy to ask those questions now. Pacifica's governors, busy people with many daily responsibilities, had little time for them then, and the vision of a great, influential, progressive radio network still beckoned. In mid-1984 KPFA's latest general manager, David Salniker, began tracking down some of the signers of the San Luis Obispo Statement in the hope that he might convince one or two to see things differently. He found Berkeley mayor Gus Newport's assistant, who had also signed the document, and they talked for a while. Pat Scott then went back to her boss. "Gus, I think we made a mistake," she said. "I think we jumped into something we didn't hear all sides of and I think we ought to back off." As a gesture of conciliation, Scott joined KPFA's local advisory board.[111] She and Salniker quickly became good friends and Scott followed Salniker as executive director of the Pacifica Foundation.

Over the next fifteen years a critical mass of Pacificans would try to turn the organization into, as Spark put it, "an instrument of social change – in our case representing a leftist viewpoint (albeit a broad, nonsectarian one)," and away from the community access model that had typified Pacifica in the 1970s. But they faced two substantial obstacles in this journey. First, as already noted, their project meant dislodging many programmers who did not fit into its framework. What would the organization do if, as was likely, these individuals did not cooperate with efforts to phase them out?

Second, what tools would Pacifica use to build greater coherence and bigger audiences? Alternative media had no system of measurement as comprehensive as Arbitron. It had no system of audience development as elaborate as the Healthy Station Project. Although Pacifica endlessly praised its praxis of listener-sponsorship, the institution had no fund-raising methods as lucrative as federal dollars, foundation grants, and corporate underwriting-techniques that in a scant ten years built a competing public broadcasting service that dwarfed Pacifica in sophistication and scale. While Pacifica radio constantly broadcast the comments of critics of these methods and institutions during fund-raising marathons in order to highlight the network's distinctiveness, its administrators had developed no alternatives to them.

Frustrated, poverty-stricken, and surrounded by an increasingly opulent, corporatized media, inevitably the latest generation of Pacificans would, in writer Audre Lorde's phrase, borrow some of the master's tools in their struggle to reconstruct Pacifica's house.[112]

But not a few of the thousands of people who depended upon Pacifica radio watched this process with suspicion. Acutely media-conscious, they had been told for a generation that Pacifica was "their" network. Who gave Pacifica's governors the right to transform the organization? they wondered. Largely dealt out of the process of change, they anxiously peered in from the cold as Pacifica continued restructuring itself. By the middle 1990s they saw a congruence similar to that which George Orwell's horses, goats, and sheep observed at the end of *Animal Farm*, as they watched their leaders, the pigs, confer with the farmers: "[F]rom pig to man, and from man to pig, and from pig to man again; but already it was impossible to say which was which."[113]

Endnotes

1 Paul Boyer, *Promises to Keep: The United States Since World War II* (Boston: Houghton Mifflin, 1999), p.403.
2 Alan Snitow, interview with author (March 20, 2003), p.20.
3 Todd Gitlin, *The Whole World Is Watching: Mass Media in the Making and Unmaking of the New Left* (Berkeley: University of California Press, 1980), p.186.
4 Edward Herman and Noam Chomsky, *Manufacturing Consent: The Political Economy of the Mass Media* (New York: Pantheon Books, 1988), p.37.
5 Ibid., p.306.
6 Peter Franck, "A Plan for Pacifica" (photocopied manuscript, April 1983), p.15.
7 Peter Franck, "Interview with Veronica Selver" (July 12, 1992, videotape transcript), pp.7-9.
8 Franck, "A Plan for Pacifica," p.2.
9 Franck, "Interview with Veronica Selver," pp.36-37.
10 Franck, "A Plan for Pacifica," p.3.
11 Franck, "Interview with Veronica Selver," p.35.
12 Ibid., pp.58-59, 69.
13 Franck, "A Plan for Pacifica," p.6.
14 Franck, "Interview with Veronica Selver," p.23.
15 Franck, "A Plan for Pacifica," p.12.
16 Ibid., pp.7-9.
17 Ibid., p.14.
18 Franck, "Interview with Veronica Selver," pp.75-76.
19 William Barlow, "Pacifica Radio: A Cultural History" (unpublished manuscript, 1992), p. 82; Joe Domanick, "Left for Dead: How KPFK Missed the Revolution," *LA Weekly* (October 4-10, 1996), p.26.
20 Ibid.
21 Clare Spark, "Pacifica Radio and the Politics of Culture," *American Media and Mass Culture* (Berkeley: University of California Press, 1987), p.578.
22 Gerald Horne, *Fire This Time: The Watts Uprising and the 1960s* (New York: DaCapo Press, 1997), pp.5-7.
23 Ibid., p.7.

24 Ibid., pp.15, 173.
25 Ibid., p.7.
26 Ibid., p.51.
27 Ibid., pp.126, 129, 141.
28 Joan Walsh, "The Battle Goes on at Pacifica Radio in Los Angeles," *In These Times* (December 7-13, 1983), p.6.
29 Spark, "Pacifica Radio and the Politics of Culture," p.579.
30 Domanick, "Left for Dead," p.26.
31 Marc Cooper, *Roll Over Che Guevara: Travels of a Radical Reporter* (New York: Verso, 1994); Marc Cooper, *Pinochet and Me: a Chilean Anti-Memoir* (New York: Verso, 2001).
32 Domanick, "Left for Dead," p.26.
33 Clare Spark, "Listening to Clio: Radical History, Not Rhetoric," *KPFK Folio* (June 1981), quoted in Spark, "Pacifica Radio and the Politics of Culture," p.580.
34 James Brown, "All's Not Quiet on the KPFK Front," *Los Angeles Times* (August 2, 1981), Calendar, p.7.
35 Jim Ladd, *Radio Waves: Life and Revolution on the FM Dial* (New York: St. Martin's Press, 1991), p.23.
36 Ibid., pp. 47-50; quotation from p.50.
37 Susan J. Douglas, *Listening In: Radio and the American Imagination* (New York: Random House, 1999), pp.278-81.
38 Jeremy Tunstall, *Communications Deregulation: The Unleashing of America's Communications Industry* (Oxford: Basic Blackwell, Ltd., 1986), p.150.
39 Mark Fowler quoted in Paul Boyer, *Promises to Keep: The United States Since World War II* (Boston: Houghton Mifflin, 1999), p.407.
40 Tunstall, *Communications Deregulation*, p.146.
41 Ibid., pp.146-51.
42 Peter Laufer, *Inside Talk Radio: America's Voice or Just Hot Air?* (New York: Birch Lane, 1995), pp.156-57; Douglas, Listening In, p.299.
43 Laufer, *Inside Talk Radio*, p.160.
44 Sharon Maeda, quoted in Minutes, Pacifica Foundation National Board, November 21, 1981, p.10.
45 "Highlights of Pacifica Radio's 50 Year History of Radio Broadcasting": http://www.pacificaarchives.org/learn/history.php.
46 Siemering quoted in Ralph Engelman, *Public Radio and Television in America: A Political History* (Thousand Oaks: SAGE Publications, 1996), p.90.
47 Ibid., pp.94, 97, 114.
48 James Ledbetter, *Made Possible By: The Death of Public Broadcasting in the United States* (New York: Verso, 1997), p.124.
49 Wetherheimer and Siemering quoted in Engelman, *Public Radio and Television*, pp.97-98.

50 Ibid., p.97; funding statistic on p.110.
51 Minutes, Pacifica Foundation National Board, March 6, 1971, p.5; Minutes, Pacifica Foundation National Board, September 11 and 12, 1971, p.7.
52 Minutes, Pacifica Foundation National Board, March 6, 1971, p.5.
53 Alan Snitow, interview with author (March 29, 2003), pp.26-27.
54 Heritage and Barnes quoted in Engelman, pp.109-10.
55 Ibid., pp.110-11.
56 Quoted in Ledbetter, *Made Possible By*, pp.130-132.
57 Alan G. Stavitsky, "'Guys in Suits with Charts': Audience Research in U.S. Public Radio," *Journal of Broadcasting and Electronic Media*, 39 (1995): 177-79.
58 Samuel G. Freedman, "Public Radio's Private Guru," *The New York Times* (November 11, 2001), Section 2, p.1.
59 David Giovanoni, *Public Radio Listeners: Supporters and Non-Supporters* (Washington, D.C.: Audience Research Analysis, 1985), p.vi.
60 Freedman, "Public Radio's Private Guru," Section 2, p. 1; Stavitsky, " 'Guys in Suits with Charts,'" p.182.
61 Ibid., p.186.
62 Ibid., pp.177-78.
63 Ibid.; Freedman, "Public Radio's Private Guru," p.1.
64 Ledbetter, *Made Possible By*, pp.125-26.
65 Lynette Clemetson, "All Things Considered, NPR's Growing Clout Alarms Member Stations," *The New York Times* (August 30, 2004), p.B1.
66 Jerold M. Starr, *Air Wars: The Fight to Reclaim Public Broadcasting* (Boston: Beacon Press, 2000), pp.4-5.
67 B.J. Bullert, *Public Television: Politics and the Battle over Documentary Film* (New Jersey: Rutgers University Press, 1994), pp.183, 190.
68 Ibid., pp.21, 50.
69 See Gail Christian, *A Strategy for National Programming* (Pacifica Foundation: September 1, 1992).
70 See David Giovanoni et al., *Audience 98* (Audience Research Analysis, 1999), p.87.
71 Engelman, *Public Radio and Television*, p.92; Walker, *Rebels on the Air*, p.144.
72 Walker, *Rebels on the Air*, pp.144-45.
73 LePage quoted in ibid., p.147.
74 Marty Durlin and Cathy Melio, "The Grassroots Radio Movement in the U.S.": www.ringnebula.com/folio/Issue-10/THE_GRASSROOTS_RADIO_MOVEMENT.htm.
75 Nicole Sawaya, interview with author (August 13, 2002), p.37.
76 Brian Kearny, "The Flaw in Community Radio: Captive Agent of the Left" (Arts Administration Paper, 1996): www.wfhb.org/agent.shtml.
77 "Community Radio . . . A Sound Business Alternative" (NFCB document, 1986).

78 Andrea Adelson, "A Wider Public for Noncommercial Radio," *The New York Times* (February 10, 1997), p.C8.

79 Jacqueline Conciatore, "CPB Asks Whether Community Radio Is Achieving Intended Purposes" *Current* (April 5, 1999), p.5; Adelson, "A Wider Public for Noncommercial Radio," p.C8.

80 "Telecommunications Act of 1996," quoted in Patricia Aufderheide, *Communications Policy and the Public Interest: The Telecommunications Act of 1996* (New York: Guilford Press, 1999), p.167

81 Robert McChesney, *Rich Media, Poor Democracy: Communications Politics in Dubious Times* (Urbana: University of Illinois Press, 1999), p.75.

82 Eric Bohlert, "Radio's Big Bully," *Salon* (April 10, 2001): dir.salon.com/ent/feature/2001/04/30/clear_channel/index.html?pn=5; Anna Wilde Mathews, "From a Distance: A Giant Radio Chain Is Perfecting the Art of Seeming Local," *Wall Street Journal* (February 15, 2001), p.1.

83 Matthew Lasar, "Broadcaster's 'Radio Show' Comes to a Troubled Region," *San Francisco Chronicle* (September 18, 2000), p.A17; Alan Ulrich, "Why Is Bay Area Radio Deaf to Classical Music?" *San Francisco Examiner* (November 28, 1999).

84 Brent Staples, "The Trouble with Corporate Radio: The Day the Protest Music Died," *The New York Times* (February 20, 2003), p.A30.

85 Spark, "Pacifica Radio and the Politics of Culture," p.578.

86 *The National News Project* (Pacifica Foundation, 1981), pp.5-7; "Prospectus" (Pacifica Foundation, no date), p.2.

87 Joan Walsh, "The Battle Goes On at Pacifica Radio in Los Angeles," *In These Times* (December 7-13, 1983), p.10.

88 Alan Snitow, interview with author (March 20, 2003), p.22.

89 Alan Snitow, letter to Sharon Maeda (May 4, 1981), *Alan Snitow Correspondence* (*ASC*); Sharon Maeda, letter to Peretz Kidron (June 15, 1981), *ASC*; Marc Cooper, letter to Sharon Maeda (March 5, 1981), p.2, *ASC*; Marc Cooper, letter to Robert Knight, cc. news directors, July 2, 1981, Los Angeles, *ASC*.

90 Alan Snitow, interview with author (March 20, 2003), p.25.

91 Walsh, "The Battle Goes On at Pacifica Radio in Los Angeles," p.10.

92 Sharon Maeda in Minutes of the Pacifica National Board, January 28-29, 1984, p.2.

93 Peter Franck, quoted in interview with Veronica Selver (July 12, 1992, video tape transcript), p.77; Robert Knight, interview with author (November 8, 2001), p.3.

94 Spark, "Pacifica Radio and the Politics of Culture," p.579.

95 Walsh, "The Battle Goes On at Pacifica Radio in Los Angeles," p.6; McDougal, "Frequency at KPFK's Human Static," p.87.

96 Walsh, "The Battle Goes On at Pacifica Radio in Los Angeles," p.10; Paul

Rauber, "Off Mike: Mid-Life Crisis at KPFA," *East Bay Express* (March 8, 1993), p.18.

97 Ibid., p.11; Minutes, Pacifica National Board of Directors Meeting, January 28-29, 1984, p. 3; McDougal, "Frequency at KPFK's Human Static," p.87.

98 Ibid., pp.86, 88.

99 Walsh, "The Battle Goes On at Pacifica Radio in Los Angeles," pp.6, 10-11.

100 Brett Harvey, "Radio Impossible: Permanent Revolution at WBAI," *The Village Voice* (September 23, 1986), p.20.

101 Nancy Clark, Ken Cloke, Osama Doumani, Peter Franck, Steve Goldfield, Richard Hanson, Judy Hirsch, Jane Hunter, Gus Newpoint, Mary Beth Roem, Herb Schulsinger, Patricia Scott, and Fernando Velazquez, "Statement of Principles, Drafted at San Luis Obispo, January 7 & 8, 1984," mimeographed.

102 Ibid.

103 Minutes, Pacifica National Board of Directors Meeting, January 28-29, 1984, p.3.

104 Franck, "Interview with Veronica Selver," p.121.

105 McDougal, "Frequency at KPFK's Human Static," p.87.

106 Ibid., p. 86; Barlow, "Pacifica Radio: A Cultural History," p.84.

107 Tom Thomas, quoted in Minutes, Pacifica Foundation National Board of Directors Meeting, May 19-20, 1984, p.2.

108 Spark, "Pacifica Radio and the Politics of Culture," p.579.

109 Issac Deutscher, *The Prophet Outcast, Trotsky: 1929-1940*, vol. III (New York: Random House, 1963), pp.33-35, 102-3.

110 Spark, "Pacifica Radio and the Politics of Culture," p.579.

111 Pat Scott, interview with author (January 31, 2003), p.3.

112 Audre Lorde, "'The Master's Tools Will Never Dismantle the Master's House,'" *This Bridge Called My Back*, ed. Cherrie Moraga and Gloria Anzaldua (Watertown, Mass., 1981), pp.98-101.

113 George Orwell, *Animal Farm: A Fairy Story* (New York: Penguin, 1946), p.128.

CHAPTER 5

Strategic Plans, 1984-1999

The Pacifica stations and the community stations have labored too long under the weight of programs that are somewhat like castor oil, good for you but not necessarily easy to take.

GAIL CHRISTIAN, PACIFICA NATIONAL PROGRAMMING DIRECTOR, 1992

Despite the debacle at KPFK in Los Angeles in the early 1980s, the Pacifica organization soldiered on in its efforts to create a more unified network. It is easy to understand why this endeavor would appear attractive to the individuals who gamely agreed to serve on the foundation's national governing board, on one of its five local advisory boards, or in some managerial position within the institution. "What sucks you into Pacifica is its potential," a longtime KPFA staffer and grant writer once told me.[1] Pacifica exuded an almost irresistible aura of possibility to progressives, who had mixed feelings about the institution's actual product but saw in its restructured future a powerful response to the increasingly rightward drift of the nation and its commercial and conventional public media.

And so from 1985 through 1999 a succession of governors continued to reconstruct the organization. Buoyed by a series of victories in national programming, the network remade the formats at the five Pacifica stations. However, the fundamental problems facing the organization could at best be managed, not eliminated. A critical mass of Pacificans, for a variety of reasons, did not want the foundation to centralize its programming operations. Aware that their views remained marginal not only to American society but to much of the Left, they understood that centralization would reduce their level of access to the regional Pacifica station with which they had a history of participation. They also knew that they had nowhere to go besides Pacifica to reach anything approaching a mass radio audience. Hence they began to mobilize in opposition to what they would describe as the "NPRization" of the network and the supposed betrayal of its hallowed past.

Pacifica's leaders, certain of the correctness of their goals, consistently underestimated these people. They derided them in public. "The left gets pissed off at anything that works," one of them would dismissively declare. "It's a whole culture of losers." In private they called them "the crazies."[2] But whatever their mental state, these dissidents, for the most part Pacifica station listeners and volunteers, showed dogged sophistication in using communications law and the Internet to block Pacifica's plans. In response, the organization's increasingly frustrated governors began to restructure the network both to make it more coherent in their own eyes and to make the institution's governing process less accessible to those who opposed their efforts. The actions they took only served as grist for the mill of a growing dissident movement within Pacifica. This spiral of conflict poised the organization for the social explosion that it would experience in Berkeley in 1999.

Is, or Was?

In 1985 the national board embarked on what its members described as a "long-range plan" for the organization, hiring civil rights activist Florence Green to produce a management audit of the network. Green came to a 1985 national board meeting held in Houston and offered her observations about the foundation's past and its future. Few of her comments were very flattering, but they appear to have been what the institution's governors wanted to hear. Green, explained the meeting's minute taker, "observed the following phenomenon at Pacifica":

1) Management of volunteers: there seems to be no workable system in place for volunteer management, evaluation or training.

2) Decision making at all levels seems to be very ineffective. Decisions are often not implemented. How decisions are made is inconsistent. People do not seem to feel they must follow decisions or directions if they disagree with the decision or direction. . . .

3) Local Board[s] are generally ineffective. National and regional Board roles are unclear. Leadership is not always strong. Board and staff do not usually function as a team, but are often adversaries. Board purpose and function is confused.

4) Relationships at all levels within [the] organization are not well defined and when defined they are not usually followed.

5) Political correctness seems more important than management or program skills. People are given jobs that they sometimes do not have the skills to do. There does not seem to be a process to train people in the skills they need or to dismiss them if their work is not effective. . . .

6) Pacifica operates as a therapeutic community or refuge for some volunteers and some staff. That aspect of Pacifica creates an atmosphere which works against the needed problem-solving process and is exhausting and draining for everyone.

7) There is a tremendous level of care about Pacifica, what it means and what it can be. There is also a kind of "missionary zeal," which works both as a strength and as a weakness for Pacifica.

8) There appears [*sic*] to be two forms of communication in use, neither of which appears to be very effective:

a) The Benevolent Dictator Approach, where memos are issued, directing people to do certain tasks. They are often sent without regard to appropriateness or knowledge of whether or not those being directed have the skill, ability or resources necessary to do the required task. Because those issues are not considered, many memos are disregarded.
b) The Passive Approach, in which communication is attempted so carefully and cautiously that the end result leaves the recip-

ient unclear as to what is really being said or asked of them. Or direct communication is totally avoided and upsets and concerns are shared only in whispers behind each other's backs.

9) Pacifica was/is a top notch, powerful, important organization. During the 70s, many of the best and brightest left. Many who have remained at Pacifica did so because they had no other place to go. They resist change and work against Pacifica upgrading itself. . . .

10) Pacifica is no longer the only game in town. Though it may be that no one does it like Pacifica, to be "Pacifica" is no longer enough to guarantee success.[3]

Very likely most members of the national board in 1985 would have resolved the ambiguity in the phrase "was/is" in observation 9 by opting for "was". Everyone who attended Green's presentation had some sense that the organization's internal growth, combined with external events, had overwhelmed the network. A station general manager commented that "her sense of isolation" within Pacifica "was profound". The national board, she explained, "needed to support all parts of Pacifica, not just the stations." Many attendees echoed her call for stronger leadership from the board.[4]

But John Simon, recently appointed manager at WBAI in New York City, commented that his station "could not afford the luxury of taking time in its planning effort." The signal desperately needed to find a new headquarters and increase its audience. No "war on programming is planned," he assured the group, but change was coming.[5] Simon's attempt in the mid-1980s to recreate WBAI continued the efforts of Clare Spark to revamp Pacifica's essentially feudal internal structure, but without Spark's attempt to rethink Pacifica's political and cultural mission. Although Simon achieved only a limited degree of success, his approach and style would be adopted throughout the network over the next ten years.

Radio Impossible

Steve Post briefly served as WBAI's general manager after the 1977 shutdown and strike. Massive debt forced the station to evacuate its

East Side former-church headquarters and flee to a rented space in the West Side garment district. Post quit as soon as he could pass the baton on to the first of a swift succession of station managers, each of whom lasted little more than a year. John Simon took the job in 1984. There he found an institution in serious disarray. Thieves preyed upon the premises. Homeless people used it as a shelter. "[W]hen you came in early in the morning and turned on the lights, shaggy strangers scrambled up from couches and out from under desks and scurried away like cockroaches," one ex-programmer later recalled.[6] The new digs were much smaller than the old headquarters, creating tension among staff. With only a skeleton crew to structure the station, personnel handed out blocks of air time to friends and allies. With no money for producers or technical equipment, most on-air hosts opted for live radio. Listener call-in shows became endemic to the format. WBAI became "nothing more than a glorified public access station," as programmer Dave Metzger put it. "A succession of talking heads."[7] Yet the station still retained a small core audience passionate about the WBAI free-form style. A young woman named Amy Goodman, who was later to play a critical role at Pacifica, chanced upon the frequency around this time, when she returned to the city from college. WBAI "just expressed all the grit, the ugliness, and the beauty of New York, in real voices, not slick advertisers that were trying to sell you something," she recalled. "It just amazed me. It was so authentic and so real, so honest."[8]

Simon came to WBAI from an effort to turn the small leftist journal *Working Papers* into a national publication. He surveyed the station and concluded that while WBAI's potential audience had changed, the frequency had not. "We have to reclaim that huge chunk of the '60s generation that's gone to careers and children," he told *Village Voice* reporter Brett Harvey. "They're not necessarily activist, but have progressive tendencies; they want the U.S. out of Nicaragua, they want divestment in South Africa. They'll come out for a demonstration if something happens. These are the folks we lost to 'All Things Considered.'"[9]

At first Simon lay low, as he told national board members he would, talking to old station managers and programmers. A consensus emerged, at least to his mind. A "magazine format" would most appropriately suit WBAI at this time. That meant adopting what managers generally call "strip programming: replacing a complex hodgepodge of individual shows with a predictably blocked-out daily format so that listeners would remember who they would be hearing tomorrow at 1 p.m. without having to look at a *Folio* schedule. "People listen to the radio differently in the '80s. They use it as a companion," Simon explained. "They turn it on and leave it on all day while they do other things."[10]

In pursuit of this audience, Simon hired as the station's new program director John Scagliotti, who had worked at a Boston alternative rock station, WBCN. Scagliotti outlined his philosophy in terms similar to Simon's. WBAI required a more coherent flow, he explained to the *Voice*, and it needed an audience that supported the whole station air sound, not just one or two programs. Thus the frequency had to turn away from "'constituency programming' to a more 'coalitionist' programming. We want progressives, feminists, gay activists to identify BAI as something they want to support because their issues will be touched on all during the day."[11]

Simon possessed the right personality for the job of general manager at a place like WBAI. He impressed Harvey as a bully. "[R]ough, tough, blunt, and aggressive," she described him, with "a reputation for flying off the handle and an air of barely restrained pugnacity." Backed by his boss, Scagliotti accomplished what three prior program directors had only dreamed of doing. He purged a huge section of the daytime schedule of its motley assortment of programmers and brought in a magazine format called *CitySounds*: a "bed of music," as Scagliotti described it, interspersed with short "modules" of documentaries, poetry readings, reviews, and feature stories. "The idea is to hook listeners in through music," Harvey explained, "zap them with a dollop of information or a dose of politics, then, quick, back to the music before they have a chance to get bored and switch stations."[12]

Chances are that Scagliotti could do what he did because after years of combat, a large portion of the station's old guard had either forgotten what they were fighting about or conceded that "it was time to let someone try to drag a kicking, screaming BAI into the 1980s." It probably helped that management did not touch WBAI's most hallowed programmer, Bob Fass. Quite the contrary, they skillfully isolated him by offering the station's late-night free-former $1,000 to produce an all-day Bob Dylan special, thereby infuriating news producer Robert Knight, who had recently been compensated $56 to produce a day-long focus on the nuclear accident at Chernobyl. Although formal opposition to the new regime quickly emerged – a small group of angry programmers who had lost air time organized the Free Speech Radio Alliance – no one stood directly in Scagliotti and Simon's way. Instead they sentenced the duo to three years of unrelenting bad will. Staff denounced *CitySounds* (or "ShittySounds," as they dubbed the format) as apolitical and superficial. "Fast food radio," Larry Josephson called it. "There's a general decline in depth and seriousness in the media symbolized by Page Six of the *Post* and 'Entertainment Tonight,' and this trend is being catered to by people like Scagliotti." The station's chief engineer and operations director resigned in protest over the changes. Two thousand letters of complaint arrived when Scagliotti (now nicknamed "Johnny Scaggs" by his opponents) tried to cut back the alternative health program of Gary Null. Conspiracy monger John Fisk – a "raving lunatic," in his own words – used his second-to-last program to denounce a stillborn attempt by WBAI management to partner with a former Pacifica board member to buy a building in which the station could rent cheap and adequate space. When Simon fired him, Fisk used his last air time to charge that "Jewish money isn't going to buy this scene. . . . If that ain't offensive, nothing is."[13]

Those staff who did not devote their free time to wearing Simon and Scagliotti out just waited them out. "Five years from now we'll all be saying, 'Oh God, remember John Scagliotti?' " commented WBAI talk show host Lynn Samuels.[14] Such smug remarks did not console Pacifica's governing board. Doubtless its members were pleased that by the end of the 1980s the frequency's audience had nearly doubled since 1976, when it had stood at about 87,000 weekly listeners in one of the world's most populous cities.[15] But the station still sustained a $200,000 debt. In 1988, a year after John Simon left WBAI, Pacifica asked a research company to assess the possibility of a capital campaign to raise money to buy a headquarters in Manhattan. The firm took a year to conclude that such a campaign was not possible, because most potential donors regarded WBAI as the home of the marginal – "hippies" or "communists," to quote from their final report. "[O]nce the infrastructure is strengthened," the study concluded, "changes in the quality and coherence of programming are made, and an aggressive campaign to promote WBAI's new image is implemented, WBAI will be in a position to consider a major capital campaign."[16]

Undaunted, management at Pacifica's other frequencies began experimenting with techniques more or less similar to those tried by Simon at WBAI. At KPFA David Salniker took on the position of general manager of the station in the early 1980s. A labor attorney, Salniker had helped some of KPFA's Third World activists negotiate with Pacifica when Roger Pritchard banned them from the premises in the mid-1970s. He also assisted KPFA's local advisory board to draft an affirmative action policy for the station. KPFA went through two general managers after Larry Bensky, one lasting only about ninety days. Then staff invited Salniker to apply for the position, which he did, intending to serve for about two years before returning to his law practice. "The best I could do was try to mediate some of the disputes that were tearing the station apart and add some stability to it," Salniker later recalled.[17]

I came to KPFA in 1983, shortly after Salniker arrived there. Raised in Manhattan, at 29 I decided to hitchhike around the country. I soon realized that I had gotten tired of my hometown. By 1982 I had relocated to Oakland, California. A dedicated WBAI listener in the 1970s, on the opposite coast I tuned into KPFA at 94.1 FM and fell in love with the station. A friend told me that the KPFA news department offered training classes for volunteer reporters. I

219

called, applied, and was accepted to Mark Mericle's news production course for the winter of 1983.

A former staff member at community station WYSO in Yellow Springs, Ohio, Mericle was new to KPFA as well. He quickly integrated himself into the station's news production schedule: morning headlines at 7 and 8 a.m., headlines again at 5 p.m., an hour of news from 6 to 7, rebroadcast at 11 p.m. Mericle co-directed the news department with Aileen Alfandary, a confident young journalist who specialized in environmental issues. Wendell Harper, the station's feisty African-American feature reporter, provided two detailed feature stories every night on Bay Area city politics. Michael Yoshida ran the live studio mixing board and kept the news department's matrix of used production and satellite equipment in good working order.

I arrived at KPFA's second-story headquarters on Shattuck Avenue in Berkeley one evening in January of 1983 and found myself in a matrix of rooms aptly described by a reporter for the *East Bay Express* as akin to "a men's dormitory that [has] been hit simultaneously by a flood and a tornado; extravagantly stacked piles of typescript, newspapers and magazines, cans of tape, graffiti, posters thumb-tacked to the walls, ancient typewriters, technical gear, staplers, and telephones that look like they've been physically assaulted."[18] After wandering about for five minutes I located the news department, where a dozen trainees like myself waited for something to happen. Mericle walked in and introduced himself. "Something about me you should know," he told us, "I'm a Marxist. But unlike most Marxists, I actually belong to a political organization: Democratic Socialists of America." Mericle and Alfandary saw themselves as both reporters and organizers. As such, they drew dozens of new volunteer trainees into the department every few months. Alternative journalists who wanted to get into radio, activists who wanted to get the word out, paralegals who wanted to do something interesting on their day off: they streamed into KPFA's rabbit warren and learned to produce feature stories for the nightly news. After a year of work at the station, a team of about 30 of us provided live coverage of the 1984 Democratic National Convention, held in San Francisco. By then I was hooked, even though I did not really want to be a journalist. I just wanted to be part of KPFA.[19]

The station gradually stabilized in the late 1970s. In 1978 KPFA's science editor, Laurie Garrett, and its public affairs producer, Adi Gevins, won a Peabody award for their ongoing documentary series *Science Story*.[20] A year later Alfandary commandeered the station during the Three Mile Island nuclear plant disaster, producing compelling round-the-clock coverage of the crisis.[21] Musicians everywhere recognized Charles Amirkhanian's music department as a radio mecca for avant-garde composers. In this context Salniker, patient and mild-mannered, offered a persona the exact opposite of John Simon's. "[A] person whose instinct is to resolve conflict, not instigate it," Don Maisel, the station's operations director, described him, "which is novel in a KPFA station manager."[22]

But, like Simon, Salniker wanted to take KPFA beyond its hallowed past. That meant getting past what he called the "bureaucratically managed individualism" that underscored the station's culture. The KPFA *Folio* of July 1984 listed no fewer than 251 people as members of the station's staff, most of them volunteers, most of them producing individual shows for one of the station's six departments: news, drama and literature, public affairs, the women's department, the Third World department, or the music department. Salniker wanted them to think about something besides their own half-hour of air time. "I have yet to have the experience of someone coming to me and urging that their program should be taken off the air," he dryly told alternative media historian John Dowling in 1983. "And rarely, of someone coming to me and saying they want to cede their time to give space to a key issue."[23]

It was in this context that Ginny Berson of the women's department began working as the station's unofficial program director, although she was not formally given the position until 1987. In the 1970s Berson had joined the Radical Furies, a lesbian-feminist collective based in Washington, D.C. ("That was then," she once grumbled, after I mentioned a reference to her role with the Furies in Alice Echols's *Daring to Be Bad: Radical Feminism in America*).[24] In 1973 Berson and singer Meg Christian founded the first women's music company, Olivia Records. Equipped with a confident, take-charge personality, at some point in the late 1970s Berson changed her on-air name to Ginny "Z" Berson. The "Z" stood for nothing but itself. "My career didn't really go anywhere until I put a 'Z' in my name," Berson once gleefully told me.[25]

Taking the opposite approach to Simon and Scagliotti's, in 1984 and 1985 Berson, Salniker, and a few others initiated a station-wide re-evaluation of programming. The event certainly introduced a lot of volunteers to one another, but it accomplished relatively little else. The staff took listener surveys, subdivided into committees, produced statements, and talked a lot. "And [at] the end of all this, we ended up with a huge staff meeting in which a new set of principles was voted on for KPFA," Berson later recalled in a distinct tone of skepticism. "They weren't actually called principles. They were called, it was almost, like, a Statement of Purpose, it was, like, Goals, it was, like, Programming Philosophy. It was very confused."[26]

Undaunted, Berson began encouraging staff to think about the station as a whole rather than just their individual program. She urged on-air hosts to say something nice about the show coming up after theirs (sometime in the early 1980s I had actually heard a KPFA interviewer say, "Well, we could talk about this fascinating matter for quite some time; unfortunately, the next program is about to start"). She got the news and public affairs departments to start promoting each other over the air. And she reminded hosts that by trashing National Public Radio during station marathon harangues, they were in effect criticizing that large portion of KPFA's audience who also regularly listened to *All Things Considered*.[27]

But eventually Berson had to deal with the actual content of the air time. Shortly before she became program director, Pacifica had sent her and her peers at the other four stations to a National Federation of Community Broadcasters extended workshop on programming that dealt with reading Arbitron ratings and how to interpret audience research (it should be recalled from Chapter 4 that such data had become popular in public broadcasting around this time). The participants traded notes on their various systems of broadcasting. The event left Berson determined to make changes when she returned to the station, which to her meant dealing with *Traffic Jam*.

A 4:30 to 6 p.m. weekday drive-time strip, *Traffic Jam* was really five almost entirely different shows produced by five different people at the same time during the week. They came and went over the years. Future *All Things Considered* reporters Richard Gonzales and Mara Liasson hosted the show in the early 1980s. So did Ginny Berson and her colleague, Bay Area writer Julia Randall.[28] And so did Robby Osman, who also hosted a weekend folk music show. Osman organized music festivals and fund-raising events throughout the region. A thoughtful on-air commentator, so popular had Osman's weekend program become that the folk singer Kate Wolf wrote a piece for it, "Across the Great Divide," which became the show's theme song. A veteran of the Mississippi Freedom Summer of 1964 and the 1968 Columbia University strike, Osman functioned in KPFA's internal life as advocate for the broad program-council model of governance that KPFA had established in the mid-1970s, one that defined "unpaid staff" as anyone who volunteered for 20 hours or more a week at the station.[29] "[W]hen I came into the station, decisions were made ... in a very group, very consensus fashion," Osman later recalled. "The important questions of the time, whether there would be a women's department, whether there would be a Third World department, whether a manager would survive or not, seemed to be made by the process of very widespread discussion and a critical mass."[30]

In 1987, shortly after Berson became program director, she decided that *Traffic Jam* needed a makeover. "The show is terrible," she frankly told its hosts at a meeting. "[N]obody's listening and it's not raising any money. So let's talk about what we can do to make it better." Berson proposed that everyone call the *Traffic Jam* programmer the day before and tell them what they had scheduled so that it could be promoted in advance over the air. She asked the quintet of hosts to call her at 10 a.m. with their plans for the day so that she could produce noon-time promotional tapes for broadcast. She even produced theme music for the strip. But this support came with a caveat. "If it doesn't get better," Berson warned, "I'm going take the show off the air."[31]

Traffic Jam did not get better, at least not in Berson's opinion. Not enough programmers called in with their schedules, she felt. They often did not use the cart or promote each other. And so Berson took the program off the air, not sparing Osman or herself. She replaced the strip with a new format called *Rhythm Drive*, five programmers playing Afro-Cuban music from 4:30 to 6 p.m. The feedback from the listeners was immediate and overwhelming. "They were screamingly against this," Osman recalled. They were sometimes screamingly against Berson as well. "I got letters from listeners that were just horrifying to me," she explained. "Really, really shook me up . . . anonymous letters talking about what a lazy bitch I was for taking *Traffic Jam* off the air and all it needed was a little attention."[32] But Berson did not back down. The rest of the station's paid staff supported her, and *Rhythm Drive* stayed.

Berson and Osman derived different lessons from this experience. "I really got a sense right away that [if] I'm going to last in this job, I've got to get a thicker skin," Berson confided. "I mean I was not going to ever be that vulnerable again." Osman regarded the change as an ominous precedent. For the first time in a long time, an unpopular decision had been made by management despite negative feedback from listeners and volunteers. "Part of the whole point was, the implicit lesson was, that if the paid staff stuck together and weathered the storm and did not obey the consensus, in the end they would prevail," he later observed. "And that was proved."[33] Indeed, Berson's decision to clear the decks for a music format at a time when research indicated that listeners wanted news and information could be read as less about audience building and more about asserting her authority. If Pacifica middle management wanted to purge the 1970s from the system, first they would have to establish who was boss.

Berson and Simon's reforms differed from those proposed by Clare Spark in that Spark's successors seemed less interested in thinking about the political content of Pacifica fare and far more concerned with format and schedule. Spark's efforts at control focused on what was to be said over KPFK in Los Angeles. Berson and Simon thought more about how and when it was to be said; they appeared to accept Pacifica's politics as a given. The problem of how to create cohesion among Pacifica's disparate audiences and programmers became a managerial rather than a philosophical dilemma. As they and their colleagues tested the limits of the system, the tensions they provoked among listeners were initially mitigated by the network's more immediately successful experimentation with national programming.

Iran/Contra to the Rescue

While Ginny Berson and John Scagliotti struggled with Pacifica volunteers, a huge political crisis swept aside most other news throughout the country. On November 3, 1986, a newspaper in Beirut, Lebanon, broke a shocking story about the Reagan administration's recent dealings in the region. The United States had secretly sold over 2,000 anti-aircraft missiles to Iran in the hopes of freeing American hostages languishing there. President Reagan had even sent Iran's Ayatollah Khomeini a Bible with his autograph, accompanying a shipment of HAWK missile parts to Tehran. These gestures made a mockery of Reagan's pledge never to negotiate with terrorists, but the most startling revelation came later that month. Reagan operatives had covertly siphoned the profits from the arms sales to the Nicaraguan Contras, a CIA-created guerrilla force attempting to overthrow Nicaragua's socialist Sandinista government. When, two years earlier, news had broken that the CIA had secretly mined Nicaragua's harbors, the House of Representatives had passed an amendment slapping a two-year ban on Contra aid. The administration's covert machinations had clearly been in contempt of Congress.[34]

In the late spring of 1987, a combined House and Senate committee announced plans to broadcast what would eventually come to 250 hours of televised hearings on "Contragate" to a nation half outraged and half fascinated by the affair. Berkeley resident Larry Bensky was walking his dog shortly before this media drama began, when his neighbor David Salniker pulled up in his car. By then Bensky had taken work as a direct mail copywriter, occasionally volunteering for KPFA on election night. He had also produced a documentary on the Nicaraguan revolution for PBS. Salniker was about to replace Sharon Maeda as executive director of Pacifica. He told Bensky that Pacifica planned to broadcast the Iran/Contra hearings from Washington. "Really," Bensky replied. "That's great. I'm glad you're doing it. Who is going to anchor it for you?" A few weeks later he was on a plane for Washington, D.C., to host Pacifica's live gavel-to-gavel coverage of the biggest foreign policy scandal in modern U.S. history.[35]

By the mid-1980s Pacifica had a little more money to play around with for projects like this, thanks, ironically, to the Reagan administration. Pacifica's FM signals, like all conventional AM and FM radio frequencies, broadcast what are called auxiliary or subcarrier signals, not audible by conventional radio receivers. Up until the Reagan years, the FCC insisted that all such Subcarrier Communications Authority (SCA) channels owned by nonprofit organizations be used by that organization or leased to another nonprofit project. They prohibited leases for commercial usage. Pacifica had over the years leased some of its subcarriers to a reading service for the blind. In 1983 the Reagan administration, in its zeal to deregulate the airwaves, lifted these restrictions. Now, in addition to the blind reading service, Pacifica began leasing its SCAs to commercial data companies, bringing in thousands of dollars of new, unexpected income.[36]

Pacifica had always been providing live coverage of some kind or another. In 1972 Bensky had anchored and produced the Democratic and Republican conventions from Miami Beach, sending narration and actuality feeds via telephone connections.

But now the network could rent satellite time with far better audio quality and reach dozens of community radio stations across the country. The Pacifica Iran/Contra coverage team consisted of Larry Bensky, his producer Bill Wax, and "occasional part-time augmentation," as Bensky later put it. But with those resources, Bensky interviewed hundreds of politicians, journalists, government officials, academics, and activists to bring context to the drama provided by the stream of government witnesses. He held national listener call-in sessions to get audience reaction to the scandal. Through it all Bensky remained open-minded, asking intellectually honest questions of his guests, while sharing his heart with his audience. "When one hears – as the Iran-Contra committees have heard repeatedly – witnesses with shady bank accounts, murderously murky pasts and obvious self-interest, talk about patriotism as motivation, one should know wherefrom one is hearing" he wrote in the *KPFA Folio* of July 1987. The production won him, Wax, and Pacifica a George Polk Award. It also put Pacifica national programming on the map. Everyone sensed that Pacifica had at last reclaimed some of the audience that had gone over to *All Things Considered*. "The question that haunts Pacifica now is how to keep those unexpected recruits," commented a reporter for *Mother Jones*.[37]

The short-term answer was: more live gavel-to-gavel coverage. The Reagan and elder Bush administrations provided excellent fodder for such events. Pacifica went back to D.C. two more times in the late 1980s and early 1990s. The first trip was to provide the only live national radio coverage of the hearings of controversial ultra-right-wing jurist Robert Bork, nominated to the Supreme Court later in 1987. Then came the electrifying hearings of nominee Clarence Thomas, accused of sexual harassment by his former assistant at the Equal Employment Opportunity Commission, Anita Hill.[38] The long-term answer, Pacifica officials concluded, was to centralize the organization's resources.

Beyond Castor Oil

On September 1, 1992, former PBS official Gail Christian, now working for Pacifica as its director of national programming, completed a study for the organization titled "A Strategy for National Programming." The document could be read in two ways – as a series of sensible recommendations for the network, or as an attack on the institutional politics of the organization. In fact, it was both.

Christian's prospectus called for just what its title implied: a centralized programming service designed to help the individual Pacifica stations build audience. The service would, over the course of five years, create a series of satellite-distributed shows available to community radio stations around the United States. The plan envisioned an expanded national news division that provided two hours of daily news, one hour in the morning, another in the evening; national syndication of Pacifica's best local programming; a late-night progressive talk show to compete with mainstream media's battalion of right-wing talk radio hosts; a regular stream of two- to five-minute feature modules adaptable to a wide variety of local programs; and the expansion of Pacifica's live coverage of key national events such as the Iran/Contra hearings. The final result would be a production service, located in Washington, D.C., that would provide about 100 hours a month of programming to 100 community radio stations, including Pacifica's. This fare would build audience size "while at the same time distinguishing Pacifica as the primary network for programming that is a positive alternative to 'mainstream' opinion."[39]

The "Strategy's" recommendations acknowledged painful truths about much of Pacifica's broadcasting. To build audience, Christian argued, these new programs would have to emphasize production values and style, as well as content:

> Simply producing new programming ... does not guarantee success. In this competitive marketplace, it is not enough to offer subject matter that is important: the material must be produced

and packaged in a manner that is interesting and entertaining. Boring programs do not redeem themselves by taking on heady topics. Since Pacifica has little to lose and everything to gain, it should position itself in the marketplace as the innovative, brash and irreverent network with programs that are on the cutting edge in format and political analysis. The Pacifica stations and the community stations have labored too long under the weight of programs that are somewhat like castor oil, good for you but not necessarily easy to take.[40]

How would the organization fund this ambitious project? Pacifica would solicit foundation grants. In an appendix to the "Strategy," Christian disclosed that Pacifica staff had recently met with three foundations with a history of giving money for public broadcasting: the Ford Foundation, the MacArthur Foundation, and the Pew Charitable Trust, foundations which also funded American Public Radio and National Public Radio. The meetings had been promising, she continued. Beyond these major funders, Pacifica had identified other prospects, "in some cases only because of particular people who are currently involved or because of formal criteria which we could try to fit." Establishing funding for programs would require not just filling out applications, but engaging in frequent "venture capital visits" designed to develop good working "partnerships" with foundation officers. Soon, the document predicted, foundation money would begin flowing for national programming.[41]

The "Strategy for National Programming" 's strengths were obvious: it was a clear assessment of the organization's weaknesses and assets. Christian had produced a carefully outlined framework for institutional growth, a proposal that showed the reader, step-by-step, how the network could become something more than the sum of its parts.

But while on a macro level Pacifica may have had "little to lose" by adopting this course of action, many of its component parts had plenty to lose. In an organization rife with jealousies and factional rivalries, who would decide which Pacifica programmers to elevate to national status? The "Strategy" offered no model by which to approach this difficult problem. In fact, the prospectus outlined nothing less than a massive transfer of broadcasting time away from the five Pacifica stations to a production center. Hundreds of hours of air time once controlled by local producers would be given over to programming created thousands of miles away. Regional activists and musicians who had come to depend upon that space for publicity or exposure would find it gone. Loyal audiences would be alienated and in some instances would surely make trouble. Such storms had always followed reformatting at Pacifica stations. But Gail Christian's master plan invited them upon the organization manifold. How could this fallout be avoided? The "Strategy" did not address this problem. And it offered little solace to those who feared what was now frequently described as Pacifica's drift toward NPR-style programming. Much of the plan – with its proposed hourly news updates and modular features – resembled the direction that much of public broadcasting had already taken. So did its emphasis on audience-building.

The "Strategy" strongly emphasized marketability over content. The word "market" appeared in some form no fewer than 25 times in the 31-page document. The proposal listed two objectives as central to its mission. First, a broadcasting goal: "to provide programming support to stations to increase their listening audiences and their financial contributions." Second, a social goal: "to provide a national voice that forwards Pacifica's mission of encouraging peace with social and economic justice." But, the "Strategy" continued, the "test" of the new national programming office's success would be its capacity "to provide programs that bring in greater audiences and revenues than those being generated on the local level."[42]

No one would deny the value to Pacifica of enlarged audiences and increased revenues. Crucial questions, however, remained unanswered. Who would decide, down the line, whether the implementation of the "Strategy" met the needs of the organization? A vaguely worded subsection titled "Accountability" merely emphasized that each position in the new national program service was associated with a definite goal.[43] What if the "Strategy" did not meet its goals? More importantly to the station staffs and audiences, what if it chose to meet its audience-building goal by toning down the organization's traditional emphasis on challenging the national security state? Christian's proposal included no mechanisms for addressing this last concern. On the contrary, it editorialized in ways likely to provoke worry about the question. Christian urged Pacifica's national news to "expand beyond its white suburban West Coast audience and become more urban oriented in its approach." Programming that addressed "one's ability to live a decent life should be emphasized. The 'October surprise' should take a back seat to the October unemployment figures."[44] This dismissive reference to 1979 presidential candidate Ronald Reagan's alleged attempt to sabotage the Carter administration's efforts to free the Iran U.S. embassy hostages would not comfort programmers already nervous about the direction in which the organization seemed headed. Unlike Bensky's Iran/Contra coverage, the "Strategy" did not demonstrate its own worth. It just called for lots of changes in an institution that hated change. Not surprisingly, then, the prospectus functioned less as a blueprint for the network's future and more as a lightning rod for local programmers and activist listeners, they now worried about KPFA's new general manager.

With Salniker moving up to the executive director's office in 1987, a hiring committee began looking for a new boss for KPFA. The name of Salniker's friend Pat Scott quickly came up as a likely candidate. Born and raised in a black working- and middle-class neighborhood in Chicago, Scott went to Illinois State University. She then moved to the West Coast to take a graduate degree at UCLA in television and film. After that she worked as an administrator for the Berkeley grocery Co-op, served as assistant to Berkeley mayor Gus Newport, and ran a horse-training ranch in the East Bay. Since the San Luis Obispo Statement controversy of 1984, Scott had also sat on KPFA's local advisory board. "I slept through many of the meetings, because they were so dull," she later recalled. But the ideas of some of her fellow board members, particularly Dick Bunce, former editor of Socialist Review, intrigued her, and so she stayed on. When Salniker asked her to apply to replace him, she agreed.[45]

I first met Scott in what was probably one of the last gestures to the 1970s consensus era at KPFA. In 1987 the entire staff gathered in the station's music library to interview her for the general manager position. We piled into the room, at least 50 of us, and asked her questions like, "What's your class background?" She seemed understandably offended by the process. It appeared to me that her hiring was a done deal. The other finalist was a white male who was asked during his staff interview whether he thought the station should hire a white male.[46] That summer, Salniker moved out of the general manager's office and Scott moved in.

Scott soon made it clear that she did not find the men's-dormitory aspect of KPFA either radical or quaint. She also found troublesome the fleas that tended to gravitate toward her clothing. "I remember the first day I was there – I had some white pants on, going out to lunch, and I got out on Shattuck Avenue and looked down and it looked like I had on a pair of tweed pants." Scott quickly noticed that staff often did not show up for work except when it was time to go on the air, and as for KPFA's air sound, "it was like hippie radio," she later explained. "It was bits and pieces here and there. Somebody would go off, you'd have dead air, nobody else was on. Or somebody would run five or ten minutes over."[47]

On the housing front, Salniker, Scott, and Pacifica's development director, Dick Bunce, performed a miracle for KPFA. They ran the first capital building project in the organization's history, quickly raising two million dollars, enough to construct a beautiful new adobe headquarters for the station on Martin Luther King, Jr., Way, just north of downtown Berkeley. In 1991, the staff gratefully moved in as composer Lou Harrison and his gamelan ensemble performed a piece called *Homage to Pacifica*.[48]

Enboldened by this success, Berson, with Scott's support, accelerated the reorganization of KPFA's format. She swept the Saturday morning schedule to make room for legendary R&B bandleader

Johnny Otis, cutting out the station's last remaining children's program. "I'm sorry I'm doing this," she later recalled telling the host. "I really would like to have a formal process, but I gotta tell you, your program is terrible. And we can go through a formal process of evaluation, but it's gonna come off anyway." Berson reshuffled the early morning hours and the noon-time programming. Volunteer programmers for the 7-8 p.m. strip called *Primetime* received notices that their shows were about to be cancelled. If they wanted to continue, they had to submit proposals for modular segments of four to thirteen weeks.[49] Berson brought in consultants to set up formal systems of evaluation for programs, and she warned programmers that she would stick to those systems. "Don't tell me that you get lots of phone calls at the end of every show telling you what a great show it is," Berson told hosts and producers. "Do you know what they say about how many phone calls each phone call represents? Each phone call represents one phone call. It's not a lot."[50]

People who had been drawn to KPFA in the 1970s saw that this process diminished their influence over the station. Prominent among the disgruntled was longtime Bay Area activist Jeffrey Blankfort, a passionate Palestinian-rights activist. In the early 1990s the Jewish Anti-Defamation League (ADL) hired a South African operative to infiltrate Blankfort's Labor Committee on the Middle East and build dossiers on him and his associates Steve Zeltzer (also a KPFA programmer) and Anne Poirier. The operative paid off a rogue San Francisco police officer to obtain legal documents on members of the group. Eventually Blankfort and his associates sued the ADL and were granted $50,000 each.[51]

But by then Blankfort felt shut out of KPFA. In the 1980s Kris Welch hosted the station's morning show. Welch was an irreverent personality with a large loyal following in Berkeley, who did her work with almost no support. I occasionally announced the morning news during her 7-9 a.m. slot and would find Welch interviewing people, trying to get to the front door to let the next interviewee in (the receptionist did not arrive until 9 a.m.), setting up reels of tape for broadcast, helping me with my newscast, and, a single mother, taking care of her eight-year-old daughter, whom she brought to work. In the early 1990s KPFA management mercifully hired a producer to assist Welch broadcast during what, after all, were and still are radio's most listened-to hours. Blankfort felt the results immediately. "The morning show . . . before Pat Scott introduced producers, had a real immediacy, had a real connection," he explained. "And so Kris Welch would frequently call me, frantic for a program for the next day. And I was very much in touch with activists coming and going and all kinds of movements and things in the city. And so I would be able to help her more often than not, or steer her to somebody who could."[52] Now Welch stopped calling. It probably did not improve matters that in 1988 station management fired his close friend Maria Gilardin from her development job at KPFA, largely over disagreements about how to promote the frequency in fund-raising materials.[53] By 1992, the two were ready to take Pacifica on.

Just before the KPFA Holiday Crafts Fair of 1992, Blankfort, Gilardin, and two longtime KPFA listeners, Marianne Torres and Werner Hertz, formed the KPFA Listeners Participation Group, which soon changed its name to Save KPFA. Blankfort went to the Fair and handed out the group's literature. Scott walked up to Blankfort and, characteristically, put her arm around him. "You and I have to talk," she said. "As soon as I pass out these leaflets," Blankfort coolly replied. Hundreds of Fair goers took a flyer, which invited concerned listeners to a meeting to be held at Ashkenaz, a dance hall on Berkeley's San Pablo Avenue, on January 25. By then word had gotten out that KPFA planned to cancel all public affairs programming broadcast after the 6 p.m. news and replace it with music. Many of these shows aired to small but dedicated communities. To the amazement of Pacifica management, no fewer than 250 listeners came to the gathering, all of them furious at their favorite listener-supported radio station.[54]

The meeting was vintage Berkeley. The agenda took about half an hour to explain, including five minutes for each participant to give their opinion about KPFA to the person sitting next to them, and five minutes for the neighbor to reply. Pat Scott had been invited to speak, but she bowed out when told that she would only be permitted to address the entire group for two minutes, the same amount of time given to everyone else. Then individuals got up to talk. "Two minutes is not enough time for me to vent all the anger I have against KPFA," declared Ashkenaz-owner David Nadel, who railed against the lack of coverage he felt the station gave to Berkeley's legendary People's Park, near campus.

Journalist Paul Rauber reported on the gathering in a feature story for the *East Bay Express*. A sometimes volunteer / sometimes paid staffer for the KPFA news department, Rauber shared the perspective of the station's paid senior staff toward this rebellion, describing it very much through their eyes:

> Marianne Torres was mad because Chris Strachwitz had played a song during the Gulf War called "Baghdad Barbecue," and laughed at her when she called to complain. Ruth Bird wanted programming about the animal rights movement. Another woman complained that all the Latin and black music made her feel guilty about being white; she would feel better about it if at least two hours of every day were devoted to Noam Chomsky and Michael Parenti. David O'Connell wanted one-third of every program devoted to listener call-ins. Greg Alexander wanted to know why certain subjects were considered taboo, like the Federal Reserve Bank, the International opium trade, and UFOs. "I get cut off all the time whenever I bring it up," he complained.[55]

The vehemence of the meeting put off even Robbie Osman. "It's appropriate for listeners to be involved," he told Rauber, "but there's a tendency to jump to the step of lighting torches and storming the castle. Of course, when you get to the castle there's only one kind of conversation you can have."[56] But however unfocused their anger might have been, these listeners instinctively understood that the keepers of the castle had adopted a new set of criteria about what constituted Pacifica's mission, and that those criteria no longer included them. There was a sense, participant

Curtis Gray recalled, "that the station was literally moving away from the community, especially the progressive, activist community that really depended on it and from which it had basically arisen."[57] The changes had come slowly and had been difficult to pin down. Now there was something concrete to attack: Gail Christian's "Strategy for National Programming." Speaker after speaker at the gathering denounced the proposal. "Shit can be prettily packaged, perfumed, and in smell-proof plastic," William Mandel, KPFA's veteran Soviet affairs commentator, indelicately declared at the gathering. "A market is a place one enters to sell goods and services for profit. Ours is a nonprofit organization."[58]

But outside of these small, heated gatherings, those who followed Pacifica politics had sympathy for Scott and skepticism, at best, for her critics. "KPFA must now carve out a new position for itself in the new, post-Cold War era: either as keeper of the flame, or pioneer in a new way of looking at the world," Paul Rauber concluded in his article for the *East Bay Express*. "The former will buy it temporary peace but ultimate irrelevance; the latter will keep it on the edge it has occupied for 44 years."[59] After setting up a table for Save KPFA at a San Francisco Mime Troupe gathering, subscriber Curtis Gray found not a few of his fellow listeners sympathetic to Rauber's viewpoint, including several members of his own family. "My brother-in-law and my sister said, 'Change can't come soon enough there. And you've got to reach out to a larger audience,'" Gray later explained. "That sort of stuff."[60] As KPFA listeners debated these questions, the staff at its sister station in Los Angeles inadvertently strengthened Pat Scott's hand.

KPFK's Wild Weekend

By the early 1990s Salniker and Scott began receiving reports of heightened anti-Semitism around Pacifica. The problem had haunted the network since 1969, when African-American writer and commentator Julius Lester read a 26-line anti-Semitic poem over WBAI's airwaves ("Hey, Jew boy, with that yamulka on your head / You pale faced Jew boy – I wish you were dead / I can see you Jew boy – no you can't hide / I got a scoop on you-yeh, you gonna die."). Actually, beyond an initial flurry of letters, the poem itself didn't cause much controversy among listeners; Lester had read it out of concern, not sympathy with the sentiments. But a teacher's strike that year had inflamed African-American/Jewish relations in New York, and the United Federation of Teachers filed a complaint against WBAI with the Federal Communications Commission. Several weeks later Lester invited black community activist Tyrone Woods onto his show to talk about the strike. Woods referred back to the poem and the UFT's objections to it. "As far as I am concerned, more power to Hitler," he declared. "Hitler didn't make enough lampshades out of them. He didn't make enough belts out of them." A veritable avalanche of protest fell upon the station, all of it unfair. Lester had broadcast none of this because he agreed with anti-Semitism. Ultimately, in fact, he was to convert to Judaism himself, a spiritual journey described in his book *Lovesong: Becoming a Jew.*[61]

But while Lester explored black cultural nationalism and anti-Semitism from the perspective of a journalist and an intellectual, the staff of KPFK in Los Angeles in the late 1980s and 1990s gave these ideologies free, uncritical rein. By 1993 I had relocated to southern California to pursue a doctorate in history at the Claremont Graduate School. One afternoon I tuned in to KPFK just as a host began interviewing three members of the Nation of Islam about African-American women in the United States. My jaw dropped as I heard one guest explain that the reason why such women work for corporations was because they were descended from African queens "and therefore have the desire for wealth in their genes." The host rudely shunted off the air a black woman who called in to disagree with this perspective. The program became known to some staff at KPFK as the "queen gene" show, one programmer later privately told me. But apparently nobody had the courage to insist that this sort of commentary discredited the station and ought not to be broadcast in an uncritical context.[62]

Such cowardice allowed the repeated airing of "Afrikan Mental

Liberation Weekend," hosted by Kwaku Person-Lynn, an instructor in African studies at Cal State Dominguez Hills. This annual event offered KPFK listeners a nearly 30-hour-long parade of prerecorded speeches by prominent black cultural separatists. A caller who phoned in to protest the content of the weekend was labeled, according to one account, a "psychotic, idiotic European," and according to another, a "psychotic, idiotic European Jew" over KPFK's airwaves.[63] The Anti-Defamation League publicly complained about the show, charging that it had included a "lengthy diatribe against the Jewish community" and had violated the FCC's personal attack rule. Despite this, KPFK management permitted the production a return engagement on the weekend of February 13 and 14 in 1993.[64] Aware that he was treading on thin ice, Bill Thomas, the station's latest general manager, assured the public that all tapes had been checked in advance and that level-headed co-hosts would challenge some of the more outrageous claims of the production. Whether anyone actually checked the tapes is unclear, but despisers of the event kept their cassette recorders running, then shared the results with southern California's formerly left-wing, now right-wing ideologue, David Horowitz. He in turn published extensive excerpts of both the 1992 and 1993 weekends in *Comint*, his journal on public media.

Defenders of Pacifica insisted that Horowitz's version of the weekend and of programming at KPFK in general had been taken out of context. Indeed, although the journal mentioned that black KPFK programmer Kenneth Carr was heard in 1992 to call UCLA "Jew-CLA" over the station's air, it did not note that he insisted that the mispronunciation had not been deliberate.[65] But even if *Comint* only got it half right, Pacifica had a lot of explaining to do. The magazine transcribed large portions of the event, and reported that the 1993 edition of "Afrikan Mental Liberation Weekend" included a noon speech by a Nation of Islam patriarch declaring, "I would not say that the white man is a descendant of Satan, because that would be wrong. We didn't have a Satan before the white man. So the white man is Satan himself." Inspirational speaker Eraka Rouzorondu told listeners that "white people are genetic mutations of blacks. And we running around here trying to look like a mutant. We have adopted their perception of reality, their life style, their values: and they are mutants! Don't call me a racist! I can't be racist! I ain't got no power." Another commentator insisted that the "same god didn't make the white man that made us. The white man was made just 6,000 years ago and we was made unlimited; we don't know nothing about any birth records to us."[66] Returning to the mutant question, KPFK listeners heard Dr. Frances Cress Welsing explain that "White supremacy is the necessity to maintain white genetic survival . . . Black people can produce white people. White people can only produce white people. They are the mutants from black people."[67] As promised, KPFK summoned UC Santa Barbara's respected historian Gerald Horne to offer a counterpoint to this flood of separatist dogma. Perhaps Horne's enthusiasm for the task declined after being introduced on-air as "KPFK's designated Negro."[68]

Doubtless KPFK's staff congratulated themselves upon learning that $15,000 had been raised for the station during pledge breaks, but they quickly discovered that they had delivered Pacifica into the hands of its enemies. Transcripts of the 1992 and 1993 weekends were mailed to Victor Gold, a member of the board of directors of the Corporation for Public Broadcasting. Enraged, Gold with great fanfare submitted a proposal to the CPB's April 1-2 meeting in Lincoln, Nebraska, ordering the agency to cut off Community Service Grants (CSGs) to any station that repeatedly broadcast materials that defamed "any race, religion, or minority." Fortunately for KPFK, which received over a quarter of a million dollars in CSG funding over that period, CPB guidelines forbade the institution from directly interfering with the programming philosophy of its recipients.[69] The board voted Gold's proposal down.

Undaunted, right-wing KPFK-haters elevated their campaign to a higher political platform: the offices of presidential hopeful and former Republican vice president Robert Dole, for whom David Horowitz had once worked as a speechwriter. Dole appeared at the 1993 Public Radio Conference in Washington, D.C., railed against "unrelenting liberal cheerleading on the public airwaves," and denounced Pacifica as "anti-Semitic" and "hate radio." Independent producer David Barsamian sat in the audience while Dole spoke. "The effect on station managers and program directors, the gatekeepers of public radio, was palpable," he later wrote.[70] Shortly after Dole's speech, Republican Representative Joel Hefley of Colorado proposed to cut the budget of the CPB by a sum roughly equal to the funding Pacifica received from the agency. Salniker promoted Scott to a new position, national affairs director, and sent her to Washington, D.C., to lobby Congress against the measure.[71]

Now "Afrikan Mental Liberation Weekend" and similar programming had Pacifica's attention. While correctly charging that the Right used the show to sabotage the network's more substantial fare, the Pacifica national office and board privately moved to assess and repair the damage done by such programming. "[W]e are in trouble," Marci Lockwood, KPFA's new manager, candidly told listener-subscribers after Dole's speech. "Quite frankly, our on-air fund raising is not doing as well as it used to."[72] Returning from Washington, D.C., Scott flew down to Los Angeles to hear for herself how KPFK's programming sounded. She quietly booked a room in a hotel and sat at her radio for some days. Finally she called Salniker at the national office. "David," Scott began, "we have a serious problem here."[73]

It was an open secret within Pacifica that Scott had once been a member of the Communist Party (CP).[74] Jack O'Dell, the latest chair of the Pacifica national board, also had a close relationship with the Party and had been forced out of Martin Luther King's inner circle because of it. Scott cherished the CP's multi-ethnic alliances. Not surprisingly, then, she distrusted black separatism and sometimes quarreled with KPFA's Third World department – which she called the "black men's department" – over its programming. KPFK had hit bottom, she told David Salniker from Los Angeles; there were "a lot of racists and a lot of anti-Semitic programs on the air, as well as programs that were endangering our license."[75]

Scott's concerns went beyond KPFK. By the late 1980s locals in

Washington, D.C., fondly or angrily dubbed WPFW "Radio Farrakhan," a reference to the leader of the Nation of Islam (NOI). Prominent among the station's on-air talent was Malik Shabazz, an "in your eyes 'Jew Jew Jew' kind of guy," as his colleague Askia Muhammad described him.[76] In early October of 1993 WPFW went through a brief crisis during that most vulnerable moment for a Pacifica station, the hiring of a new general manager. When 53-year-old staffer Tom Porter discovered he had not been selected for the post, he organized an on-air "teach-in" for WPFW's listeners to protest the decision. Pacifica dispatched its Washington bureau chief, Bob Daughtry, to "restore regular programming" as soon as possible, or, if that could not be accomplished, to take the station off the air until new management could come in. Daughtry opted for the latter course. WPFW listeners heard a low-pitched hum until 6 a.m. on October 4, when Phil Watson, one of the signal's founders, took over as interim general manager.[77]

Following the debacle, Muhammad stepped in as WPFW's interim program director and news director. A talented journalist, Muhammad had done commentaries for National Public Radio and produced no fewer than five documentaries for the award-winning NPR series *Soundprint*. He was also a member of the Nation of Islam, but Scott respected him. In a meeting with Muhammad, she and Gail Christian insisted that WPFW's black nationalist commentators must not use the station as a soapbox. "I just said that you can have these people on the air, but I'm telling you, you better ask some provocative questions," Scott later recalled. "You better deal with it . . . you've got to have some counterpoint." According to Scott, Muhammad attempted to implement this policy, but, not surprisingly, found the station's commentators uncooperative. To his disappointment, Pacifica chose another for the job of permanent program director, a setback he attributed to his affiliation with the Nation.[78]

Then in the spring of 1994 the Pacifica national board passed the following resolution. Program directors posted copies of it on the bulletin boards of on-air studios throughout the network:

RESOLUTION

PACIFICA BOARD OF DIRECTORS MEETING

MAY 14, 1994

MOTION: RACIST, HOMOPHOBIC, SEXIST, ANTI-SEMITIC
OR MISOGYNIST PROGRAMMING HAS NO PLACE
IN PACIFICA AND SHALL BE GROUNDS FOR
THE SUMMARY REMOVAL OF A PROGRAMMER.
THE TOLERATION OF SUCH PROGRAMMING SHALL BE
GROUNDS FOR REMOVAL OF A PROGRAM
DIRECTOR OR PROGRAM HEAD.[79]

Shortly after the release of this declaration, KPFK dropped two programs accused of broadcasting hate speech: *Family Tree*, hosted by Jan Robinson Flint, and Ken Carr's *Freedom Now*. "There have been problems with those programs," Clifford U. Roberts, who had recently replaced Bill Thomas, told the *Los Angeles Times*. "I felt that they were using language in those programs in a way that was counter to our mission, which is to bring people together." Apparently the terminations took place without any meeting between management and the programmers. "If they had a griev-ance with 'Family Tree,'" Flint asked a reporter for the *Times*, "why was there no verbal warning, no suspension, no due process?" The move drew praise from the ADL. "I'm very pleased and we think it's been a long time coming, but it's certainly welcomed," declared the group's regional director in Los Angeles.[80]

Pat Scott's opposition to ethnic nationalist chauvinism and separatism deserved praise as a principled and courageous stance. But it also gave her enormous power over her friends and enemies at Pacifica. White board members and white staff at the national office knew that their attempts to curtail ethnic nationalist program-ming that contained racism or anti-Semitism would be met with loud countercharges of racism. Nonwhite board members often felt defensive about the matter. Almost everyone preferred getting a root canal to dealing with the problem. While Pacificans love telling truth to power, they dread telling truth to the powerless. Now they had a smart, decisive African-American woman who would fight the battle for them and function as an ideological gatekeeper. Meanwhile Pacifica's dissidents hedged on the issue. "The problem," Jeff Blankfort later contended, "is [that] the role of the organized Jewish community, which unfortunately will be extrapolated by certain black activists as all Jews, in controlling or dictating to the black community what its leaders should or shouldn't say, is very much resented in the black community."[81] Doubtless "Afrikan Mental Liberation Weekend" speakers who called Jews "psychotic, idiotic Europeans" or called white people "mutants" disliked being told they should not. The question remained whether the network's credibility and its station licenses would survive 1970s-style management. The struggles over black cultural nationalism in the early 1990s convinced many progressives that Pat Scott was moving the foundation in the right direction. By 1994 David Salniker had stepped down as executive director and Scott had taken his place.[82]

Once formally ensconced as Pacifica's top administrator, Scott moved quickly to finish what she had started at KPFK. On Wednesday, January 4, 1995, she came to North Hollywood and, to the amazement of staff, asked general manager Roberts and program director Lucia Chappelle to leave the station. Someone called reporter Claudia Puig of the *Los Angeles Times*, who found KPFK in shock when she arrived on the scene several hours later. "Scott . . . cited past programs by African American producers that were branded as anti-Semitic by the Jewish community as potentially divisive and not helpful to the Pacifica Foundation's stated mission," Puig concluded in her story. Pacifica's new executive director even eliminated the position of assistant general manager, but assured staff that its occupant, Mary Fowler, would remain at the station in some capacity. Two weeks later Fowler was out the door as well. Forty paid and unpaid staff members signed a letter to Jack O'Dell demanding her return "or an era of cold and tense relations between this station and Pacifica is on the horizon," they warned. Meanwhile the heat was about to turn up again at KPFA.[83]

Shedding People

By July of 1995, senior staff at KPFA had met, had strategized, and were poised to reorganize the station. "KPFA is about to transform its air sound," general manager Marci Lockwood promised Paul Rauber of the *East Bay Express.* Lockwood wouldn't go into details, but Rauber suggested to readers that "the new schedule will emphasize identifiability of air sound during large blocks of time."[84] At the end of the month the announced changes went into effect. Programmers who had hosted shows at the station for decades received notice that their programs would terminate in a week. Folk music expert Chris Strachwitz, African-American vocal music specialist Opal Nations, jazz aficionado Phil Elwood, who was music critic for the *San Francisco Examiner*, and feisty talk show host Mama O'Shea all lost their shows in a massive restructuring of the station. Several months earlier William Mandel had gotten into a fight with KPFA management. He had criticized Berson and Lockwood on his morning show and was dismissed for so doing. Now about a dozen volunteer programmers and programming groups joined him looking in from the outside. Berson assured staff that the changes did not mean individual programmers could not return in some other context. "No one has been permanently removed from the air," she told a reporter. "They may not believe that, but it's the truth." And it was, sort of. A slow trickle of volunteers gradually returned to KPFA's airwaves, but no longer as members of autonomous collectives like *Music in America, Living on Indian Time,* or *Freedom Is a Constant Struggle.*" Instead, they hosted modular air slots in strips designed by paid staff.[85]

At KPFT in Houston, management brought the Healthy Station Project to town. Lynn Chadwick and David LePage arrived in 1991 and assembled the predominantly volunteer staff to "brainstorm" about the station. LePage "drew circles on newsprint into which he narrowed our statements into single words," Native American programmer Jacquelyn Battise later bitterly recalled. The brainstorming appears to have been a formality, prelude to a succession of general managers who trimmed the station's volunteer public-affairs programmer base. According to one account, in 1992 KPFT manager Barry Forbes removed 37 out of 90 hosts.[86] It appears that Ray Hill managed to keep his program by sheer bluster. "Now, Barry, I am an ideological bastard," he told Forbes in a private meeting. "I'm probably the only one left at the station that actually believes in the kind of pacifism that Lew Hill believed in, but if you fuck with my program I will kick your L.A. queer ass out in the middle and leave blood in the street. Do you understand me?"[87] Hill stayed on the air. Many others did not. "Public affairs does not work in Houston," a KPFT program director told a station gathering in 1995. "[T]he decision has been made to be a music station featuring Texas based music." Soon former KPFT news director Garland Ganter presided over a frequency whose "Sounds of Texas" schedule had clearly moved away from the tradition of a station once proudly described as "the most integrated place in Houston." The weekend lineup had gone to an all-music format. During the week, local public-affairs programming only broadcast before 7 a.m. and after 7 p.m. Between those hours listeners heard popular music, the *BBC Newshour*, WXPN's *World Café*, NPR's *Fresh Air* with Terry Gross, and the *Pacifica Network News*. Ganter "turned the station around and made money," KPFT programmer Torry Mercer later conceded. "But to do that he compromised everything. He took the station away from the community."[88]

Changes such as these accompanied the evolution of all five Pacifica stations to varying degrees from the mid-1990s onward. Strip schedules, satellite programming, and professionalization: this praxis represented the core of the new Pacifica. A tense, ongoing standoff persisted at WBAI, where Scott's management negotiating team and the station's union stewards dug in over who would be included in the bargaining unit. WBAI's contract gave its 170 volunteers, or "unpaid staff," union recognition, making it harder for management to make programming changes. Scott wanted them out of the collective bargaining agreement. Both sides clearly understood what was at stake in the fight. "Scott would like the ability to make, without notice, radical or fundamental changes in the programming and format of the various Pacifica stations," WBAI shop steward Errol Maitland told Joel Bleifuss of *In These Times* in 1995. "Right now, there is constraint at WBAI, and that is the union."[89]

At the same time a different kind of station manager arrived to implement the new regime, someone who functioned as an enforcer rather than a conciliator. No one exemplified this new persona better than did former actor Mark Schubb, hired to run KPFK in 1995. A local reporter interviewed Schubb about a year into the job and described him as having a "focused, even self-righteous anger."[90] KPFK morning show host Marcos Frommer put his assessment less delicately. "I've never met anyone quite as bright and socially inept at once, kind of a management idiot-savant, able to deal with complex technical and administrative issues, completely incapable of dealing with human beings," Frommer wrote upon quitting the station in 1999, adding that Schubb was "unwilling and unable to accept any criticism, and if such criticism is brought up in a meeting, it usually ends with him screaming, shouting, and exiting the room." The station's new manager drew the most visceral reaction from former KPFK employee Lyn Gerry, also terminated from her job in 1995. "All I wanted to do was kill Mark Schubb. Okay?" she later told me. "I'm going to speak honestly. I hated him and I wanted to kill him."[91]

Schubb definitely matched shouting words with deeds. On February 27, 1996, KPFK programmer Ron Wilkins, a self-described pan-Africanist, decided that he had had enough and would raise the question of KPFK's direction on his regular Tuesday night program, *Continent to Continent*. Shortly after this show, KPFK staff would receive the following memo from their boss:

Dear Programmers and Board Ops:

We need help in honoring KPFK's long-standing policy against airing "dirty-laundry," including "event announcements" for that purpose.

Even if the offense is by a guest or a caller, please remember that it is your responsibility to cut it off and move on.

This is one of the few rules we have that will absolutely lead to permanently being banned from the station . . .

[signed] Mark Schubb"[92]

Nothing infuriated Pacifica's volunteer programmers and listener activists more than Pacifica management's refusal to allow discussion over the network's airwaves of the dramatic changes taking place throughout the foundation. Writing about Pacifica in the mid-1990s, *Village Voice* "Press Clips" columnist James Ledbetter noted that even National Public Radio during its 1983-1984 financial crisis spent less time keeping its troubles off its air than Pacifica, where the "gag rule," as it was called, sometimes pushed station hosts to the edge.[93] Defiantly, Wilkins brought local advisory board chair Ruben Lizardo and several dismissed African-American programmers into the studio with him. Perhaps to prevent management from immediately sensing the show's subject matter, Wilkins began by reading a timeline of what he saw as important events in history correspon-ding with the present month. "Feb. 14, 1989," began Wilkins's last date. "Salman Rushdie retreats into hiding after receiving a death sentence for blaspheming Islam in his racist novel *The Satanic Verses*." Following this came 15 minutes of grievances against KPFK management. The station's problems stemmed from "the white left," commented Lizardo. Former KPFK programmer Nzinga Heru agreed. "I am a firm believer that we in fact are at war. I'm not surprised what the enemy would do in order to attack us and to suppress truth," he declared. Heru's program *Hotep* had recently been cancelled. "Black people and white people do not think alike. We do not think alike and we have the right to our own critical thoughts."[94]

Soon the trio noticed Schubb approaching from beyond the studio's pane of glass. "I see the manager in master control," Wilkins told his listeners. "Maybe he may want to join us. I'm sure he can hear our signal." Indeed he could. Within seconds of Schubb's appearance, Wilkins's voice was interrupted by a promotional cart announcing an upcoming feminist show. Schubb had cut the studio's signal off. "I only heard five minutes of it but I knew it was garbage," he told a reporter. Shortly after that, Wilkins's program was cancelled.[95]

At WPFW Pacifica hired as program director a kindred spirit to Schubb. The appointment of Lou Hankins in 1994 infuriated Askia Muhammad in large part because Hankins's prior work had been primarily with an AM gospel outlet. Hankins had served in Vietnam, however, a fact he proudly shared with station staff. He also gave a show to a black D.C. police detective, allegedly argued with others about the significance of police brutality in the city, and told programmers that he disliked Nina Simone's song "Mississippi Goddamn."[96]

Muhammed conceded, however, that despite what he considered Hankins's "Neanderthal political view," the new general manager made a contribution to the station. "I thought he was a smart guy. He [knew] the radio game, the turn-ons, how to make people listen to you, not make people turn you off," Muhammed recalled. "And those are the fundamentals that he tried to teach."[97] Hankins made no secret of where programmers who disagreed with him could go. He distributed a memorandum to all WPFW staff titled "Toxic People." The upper righthand side of the memo featured a caricature drawing of Hankins that one presumes he found flattering. It showed him seated, wearing a black military beret, sunglasses, and what resembled a football jacket with shoulder pads. The memo extolled the progress WPFW had made over six years: larger audience share, more listeners, and a higher pledge fulfillment rate. The problem, Hankins declared, was the "toxic people" who insisted on remaining at the station:

> To let the toxic people tell it they hate what's going on at WPFW and they can't stand this one and that one. This is the real killer. . . . There are actually people they don't speak to here. Can you believe it? Volunteering your time or getting paid for it at some place that you hate, that doesn't treat you fair and in your mind the manage-

ment doesn't know what they are doing.

Why are you still here? The only thing I figure is that you think the station can't make it with out [*sic*] you. Well you are wrong. . . . As a matter of fact WPFW would be better off with out [*sic*] you. You are TOXIC! You steal the joy of others! You are slowing us down! You are in the way! So do everybody a favor and leave please.

I'M BEGGING YOU! PLEAS . . . PLEASE LEAVE.[98]

Schubb and Hankins exemplified the managerial culture of the new Pacifica, a culture of toughness, of thick skins and pink slips. The network's leadership had resolved to lock arms and bare-knuckle their way through any resistance they might encounter on the path to a more centralized and streamlined organization. Scott's resolve often drew admiration from others, occasionally even from her enemies. "I didn't agree with the things that she was doing," Lyn Gerry later commented, "[but] there was something about her. She was a hard ass, and I love hard-ass women."[99] Community station KZYX of Mendocino's Nicole Sawaya ran into Scott, Hankins, and Gail Christian at a 1995 National Federation of Community Broadcasters conference. "They never smiled. They all wore black leather," Sawaya later remembered. "They reminded me of gangsters."[100]

At KPFA listeners got a taste of this stance when outrage over the 1995 changes became so pronounced that the station decided to clear the air at a general meeting at the North Berkeley Senior Center. Hundreds of KPFA listeners, advisory board members, and staff packed the room. Furious listener-subscribers sat in the audience; Ginny Berson and general manager Marci Lockwood put on their best stone faces, stood before microphones, and fielded questions, most of them rhetorical.

"Since KPFA is listener-supported, I'd like to know why the listeners weren't consulted before these drastic program changes were implemented," one attendee asked. The audience applauded and cheered.

"We had an incredible amount of listener input," Lockwood

calmly explained, probably referring to an Arbitron-based audience research report the station had commissioned in 1995. "We may not have gone to each and every one of you in this room and said, 'What do you want?'" The listeners jeered and interrupted as she spoke, making it difficult to continue. "We don't want a commercial station!" one shouted. "We don't want a commercial station either," an obviously exasperated Berson replied.[101]

Had Lockwood chosen to be franker with her audience, she might have responded to the question as follows: "We did not consult you about these changes because we knew what your answer would have been: No." Pacifica managers now regarded the station's volunteers and activist listeners as anachronisms, tethering the organization to what they saw as its dysfunctional past. "Everyone wants a piece of it," Pat Scott told an interviewer around this time, referring to KPFA. "And because there is nothing else, that people don't have access to anything else, they want to make sure that they keep this. This is theirs, this is their special treasure. And sometimes what they see as individuals in terms of how the station can be used is not necessarily what's best for a larger group of people."[102]

This determination to move forward under any circumstances turned Pacifica national board meetings into combat zones. The 1993 meeting in Berkeley was particularly ugly. A crew of KPFK hosts furious at program cancellations showed up along with Blankfort and Gilardin. By the end of a weekend of shouting matches, Pacifica literally banned Gilardin from entering the premises of any Pacifica station.[103] Subsequent meetings were characterized by endless tussles over which sessions would be open to the public and which could be tape-recorded by listener attendees. At one board gathering in Galveston, Texas, Pacifica brass ordered guards to escort Blankfort out of the conference hotel.[104]

Frustrated by constant resistance to schedule changes on the part of local advisory boards, the national office decided to resolve the issue by fiat. On July 12, 1995, the executive committee of the board warned the network's five local advisory boards that managers and program directors could make changes with or without the approval of the LABs. The executive committee memorandum went so far as to threaten those LAB members who did not concur with national office policy. "Members of any local Board who do not feel that they can assist Pacifica in its present mission are advised to resign," the letter declared. "If there are indications that actions are being taken collectively or individually to countermand the policies, directives, and mandates of the Pacifica Board, the [national] Board will take appropriate actions."[105]

After the Texas board meeting, Blankfort received an unexpected telephone call from a government official. An investigator for the Corporation for Public Broadcasting had read an article in *Current*, public broadcasting's trade magazine, about the conflicts at the Houston station. He explained that he had embarked on an investigation of Pacifica's governance practices. Blankfort, delighted, outlined his concerns. Then he and his colleagues, newly renamed Take Back KPFA, filed a complaint with the CPB's Office of Inspector General.[106] A long series of false starts ensued, in which an investigator was fired and his replacement suffered a heart attack. Finally in April of 1997, CPB operative number three, one Armando Arvizu, published a lengthy and critical audit of Pacifica's governance policies.

Arvizu's report suggested that a veil of secrecy had descended over the organization. Pacifica's listeners received practically no notice of upcoming governing board meetings. Although the national office placed brief advertisements about the meetings in newspapers, they appeared only days before the event and offered no information about open sessions and no contact information. Furthermore, the auditor could find no evidence that they had been announced over the airwaves at the five Pacifica stations.[107] Even worse, he concluded that the national board held most of these meetings in closed session – a violation of the Telecommunications Act. Pacifica now only allowed the public into their board meetings for one hour, according to Arvizu – the hour devoted to public comment. In other words, the deliberations of the board were secret. The minutes of board meetings held since May 1994, he wrote, indicated that subjects such as finance and financial audits, bylaw amendments, and development were discussed in closed sessions. Arvizu asked Pat Scott why it had come to this. "The Executive Director explained that all governing board meetings used to be open to the public until the board and staff started experiencing problems with the public," he wrote. "The Executive Director and her staff cited acts of violence and written hate materials directed at the staff." The auditor sympathized, up to a point. "While we care for the safety of Pacifica volunteers and staff," he concluded, "the issue of violent acts against the staff cannot be addressed by closing all governing board deliberations."[108]

Finally, Arvizu found that, for all practical purposes, the network's local advisory boards had been left by the wayside. The minutes of the past few years indicated that LAB members had played no role at national board meetings. They offered no presentations and made no recommendations. "If the advisory boards were performing their mission of assessing the education and cultural needs of the communities being served, they were not reporting those findings to anyone."[109] The auditor's prose suggests that he may have been particularly disturbed by a discussion he had had with Scott regarding the sweeping transformations that took place throughout the network in 1995. "The Executive Director informed us that she [Arvizu's italics] had directed the 1995 programming changes that caused so much concern at all five stations," he wrote. "[S]he was interested in increasing listening ratings. The five Advisory Boards had been left out of the loop."[110]

Pat Scott's written reply to Arvizu revealed the extent to which the organization now resisted openness in governance. Scott claimed that Pacifica held open meetings after 1995, but only cited a subsequent open board retreat, rather than a board meeting, as an example. Resorting to legal logic, she rejected Arvizu's sensible suggestion that the foundation release board meeting minutes. "If Congress had intended for minutes to be made available to the public," she wrote, "it would have required governing boards to keep minutes of their meetings and to place copies of such minutes in their public inspection file.... Congress imposed no such requirements." She distorted his concerns about the marginalization of local advisory boards. "The IG's [Inspector General's] view of advisory boards as autonomous entities designed to be interjected into, and to exercise virtual veto power over, all the planning and decision making processes of the governing board must not be sustained." Arvizu had only suggested that the LABs be consulted, not given dictatorial powers. Then she attacked Arvizu himself. "The IG arrived at Pacifica's offices, camped there for five days, persistently demanded to examine documents completely unrelated to his inquiry, and conducted unscheduled late-evening telephone interviews with Pacifica board members." Finally Scott demanded a meeting with the CPB Board at its regularly scheduled meeting of May 19, 1997, to refute the audit.[111]

The CPB agreed to give Pacifica and Take Back KPFA their day in court. Blankfort arrived and nodded hello to Jack O'Dell, there to represent the Pacifica governing board. But before either man could make his presentation, CPB board chair Alan Sagner announced his decision. No sanctions would be imposed upon Pacifica, he declared. While accepting the findings of Arvizu's report, Sagner praised Scott and O'Dell for their attempts to build audience and centralize the operations of the network. He only asked that Pacifica publicize its board meetings more rigorously.[112]

Blankfort drew sinister implications from this defeat. "There's something really wrong when CPB, which is a quasi government agency representing a propaganda arm of the United States, embraces or protects Pacifica when they could actually go after Pacifica and take its funding if they wanted," he later commented.[113] Indeed, the apparent contradictions could not be richer. Here was a nonprofit agency that used federal money to facilitate the commercialization of public broadcasting giving a clean bill of health to a radio network presided over by an ex-Communist. One could easily extrapolate from this the claim that the agency smiled upon Scott and O'Dell's efforts because both camps were attempting to "NPRize" the network. But this formulation missed a critical point.

Many people within the progressive community approved of Scott and company's efforts, or at least sympathized with them.

In 1996, for example, Scott received a Media Hero prize during the annual Media and Democracy conference of the Institute for Alternative Journalism's (IAJ) in San Francisco. The award set off a storm of protests, along with accusations that the IAJ had shut out from various conference panels dissidents attempting to reform the network.[114] But many progressive media producers regarded the controversy as symptomatic of the very marginal attitude that Scott and her allies seemed intent on repairing. Journalist and filmmaker Michael Moore, dismayed at the conference's focus, wrote an exasperated column for the *Nation* magazine. "Is it me or is the left completely nuts," his essay began. "I won't bore you with the details of October's Media and Democracy Congress, but suffice it to say that the left is still in fine form, completely ignoring anything that really matters to the American public. I'm convinced there's a good number of you who are simply addicted to listening to yourselves talk and talk and talk – MUMIA! PACIFICA! CUBA! ENOUGH ALREADY!"[115] Even syndicated columnist Alexander Cockburn, who would later excoriate the organization for allegedly selling out, confessed in 1997 that he had taken a wait-and-see attitude toward Pacifica through much of the 1990s. "I've held off for many months, years actually, from discussing Pacifica affairs on the grounds that some house-cleaning was necessary at the various Pacifica stations," he wrote in the *Anderson Valley Advertiser*.[116]

And despite qualms over his personality, Mark Schubb enjoyed substantial support for cleaning house at KPFK in Los Angeles. In late October of 1996, the *LA Weekly* published a long feature story about the station's history titled "Left for Dead: How KPFK Missed the Radio Revolution." Writer Joe Domanick all but represented Schubb as heaven-sent to save KPFK from certain doom. Marc Cooper had rejoined the staff by that year, producing a very successful weekly show called *Radio Nation* which broadcast interviews with writers from *The Nation*. Dominick's essay characterized the Spark/Cooper years of the early 1980s as an opportunity lost, followed by more than a decade of drift and decline. "But the marginal, strident, straight-outta-Berkeley multiculturalism that had ingrained itself at KPFK wasn't really the issue," Dominick wrote:

> More troublesome was the managerial style, the propensity to tolerate unaccountable programmers and weak-kneed program directors – the kind most of the people at the station liked because if their shows were hollow, technically inept or woefully underproduced, nobody bugged them. Two hours of music from Belize on Friday morning was what the station put up against Michael Jackson [a talk show host] on KABC. And when Rush Limbaugh came along in the same time slot on KFI, the Belizean music blared on. The question of whose vision of the station would dominate had been settled. The answer was everybody's.[117]

Dominick framed the challenges facing KPFK in a way that spoke to the anxieties and concerns of many people throughout Pacifica. Most of them publicly avoided defending Pat Scott and her lieutenants for fear of falling into the crossfire that had become part of the daily life of the network. A sense that the foundation was sleepwalking overshadowed whatever concerns they had about the extent to which Scott had abrogated the authority of others or run roughshod over legal process. What good were principles of democracy and openness, they wondered, if they resulted in bad, sloppy programs, or, worse, endangered station licenses? For every throng of listeners who angrily asked why the dramatic changes taking place at a Pacifica station had not been discussed openly first, there were others who quietly approved of the reforms. They knew that for decades Pacifica had been discussing the problems the *LA Weekly* described. Now someone was finally doing something about them. Domanick's essay crowed about Pat Scott's 1995 firings at KPFK. "Pat did what nobody else before her had the courage to," Marc Cooper was quoted as saying, "which was to say 'This radio station stinks, and you're out of here.'"[118]

If Domanick's article was a bit of a puff piece (Schubb would later sign him on as a talk show host at the station), the changes he described did indeed win support from old and new KPFK listeners.

Nonprofit consultant and entrepreneur Nalini Lasiewicz was a typical fan from this period. She had been listening to KPFK since the late 1960s and experienced Schubb's reforms as significant improvements. Lasiewicz loved the *Global Village* music strip that now broadcast on weekday mornings, as well as Cooper's and other recently inaugurated talk shows. KPFK's "tone of voice was intelligent and uplifting and smart," Lasiewicz later recalled. "There was a feeling of good energy." So enthusiastic was she about the new KPFK that Lasiewicz and her husband donated thousands of dollars to the station, as well as office furniture and a Christmas party, "just as a thank you," as she later put it, for the staff's efforts.[119] But while KPFK seemed poised on the brink of greater things, the centerpiece for the new Pacifica would come from another part of the network.

The Exception to the Rulers

When she chanced upon WBAI in New York, Amy Goodman had just graduated from Harvard College and returned to the city. She had been raised in Bay Shore, Long Island, by a family of activists; her mother had spent much of the 1980s working for the Nuclear Weapons Freeze. Her father, an ophthalmologist, had been a civil rights advocate in the 1960s, taking a stand for school integration in a predominantly white suburb. "I would go to the night meetings," Goodman later recalled. "A thousand people would be screaming, and I would watch him stand his ground. There were death threats, but he just went on. I think that very much shaped my feeling about what was just in the world." Now out of school and on her own, she had just finished a series of articles for Ralph Nader and Alan Nairn's *Multinational Monitor* on Depo-Provera, the controversial birth-control shot. Goodman was about to enroll in Hunter College for graduate classes in biochemistry when a course on radio production caught her eye. WBAI's Andrew Phillips taught the class. At the time Phillips hosted a show called *"Investigations*, a program dedicated to what radio producers call "actuality" – the sounds of people talking and doing things on tape, speeches, demonstrations, street interviews. Goodman sat in on the first lecture, then talked with Phillips afterwards. The latter knew a true believer when he saw one. He asked her if she wanted to apprentice for him at WBAI. She protested that she had no radio experience. "That's fine," Phillips replied. That evening the two walked the mile from Hunter on the East Side to WBAI's West Side headquarters. Phillips put his new student to work editing tapes for an upcoming program on the fortieth anniversary of the nuclear bombing of Hiroshima. "And I never left," Goodman later explained.[120]

Following the departure of Scagliotti and Simon in the late 1980s, WBAI experienced a significant ethnographic shift. Many of its older white programmers moved on, some lured away by jobs at National Public Radio or WNYC, the city's then municipally owned station. Into the gap stepped producers determined to reach beyond the frequency's predominantly white air sound. Prominent among them was Samori Marksman. Born in St. Vincent in 1948, Marksman studied political science and cinematography at New York University before coming to WBAI. In 1977 he began producing interview shows for the station while working for the government of Grenada as a researcher and publicist. His friend and admirer Louis Proyect remembered him "as belonging to the grand tradition of Afro-Caribbean Marxism" exemplified by C.L.R. James, Walter Rodney, and Eric Williams. Radical intellectuals of all backgrounds throughout New York cherished his daily interview show *Behind the News*, on which one could hear Marksman grapple with figures as diverse as the British Labor Party's Tony Benn or former CIA director William Colby.[121] Long before Marksman became program director at WBAI he exemplified a postcolonial cosmopolitanism that became characteristic of the station's news and public affairs focus. Marksman's tenure also signaled the emergence of a new audience for Pacifica's second frequency: Caribbean immigrants. By the 1980s New York City had become "the Caribbean cross-roads of the world," in the words of anthropologist Constance Sutton. Over 324,000 women and men hailing from Jamaica, Trinidad, Barbados, Haiti, and a dozen other Caribbean countries lived in the city, according to government census data.[122]

257

WBAI's latest generation of programmers took note of and inspiration from their presence. African-American producer Valerie Van Isler traveled through the Caribbean for WBAI, producing features on Grenada's ill-fated New Jewel movement and democratic struggles in Haiti. Robert Knight and the public affairs show *Undercurrents* won a Polk award for his coverage of the U.S. invasion of Panama.[123]

Goodman thrived in WBAI's atmosphere of diversity and political commitment, switching off with Robert Knight and Marksman as news director for the station. In 1991 she and Alan Nairn traveled to East Timor, barely escaped with their lives, and won awards for an eyewitness account of a massacre on the island.[124] Then in 1992 Goodman teamed up with Bernard White, a droll, witty producer who excelled at live talk, to co-host the station's morning program, *Wakeup Call*. The show both reported the news and championed causes, among them the case of Moreese Bickham, incarcerated in Louisiana's Angola prison since 1958. Tipped to Bickham's plight by independent producer David Isay, *Wakeup Call* told his story, that of a man who defended himself against armed Klansmen, only to be convicted of murder and placed on Louisiana's death row. Heart attacks induced by terror just hours before his two scheduled execution dates had saved Bickham from state-sanctioned extermination. White and Goodman publicized his plight and urged WBAI listeners to call authorities for a reconsideration of his sentence. Upon his release, Bickham came to WBAI and thanked the staff over the airwaves.[125]

Ever since Gail Christian completed her "Strategy for National Programming," Pacifica had been shopping around for some kind of national daily public-affairs show to prove the viability of the concept. In 1995 the network briefly distributed an interview program hosted by economist and syndicated columnist Julianne Malveaux. Publicist Tony Regusters produced the show out of WPFW. Malveaux brought fire and erudition to her work, but she had little patience with the poor studio conditions Pacifica had given her. The experiment lasted only three months. At the same time a former governor of California accepted KPFA's invitation to host a news and talk show at 4 p.m. Jerry Brown titled his offering *We the People*. Although the program invariably featured a guest or two, most of the hour focused on the rambling meditations of the host. One Pacifica staffer privately referred to the segment as "I the People." WBAI and KPFK picked up the program. The show lasted for some time, ending when Brown ran for mayor of Oakland.[126]

In the midst of all these fits and starts, Pacifica asked Goodman to produce a national show on congressional politics. It was early 1995. The Republican Party had just swept Capitol Hill, enabling Georgia Congressman Newt Gingrich to become Speaker of the House of Representatives. Right-wing talk show hosts hailed his "Contract with America," for the most part a glorified array of privatizations and budget cuts. Goodman moved to Washington, D.C., and accustomed herself to the daily routine of a national reporter. By the end of the series she was seething with anger. She covered House committees where Representatives spent most of their time discussing ways to fiscally penalize states where women on welfare had "too many" abortions. "They wanted to go after women on welfare," Goodman later recalled, "keep down the number of children that they have, but at the same time they didn't want to encourage abortion. And so they started to discuss why women have sex." Ways to cut social services, especially for poor women, were always high on the agenda. Meanwhile Gingrich had figured in a minor scandal. In January of 1995 television reporter Connie Chung had just interviewed his mother. When Chung asked mom what her son thought of then First Lady Hillary Clinton, she got hesitation at first. "Why don't you just whisper it to me," Chung pressed, "just between you and me." A "bitch," came the smug reply.[127]

On Goodman's final day in Washington, March 3 of that year, she had not intended to go to Gingrich's daily press briefing. But the crescendo of anti-woman legislation coming out of D.C. had become too much for her, as had the silence of most of the press on the subject, especially at Gingrich-related events. "It seemed like there was a kind of agreement, a protocol, between the press and the

Speaker," she explained. At the last minute she rushed over to his media appearance. Dressed in sneakers and jeans, she positioned herself next to the television camera so that she would be heard but not seen; the focus would be entirely on Gingrich.[128] Goodman raised her hand and charged that Congress had over the past two years essentially declared "war on women." Then she got down to specifics.

"You fired the first salvo when you called the First Lady a bitch," Goodman continued. "So why don't you apologize?"

Gingrich became furious. The two snarled back at forth at each other. "To the best of my knowledge, I never said what you said I said," he responded.

"Are you calling your mother a liar, then?" Goodman asked.[129]

The broadcast hit the Pacifica network like a fireball. I was visiting KPFA when the piece aired. People stood around the halls and talked about the exchange. Some thought that Goodman had come off as a bit juvenile, a criticism that would follow her over the years, even from colleagues who admired her. "She is earnest to a fault, with little patience for folks who may have a more nuanced stance on certain issues than she does," commented journalist Danny Schechter. "She has only fastballs, and she throws at the head," observed *Time* magazine's Steve Lopez.[130]

But most Pacifica listeners quickly came to identify with Goodman's intense, insistent tone. They could see themselves standing in Goodman's place, asking the same angry, obvious questions that most journalists never ask. The Gingrich confrontation did not just report the news, it made news, and not just at Pacifica either. "Gingrich Can't Ditch Bitch Remark," ran one headline after the fight. Soon right-wing talk show hosts were talking about Goodman, demanding that *she* apologize for upsetting the Speaker of the House.[131]

What Amy Goodman's critics and supporters both missed, however, was that her style represented a decisive break with earlier Pacifica public affairs broadcasting. Since the late 1960s, most Pacifica programmers had shunned any kind of on-air contact with the Right, arguing that the network's resources were better used airing rarely heard voices from the Left. Indeed, KPFA listeners sometimes complained when the station broadcast a presidential State of the Union address. Goodman emphatically rejected that stance. She constantly pushed to get government officials, right-wing ideologues, and corporate flaks on the air so that she and her favorite progressive activists could pelt them with critical questions.

Nothing better characterized her approach than her telephone dogfight with Bill Clinton. In November 2000 the President thought he would pleasantly surprise New York radio stations by calling in urging listeners to vote. Chances are that if he had called WBAI in 1977, staff would have hung up on him. But when Clinton phoned in to give what he thought would be a routine thirty-second "get out and vote" pitch, Goodman rushed to the receiver, turned on the tape recorder, and challenged him for thirty minutes on everything from welfare reform to the embargo against Saddam Hussein's Iraq. "You are calling radio stations telling people to vote," she began. "What do you say to people who feel the two parties are bought by corporations and that at this point their vote doesn't make a difference?"[132] Whatever problems anyone had with Goodman's tone, no one could dismiss her work as the Left talking to itself.

Shortly after the Gingrich fight, Pacifica development staffer Julie Drizen asked Goodman to continue the program indefinitely. In early 1996 the two came up with a title, *Democracy Now!*, and an on-air slogan that reflected the show's sassy spirit: "The Exception to the Rulers." Larry Bensky signed on as a political commentator. Columnist Juan Gonzalez of the *New York Daily News* joined as co-host twice a week. Almost immediately the show began making waves across the community radio system. In early 1997 WRTI in Philadelphia unceremoniously dumped *Democracy Now!* just as it prepared to air commentaries by controversial Pennsylvania death-row inmate Mumia Abu-Jamal, convicted of killing a police officer. But most community stations enthusiastically stayed with *Democracy Now!* – once they joined.

The trick was getting them to join, which meant getting them to apportion an hour every day for the show, which meant getting at least three or four volunteer hosts at each station to move aside. "We all feel very strongly about how good a program [*Democracy Now!*] is," a manager for radio station WORT in Madison, Wisconsin, told a reporter for *Current* magazine. "But our commitment by mission statement is to provide as much local access as we can, to provide our community with a window to the airwaves." Within Pacifica, Scott pushed hard to make sure that all five network stations ran the program. Then in December of 1997 the foundation launched its own satellite service, a less expensive alternative to NPR's Public Radio Satellite System. Pacifica's new service distributed *Democracy Now!* and 17 other programs, including a half-hour *Pacifica Network News*. Soon dozens of community radio stations began affiliating. In 1998 Pacifica listed 56 community station members. By 2000 one audience research analyst estimated that Pacifica radio alone reached approximately 800,000 people a week – with affiliates, the total came to about one million a week. Some Pacifica stations played *Democracy Now!* twice a day. KPFK ran it twice every morning. Amy Goodman and Pacifica quickly became synonymous. Even the network's dissidents praised her work. "It is, among those critics of Pacifica, considered to be the exception to Pacifica rulers," Jeff Blankfort told *Current*. But few acknowledged that Goodman's breakthrough program was a direct beneficiary of the foundation's stronger, more centralized system of management. The Pacifica network circa 1979 could never have harnessed the level of cooperation necessary to launch and promote *Democracy Now!*, much less get all five Pacifica stations to play it.[133]

Meanwhile, back in Berkeley, Scott found a new general manager to replace the departing Marci Lockwood. Once Nicole Sawaya got past the gangster-like aura that Scott and her associates seemed to exude at the NFCB conference, she chatted with them about ways that Pacifica and KZYX in Mendocino could cooperate. Sawaya had come to the event to protest new CPB guidelines that would have cut funding for rural stations such as KZYX by relying solely on Arbitron ratings to determine funding (Arbitron did not even bother to measure many rural frequencies). Sawaya knew that Mendocino's Republican Congressmember Frank Riggs had voted to continue CPB funding despite Newt Gingrich's denunciations of the agency. "I come from KZYX, Representative Frank Riggs's station," she angrily began during a conference open-mike session. "I see that my station's about to lose funding.... So what are you going to do about all the rural stations? Because we're the ones that won the fight for you on the Hill."[134] Soon the CPB added a "community service index" to the funding formula, allowing rural community radio outlets that generated sufficient local financial support to continue to receive CPB grants.[135]

Scott was impressed. She first asked Sawaya to take the position of program director at KPFK in Los Angeles, but Sawaya declined. Then Scott offered sweeter bait – the job of general manager at KPFA. Longing to return to San Francisco, Sawaya accepted the position in 1997. Writing about the hire, *Current* magazine noted that by then women managed public radio stations in six of the top ten markets in the United States. Why? reporter Geneva Collins asked. "Women are more risk-takers," bragged one woman manager interviewed for the story. "They're used to juggling a number of duties at the same time." Another interviewee offered an equally plausible theory. "It seems to me that women and minorities get a chance at leadership in places that are really in trouble," she commented.[136]

By 1997 Pacifica radio was, paradoxically, in better shape and in bigger trouble than it had ever been. Pat Scott and company had reconstructed the organization, helped make it sound more professional, and delivered its programming to the largest national audience in Pacifica's history. *The New York Times* followed Pacifica's evolution with interest. "Clamorously, Pacifica Radio Dances Towards Mainstream," ran Iver Peterson's business desk column on May 12, 1997. In December Peterson followed up with a longer piece, "Ruffling Left-Wing Feathers to Recharge Pacifica Radio."[137] The list of accomplishments Peterson assembled spoke for itself: a widely praised syndicated program, new headquarters for KPFA, a

$100,000 refurbishing of KPFK's transmitter, a $300,000 reconstruction of KPFT's studios, and WBAI about to move from its dilapidated 34th Street flat to spacious studios in Wall Street. At KPFT and WPFW the audience had, by fits and starts, grown an astonishing 50 percent.[138]

But the price for this external and internal growth was apparent everywhere in the organization. In pursuit of centralization, Scott could manage the challenges impeding her agenda, but she could not eliminate them. Lacking any consistent means of capitalization, the foundation still depended primarily on the voluntary or low-paid labor of thousands of people to do almost everything from hosting shows to taking out the garbage. These unpaid staff members adhered passionately to Pacifica's mission – however they understood it – and they had no access to any other air time like Pacifica's five radio stations, each now surrounded by a growing population of exiles, scores of people who had been declared incompatible with the revised purposes of the foundation. Each of these groups had small, loyal listener followings. And suddenly they had a new, powerful organizing tool that, just a few years earlier, hardly anyone had foreseen.

Free Pacifica!

By 1995 the Internet had arrived. A critical mass of Americans owned the number of personal computers necessary to make commercial email services economically viable. They proliferated across the country: America Online, CompuServe, Prodigy, in addition to the thousands of college campuses and public institutions that now provided email for their students and employees.[139] In that year Take Back KPFA started what was probably the first Pacifica dissident listserv, a program that sends each member's email message to all members of the group. It quickly proliferated to hundreds of people – mostly listeners and volunteers – and, although few people immediately noticed, almost instantly it transformed the internal life of the Pacifica organization.

Before the 1990s, Pacifica listeners had periodically attempted to organize themselves. In the early 1970s these efforts had become common enough to fall into a pattern recognizable by Pacifica's first institutional historian, Vera Hopkins. "Periods of crisis, " she wrote after the KPFA staff strike of 1974, "have repeatedly been followed by moves for subscriber-elected control."[140] Invariably these movements sprang into action during controversies over programming and format scheduling. And invariably they failed to achieve their goals.

To cite only one example, in 1972, after Elsa Knight Thompson and a noticeably large number of programmers had been fired or had left KPFA, a small group organized a Subscribers Organizing Committee (SOC) and called upon station management to explain why they had not been consulted about the changes. "KPFA: LISTENER SPONSORED BUT NOT LISTENER CONTROLLED," their literature protested. When the regular station marathon began in February, several members of the committee went to KPFA's offices to "free KPFA." The marathon had not been doing well, and so they offered a $100 matching grant – a donation to be given only after the staff had raised the same sum during a short segment of the on-air pledge drive. This particular grant, however, had a string attached. KPFA also had to agree to take on-air contributor telephone calls for 30 minutes, presumably from disgruntled subscribers.[141]

Not only did KPFA staff decline the gift, they refused to allow members of SOC into the building. Negotiations over the proposal took place in the form of letters exchanged up and down KPFA's front steps. Eventually the program director sent a final note to the protestors. "The governance of the station does not lie in the streets," Larry Lee explained, and then declared the offer "neither [in] the public interest, convenience, necessity, nor ours (KFPA's)." SOC subsequently asked station staff to include its meetings in KPFA's on-air Calendar of Events listings. Management turned them down. The group inquired as to whether they could purchase ad space in the *Folio* to announce their meetings. The *Folio* editor denied them that as well.[142]

Undaunted, SOC members drafted a proposal that would reorganize KPFA as a subscribers cooperative-decision-making placed in the hands of those who donated money and labor to the station. They presented the idea to openly hostile KPFA personnel at a staff meeting on February 24. Staffers refused to offer even an informal reaction to the idea. One listener arrived at the meeting with a cassette recorder and tried to tape the proceedings. Furious programmers demanded that he leave. When he refused, someone grabbed his microphone and "physically removed" him, according to one account, from the building. Everyone fussed about the incident for a while, then the listener movement gradually faded away.[143]

This brief campaign proved typical of Pacifica listener-empowerment movements through the years. First subscribers found themselves provoked by sudden format shifts at a Pacifica station. Then they gathered to discover why, after constantly hearing about their indispensability during station marathons, they hadn't been consulted about the changes. Enraged by staff stonewalling over the matter, they called for subscriber control. But the very lack of institutional access they lamented always did their rebellion in. Although usually some station staff sympathized with the logic of subscriber elections, most, like the founders of the network, had little interest in sharing power.[144] Short on funds, denied access to the station microphone, the station program *Folio*, and, most important, the station subscriber list, these movements always ran out of gas after a few months.

But now, using the Internet, disgruntled listeners could begin to build their own subscriber lists. Listservs allowed Pacifica subscribers and volunteers to hold what were essentially round-the-clock meetings about Pacifica politics. In the late 1990s they proliferated around the network. These lists were often combative, to put it mildly. But they enabled staff and subscribers at different stations to communicate with one another. By 1997 there were three prominent dissident listener groups: Take Back KPFA in Berkeley, the Pacifica Accountability Committee in Los Angeles, and Save Our

266

Station at WBAI. In Houston, KPFT listener Torry Mercer and four disgruntled colleagues organized Montrose Radio, a low-power FM station, just a few blocks away from KPFT, "basically as a response to all the public affairs programming being taken off of KPFT by Garland Ganter," as Mercer later explained.[145]

The Internet also provided these activist listeners with another means to get the word out. In 1996 former KPFK employee Lyn Gerry embarked on what would become a crucial resource for what its participants came to call the "independent media movement." Furious at Pat Scott's housecleaning at KPFK the previous year, Gerry joined the Pacifica Accountability Committee. Her roommate, dumped KPFK assistant manager Mary Fowler, helped Gerry learn the new Internet formatting language called HTML. Gerry used it to build a Web site, www.radio4all.org, which provided links to dozens of low-power FM or "micro-radio" stations in the United States and around the world. One link led to a site germane to Pacifica, Gerry's freepacifica site. www.radio4all.org/freepacifica quickly became saturated with documents intended to expose what Gerry called the "regressive/corporate/fascist attitude" of Pacifica management.[146]

Email and the Web did more than enable Pacifica dissidents to communicate with one another and build membership lists. It allowed them to forge a collective identity. Take Back KPFA's listserv, to which I subscribed, included ethnic nationalists, libertarians, John Whiting – a producer from the early 1960s who now lived in England – former Pacifica president Peter Franck, several conspiracy theory fans, a gun enthusiast, and dozens of ex-Pacifica programmers who had little in common besides their anger toward or alienation from current Pacifica management.[147] A decade earlier, time and distance would have made it impossible for them to establish a sense of unity. Now they joined hands to share one task: hurling gigabytes of negative data and opinion about the Pat Scott administration across cyberspace.

And Scott gave them plenty of material to hurl. She did things that either were bad or could easily be made to look bad. The

American Consulting Group (ACG) fit into the first category. Scott hired the notorious anti-union negotiating firm in 1995. They met with KPFK's workers that year and offered a contract that focused on management rights. "This is the 90s. This is reality," one ACG rep told KPFK's staff. "Get used to it." Lyn Gerry did some research, put her findings up on freepacifica.org, and delivered unto the network a minor scandal. ACG literature boasted that "the firm has been involved in more than 700 union elections" and "three times that many union efforts that were neutralized," she reported. A promotional video bragged that the ACG had been helping companies "stay union free" since 1979. Scott admitted that hiring the firm was a mistake and replaced ACG with a management rep team recommended by California unions.[148]

Burt Glass qualified for the second group. Around the same time Scott hired Glass as Pacifica's communications director, he sat on the board of Peace Action (PAC) and had served as spokesperson for conservation and anti-nuclear weapons groups. But he had also worked for former Attorney General Janet Reno's Community Policing Program (COPS). The dissidents made a meal of it. "Pacifica Hires Former Justice Department Spokesperson to Fill Newly Created Position of 'Communications Director'!" ran a freepacifica.org headline.[149] If it bled, it led.

Being Smart for People

Even hard-ass women get tired, and by late 1997 Pat Scott was ready to move on. She seemed to have lost perspective on her own accomplishments, giving the impression of someone bent on establishing her authority more than on defining her purpose. Scott's public comments suffered from an increasingly rote quality. "People are not listening," she told Iver Peterson of *The New York Times* in the same article that reported the network to have one million listeners. "And we can't fulfill our mission if we just keep on talking to ourselves."[150] While talking to the *Times*, Scott was already thinking about her post-Pacifica future, as were her development director, Dick Bunce, and her national program director, Gail Christian. But before changing the guard, Pacifica's executive director had two more tasks on her checklist: first, to recruit a new foundation chair; second, to consolidate the board's power.

In 1996 Jack O'Dell, who had been on the Pacifica national board in some capacity for twenty years, announced that he was stepping down.[151] The internal process by which the board decided upon his replacement, Dr. Mary Frances Berry, the head of the U.S. Civil Rights Commission, is probably lost to the organization's history. No one I spoke to even informally would privately, much less publicly, admit that they took the initiative in recruiting her. But in retrospect it is not surprising that a group of people seeking greater legitimacy in the world of media and politics would find Berry an attractive candidate for the position.

Mary Frances Berry was born in 1938 in Nashville, Tennessee, to a family so poor that she spent some of her childhood in an orphanage. The racism she encountered growing up only girded her ambition. Her mother's advice became her motto. "Be overeducated," Berry later summarized it. "If someone else has a master's degree, you get a Ph.D. If someone else has that, then you get a law degree too." She won fame as a talented and prolific historian, took the job of university provost, then occupied various slots in the Carter administration and on the U.S. Commission on Civil Rights. In 1984 the Reagan administration fired her. Berry sued and got her job back. "[T]he happiest day in my life was when Reagan fired me," she later said. "I was fired because I did what I was supposed to do." She became head of the commission under the Clinton administration.[152]

Berry's own description of one of the more celebrated events in her life illumined her perspective on political work. On Thanksgiving Day in 1984, Berry and two associates paid a visit to the South African embassy in Washington, D.C., with a list of demands, including freedom for Nelson Mandela. They refused to leave the office until the ambassador contacted Pretoria with their concerns. The action had been planned for a slow news day. Scores of reporters watched as police led Berry and her associates into a police wagon. "Here was not just another campus radical," gushed

Ms. Magazine. "[H]ere was Dr. Mary Frances Berry, a member of the Commission on Civil Rights, a professor of history and law, a member of the bar, a scholar with published books to her credit, with more citations and honorary degrees than her wall could hold." Berry offered the lesson of the day: "If you're going to help people in their struggle, you should be smart for them. . . . If your demonstration doesn't get media coverage, you might as well not have it."[153]

Here was a prestigious, media-savvy figure to lead the Pacifica network, someone with perfect progressive credentials. At strategic public moments, Berry exuded reasonableness. She denounced Nation of Islam Louis Farrakhan's Million Man March, calling its initiator guilty of "the most despicable, anti-Semitic, racist, sexist and homophobic attitudes imaginable."[154] She could speak and write eloquently about the complexity of race relations in America, as in her November 29, 1997, *New York Times* op-ed column entitled "Ashamed of George Washington?" In the essay Berry chided the New Orleans School Board for changing the name of a local elementary school from that of the nation's first president to Dr. Charles Drew Elementary, in honor of the celebrated African-American surgeon. Berry called the decision "petty." She acknowledged that Washington had owned slaves – the reason the board switched names – but noted that, unlike Thomas Jefferson, he provided for the freeing of his slaves after his death. Nor did Washington apologize for slavery. Lincoln, on the other hand, famously told a newspaper editor that "if I could save the Union, without freeing any slave, I would do it." Ultimately, Berry asked, should slaveholding count as "the sole issue by which we judge Presidents?" The board's summary action, she concluded, denied students a chance to understand the "context and ambiguities" of the times in which Washington lived.[155]

But as an administrator Berry had a reputation for leaving such ambiguities by the wayside, as *Salon* journalist Judith Coburn discovered when she conducted a series of off-the-record interviews with Berry's associates. "[A] vitriolic brawler who doesn't know when to stop fighting," Cockburn characterized Berry, "and who turns on anyone who disagrees with her – even African-Americans with civil rights records equal to or more impressive than her own."[156] Long before Coburn's 1999 article, the liberal *Washington Monthly* had come to the same conclusion. In 1987 the magazine published an exposé titled "The Powers That Shouldn't Be: Five Washington Insiders the Next Democratic President Shouldn't Hire." Mary Frances Berry figured prominently on the list. Author Paul Glastris easily located former government officials and academics who described her as "a bull in a china closet," someone who "so distrusted people as to not be trustworthy herself," in the words of a former Carter administration colleague. "The question was always 'What do we do about Mary?'"[157]

But no one at Pacifica had any sense of foreboding in 1997. Quite the contrary, they experienced Dr. Berry, as she quickly came to be called, as a deliverance from the Scott administration. And at first she played the role. In 1998 the network's new board chair arrived with great fanfare to visit KPFA in Berkeley. Two Bay Area newspapers wrote stories about Berry's tour. "New Chairwoman Hopes to Soothe Tempers at KPFA," Metro section writer William Brand headed his article in the December 12, 1997, *Oakland Tribune*. Berry had already taken steps to mend fences, his article disclosed. Shortly after assuming office, she hired a court reporter and had Pacifica staff post complete transcripts of board meetings on the foundation's new Web site, www.pacifica.org. She also appeared on a call-in show at KPFA and fielded questions in person at a local advisory board meeting. These gestures won Berry praise from everyone, including KPFA dissidents. "She's like a fresh breeze," declared Jeff Blankfort of Take Back KPFA. "She actually came to seriously listen to what people had to say. It's been very depressing here for a while."[158]

Berry made no secret, however, of her plans to continue moving in Pacifica's present direction. "What I want is programs that reflect community interest and needs and are programs that people listen to," she told reporter Brand. "[W]e need to present different points of view and it needs to be presented in a way that people will listen."[159] Her true priorities quickly manifested themselves in her choice for a new executive director to replace Pat Scott. The announcement came in October 1998, shortly after Scott's resignation: none other than Lynn Chadwick, former president of the National Federation of Community Broadcasters and co-founder of the Healthy Station Project. Already employed as Pacifica's operations director (yet another new position), Chadwick had made a career out of working with the Corporation for Public Broadcasting to rein in what she and her colleagues saw as the rough edges of community radio stations. Her colleague Bessie Wash, new general manager at WPFW, praised the choice in *Current* magazine. "Lynn is a strong leader, not afraid to face challenges. She doesn't duck controversy, but faces it head-on," Wash said.[160] That was putting it mildly. "Lynn, just in the way she is built, does not allow for group process," a Pacifica national board member would soon tell *Salon* magazine. "She's an autocrat to the core, and a bulldog."[161] Chadwick quickly established the tone of her leadership in a statement to the national board. "We have to stop the rudeness, the bullying, the you-can't-tell-me-what-to-do attitude," she declared.[162] Together Berry and Chadwick would implement the last item on Pat Scott's agenda: the creation of a self-appointing governing body for Pacifica.

In January of 1999 syndicated columnist Alexander Cockburn published a long essay in his and Jeffrey St. Clair's Web newsletter *CounterPunch*, warning that impending bylaws changes were likely to transform the nature of governance at Pacifica and make it much less democratic. Since the late 1970s, Cockburn wrote in "The Neutering of Pacifica," the network's five local advisory boards had nominated members to serve on the national board.[163] Cockburn was correct. In a pro-forma process, the LABs nominated members of their local boards to membership on the national board, and the national board accepted them. An attachment to a March 1998 Pacifica Foundation document titled "Policies Governing Local Station Advisory Boards" listed responsibility number 12 as "To elect representatives to the Board of Directors."[164] Some Pacifica board members later claimed that this practice never took place, but even one of Berry's staunchest supporters on the national board acknowledged the process. "I was voted onto the national board by the local advisory board," Ken Ford told me in the course of our interview for this book.[165]

But in the autumn of 1998, following a CPB memorandum on governance requirements sent to all recipients, Pat Scott called the Corporation for Public Broadcasting and asked whether this arrangement was legal. In September she received a formal response from Robert Coonrod, president of the CPB. Probably not, he replied. The Telecommunications Act stipulated that community advisory boards (what Pacifica called local advisory boards) "shall be solely advisory in nature" and shall "in no case have any authority to exercise any control over the daily management of the station." In addition, Coonrod warned, CPB guidelines declared that the law "segregates the management and operational functions of the governing board from the advisory board's functions to assure a clear demarcation between the governing board and the advisory board." Based on his understanding of the law, Coonrod concluded, Pacifica's governance structure "appears to be at variance with both the law and our guidelines" and could jeopardize the foundation's CPB funding. Scott then asked Pacifica's FCC lawyer, John Crigler, for an opinion. He agreed: "To avoid the risk of losing CPB funding, Pacifica would be wise to structure its Community Advisory Boards in a way that clearly distinguish[es] the purpose and composition of such Boards from the purpose and composition of Pacifica's Governing Board."[166] Soon Chadwick issued a public notice of bylaw change to be enacted at the foundation's board meeting to be held in Berkeley in the last days of February 1999.[167]

I read Cockburn's column and looked up the complete, unedited statute to which Pacifica's lawyer referred regarding local advisory boards cited by Pacifica. I could not see how the current board structure could be construed as a violation: "The role of the board shall be solely advisory in nature, *except to the extent other responsibilities are delegated to the board by the governing body of the station.* In no case shall the board have any authority to exercise any control over the daily management or operation of the station."[168] The language did not seem to deny the board the power to allow individual local advisory board members to sit on the national board. In truth, the national board's minutes indicate that Pacifica had been electing local board members to the national board since the late 1970s with no CPB objection noted.[169] And Coonrod's stipulation that there be a "clear demarcation" between the two types of boards represented a CPB interpretation of the statute, not the statute itself. But it was obvious that Chadwick was determined to remove LAB members from the governing board, and possibly to remove the rights of LABs to nominate individuals to the governing board, changes that would leave a dangerous political void. "Whose institution is it?" wondered Cockburn. "Whose will it be? Is this Governing Body likely to choose a structure of governance giving any other group within Pacifica, including its subscribers, any say in who gets to make the meaningful decisions at Pacifica? Or will it instead grant itself permanent control [over] its own composition?"

Cockburn continued:

> The most confounding part of this sad saga is the likelihood that most of the men and women making this decision are well meaning people who hold dear one or another stripe of "progressive" values. From their position, they may well believe that they are acting to save Pacifica, protecting it from assault by present and future foes. They may not trust the motives of programmers, staff, volunteers, or subscribers. If one is to believe their public statements, they are solely concerned with expanding Pacifica's audiences beyond their present scope, and insuring financial growth. Yet the vision they have of how this is to be done, and why, is not now or ever to be open to challenge. It is hard for autocrats to find their own power objectionable.[170]

These were the last kind words to be said of the Pacifica governing board for the next three years. Alerted to the foundation's plans, hundreds of dissidents from New York City, Houston, Los Angeles, Washington, D.C., and the San Francisco Bay Area rushed to the board's February 28, 1999, gathering in Berkeley. The meeting had been scheduled at a local Berkeley hotel – until its owner got news of the impending confrontation. Then it was relocated to a UC Berkeley conference hall. Protestors gathered along a nearby off-campus road, "safe from the billy-clubs of the UC Police," wrote one amused journalist, "spreading news of the outrage to incoming shoppers from Orinda."[171]

Station volunteers and activist listeners packed the hall, watching Pacifica's board members nervously deliberate the bylaws changes. Perhaps the most prophetic plea for the board to reconsider its restructuring plans came from Sherry Gendelman, chair of KPFA's local advisory board, speaking for the heads of all five Pacifica LABs, known as the Council of Chairs. "How will you govern if you are perceived as a completely self-appointed entity?" she asked Berry and Chadwick. "How will you guide the network through the very difficult decisions that national boards historically had to manage, such as testifying before hostile government committees, engaging in difficult union negotiations, handling public reaction to very controversial programs, or station staff personnel meltdowns that have taken place from time to time within Pacifica? How will you handle these if no one can figure out why you are in charge?"[172]

But the board had already made up its mind, or, more precisely, Berry and Chadwick had made up their minds for the board. "[W]e want to centralize, as much as possible, administrative services," Berry declared. "All of the managerial and administrative aspects of this place that can be centralized in order to save money and in order to find ways to [do] things more effectively so that there will be more money to go into programming."[173] At the last minute an advisory letter from CPB vice president Richard Madden arrived with a troubling timeliness. The faxed document threatened the loss of CPB funding if Pacifica didn't cut LAB members loose from the national board. Clearly cornered, Berry's nine colleagues on the board unanimously passed a resolution that prohibited local board members from sitting on the national board. New board members would be nominated by the national board's governance and structure committee. The board no longer had any obligation to accept nominees proposed by local boards.[174] Then, to the dismay of the audience of activists who had packed the auditorium, governing board members resigned from their own LABs so that they could remain on Pacifica's now self-appointed governing body. "All right," Berry concluded with a tone of satisfaction in her voice. "Hearing from the persons whose status was as local advisory board members, that they have duly resigned from that, I hereby announce that they remain as members of the governing board of Pacifica Foundation to serve the terms that are now their stated terms as of this date."[175]

With the board's business accomplished, the meeting moved on to its one-hour public comment period, insultingly scheduled after all the decisions had been made. Apportioned two minutes each, speaker after speaker railed against the vote that had just been taken. Larry Bensky brought a series of flip charts that illustrated the ever larger share of income taken by the national office (3 percent in the 1970s, 17.2 percent in 1999) in contrast to the amount of national programming provided. "I'm asking that you consider instituting an immediate hiring freeze on all national office positions, institute an immediate review of all personnel, and consider restructuring our administrative entity along the lines of what we should have," he concluded.[176]

In the middle of Bensky's talk, Berry walked out of the room. "Where's Mary Berry?" audience members began to ask. "Mary had to step out," June Makela, another board member, explained. "Don't talk without her!" people shouted. "Mary! Get Mary Berry! . . . You're going to hold us to two minutes and walk out?"

Makela tried to reassure the crowd. "Please go ahead," she said. "We're doing a total transcript of all speakers."

But the audience would not be silenced. "We want Mary! We want Mary!" they chanted.

Finally board member Robert Farrell of Los Angeles lost his patience. "[A]s members of the board," he warned, "we're here as a matter of courtesy, listening to folks up here in the Berkeley area. I'm not from here." If people did not want to speak, Farrell declared, they should make room for those who still did.[177] For the caretakers of this public corporation, listening to the public had now become a courtesy rather than an obligation.

Toward the end of the conference, another fax arrived, this one signed, not by an official of the Corporation for Public Broadcasting, but by three of the most important academic scholars on the American Left. "As long-time admirers and supporters of Pacifica, we are troubled by apparent tendencies toward increased centralization of power and decision-making that bring Pacifica closer to the private corporate model," wrote Noam Chomsky, Edward S. Herman, and Howard Zinn. "Pacifica's strength and legitimacy grew from the knowledge and confidence of its listeners that [were] based and directed from within their respective communities and spoke to their interests. . . . With the question of the mode of governance at issue in the forthcoming board meeting, we would strongly urge the board to celebrate Pacifica's 50th birthday by a firm commitment to democratic forms of governance."[178]

Berry acknowledged the letter – sort of. "I received, as many of you did[,] all of you did, many communications," she began. "I got a letter, which purported to be from Howard Zinn, who I very much respect and am very fond of, Noam Chomsky . . . Ed Herman concerning this change in which they said that as the 50th anniversary of Pacifica, we should continue to operate in a democratic – small d – fashion. Let me just say I would be responding directly to them, but what we have done here is no less democratic, as I said before, than we were before."[179] The board meeting ended shortly afterward. Hundreds of troubled Pacificans streamed out into the Berkeley afternoon sun and talked among themselves.

Several days later Chadwick received another message from Richard Madden of the CPB. The email, subject "Closure," hinted at his own misgivings. "Again, congratulations!" Madden wrote, then added, "Assuming there's such a thing as closure on any public radio issue."[180] Current magazine made no such assumption. "Tempers Rise as Pacifica Lets Board Select Itself," ran its headline. "What are they going to do now that they have absolute power?" rhetorically asked R. Paul Martin, WBAI's staff steward, of the journal's reporter

Jacqueline Conciatore.[181] "One of the staples of the Pacifica broad-casting diet is constant alarums about unaccountable corporate power," wrote Alexander Cockburn in a follow-up piece to the board meeting. "The present governance struggle at Pacifica is thus rich with a sorrowful irony."[182]

A Profitable Paradox

In 1997, to give the foundation's staff and governors a sense of direction, development director Dick Bunce drafted a Strategic Plan for Pacifica's next five years of operation. The 25-page document, produced during a series of staff retreats, often read like a fund-raising brochure, which was probably intentional. The Strategic Plan's critical prose, however, could be found not in its laundry list of institutional goals, but in an introductory essay subtitled "The Crisis of Democratic Communications." Noting the effect of mergers and conglomerates on the "public sphere" in general and in the public radio environment specifically, the prologue recognized the impact of the fall of the Fairness Doctrine. "By restricting the flow of information essential to political discourse and citizen participation, media trusts imperil democracy." But instead of exhorting the Pacifica network to take the lead in harnessing forces against this trend, it urged the network to take advantage of the situation. "The expansion of media trusts simultaneously illustrates the distinctive-ness of Pacifica's programming and mission," read another sidebar. "By diminishing the supply of informational programming-Pacifica's and public radio's stock-in-trade-the commercial trusts have paradoxically increased audience demand for Pacifica and other public radio services."[183] The strategy was clear: Pacifica would accept its containment, centralize its authority, and build listener-supported socialism in one small radio network.

The external changes that made this vision attractive, however, would also make it impossible to achieve. Sure enough, after fifteen years of bureaucratic struggle, Pacifica had transferred practically all formal authority from the peripheries of the network to itself. The local boards no longer had the automatic right to appoint members to the national board (although technically they could still nominate them). They had little, if any, input into the hiring of station managers, or even the overall direction of station program content. That meant that the network's active listeners had lost whatever real influence they had enjoyed over the network's affairs. The vast majority of weekday programming had been taken from volunteers and placed in the hands of paid staff.

But if Berry and her associates imagined that they had just cleared the way for a new golden age, the opposite would soon become apparent. Having converted itself into a self-appointing body, the Pacifica national board signed a warrant for its own slow political death. And the people who would carry out the contract were not the vocal dissidents who thronged to national board meetings and filled the Internet with their anger and frustration. Instead a revolution that would for the first time make Pacifica a truly democratic organization would be reluctantly led by forces that had, until this point, supported the institution's attempts at centralized reform – starting with the paid staff of KPFA in Berkeley, who, having cooperated with various purges up to this point, knew that they could be next, and continuing with progressives elsewhere, who, like Alexander Cockburn, had kept quiet over the years in the hope that "housecleanings" from above would improve the network.

On February 28, 1999, these forces found themselves asking the same question. Who were these people who, now completely unaccountable to anyone else in the organization, held the keys to the kingdom? Could they be trusted? Why, as Sherry Gendelman had pointedly asked, were they in charge? Paradoxically, in an attempt to strengthen itself, the already weak board had made itself even weaker. A governing structure is only as strong as its ability to make unpopular decisions. What power did this board and its national office now have to do that? Since everyone knew that it took funds rather than raised them, the Pacifica board could offer no carrots to entice others to carry out its will. And what legitimacy did it enjoy as a reconstituted oligarchy in charge of the forces of "democratic communications"? The new and improved Pacifica apparently regarded this glaring contradiction as irrelevant – indeed, its chair could not quite bring herself to believe that others saw it as a problem, but they did. The Pacifica network now swarmed with exiles, displaced programmers and listeners with nowhere to go, ready to pounce at the first sign of weakness.

Sandbagged with contradictions, the Pacifica governing board and executive officers' base of support was now a mile wide and an inch deep. Its leaders had only their own personal toughness to sustain their efforts. Chadwick had ridden the bureaucratic bronco at dozens of community stations and had come out on top. Berry had dueled with apartheid and the President of the United States and won. As they left the February 1999 governing board meeting, Chadwick doubtless wondering what to do about Nicole Sawaya, it is unlikely that either foresaw what was about to happen to the organization that they had chosen to lead.

Endnotes

1   Recollection of author.
2   Kate Coleman, "Tuned In, Turned On and Locked Out," *The LA Weekly* (July 30-August 5, 1999): http://www.laweekly.com/ink/99/36/news-coleman. php; recollection of author, who sometimes called them "the crazies" himself.
3   Minutes, Pacifica Foundation Board of Directors, October 5-6, 1985, Houston Metropolitan Ministries, pp.2-3.
4   Nancy Angelo, quoted in ibid., p.12.
5   Ibid., p.11.
6   Brett Harvey, "Radio Impossible: Permanent Revolution at WBAI," *Village Voice* (September 23, 1986), p.15.
7   William Barlow, "Pacifica Radio: A Cultural History" (unpublished manuscript, 1992), pp.76-77; Harvey, "Radio Impossible," p.19.
8   Amy Goodman, interview with author (August 15, 2003), p.2.
9   Harvey, "Radio Impossible," p.15.
10   Ibid., p.16.
11   Ibid.
12   Ibid.
13   All quotes from Ibid, p.22.
14   Ibid.

15 Jay Sand, "The Radio Waves Unnameable: BAI, Bob Fass, and Listener-Sponsored Yippie!" (November 26, 1995): www.wbaifree.org/fass/fasschp8.html. William Barlow quotes former WBAI station manager Valerie Van Isler estimating the late 1980s WBAI weekly audience at 140,000 listeners: see Barlow, "Pacifica Radio: A Cultural History," p.78.

16 Caesar and Washburn report, quoted in Barlow, "Pacifica Radio: A Cultural History," p.84.

17 David Salniker, interview with author (May 30, 2003), p.4.

18 David Lerner, "Radio Free Berkeley," *East Bay Express* (January 14, 1983), p.7.

19 Recollection of author.

20 Richard Wolinsky, "Gevins and Garrett Win Award for Science Story," *KPFA Folio* (May 1978), p.1.

21 Helen Mickiewicz, "How to Cover a Disaster," *KPFA Folio* (May 1979), p.1.

22 Maisel quoted in Lerner, "Radio Free Berkeley," p.10.

23 Salniker quoted in John Downing, *Radical Media* (Boston: South End Press, 1983), pp.82-83.

24 Alice Echols, *Daring to Be Bad: Radical Feminism in America* (Minneapolis: University of Minneapolis Press, 1989), p.229.

25 "The Rainbow History Project," p.9: www.rainbowhistory.org/timeline.pdf; recollection of author.

26 Ginny Berson, interview with Veronica Selver (no date, probably November 1994, video tape transcript), p.8.

27 Recollection of author.

28 *KPFA Folio* (April 1982), pp.12, 19, 21.

29 Lerner, "Radio Free Berkeley," p.10.

30 Robbie Osman, interview with author (March 3, 2002), p.1.

31 Ginny Berson, interview with Veronica Selver (no date, probably November 1994), p.12.

32 Ibid., 13.

33 Ibid., pp. 12-14; Robbie Osman, interview with author (March 3, 2002), p.1.

34 Paul Boyer, *Promises to Keep: The United States Since World War II* (Boston: Houghton Mifflin, 1999), pp.412, 417-18

35 Larry Bensky, interview with Veronica Selver (April 1983, video tape transcript), p.26; *KPFA Folio* (July 1987), p.2.

36 David Salniker, interview with author (May 30, 2003), p.15; "SanDisk Debuts 802.11b Compact Flash and Secure Digital Cards + 128MB, 256MB," *Reiter's Wireless Data Web Log*, (January 9, 2003): reiter.weblogger.com/2003/01/09.

37 Larry Bensky, interview with Veronica Selver (April 1983, video tape

transcription), pp. 26-27; Larry Bensky, "The Iran-Contra Hearings Continue," *KPFA Folio* (July 1987), p.1; M. Fisher, "Pacifica's Next Wave," *Mother Jones* (May 1989), pp.50-52, cited in Ralph Engelman, *Public Radio and Television in America: A Political History* (Thousand Oaks, SAGE: 1996), p.78.

38 "Pacifica History," *Pacifica Radio Archives*: www.pacificaradioarchives.org/learn/history.php; Paul Rauber, "Off-Mike: Mid-Life Crisis at KPFA" (March 5, 1993), p.11.

39 Gail Christian, "A Strategy for National Programming" (September 1, 1992), pp.1, 5.

40 Ibid., p.7.

41 Ibid., "Appendix, Foundation Grantseeking," (appendix unpaginated).

42 Ibid., p.1.

43 Ibid., p.20.

44 Ibid., p.8.

45 Pat Scott, interview with author (January 31, 2002), p.4; Iver Peterson, "Ruffling Left-Wing Feathers to Recharge Pacifica Radio," *The New York Times* (December 29, 1997), pp.D1, D9.

46 Ibid., p.1; recollection of author.

47 Pat Scott, interview with author (January 31, 2002), p.6.

48 Veronica Selver and Sharon Wood, *KPFA on the Air*, video documentary (Selver Productions, 1999).

49 Paul Rauber, "Off-Mike: Mid-Life Crisis at KPFA," *East Bay Express* (March 5, 1993), p.16.

50 Ginny Berson, interview with Veronica Selver, pp.17, 19.

51 Dan Evans, "Adversaries Go Inside the ADL's Spying Operation," *San Francisco Examiner* (April 1, 2002): www.examiner.com/news/default.jsp?story=n.adl.0401w.

52 Jeff Blankfort, interview with author (February 16, 2002), pp.9-10.

53 Maria Gilardin, interview with author (August 2, 2002), p.6.

54 Paul Rauber, "Off-Mike: Mid-Life Crisis at KPFA," *East Bay Express* (March 5, 1992), p.11; Jeff Blankfort, interview with author (February 16, 2002), p.3; Curtis Gray, interview with author (July 28, 2004), p.1.

55 Rauber, "Off-Mike," 11,

56 Ibid.

57 Curtis Gray, interview with author (July 28, 2004), p.1.

58 Ibid., p.12.

59 Ibid., p.18.

60 Ibid., p.2.

61 Andrew Lumpp, "The Pacifica Experience, 1946-1975: Alternative Radio in Four United States Metropolitan Areas" (doctoral dissertation: University of Missouri, 1977), pp.230-37; Julius Lester, *Lovesong: Becoming a Jew* (Seaver Books, 1995).

62 Recollection of author.

63 Alex Safian, "Pacifica: Broadcasting Hate" *Comint* (Spring-Summer 1993): 32; Claudia Puig, "KPFK Confronts Charges of Anti-Semitism," *Los Angeles Times* (February 29, 1992), p.F4.

64 Safian, "Pacifica: Broadcasting Hate," 33.

65 Ibid., p.33; Kenneth Deda-Kemathi Carr, community comments, Minutes of the Interim Pacifica Board, March 9, 2002, Los Angeles, California (taken from audio). Despite the ambiguity of the moment, Carr was suspended from KPFK.

66 "From Pacifica's Classroom of the Air," *Comint* (Spring-Summer 1993): 36.

67 Ibid., 37.

68 Safian, "Pacifica: Broadcasting Hate," p.33.

69 Exchange Between Victor Gold and CPB Chair Sheila Tate, "Special Reports," *Comint* (Spring-Summer 1993): 24-25.

70 David Barsamian, "The Pacification of Public Radio, NPR, Pacifica, and Community Radio: Crises and Prospects," *Z Magazine* (October 1997): zena.secureforum.com/Znet/zmag/articles/barsamianoct97.htm.

71 David Salniker, "Emergency Statement to Pacifica Subscribers" (July 28, 1993), p.1; "Chronology of Abuses by Pacifica Management and Board of Directors": www.radio4all.org/freepacifica/pacifica_chrono.htm; James Ledbetter, *Made Possible By . . . The Death of Public Broadcasting in the United States* (New York: Verso, 1997), p.128.

72 Marci Lockwood, letter to KPFA subscribers (September, 1993), p.1. The pressure from Congress continued through January of 1995, when the Republican senator from South Dakota, Larry Pressler, demanded that the CPB disclose how many reporters for National Public Radio had previously worked for Pacifica: see Lars-Erik Nelson, "GOP Is Sneaky with Public TV," *New York Newsday* (January 29, 1995), p.2.

73 Pat Scott, interview with author (January 31, 2002), p.7; Taylor Branch, *Parting the Waters: America in the King Years, 1954-63* (New York: Touchstone, 1988), pp.573-74, 850-51.

74 In our interview, Pat Scott did not want to talk about her time with the Communist Party. But while station manager at KPFA, Scott had told me and others of her involvement. Jeff Blankfort mentioned it in his interview: see Jeff Blankfort, interview with author (January 31, 2002), p.3. I regret having to bring this up, but it is a crucial aspect of the story, about which practically no one except journalist Jesse Walker has written. See Jesse Walker, "A War at Pacifica," *Alternative Press Review* (Spring-Summer 1998): www.radio4all.org/fp/war-walker.htm.

75 Pat Scott, interview with author (January 31, 2002), p.7.

76 Askia Muhammad, interview with author (October 2002), p.13.

77 Ibid, p.13; Jeffrey Yorke, "WPFW, Gone and Back Again," *Washington Post*

(October 5, 1993).

78 Pat Scott, interview with author (January 31, 2002), pp.14-15; Askia Muhammad, interview with author (October 2002), pp.4-5.

79 Resolution, Pacifica Board of Directors Meeting, May 14, 1994, p.1.

80 Claudia Puig, "KPFK Drops Two Programs Accused of Using Hate Speech," *Los Angeles Times* (July 23, 1994), pp.F2-F15.

81 Jeff Blankfort, interview with author (January 31, 2002), p.10.

82 "Chronology of Abuses by Pacifica Management and Board of Directors": www.radio4all.org/freepacifica/pacifica_chrono.htm.

83 Claudia Puig, "Top KPFK Executives Fired in Management Shake-Up," *Los Angeles Times* (January 5, 1995), p.F2; "KPFK Staff Letter, 1/95:" http://www.radio4all.org/fp/pawmary.htm.

84 Paul Rauber, "Sticks and Stones," *East Bay Express* (July 7, 1995), p.2.

85 Craig Marine, "Familiar Voices Disappearing from KPFA," *San Francisco Examiner* (August 1, 1995), p.B-1; recollection of author.

86 "You Wouldn't Want to Work for These People": www.kpftradio.com/aug11.html.

87 Ray Hill, interview with author (January 15, 2003), p.14.

88 Program director quote from Jacquelyn Battise, "Radio Lost," *Houston Peace News* (August 1999), p.6; "most integrated"quote from William Barlow, "Pacifica Radio: A Cultural History" (unpublished manuscript, 1992), p.70; KPFT Program Guide (August 8, 1995); Jacqueline Battise, interview with author (September 22, 2002), p.5; Torry Mercer, interview with author (September 21, 2002), p.10.

89 Joel Bleifuss, "Pacifica's Uncivil War," *In These Times* (December 14, 1997), p.17.

90 Joe Domanick, "Left for Dead: How KPFK Missed the Radio Revolution," *LA Weekly* (October 4-10, 1996), p.10.

91 Marcos Frommer, "The Scoop on KPFA from Marcos Frommer," email message (October 13, 1999): www.radio4all.org/fp/102099frommer.htm; Lyn Gerry, interview with author (March 8, 2003), p.12.

92 Mark Schubb, memo to staff (February 28, 1996): www.radio4all.org/fp/gag.gif.

93 James Ledbetter, *Made Possible By . . . : The Death of Public Broadcasting in the United States* (New York: Verso, 1997), pp.129-30.

94 Hector Tobar, "Mixed Signals at KPFK," *Los Angeles Times* (September 17, 1996), p.A1.

95 Ibid.; Per Fagereng, "Pacifica Battles Blacks and Labor," *Portland Free Press* (July 1996): www.radio4all.org/fp/pfp796.htm.

96 Ruben Casteneda, "A Different Kind of Blues: On Weekends Police Officer Becomes Jazz/Soul Deejay," *Washington Post* (August 12, 1995), p.B3; Askia Muhammed, interview with author (October 2002), p.3; Verna Avery

Brown, interview with author (October 2002), p.16.

97 Askia Muhammed, interview with author (October 2002), p.2.

98 Lou Hankins, memo to staff, "Re: Toxic People," no date; possession of author.

99 Lyn Gerry, interview with author (March 8, 2003), p.10.

100 Nicole Sawaya, interview with author (August 13, 2002), p.16.

101 Berson quoted in Veronica Selver and Sharon Wood, *KPFA on the Air*, video documentary (Selver Productions, 1999).

102 Scott quoted in ibid.

103 Maria Gilardin, interview with author (August 8, 2002), p.19.

104 Jeff Blankfort, interview with author (February 16, 2002), p.8.

105 Quote from Armando J. Arvizu, "Compliance Audit of Pacifica Foundation, Berkeley, California, Audit Report No. 97-01" (April 9, 1997), p.13.

106 Armando J. Arvizu, "Compliance Audit of Pacifica Foundation," p.1.

107 Ibid., p.7.

108 Ibid., p.9.

109 Ibid., p.12.

110 Ibid., p.13.

111 Pat Scott, letter to Alan Sagner, Chair, Board of Directors, Corporation for Public Broadcasting (no date), pp.1-5.

112 "No Sanctions Against Pacifica Closed Meetings," *Current* (June 27, 1997): www.current.org/rad/rad710p.html; Jeff Blankfort, interview with author (February 16, 2002), p.5.

113 Ibid., p.9.

114 Ron Curran, "Following the Money: Is Alternative Press Wire Service Compromised by Secret Foundation Support?" *San Francisco Bay Guardian* (October 8, 1997): www.sfbg.com/News/32/02/Features/follow.html.

115 Michael Moore, *Nation* (November 17, 1997): www.a4a.mahost.org/moore.html.

116 Alexander Cockburn, "National Notes," *Anderson Valley Advertiser* (April 16, 1997).

117 Joe Domanick, "Left for Dead: How KPFK Missed the Radio Revolution," pp.26, 28.

118 Ibid., p.28.

119 Nalini Lasiewicz, interview with author (January 19, 2004), p.1.

120 Fred Bunning, "An Advocate for Advocacy," *Newsday* (April 21, 2003); Amy Goodman, interview with author (August 15, 2003), pp.3-4.

121 Louis Proyect, "Remembering Samori Marksman": www.columbia.edu/~lnp3/mydocs/american_left/samori.htm.

122 Constance R. Sutton, "The Caribbeanization of New York City," p.19, and Roy Simón Bryce-Laporte, "New York City and the New Caribbean Immigration: A Contextual Statement," p. 59, in Constance R. Sutton and

Elsa M. Chaney, *Caribbean Life in New York City* (New York: Center for Migration Studies of New York, Inc., 1987).

123 Barlow, "Pacifica Radio: A Cultural History," p.79.

124 Ibid.

125 Bernard White, interview with author (November 1, 2002), p.7; Jacqueline Conciatore, "Tenaciousness and Hope on FM: Amy Goodman's 'Democracy Now'" *Current* (November 17, 1997): www.current.org/people/peop721g.html.

126 Tony Regusters, interview with author (October 2002), pp.6-7; Jack Stenz, "How Jerry Got His Soul Back," *Sonoma Independent* (October 27, 1996): www.metroactive.com/papers/sonoma/10.17.96/jerry-brown-9642.html; recollections of author.

127 Amy Goodman, interview with author (August 15, 2003), p.6; Jenn Shreve, "America's Most Bitchin' Broadcaster," *Salon* (July 10, 1999): www.salon.com/people/rewind/1999/07/10/chung/.

128 Amy Goodman, interview with author (August 15, 2003), p.8.

129 Conciatore, "Tenaciousness and Hope on FM."

130 Danny Schechter, "Saving Amy: 'The Exception to the Rulers,'" MediaChannel (October 27, 2000): www.mediachannel.org/views/dissector/amy.shtml; Steve Lopez, "This Just In: We're Fired," *Time* (January 29, 2001), p.6.

131 Ibid.; Amy Goodman, interview with author (August 15, 2003), p.13.

132 "ON ELECTION DAY, PACIFICA RADIO'S DEMOCRACY NOW! AND WBAI ASK CLINTON THE HARD QUESTIONS," *Democracy Now!* press release (November 7, 2000).

133 "Pacifica Lofts Alternative Radio Satellite," *Current* (December 15, 1997), quoted in *Pacifica Radio Network* newsletter (June 1998), pp.1-6; Conciatore, "Tenaciousness and Hope on FM"; David Giovanoni, "To: The Pacifica Foundation Board of Directors," statement, (February 25, 2000), p.1; Pat Scott, interview with author (January 13, 2003), p.13; Iver Peterson, "Ruffling Left-Wing Feathers to Recharge Pacifica Radio," *The New York Times* (December 29, 1997), p.D1.

134 Nicole Sawaya, interview with author (August 13, 2002), p.18.

135 Ibid., p.20.

136 Ibid., pp.18, 22-23; Geneva Collins, "Women Head Many of the Country's Largest Public Radio Outlets," *Current* (October 6, 1997): www.current.org/rad/rad718b.html.

137 Iver Peterson, "Clamorously, Pacifica Radio Dances Toward Mainstream," *The New York Times* (May 12, 1997), p.D9; Iver Peterson, "Ruffling Left-Wing Feathers to Recharge Pacifica Radio," *The New York Times* (December 29, 1997), pp.D1, D9.

138 Ibid, p.D9.

139 Janet Abbate, *Inventing the Internet* (Cambridge: MIT Press, 2000), p.212.
140 Vera Hopkins, "Statement About 'Listener' Representatives on the KPFA Board" (May 19, 1975), p.1.
141 "KPFA: LISTENER SPONSORED BUT NOT LISTENER CONTROLLED," *New Morning* (April 1972), p.15.
142 Ibid., p.16.
143 Ibid.
144 Hopkins, "Statement About 'Listener' Representatives," p.1.
145 Torry Mercer, interview with author (September 21, 2002), p.11.
146 See www.radio4all.org/freepacifica for details about the site itself; Lyn Gerry, email to author (June 13, 2003); Bleifuss, "Pacifica's Uncivil War," p.16.
147 Recollection of author.
148 Bleifuss, "Pacifica's Uncivil War," p. 17; Lyn Gerry, "Pacifica Foundation Hires Union Busters, Preliminary Investigation Results": www.radio4all.org/fp/ubust.htm.
149 "Pacifica Hires Former Justice Department Spokesperson to Fill Newly Created Position of 'Communications Director!'": www.radio4all.org/fp/burtglass.htm.
150 Iver Peterson, "Ruffling Left-Wing Feathers to Recharge Pacifica Radio," p.D9.
151 Pat Scott, interview with author (January 31, 2003), p.18.
152 "Mary Frances Berry," *Contemporary Black Biography*, vol. 7 (Gale Research Inc., 1994), pp.11-15.
153 Ibid.
154 Judith Coburn, "There's Something About Mary," *Salon* (Oct. 12, 1999): www.salon.com/news/feature/1999/10/12/berry/print.html.
155 Mary Frances Berry, "Ashamed of George Washington?" *The New York Times* (November 29, 1997), p.A25.
156 Coburn, "There's Something About Mary."
157 Paul Glastris, "The Powers That Shouldn't Be: Five Washington Insiders the Next Democratic President Shouldn't Hire," *The Washington Monthly* (October 1987), p.46.
158 William Brand, "New Chairwoman Hopes to Soothe Tempers at KPFA," *Oakland Tribune* (December 12, 1997), pp.B1-B2; "Pacifica's New Face," *Berkeley Voice* (December 11, 1997), pp.1, 28.
159 Brand, "New Chairwoman Hopes to Soothe Tempers at KPFA," pp.B1-B2.
160 Jacqueline Conciatore, "NFCB Veteran Lynn Chadwick Promoted to Head Pacifica Radio" (Oct. 26, 1998): www.current.org/rad/rad819p.html.
161 Anthony York, "The War over KPFA," *Salon* (July 17, 1999): www.salon.com/news/feature/1999/07/17/kpfa/index2.html.
162 Lynn Chadwick, My First Hundred Days, Pacifica Foundation Executive

Director Report, Board of Directors Meeting, Berkeley, CA, February 1999, p.1.

163 Alexander Cockburn, "The Neutering of Pacifica," *CounterPunch* (January 15-31, 1999): www.counterpunch.org/pacifica.html.

164 "Pacifica Foundation Station Board Position Description," in "Pacifica Foundation Policies Governing Station Advisory Boards" (March 1, 1998), p.2.

165 Ken Ford, interview with author (February 22, 2004), p.2.

166 Robert Coonrod, letter to Pat Scott (September 14, 1998), pp.1-2; John Crigler, letter to Lynn Chadwick (October 12, 1998), pp.1-2, cited in *The Pacifica Files: A Reference Source and Manual for Activists on the Crisis at the Pacifica Radio Network* (New York: The Campaign to Stop the Corporate Takeover, no date), pp.57-60.

167 "Notice of By-Law Change," in *Pacifica Foundation National Governing Board Meeting Booklet* (Berkeley: Pacifica Foundation, 1999), p.ii.

168 United States Code, Title 47-Telegraphs, Telephones, and Radiotelegraphs, Section 396(k)(8)(C) (italics added).

169 Pacifica National Board Meeting, September 14-15, 1979, Berkeley, California, p.7.

170 Cockburn, "The Neutering of Pacifica": www.counterpunch.org/pacifica.html.

171 Paul Rauber, "Bad Blood," *East Bay Express* (March 5, 1999), p.5.

172 Minutes of the Pacifica National Board, February 28, 1999, pp.23-24.

173 Ibid., p.54.

174 Richard Madden, letter to Lynn Chadwick, February 24, 1999, cited in *The Pacifica Files*, pp.1-2; Pacifica Foundation By-Laws, as amended, 2/28/99, p.1. In a footnote on p.5 the new bylaws stated that local boards would retain the right to nominate directors "as a body or individually," but the board's obligation to honor those nominations had been eliminated.

175 Minutes of the Pacifica National Board, February 28, 1999, p.16.

176 Ibid., pp.76-77.

177 Ibid., pp.75-78.

178 Noam Chomsky, Edward S. Herman, and Howard Zinn, letter to Dr. Mary Berry (February 24, 1999).

179 Minutes of the Pacifica National Board, February 28, 1999, p.18.

180 Richard Madden, email to Lynn Chadwick, March 2, 1999, p.1.

181 Jacqueline Conciatore, "'Tempers Rise as Pacifica Lets Board Select Its Own Members," *Current* (March 8, 1999): www.current.org/rad/rad906p.html.

182 Alexander Cockburn, "The Capturing of Pacifica," *CounterPunch* (no date; probably March 1999): www.counterpunch.org/pacifica2.html.

183 Dick Bunce, "The Crisis of Democratic Communications," in *A Vision for Pacifica Radio: Creating a Network for the 21st Century* (Berkeley: Pacifica Foundation, 1997), pp.4-5, 7-8, 12, 17.

CHAPTER 6

In Defense of the Realm, 1999–2000

I keep asking, . . . How are we going to get past this?

SAUL LANDAU

Much of the American progressive community experienced the KPFA crisis of 1999 as a slowly exploding information bomb. Shocking headlines appeared in newspapers; frantic messages flooded email browsers, forwarded by friends from KPFA's staff, or from Pacifica, or from one of the many station solidarity groups that had formed in response to the crisis. On top of all this, residents of the Bay Area endured nightly live television coverage of the firings, demonstrations, armed guards, rumors of a station sale, and expulsion of KPFA's staff. As the bad news radiated outward across the country, prominent leftists tried to make sense of what was happening. Most of them had, like filmmaker Michael Moore, been dismissing the "Pacifica struggle" as an exercise in marginality, but no longer. On August 2, the *San Francisco Bay Guardian* published a letter to Pacifica from Moore, who had been interviewed on KPFA at least nine times over the previous fifteen years. Once again questioning the sanity of others, Moore's opening paragraph reflected the astonishment with which many progressives received the situation in Berkeley:

> Dear Ms. Chadwick and Ms. Berry:
> You seem like two decent human beings. So just what in hell's beans

do you think you are doing? Are you nuts? You must rue the day you decided to get involved in Pacifica Radio. All those years of hard work fighting for people's rights and – poof! – you will now be remembered as the individuals who sent police in to shut down a newscast! That's it. That's your whole damn legacy wrapped up in that one sentence. Jeez, I'd want out of that, wouldn't you?[1]

The national and even international spotlight now shone on Pacifica radio for all the wrong reasons. Its travails received coverage from the nation's top newspapers, as well as from the European press. Dozens of writers on media and progressive politics struggled to answer Michael Moore's question. What "in hell's beans" was this fight all about?

Thus from the autumn of 1999 onward, Pacifica's civil war expanded into two stories. The organization's management fought with the network's component parts in a struggle to maintain authority and control. These efforts only contributed to the growth of Pacifica's dissident movement, which had taken on aspects of a holy crusade in Berkeley, Los Angeles, Houston, New York City, and Washington, D.C.

But in the background a second dynamic supported the first. Various writers and activists operating both within and beyond the organization endeavored to explain the Pacifica struggle to a mystified general public. They constructed narratives of the conflict that varied depending on their political perspective or their stake in the institution's future. Within the organization, most of these writers were dissidents. But the senior staff of KPFK in Los Angeles saw the fight differently from Pacifica listeners in northern California. They sought to convince the public that the battle that had taken place in Berkeley was essentially a detour on the road to a more effective Pacifica radio network. While *The Nation* magazine made its pages available to a variety of perspectives on the crisis, it reserved its editorial section for a KPFK staff member and *Nation* editor who argued this case.

In the debate that ensued, a dialogue emerged between two narrative explanations competing for the attention of the public: a democracy narrative, and a relevance narrative. Both had their roots in tensions that went back to the very beginnings of the Pacifica organization and could be found in Lewis Hill's public writings and letters. The debate between these two narratives generated widespread attention as the Pacifica fight became a metaphor for the anxieties many progressive Americans felt about the rightward drift and consolidation of the media. In this context, a defense of the general direction in which Pat Scott had taken the organization made its last stand.

Revolt of the Spoonerites

By the winter of 1999 Pacifica's dissidents were throwing everything they had into a concerted attempt to undo the changes in the bylaws enacted at the foundation's February meeting in Berkeley. Lawsuits became central to their strategy – the first had been filed by attorney Dan Siegel while the KPFA staff had been locked out of their building. The primary impetus for the suit came from David Adelson, a research biologist at UCLA. Adelson joined KPFK's local advisory board in the 1990s and followed the purges at the station with alarm. He shared concerns about hate speech, but worried that the elimination of ethnic nationalist and pan-Africanist programming put KPFK on a trajectory that would strip the station of any real ethnic and political diversity. Adelson found the removal of Ron Wilkins's program particularly disturbing. "[KPFK manager] Schubb could have handled it another way," Adelson later commented. "He could have announced an event to deal with these issues. He could have said we're going to have a public forum. This is crucial, because here we had this radical African-American community listening, and Schubb just cut them off completely. Bad for the city. Terrible."[2]

Adelson quickly absorbed the intricate history of Pacifica's bylaws and the plan to centralize the board. Shortly before the national board met in Berkeley in February, he began calling prominent progressive journalists in the hope that one of them would write about the controversy. He appealed to Molly Ivins, Jim Hightower, and David Corn, to no avail. Finally Alexander Cockburn showed interest in the subject, taking from the biologist's 2,300-word backgrounder the material that would comprise his "Neutering of Pacifica" essay.[3] At the same time, anticipating Pacifica's plan to create a self-appointing board, Adelson and several associates began poring over the California Corporations Code. They also raised enough money for Siegel to explore the legality of the move.

By the summer of 1999 Adelson and Siegel had put together a case. Its central argument was simple. Pacifica had violated state corporation law, because the foundation had "failed to submit the proposed bylaw changes to members of Pacifica's local advisory boards for their consideration and vote." The LAB members, now excluded from sitting on the national board, were in fact members of the Pacifica Foundation, a non-profit corporation licensed in California. Thus, by denying them the chance to vote on the question of their exclusion, Pacifica had acted illegally.[4] Only one more task remained. Someone had to convince 5 percent of all Pacifica LAB members to sign on to the suit. Adelson sat down at the telephone again. While Pacifica installed armed guards at KPFA, he persuaded 23 of them to join the cause. Siegel filed *David Adelson et al. vs. Pacifica* in Alameda Country Superior Court three days after Chadwick shut the station down. TV news reporters filmed him handing papers to the court clerk.[5]

At around the same time, Sebastopol resident Carol Spooner sat at her radio, fuming. A grandmother and paralegal on her way to becoming a lawyer, Spooner had been listening to KPFA for almost 40 years, depending on it to cure her periodic blue moods. "I tend to be very, very introspective and sometimes withdrawn," she later confided. "From time-to-time over the years I would hear something on KPFA that just went straight in and rang for me and helped me to feel connected to the rest of the world again." Like tens of thousands of subscribers, Spooner thought that KPFA was her station. While driving to work on April 1, 1999, she tuned to KPFA and heard morning show host Kris Welch talk about the dismissal of Nicole Sawaya. Subsequent events infuriated her. Spooner went to

Lyn Gerry's freepacifica.org Web site, found out about the Adelson lawsuit, and read it. The action disappointed her. It did not go far enough, Spooner thought. Specifically, it did not demand the removal of the Pacifica board of directors for breach of trust. "So I said, 'Well, okay, I'll have to do it.'"[6]

The problem was, how? At first Spooner was not sure. But since she knew that it had to be done, she started her own organization. Its Web site went up on July 26, 1999, while KPFA was locked down:

THE COMMITTEE TO REMOVE THE PACIFICA BOARD ANNOUNCES ITS FORMATION TODAY TO END THE GRIP OF TYRANNY ON THE 50 YEAR OLD RADICAL INSTITUTION FOUNDED BY VISIONARY PACIFISTS TO SERVE AS A MEDIUM FOR ARTISTS, THINKERS AND DISSENTERS IN AMERICA.

THE PACIFICA BOARD HAS BECOME AN INTOLERABLE ADVERSARY OF THE FOUNDING PRINCIPLES OF THE PACIFICA FOUNDATION AND MUST BE REMOVED.

OUR GOAL IS THE REMOVAL OF THE ENTIRE PACIFICA BOARD OF DIRECTORS – EITHER VOLUNTARILY BY RESIGNATION, OR INVOLUNTARILY BY COURT ORDER.[7]

By then Spooner had decided on a class action lawsuit. She and her husband, Gregory, went to Save KPFA rallies and demonstrations with statements for listener-subscribers to fill out. "NOTICE," the form began. "KPFA LISTENER SUPPORTERS. YOU MAY HAVE LEGAL RIGHTS!" The document asked the holder to sign a declaration that he or she subscribed to KPFA, had done so, or had volunteered for the station in the past, and "believe the Board of Directors of The Pacifica Foundation has acted with gross abuse of their authority or discretion, dishonest acts, and /or fraud and should be removed as directors of The Pacifica Foundation."[8]

Had Spooner attempted this in the pre-Internet era, she might have gotten around 100 declarations. But now her experiment in radical ambulance chasing went up on her Web site, along with similar statements for listener-subscribers at WPFW, WBAI, KPFK, and KPFT. Spooner posted her appeal on all Pacifica-related email lists and waited for a response. By late October about 4,000 signed forms had come in through the mail. Eventually the committee would possess well over 10,000 subscriber statements, from over a tenth of the entire foundation's subscription base.[9]

With that, Spooner needed three more big things: an attorney, money, and standing to sue. After some searching she found a lawyer who specialized in class action cases and was willing to represent her – for $25,000. Undaunted, Spooner combed her contact list and found an anonymous donor to front the money. The standing question proved a bigger challenge. Despite the rhetoric of moral ownership Pacifica had cultivated over the decades, the network's listener-subscribers were not members of the foundation in any legal sense. Only the board of directors and LAB members enjoyed that status, the latter only until February of 1999. Therefore the listener-subscribers' rights as members of the foundation could not have been violated by Pacifica. If Spooner and her followers wanted standing to sue, they had to win "relator" status from the office of the California Attorney General, which was rarely granted. This special dispensation would literally put the lawsuit under the auspices of the state of California.[10]

From the outside, it looked like a long shot-an obscure paralegal asking one of the state's highest elected officials to come to the assistance of a community radio station. But during the shutdown of KPFA outraged Bay Area state senators and assembly members staged a special legislative hearing on Pacifica's behavior. Dozens of KPFA staff appeared as witnesses.[11] Following the August 20 hearing, legislative staff produced a report on the crisis. It hedged on a lot of issues; the phrase "Pacifica may have violated" appeared repeatedly in the conclusion. But on one matter the audit stood firm. Pacifica's actions over the summer of 1999 "breached an implied contract with its local programmers, subscribers and volunteers," the report declared.[12]

With that on paper, throngs of "Spoonerites," as they came to be called, flooded Attorney General Bill Lockyer's Web site with pleas for relator status. Over 1,000 of them signed a petition requesting his help.[13] Another constituent made a personal appeal. In the late 1950s former Pacifica president Peter Franck and Lockyer had been comrades in Slate, UC Berkeley's legendary student group. Franck looked for his old colleague at a Slate commemorative dinner party. He gave the Attorney General a copy of the audit and a recently released television documentary on the history of KPFA, *KPFA on the Air*. In September of 2000 Lockyer granted Spooner relator status to sue Pacifica.[14] By now Spooner and her followers were demanding a listener-subscriber-elected national board. Exultant activists at KPFA pushed for the station local advisory board to become subscriber-elected. The paid staff and management at KPFA would never have agreed to such a move prior to their expulsion in July 1999. Now they not only acceded to the proposal, they ran eight-track carts urging listeners to run and vote in the election.[15]

Meanwhile public attacks on the national board mounted. On August 18, 1999, Robbie Osman and Barbara Lubin's Friends of Free Speech Radio ran an ad in *The New York Times* demanding the resignation of Mary Frances Berry and Lynn Chadwick. "Intentionally or not, you have done what decades of right-wing attacks failed to accomplish," the statement concluded. "You have weakened Pacifica to the point of collapse." Seventy academics, organizers, politicians, and artists signed the statement, including Jerry Brown, now mayor of Oakland, author Barbara Ehrenreich, actor Danny Glover, scholar Angela Davis, and Juan Gonzales, co-host of *Democracy Now!*.[16] But a much larger national discussion both overshadowed and created the anxieties that fueled this protest.

The Big Picture

By the mid 1990s, liberal and progressive Americans felt a deep sense of powerlessness about the rightward drift and inaccessibility of newspapers and broadcast media. A generation of writers and scholars spoke to this discontent. Study after study on the question of media democracy lined the shelves of radical and even mainstream bookstores. UC Berkeley journalism professor Ben

Bagdikian's continuously updated *The Media Monopoly* offered a compelling account of the decline of independence among news providers. Noam Chomsky and Edward Herman's *Manufacturing Consent* provided statistical evidence on the extent to which television news took its cues from the U.S. State Department. Former rock-and-roll magazine publisher, now historian, Robert McChesney's *Telecommunications, Mass Media and Democracy,* recounted the unequal struggle between media activists and corporations in the 1930s that had led to the nation's commercial system of broadcasting.[17] As the Pacifica crisis raged, the demand for books on media bias and conglomeration appeared to exceed the capabilities of publishing houses. Out they came on a monthly basis with titles like *Breaking the News: How the Media Undermine American Democracy*; *Megamedia: How Giant Corporations Dominate Mass Media, Distort Competition, and Endanger Democracy*; and *Derailing Democracy: The America the Media Don't Want You to See.*[18] Writers such as Norman Solomon and Danny Schechter made careers out of dissecting the media, exposing the ways television and newsprint stories favored corporate executives over workers, men over women, white people over those of other colors, and the warlike over the peaceful.[19]

The mid-1990s also saw the rise of the progressive media activists. These crusaders roughly divided into two categories: those who wanted to create new media, and those who wanted to fix the old. Fairness and Accuracy in Reporting (FAIR) qualified for the latter group. Founded in 1986 by a former lawyer for the American Civil Liberties Union, in the 1990s members of the FAIR collective issued regular "action alerts" over the Internet against egregious examples of newspaper or television news distortion, urging its subscribers to call and protest. The Pacifica satellite distributed FAIR's weekly radio show, *CounterSpin.*[20]

The micro-radio and independent media movements fell into the former category. In the early 1990s hundreds of activists across the country began building low-power FM radio stations, in defiance of the FCC's 1979 ban on them (see Chapter 4). These 10-watt or less stations delighted radio listeners and infuriated commercial station owners, who charged signal interference whether there was any or not. In Springfield, Illinois, a blind black man named Dwayne Readus outraged the police by documenting news of officer brutality over his half-watt station. In Berkeley, California, former Free Speech Movement activist Stephen Dunnifer, alarmed at media coverage of the 1991 Persian Gulf war, started Free Radio Berkeley, broadcasting at first from the East Bay hills. When the FCC fined him $20,000 in 1993, a penalty twenty times what the law allowed, the National Lawyers Guild took his case. Dunnifer's David vs. Goliath fight with the FCC captured the media's attention, but a judge ruled against him in 1998.[21]

In November of 1999, three months after the KPFA staff returned to work, "indymedia" fever swept the world. Thousands of anti-globalization activists converged upon Seattle, Washington, to protest the meeting of the World Trade Organization there. A small group of technicians feared that the media would ignore the event, especially the many groups protesting the WTO's policies. So they raised money and built their own open Independent Media Center, complete with computers, digital editing systems, Internet connectivity, and streaming audio/video. www.indymedia.org, the portal to this resource, made information available to a host of volunteer journalists whose accounts of the "Battle of Seattle" streamed around the world. Perhaps for the first time, the Internet demonstrated its ability to circumvent mainstream information providers in the coverage of a major international event. Soon 60 independent media centers flourished in the big cities of North America, South America, Europe, Asia, and Africa.[22]

The Battle of Berkeley exploded in the midst of this concern, activity, and fervor. Most of the media writers already mentioned would quickly take sides over the Pacifica fight, supporting the forces of democratic reform. The contrast between the micro-radio/independent media movement and the organizational direction in which Pacifica seemed headed could not have been more stark. Many low-power FM stations and almost all independent media centers operated as democratic collectives. A self-appointing board now governed Pacifica. While KPFK threatened with expulsion hosts who wanted to talk about the network's policies over the air, indymedia centers thrived on openness. "Anyone may publish to the [indymedia] newswire, from any computer that is connected to the Internet," indymedia.org's Web site proudly declared, "by clicking the 'publish' link on the www.indymedia.org page and following the easy instructions."[23]

Not surprisingly, then, media activists framed the Pacifica fight in that context. The sum of their writings comprised the dominant narrative in the Pacifica discourse – the democracy narrative.

Pacifica dissidents focused on two essential demands: the Pacifica Foundation had to broaden its governance structure, and it had to become a more transparent organization. But in its most coherent form, the Free Pacifica movement's democracy narrative was really a history, a tale of slow corruption and silent collusion with outside influences that had only recently shown their true face. In some ways this narrative resembled the story American colonists constructed about their deteriorating relationship with England during the war for independence. In fact, the Pacifica version of this story was best told by a radio producer who had worked at KPFA in the early 1960s and then emigrated to England. John Whiting returned to the United States in the 1990s to write a book about the history of Pacifica and KPFA. What he saw so infuriated him that, upon going back to Britain, he wrote a narrative of the institution's decline, "Pacifica in Vincula."[24]

Whiting's essay began in classic Rousseauian style. "Free media everywhere are in chains," he began. "Pacifica Radio, America's uncompromising listener-supported, non-commercial FM network, now passes its programs through the fine mesh of the Arbitron rating sieve to make them more easily digestible." It was the same in England, the author lamented. "In Britain, the BBC's intellectually up-market Radio 3 is, like Pacifica, being made more 'user-friendly' with personality-led 'strip' programming which, unlike strip poker, removes the content and leaves the clothing."

But it had not always been that way. Like Rousseau, Whiting

recalled a golden age of the organization, the 1950s and 1960s:

> The culture shock of tuning in to KPFA in 1949 was like hearing an atheist sermon preached from the pulpit of Grace Cathedral. The airwaves had never been available to iconoclasts, but now they were reaching not just a handful of people at a meeting or a concert, but an indeterminate mass of the general public. "Indeterminate" is the operative word. The Nielsen ratings, with their little boxes attached to consoles in a few living rooms, were already up and running for AM radio, but FM was still only a gleam in an ad man's eye. Lew Hill could ignore with impunity the size of KPFA's audiences because there was, mercifully, no way of measuring them.[25]

To Whiting, the poverty KPFA endured ennobled its cause. "Engagement typified the staff as well; they worked for peanuts and the shells were often empty," he wrote. "Idealists came to work, usually unpaid, remained as long as penury would allow, and then went on to other employment where the skills they had acquired might lead to a distinguished career." The staff made decisions as Lewis Hill had first intended, as a democratic collective.

Then came the 1980s and the beginnings of temptation. The subcarrier signals Pacifica acquired and leased out (see Chapter 5) brought in a steady stream of money. "Suddenly Pacifica had moved into the bottom of the Big Leagues," Whiting wrote. "There was money coming in which one could actually control, rather than simply handing it over to whatever creditor happened to be banging on the door. There was scope for management, for planning, for financial rationalization, for serious fund-raising."

This led to "delusions of grandeur" for Pacifica, exemplified by Gail Christian's "Strategy for National Programming." "The power structure of the American networks, which had motivated the creation of listener-sponsored local radio, was now to serve as its model," Whiting continued. Ambition led to greater expenditures, such as the purchase of KPFA's new headquarters in 1991. Saddled with a huge mortgage, KPFA began bringing in audience research specialists. Whiting summarized their counsel: "More pop music. No speeches. More chat. No big words. Same programs every day. Go down-market. Purges began. Soviet Affairs analyst William Mandel went first. Then jazz programmer Phil Elwood. Then others."

Then came secrecy, private board meetings, relatively well-paid managers, the curtailing of the station *Folio*, and a more rigorously enforced gag rule. The bureaucracy Pacifica had created in the 1980s and 1990s needed money to support it, and that meant resorting to audience-rating strategies and expensive national programming. "You can't have it both ways," Whiting warned, "either you run a station in which direct, inexpensive, accessible communication is the sine qua non, or you establish a self-supporting, self-justifying hierarchy in which the preservation of your professional and personal life-style must necessarily take precedence over all other priorities. Following the latter path, KPFA has changed from the station many people listened to but didn't support to the station some people still support but don't listen to."[26]

Critics of Pacifica replicated some version of this narrative over and over through the later 1990s: community radio had succumbed to the blandishments of power and now paid the price as a soulless bureaucracy. This summed up libertarian writer Jesse Walker's essay "With Friends Like These: Why Community Radio Doesn't Need the Corporation for Public Broadcasting," published by the Cato Institute in 1997. Like Whiting, Walker saw a golden age in the 1950s and 1960s, when nonprofessional, predominantly volunteer staffs ran the Pacifica stations and pioneer Lorenzo Milam instituted the KRAB Nebula, a loose confederation of community radio frequencies. "[C]ommunity radio came to represent a third model of broadcasting," Walker wrote, "different from both commercial and institutional radio, though it overlapped in certain ways with both. In its ideal form, it was broadcasting rooted in civil society, a phrase whose recent transformation into a Beltway cliché should not blind us to the richness of the institutions it describes."[27]

Then came the Corporation for Public Broadcasting. The CPB's funding for community radio came with a price: a demand that its grantees hire a minimum number of paid staff, achieve a baseline level of listenership measured by Arbitron ratings, or demonstrate a certain amount of community financial support. This created a set of "perverse incentives," Walker wrote. "Community stations that previously got by on listener pledges and local underwriting might be eligible for thousands more – if they hire more full-time staff, increase their broadcast hours, seek more funds, and, under the new rules, make their programming more mainstream in pursuit of higher Arbitrons."[28] Walker and Whiting both saw large infusions of government or private money as harmful to the grassroots cultures community radio stations had fostered in the 1950s and 1960s with their emphasis on altruism, iconoclasm, and spontaneity.

More prominent writers dealing with Pacifica tended to shy away from these analyses. They usually supported a democratized Pacifica because the national office and board's behavior during the Battle of Berkeley simply appalled them. Like Alexander Cockburn, they often focused on the contradiction between the democratic rhetoric Pacifica promulgated on the air and its undemocratic system of governance. "Public radio's evocations of democratic values on the airwaves are undermined when stations treat democracy as a concept that should not intrude past their own front doors," wrote Norman Solomon, who took a partisan stand on behalf of KPFA after the firing of Sawaya in March 1999. "In such a context, the governance of the medium is the message."[29] Robert McChesney put the dilemma more starkly in an interview with alternative media producer David Barsamian:

> [Y]ou have a form of management [at Pacifica] that's in the hands of a self-appointed board who basically have little or no experience with community radio themselves who have all the legal cards to do whatever they want. They have more power over those five Pacifica stations than Rupert Murdoch has over his enterprises. They have more power than a capitalist organization because they don't have shareholders to account to.[30]

Given this power and Pacifica's recent behavior, what were they going to do next? worried McChesney. "There's more secrecy around Pacifica than you'd find at the CIA. It's probably easier to go into the CIA or the NSA and ask them what they're doing under-cover in some country than it is to find out what Pacifica's board's plans are for their stations."[31] By the end of the Pacifica crisis almost all the prominent writers mentioned so far would ally themselves with the Free Pacifica movement in one way or another. Ed Herman and Chomsky had signed a plea for democracy sent to the February 1999 board meeting with Howard Zinn. *Media Monopoly* author Ben Bagdikian signed Lubin and Osman's letter to Berry in *The New York Times*.[32]

In the face of this opposition, Mary Frances Berry held the board together by dint of personality and prestige. Even Bay Area board representative Pete Bramson, who had publicly denounced Pacifica for considering selling KPFA, regarded Berry with awe. At board meetings Berry was "shrewd, totally adept linguistically, icy steely sharp, intimidating," Bramson recalled, with "a capacity to maintain her composure and to give shit as well as accept it."[33] Her position on the U.S. Civil Rights Commission and the fact that she was an African-American woman probably helped. Black board members felt defensive about her; white board members feared to criticize her.

But Pacifica's chair had few personal connections to the founda-tion's five radio stations. Unlike Pat Scott and David Salniker, Berry had had little experience with Pacifica and its various personalities prior to taking over the board. Chadwick had burned all bridges at KPFA and could not fill the gap anywhere else. "It seemed like her breadth of experience was more in the national arena, the arena with CPB and the larger issues versus dealing with a radio station," Bramson remembered. "And I say that because of the discomfort that I sensed from her when she was interacting at the staff level."[34] For the most part, both women resorted to rote statements about diversity and audience size in defense of their leadership. If anyone was going to persuade the public to give Berry and Chadwick a second chance, it would not be themselves. By early May, however, someone else had volunteered for the task.

Where Was Dennis?

On May 10 an editorial appeared in *The Nation* magazine titled
"Whose Pacifica?" written by one of its contributing editors, Marc
Cooper.[35] Having returned to KPFK in the late 1990s, Cooper now
hosted *The Marc Cooper Show* from 5 to 6 p.m. most weekdays, in
addition to his modular public-affairs program *Radio Nation*, which
billboarded the latest features published in *The Nation* magazine.
Ironically, fifteen years earlier Cooper had been a Pacifica trouble-
maker himself. Now his editorial marked the beginning of a
concerted campaign by himself, his allies in southern California, and
The Nation to convince the progressive community that Pacifica was
simply experiencing a rough patch on the way to becoming a more
effective broadcasting organization. Cooper's intervention marked
the emergence of the second narrative competing for dominance in
the Pacifica crisis: the relevance narrative.

"Whose Pacifica?" began with a bit of gallows humor. "There's a
scene in *The Godfather* when Clemenza," Cooper wrote, "anticipating
the outbreak of a full-scale war between the families, nonchalantly
remarks to young Mikey Corleone: 'This thing's gotta happen every
five years or so . . . every ten years – helps to get rid of the bad
blood.' You could almost say the same thing about Pacifica Radio."
Then Cooper got serious. Sawaya's firing had been a mistake, he
declared, "a gigantic and inexcusable blunder." But the crisis over
KPFA overshadowed a "deeper conflict," Cooper argued, one that
had been unsettling the organization for the past five years:

> Fueling the conflict is a tension between two visions of what Pacifica
> Radio can and should be as it completes its first fifty years. One
> view is that the five stations should be a high-frequency tom-tom for
> activists, the equivalent of a mimeographed bulletin of the left that
> makes little effort to reach beyond its current constituencies. The
> competing view is that Pacifica should be a newspaper of the left, an
> electronic *Le Monde* or *Guardian* with some intellectual heft and
> depth and – yes – even some occasional analytical distance from the
> movements to which it is sympathetic.[36]

"Both visions can be defended, and they're not mutually exclusive," Cooper continued. "But as a Pacifica programmer going back, on and off, twenty years, I unabashedly support the latter strategy as the only way for Pacifica to stop occupying only the fringe. And it is toward that second vision that Pacifica has tried over the past five years – in its awkward and inefficient way – to move."[37]

Cooper's framing of the issue was eloquent, if not original. Peter Franck had articulated the same basic dichotomy years earlier, asking whether Pacifica should function as the newspaper or the newsletter of the Left. Cooper, however, put the framework into practice in his own programming at KPFK. He broadcast interviews with scholars who criticized Fidel Castro's four decades of uninterrupted control over Cuba. He argued that the Free Mumia Abu-Jamal movement hurt the anti-death penalty cause, tying it to a "politically dubious cult-groupie."[38] Cooper's commentaries, often published in the *LA Weekly* or the *Los Angeles Times*, sometimes came off as condescending, even snotty, with exhortations to the Left to learn "to walk and chew gum at the same time."[39] Still, he walked almost alone within the Pacifica organization as someone willing openly to ask questions about American peace and social justice movements that others would only discuss in private.

"Whose Pacifica?" tapped into the anxieties of many progressives who had supported Pacifica's overall direction through the 1990s and who had been part of the Left for decades. They knew that leftists make mistakes, sometimes big ones. The essay rejected a philosophy of community radio exemplified by WPFW news director Paz Cohen's 1977 directive to her staff: "[W]e are here to tell people what PARTICIPANTS (the perpetrators and those affected) are saying, doing, planning and thinking" she wrote, "NOT what WE THINK they stand for or really mean. Their actions speak louder than your adjectives."[40] Marc Cooper spoke for a generation of Pacificans who, 22 years later, thought that leftist radio programmers had an obligation to think. What did it matter, they wondered, whether Pacifica ran itself democratically if KPFK answered Rush Limbaugh with programs claiming that white people were mutants?

But in his campaign to stay the course at Pacifica, Cooper had to do more than outline a philosophy of relevance worth supporting. In order for him to convince progressives that Pacifica was moving in the right direction, he had to prove that KPFA bore substantial responsibility for the crisis in Berkeley. Here his arguments began to fail.

Shortly after the expulsion of the KPFA staff in July, *The Nation* published another Cooper editorial, "Pacifica on the Brink." Cooper insisted that the KPFA staff deserved equal blame for the shutdown, characterizing station personnel as "a group of committed leftists ripping apart their own institution in a factional dispute. Pacifica's critics claim they have been muzzled. On the contrary, for more than three months KPFA staff have had unfiltered access to the air to put forward their grievances. Off the air, some full-time Pacifica critics have been running a vigorous Internet and e-mail campaign hinting at some sort of dark conspiracy."[41]

By August Cooper had come up with his own version of the incident that precipitated the police expulsion, the suspension of Dennis Bernstein. In the *LA Weekly*, Cooper accused Bernstein of having deliberately staged an incident. "Instead of using KPFA's ample union protections to protest what he thought an unjust attack, Bernstein went running through the station claiming he was in physical peril and lodged himself under an equipment console in the news studio," Cooper wrote. "The *Evening News* was on the air, but it was being interrupted by a jostling of the tape machine under which Bernstein was nesting." Under those circumstances, "KPFA's acting manager then did what any responsible person would do in his place. He shut down Bernstein's histrionics by shutting down the station signal." Cooper conceded that it might have been better not to have involved the police. "But to believe that Bernstein was anything more than a reckless provocateur is a delusion."[42]

Aside from the fact that Bernstein never hid under a tape console, the situation at KPFA was far more serious than Marc Cooper portrayed it for *The Nation* and *LA Weekly* readers. Pacifica had tried to muzzle KPFA, firing or suspending three programmers for talking about the crisis over the airwaves and threatening everyone else with suspension as well. In his description of Bernstein's suspension, Cooper neglected to mention the program for which Bernstein had been disciplined – a press conference announcing, among other things, the discovery of an email memorandum by a member of the national board proposing the sale of KPFA. That same memo advocated the shutdown of KPFA prior to the Bernstein confrontation. "But seriously," Michael Palmer had written, "I was under the impression there was support in the proper quarters and a definite majority, for shutting down that unit and reprogramming immediately. Has that changed? Is there consensus among the national staff that anything other than that is acceptable/bearable?" This alarming question simply did not exist in Cooper's representations of the hours preceding the expulsion of the KPFA staff.[43]

In his second Nation editorial, Cooper demanded that the KPFA staff "find ways to distance themselves from the Internet strategists who wish only to exacerbate the conflict." But where else was the staff to turn? Pacifica had fired their general manager and replaced her with a functionary who devoted her career to constructing government-subsidized programs to get rid of the "bad blood," as Cooper himself put it, at community radio stations. Private pleas to national board members had gone unheeded. The station's local advisory board had been rendered powerless to do anything at all meaningful at Pacifica, let alone force Sawaya's rehiring. What choice had KPFA personnel but to use the airwaves and forge alliances with the station's activist community?

During her May 5, 1999, talk over the KPFA airwaves Mary Frances Berry had confided that she had read Cooper's first editorial in *The Nation*. It had not persuaded her to rehire Sawaya, but she said that she liked it anyway. "I don't agree with everything in the article, but I think he's right about saying that one issue is whether the stations and Pacifica should be, simply reflect a small group of people speaking and having radio stations to use to express their vision, or whether it should be a newspaper, sort of, like, for the Left or for progressives, and that this is one of the issues."[44] Cooper's arguments could be read as a call to stay the course and to continue to struggle for greater relevance, which undoubtedly was his intent. They could also be interpreted as an effort to protect the author's own institutional base. Many of the senior staff at KPFA had worked at the station for years and enjoyed, as Cooper observed, solid union protection. But Cooper had only recently been rehired by a relatively new and controversial general manager to produce drive-time programming for KPFK. He had openly crowed about the firings that helped clear the space for his renewed tenure. The station was surrounded by dissident ex-programmers who wanted their shows back and by local advisory board members furious at their impotence. They were also angry about something else.

Mark Schubb built an impressive public affairs lineup for KPFK, including Cooper, journalist Joe Domanick, and UC Irvine history professor Jon Wiener. But with the departure of Marcos Frommer in 1999, critics began to call into question the station's commitment to local diversity. By the spring of 2001, white people dominated KPFK's afternoon drive-time schedule. Marc Cooper now appeared on KPFK's airwaves no fewer than six times a week: 4–5 p.m. Monday through Thursday, then for a half-hour on Fridays and Sundays as the host of *Radio Nation*. Following Cooper on weekdays came another hour of local public-affairs programming, *Beneath the Surface*, whose three hosts, Weiner, Suzi Weissman, and Domanick, were all white. A white woman hosted the 1 p.m. health and spirituality hour.

In fact, people of color did host drive-time public affairs shows, most notably morning show host Jon Beaupre, former programmer for NPR's *Latino USA*. But Beaupre did not make minority issues his primary focus. Those who did so broadcast after 7 p.m. or on weekends, when radio listening in urban areas declines. The station aired African-American writer Earl Ofari Hutchinson's *Tuesday Live* and *IMRU*, KPFK's historic program on lesbian/gay/bisexual/transgender issues in the evening. Late on Friday nights Fidel Rodriguez hosted his talk/music show *Seditious Beats*. On weekends listeners could tune in to Assumpta Oturu's *Spotlight Africa* and Rubén Tapia's *Enfoque Latino*, the station's Spanish-language public affairs program.[45]

Not a few observers commented on the degree to which Pacifica's chair focused on diversity issues at KPFA while rarely complaining about the matter elsewhere in the network. "[W]hen KPFK in Los Angeles had two choice drive-time slots available recently (one of them formerly held by a Latino), Pacifica hired two white guys, Joe Domanick and Jon Wiener," Alexander Cockburn wrote in his online journal *CounterPunch*. "Berry is not shy about playing to the PC gallery about the need to diversify."[46] (In fact, Wiener was not "hired" – he signed on as a volunteer.) Robert McChesney noted the phenomenon elsewhere. "Berry has stated that her desire is to expand Pacifica's reach among people of color," he wrote. "But the opposition to her actions by virtually all of KPFA's minority programmers and active listeners, as well as the low minority listen-ership at Houston's KPFT – a Pacifica station she does not hassle – reveals how bogus her claim is."[47] Indeed, it appeared to many that diversity problems at Pacifica stations rose and fell depending on the degree of loyalty their staffs showed to Mary Frances Berry.

In this tenuous context the overthrow of Pacifica's board could hardly have seemed an attractive prospect to KPFK senior staff and their supporters. Perhaps that was one reason why none of them realized the full gravity of the crisis in Berkeley. The KPFA staff were not rebelling for the hell of it. They had supported Pat Scott's reforms and Strategic Plan all down the line, faithfully enforcing the gag rule up until the firing of Sawaya. Even Scott acknowledged as much during the shutdown. "KPFA has been doing everything it could for years and was on the right track," she told Judith Coburn in *Salon*. "This whole issue is crazy."[48] Cooper scoffed at evidence that the shutdown had been planned. "And why would Pacifica plan a shutdown of KPFA, which has resulted only in the loss of untold thousands of dollars and tons of precious credibility?" he asked, responding to *Nation* letter writers.[49] The answer was depressingly simple. The culture of toughness Pacifica had encouraged in the

1990s now ran amuck. Pacifica's agenda was no longer relevance, as Cooper claimed, or a gradual drift toward NPR-style programming, as dissidents had been complaining ever since Clare Sparks' charge in 1984. The agenda was now about little more than authority and control. The director of the *Pacifica Network News* (*PNN*) would find that out first.

"That Was Bullshit"

On Tuesday, October 26, 1999, *PNN* Director Dan Coughlin sat at his desk wondering what to do. He had a press release in his hand. It came from Marty Durlin, manager of community radio station KGNU in Colorado. "16 Radio Stations to Boycott Pacifica Network Programming on October 27," ran the title. The stations all broadcast *PNN's* half-hour daily feed produced in Washington, D.C., and *Democracy Now!*. But on Wednesday they would refuse to air any Pacifica programming on their stations for one day, in protest of the centralization of the national board and the expulsion and arrest of KPFA staff. "A Day Without Pacifica," some stations called it. Many would open up their studio phone lines to listeners to talk about the crisis. "The Pacifica debacle is the single best example of the cancer that has been eating at noncommercial media for more than a decade," Durlin's release concluded, "disempowering communities in the name of professionalization, commercializing the airwaves in the guise of development, centralizing authority in the name of efficiency, and promoting high production values at the expense of local color."[50]

Behind this protest lay another concern. Satellite distribution to Pacifica's 65 subscriber stations rapidly deteriorated after the chaotic lockdown of KPFA in July and August of 1999. The responsibility for the system had been taken away from the two people who knew it the best, Jim Bennett and Michael Yoshida, and been transferred to less experienced staff in Washington, D.C. Since then, complained community station WORT operations director Norman Stockwell in a letter to Pacifica, "service has been frequently interrupted, unpredictably cut off and often simply not delivered (e-mail messages received just before, or significantly after, missed uplinks do not constitute ample notice of refeeds for programs that are time contingent)."[51] Many stations were furious at Pacifica for reasons beyond how the foundation handled its internal affairs.

Dan Coughlin was aware of that anger. 36 years old, he had been born in Caracas, Venezuela, and raised in England, where he soaked up the punk/West Indian/South Asian youth culture of the 1980s. Concerned about police brutality, he became a crime reporter for Interpress Service, then moved to New York City to cover United Nations affairs for the agency. Not surprisingly, Coughlin quickly fell in with the crowd at Samori Marksman's WBAI. In 1996 he became producer for Amy Goodman's *Democracy Now!*, then *PNN* director in 1998.[52]

By 1998, however, serious tensions had emerged within the network over Amy Goodman and *Democracy Now!'s* coverage of issues. According to Coughlin, WPFW manager Bessie Wash and KPFK's Mark Schubb disliked the program. According to Pat Scott, Schubb did not want to run it. According to Amy Goodman, he "couldn't stand it," as he told her directly.[53] Chances are that Schubb and Cooper agreed with the assessment of their ally Ella Taylor, who reviewed films for KPFK. Goodman was "excellent at providing a voice for the wretched of the Earth, from Ohio to Afghanistan," Taylor wrote for the *LA Weekly*:

> But one doesn't turn to her show for open debate about leftist thought. On almost any issue, she will trot out verbatim speeches of a small circle of like-minded friends – Noam Chomsky, Howard Zinn, Michael Parenti, Cornel West . . . when Goodman rightly scolds the commercial media for their distortions, she's not above replacing those distortions with others of her own. As the conflict in the Middle East escalates, she routinely reports Palestinian casualties – which the mainstream media have also been doing [for] some time – while ostentatiously omitting those on the Israeli side.[54]

In fact, Goodman did sponsor very open debates on issues controversial within the Left, from the administration of Zimbabwean president Robert Mugabe to Ralph Nader's candidacy for president in 2000.[55] But on certain topics she drew an ideological line, nowhere more rigidly than at the case of Mumia Abu-Jamal, whose cause Cooper was about to criticize very publicly in *Mother Jones* and the *New York Observer*. Both Coughlin and Goodman were disappointed when their colleagues balked at Pacifica making a cause of Temple University's radio stations banning *Democracy Now!* just before the program broadcast Abu-Jamal's commentaries. "[W]e saw that as an opportunity to get our name out and to get our message out and to build. Like being banned in Boston, or banned by the BBC," Coughlin recalled. "But that was opposed because it was seen as being part of the 'old' Pacifica."[56]

This was the context in which the Battle of Berkeley reached Coughlin's corner of the Pacifica network. The fight quickly polarized national staff already deeply divided over the approach that Pacifica should take to news and public-affairs programming. One side, Goodman's and Coughlin's, felt strongly that coverage should identify with voices for peace and social justice throughout the United States and the world. The other side, Schubb's and Cooper's, wanted more inter-Left debate and "analytical distance," as Cooper put it, in national programming. Up until 1998 Pat Scott had held things together by sheer bureaucratic willpower and not infrequent telephone shouting matches. Now she was gone. So were development director Gail Christian and national programming executive producer Julie Drizin. Indeed, after the shutdown in Berkeley, nobody was handling the affiliates. Chadwick was often unreachable, absorbed in the fight at KPFA.[57] And so a difficult question fell into Coughlin's lap. To what degree should *PNN* provide coverage of the Pacifica crisis?

Wherever his sympathies may have been, Coughlin had said nothing publicly about the situation at Pacifica so far. But he felt that he could not completely ignore an ongoing story that was being covered by the *New York Times* and the *Washington Post*. If one-quarter of CBS's affiliates went on strike, wouldn't that be news? And wouldn't Pacifica make hay over it if CBS said nothing about the matter over its own newscasts? WPFW's Wash and Hankins felt otherwise. By April of 1999 FAIR's program *CounterSpin*, distributed over the Pacifica satellite, had begun broadcasting stories about the Pacifica crisis. When they did, WPFW management interrupted the show with music. KPFK pulled an edition that included an interview with Larry Bensky. In July WPFW once again drowned out a *CounterSpin* program on Pacifica with jazz.[58] Everyone was doing whatever they wanted (or suppressing what someone else was doing) as far as coverage of the crisis was concerned. The buck no longer stopped anywhere. "A Day Without Pacifica," Wednesday, October 27, arrived. Coughlin made a decision, permitting a 37-second "reader" mentioning the event over the *PNN* newscast:

> Sixteen affiliates of the Pacifica Radio network today boycotted Pacifica programming to show their concern about the handling of a labor-management dispute at Pacifica station KPFA in Berkeley. This summer, more than 100 persons were arrested, and thousands took to the streets at the oldest listener-sponsored station in the country to protest Pacifica staffing decisions. Hurt during the dispute was Pacifica's satellite distribution system, which provides programming to some 63 stations nationwide. The sixteen Pacifica affiliates from eleven states called for the network to adopt new open, accountable governance and to continue to support community-based journalism, which they said had made Pacifica great.[59]

It seemed to Pacifica's soon-to-be ex-news director like a gesture toward transparency for the affiliates. Then he took a long weekend.[60]

According to Coughlin, when he returned to work on Monday, an email message was waiting for him from Chadwick. "Dan," it read, "take the day off. You're no longer news director." Coughlin called his boss. "Dan, you're trying to fuel the flames," he recalled Chadwick exclaiming. "What was that news story you did? That was bullshit. That's such horseshit. You're just trying to fuel the flames of the crisis at KPFA. You're trying to destroy the network." The next day, however, he received more email from Chadwick. He "did not understand" their conversation, it said, adding that "appreciation is the only basis for your reassignment, not a disagreement over news content." Coughlin looked at Pacifica's Web site and saw a press release. He had a new job, "Development Specialist for News Operations for Pacifica." Coughlin would be working with a newly created Task Force on Programming and Governance. The release quoted an exuberant Lynn Chadwick. "Because we are dedicated to including opinions from every spectrum of our audience and want a shared programming vision, we wanted someone with Dan's news experience to consult with the Task Force," she declared. *PNN* reporter Mark Bevis would step in as acting news director.[61]

Coughlin was stunned. Yesterday he had supposedly tried to destroy the network. Today he was supposedly in charge of reconstructing it. "They didn't even talk to me," Coughlin recalled. Nor did Chadwick and her assistants talk to the four people who proposed the task force – broadcasting historian and former WBAI LAB chair Ralph Engelman and WBAI programmers Mimi Rosenberg, Pepsi Charles, and Karen Frillman, or contact another former LAB chair, Nan Rubin, who helped develop the proposal. None of these people believed that Coughlin had been reassigned out of appreciation. Engelman rushed to distance his group from Chadwick's decision. "Our desire was to help provide a mechanism for establishing a renewed sense of purpose and unity, not a fig-leaf for arbitrary and divisive action," he wrote in a public letter to Pacifica. Rubin, appalled, sent a memo as well: "You must remove my association from this action. I will have no part of it."[62]

Worst of all, Coughlin's removal horrified two of his friends, Amy Goodman and *PNN* anchor Verna Avery Brown. They wrote a letter to the Pacifica governing board asking for an explanation. "We are not questioning whether Lynn Chadwick as a manager has a right to make staff changes, but whether she is right to do this," they explained. "This decision has grave implications for our future as a credible news organization. Our integrity and independence are at stake. Pacifica cannot afford to be rocked again by another scandal."[63]

It was too late. The scandal was in progress. "Did Coughlin Lose His Job for Breaking the 'Dirty Laundry Rule'?" ran a headline in

Current magazine. Chadwick had insisted to the reporter, Steve Behrens, that Coughlin's instant transfer had nothing to do with the affiliates reader. It does not appear that Behrens found her very convincing. "Dan and I did have a conversation about that story," he quoted Chadwick as saying, "and I'd better stop that sentence right now."[64] The precedent Chadwick appeared to be establishing was obvious. Pacifica managers now reserved the right not only to remove employees for breaking the gag rule, but for running news stories they found displeasing. Verna Brown went to national board members and asked them to reinstate Couglin, to no avail. "I started to feel like the whole ship was out of control," she later explained. After protesting Chadwick's action for some weeks, she resigned.[65]

Dan Coughlin's "reassignment" and the widespread perception that his supervisor, Lynn Chadwick, had moved him because of a *PNN* story she did not like, validated the claims of longtime Pacifica dissidents. More important, the response confirmed fears that Chadwick simply could not manage the organization.

We're Irrelevant

Aaron Glantz worked for *PNN* as a stringer, an independent journalist whom the news agency paid by the story. He often filed as Pacifica's reporter in Sacramento, California. Coughlin's controversial dismissal put him and his fellow stringers in an awkward position. How should they respond? Coughlin had commissioned Glantz to cover the protests in Seattle against the World Trade Organization. He decided to go despite the scandal.

Upon arrival at the WTO protests, Glantz got a call from KPFK-based reporter Robin Urevitch. She started yelling at him for filing stories for *PNN*. In September, Urevitch had been barred from KPFK's newsroom for publishing in a local newspaper a piece about the Pacifica crisis that had angered Mark Schubb.[66] "I had told her [Urevich] that I thought that what was happening was really screwed up but that I was not just going to take action all by myself," Glantz later explained. "And that I thought that it was really important that if I do something it is part of a collective action so that it is useful and I don't just screw myself over." So Urevich began writing a letter of protest that she and Glantz would distribute. Meanwhile he continued filing stories for *PNN*. To his dismay, the Independent Media Center voted to expel him. Then former *PNN* reporter Jeremy Scahill, also at the protests, confronted Glantz and shouted at him. Next he got a call from WBAI reporter Eileen Sutton, "who I didn't even know, and she yelled at me."[67]

When Glantz returned to Berkeley, he noticed something that he considered odd. *PNN* now showed an interest in just about any story on which he was working, including stories that even Glantz considered marginal. He concluded that *PNN* was running short of reporters. "It became clear that it wasn't just people who were yelling at me who were boycotting Pacifica," he recalled. Soon Sutton, Urevich, and KPFA reporter Vanessa Tait formed an organizing committee for Pacifica Reporters Against Censorship. Glantz joined the cause.[68]

The group held a press conference in front of KPFA on January 24, 2000. They announced that dozens of reporters had signed a document protesting the widespread censorship throughout the network of programs on the Pacifica crisis. Their statement cited 14 acts of tampering with stories, drowning them out with music, cutting them out of newscasts, or somehow punishing their producers. "It is clear that censorship at Pacifica is becoming a way of life," the text declared. Unless that censorship ended, the undersigned would stop filing stories with *PNN* for the next three months.[69]

A few weeks earlier reporters at KPFA might have been able to walk next door and hand the document to Lynn Chadwick. But by then Chadwick had relocated to Washington, D.C., and would soon move the entire Pacifica national office, with all its files, equipment, and furniture, to the nation's capital. "Last summer there was a 10,000-person free-speech march against Pacifica in Berkeley," Chadwick joked with a reporter from Current. "Here in the District of Columbia, WPFW has been relatively unbothered. Do the math." She also told the reporter that she had hired George Strait, 22 years an ABC correspondent, to reorganize Pacifica's national program-ming.[70] To solidify her relationship with the city of Berkeley, Chadwick requested Mayor Shirley Dean to authorize the city to pay for Pacifica's security costs, "due to the inability or unwillingness of the Berkeley Police Department to provide adequate protection." The demand enraged Dash Butler, Berkeley's chief of police. Chadwick's crackdown on KPFA had cost the police department $200,000 in overtime pay. "This occurred in spite of our advice to their management," Butler wrote in a public letter. "How ironic that after ignoring [police] advice and deciding to make so many arrests, they have NOW decided that they do not wish to follow through with the prosecution of those arrested. . . . Lynn Chadwick and the rest of Pacifica Foundation should pull out an appropriate sized mirror and take a good look at the real culprits – those who made their decisions during the dispute."[71]

PNN's Mark Bevis issued a public statement in response to the stringers' strike similar to the legalistic claim that Pacifica had not fired Nicole Sawaya. The action wasn't a strike, he told *Current* magazine. It was a boycott. Pacifica would not recognize it. "PNN is unionized, and its bargaining unit represented by AFTRA," Bevis explained, and rebuked charges of censorship. "Every news organi-zation decides what to publish or broadcast; that is called news judgment."[72] While Bevis turned strikes into boycotts and what many saw as censorship into news judgment, the Pacifica national board met and considered a three-page memorandum, "The Pacifica State," by audience research analyst David Giovannoni. Over 800,000 people tuned in to Pacifica radio each week, Giovanonni began. "But roughly 40,000,000 people live under a Pacifica signal. For most Americans, Pacifica simply does not exist." The organization had lost its influence. "It is a faded reflection of its proud history," the consultant continued. "At one time, we could say that Pacifica was simply 'under-performing.' The time for polite euphemism is over. By any objective measure of public service, Pacifica has crossed the line from 'under-performance' to 'irrele-vance.'"[73]

Giovannoni's statement went on to make various vague recommendations for the network. Pacifica management put the document on its Web site beneath a colorful banner headline, "Pacifica Foundation Announces a Transition." Now when potential donors went to www.pacifica.org, they learned that the organization had become irrelevant.[74] Clearly, Chadwick and Berry still needed help with public relations. Once again, someone volunteered to save the show.

Stop the Pacifica Bashing!

Saul Landau had been associated with Pacifica for years. In 1962 as a student activist he defended the Cuban revolution on a KPFA panel with Stanford economist Paul Baran and public opinion expert Richard Brody. The rabidly anti-Communist Senate Internal Security Subcommittee, about to subpoena Pacifica board members to Washington, D.C., demanded a copy of the program.[75] From this point of departure Landau went on to a remarkable career as a writer and filmmaker. His work won most major awards for documentaries, including an Emmy for "Paul Jacobs and the Nuclear Gang," the poignant story of one research scientist's attempts to uncover government suppression of radiation hazards in Utah and Arizona.[76]

Perhaps the most dramatic episode in Landau's career came in 1976, when agents of Chilean dictator Augusto Pinochet assassinated Landau's close friend Orlando Letelier in Washington, D.C. Letelier had served as ambassador to the United States under the socialist government of Salvadore Allende. Outraged, Landau spent years tracking down the murderers. His research, included in a Pacifica radio documentary, helped bring them to justice. In 1980 he and an associate published their findings in *Assassination on Embassy Row*.[77]

Pacifica stations often offered Landau's recorded talks on Latin American revolutions as premiums during Pacifica radio fundraising marathons. His film documentaries on Cuba, such as *The Uncompromising Revolution*, packed repertory movie houses.[78] In the late 1990s he became a regular commentator for *PNN*, turning his offerings into a popular anthology of essays, *Red Hot Radio: Sex, Violence, and Politics at the End of the American Century.*[79] It is safe to say that by then Saul Landau had become one of the heroes of the Pacifica radio network. All that changed in one month.

In early February, Pacifica activists discovered that Landau was circulating a petition among prominent progressives asking for the Free Pacifica movement to stand down. It is likely that one of the people to whom he sent the petition forwarded it to dissidents. In any event, they got it and quickly emailed it everywhere. Apparently someone had asked Landau to join the stringers' strike and he was upset. "I am horrified at the new wave of Pacifica bashing," Landau wrote to potential petition signers, "this time by a group of people who allegedly produce the news show and demand of me and others to stop offering our commentaries and reports on the air." Landau claimed that most of the strikers did not produce anything for *PNN*. "This is a first in labor history, where 'strikers' who don't belong to a union, strike against union members" – the union members being *PNN's* salaried employees.

With that came Landau's statement, "An Appeal to All Progressives! Stop the Pacifica Bashing!" The text urged an end to "[t]he continuation of what has become a veritable war against Pacifica [that] could lead to the death of the only alternative radio network progressives possess. This would be tragic." Then the statement denounced the *PNN* stringers' "boycott":

> We call for an immediate end to such tactics. There is, indeed, no sanctioned strike or authorized labor dispute underway at Pacifica National News. Some of those urging the boycott have differences with Pacifica news management. That is their right. But they do not have the right to cloak their factional grievances in the language of a bona fide labor dispute.

> Boycotts, defunding campaigns and negative public relations strategies are powerful tools that can be used against recalcitrant and abusive corporate employers. To turn them against Pacifica is unconscionable. The only victims of such actions are the listeners, many of whom are activists who need information, analysis and

debate from radio to help nourish their world views. While the inner workings and conflicts of Pacifica might be of some interest to some of these listeners, the chief mission of Pacifica is to bring much bigger and universal issues to its audience.

Sadly, the amount of time spent this past year bashing Pacifica, we calculate, was subtracted from the time available to fight against racism, sexism, exploitation, injustice, inequality, environmental contamination, corporate capitalism and imperialism.[80]

Landau's statement conceded that Pacifica had made "mistakes." But so had the dissidents. "Surely, Pacifica's shortcomings should be seen as such: shortcomings and mistakes, not betrayals and conspiracies." It was time for everyone "to reunite as a Pacifica family and seek greater cooperation."[81] Forty-three prominent scholars and activists signed the document, from sociologist Frances Fox Piven to actor Ed Asner. Two of Landau's colleagues at the Institute for Policy Studies in Washington, D.C., endorsed the text. So did Barbara Ehrenreich and Jerry Brown, who, just three months earlier, had both signed a statement demanding that Mary Frances Berry resign.

Most people in the organization immediately recognized the appeal for what it was – a partisan statement couched in the language of reconciliation. Landau's petition made no specific demands on Pacifica management, only on the opposition. The statement legalistically insisted that because *PNN's* stringers did not belong to a "bona fide" union, they could not be on strike (since when did workers have to belong to a union to go on strike?). And it incorrectly claimed that few of the stringers had anything to do with *PNN's* broadcast. Shortly after the appeal came out, the stringers tabulated a detailed chart of the stories they had contributed to *PNN*. Twenty-two reporters who had filed stories for *PNN* since July of 1999 were now on strike against the service.[82]

A wave of indignation traveled across the Internet to Landau. Economist Ed Herman led the charge. "One revealing feature of your letter that shows its apologetic quality is its reference to 'Pacifica bashing' without recognition of the fact that there are two Pacificas," he wrote:

One comprises the long-time employees, volunteers, and devoted audiences who have gotten out into the streets by the thousands, petitioned the management for more local control and democratization and against the censorship, firings, and program alterations imposed from above. . . . A second Pacifica is the management and policies of the Scott-Chadwick-Berry regime, which has moved to Washington, D.C., away from its bothersome listener audience and closer to the power brokers that constitute the key element in its evolving constituency. This is obviously what you mean by "Pacifica.".[83]

Fifty progressives signed a public counter-petition against Landau's call for a truce. "If this 'Appeal' were written a couple of years ago, when criticism of the network's leadership seemed more alarmist and exaggerated, it might have been defensible," they wrote. "This is not the time for a moratorium, but for well-calibrated action aimed at changing the current leadership before more damage is done."[84] Pacifica's leadership, too, knew a gesture of support when they saw one. Mary Frances Berry repeatedly praised Landau's efforts at the next Pacifica board meeting.[85]

In fairness to Landau, it must be acknowledged that his statement resonated with the enormous frustration and confusion progressives felt over Pacifica's worsening civil war. Many of them found it incomprehensible. Was it ever going to end? they wondered. Landau spent the weeks after his petition surfaced trying to resolve his own crisis within a crisis. He talked to dissidents from Berkeley. "I keep asking, what is the strategy?" he told a reporter from *Mother Jones*. "How are we going to get past this? And I hear accusations: They did this, and they did that. I say that may be so, but what's the strategy to move on?"[86]

It was not surprising that Landau could not find the answer he wanted. Doubtless the people of whom he asked his question gave him a wide assortment of replies. By now there were an untrackable number of protest groups throughout the Pacifica organization: The Pacifica Listeners Union, North Bay for KPFA, Center for a Democratic Pacifica (New York and Berkeley chapters), Radio4Houston, and the Pacifica Accountability Committee, to name a few. North Bay for KPFA in Sebastopol could have started its own radio station, given its membership of 400 activists whose matrix of affinity groups organized constant Save Pacifica demonstrations, town hall meetings, and financial support for Carol Spooner's lawsuit.[87] Landau apparently could not hear the theme upon which all these dissidents played striking variations: they knew that they had been shut out of the governance of the only broadcasting organization they felt they had, and that it was morphing into something that frightened them, something that had moved to Washington, D.C., talked about selling radio stations, and hired ABC correspondents to reorganize national programming. There was only one remedy: the overthrow of the present board and establishment of something that had never before existed, a listener-subscriber-elected network. That, not dialogue, was their exit strategy. The democracy narrative and the relevance narrative were talking past each other. If the first could not explain its vision in one coherent voice, the second could not explain how its ends could morally survive Pacifica's coercive means.

In August of 1999, Marc Cooper gave the rhetoric of moral ownership one more try. "Back in the early '70s, when I worked as a translator for Chilean President Salvador Allende, and his democratic socialist government was under fierce attack from an outraged right wing," Cooper wrote in the *LA Weekly*, "there was one slogan that became a favorite. In the last days before the 1973 military coup, when Allende supporters would rally in the streets to defend him, their banners read: 'This Government Is Full of Shit. But It Is Our Government.' That's pretty much how I feel today about embattled Pacifica Radio, on whose local affiliate KPFK I host two programs: The organization is full of shit, but it's our organization."[88]

The thousands of people who signed Carol Spooner's lawsuit declaration no longer trusted such analogies. The Chilean people voted for Allende, but Pacifica's listener-subscribers and staff did not vote for Lynn Chadwick. They knew now that the rhetoric of moral ownership was nothing more than sweet talk. Pacifica radio was not their organization – yet.

Endnotes

1   Michael Moore, "A Letter," *San Francisco Bay Guardian* (August 2, 1999): www.superlists.com/kpfa/moore.html.
2   David Adelson, interview with author (December 27, 2002), p.3.
3   Ibid., p.26.
4   *David Adelson et al. vs. Pacifica*, In the Superior Court of the State of California, Docket No. 814461-0, Preliminary Statement (November 8, 1999), First Claim for Relief, pp.45-47.
5   See *David Adelson et al. v. Pacifica Foundation*, Case No.: 814461-0 (Alameda Co. Superior Ct.); David Adelson, interview with author (December 27, 2002), p.30; recollection of author.
6   Carol Spooner, interview with author (December 1, 2002), pp.3-5.
7   Committee to Remove the Pacifica Board, "For Immediate Release," press release, July 26, 1999.
8   "NOTICE [TO] KPFA LISTENER SUPPORTERS. YOU MAY HAVE LEGAL RIGHTS!" no date: home.pon.net/wildrose/kpfanotice.htm.
9   Carol Spooner, interview with author (December 1, 2002), pp.12, 14.
10 Ibid., pp.5-7.
11 Charles Burress, "Lawmakers to Investigate KPFA Dispute, Audit to Focus on Pacifica's Actions," *San Francisco Chronicle* (August 5, 1999), p.A-18.
12 Joint Legislative Audit Committee [California], "The Pacifica Foundation and the Crisis at KPFA Listener Sponsored Radio-Report of the Joint Legislative Audit Committee," (Oakland, California, August 20, 1999), p.15.
13 "To: Bill Lockyer, California Attorney General, RE: Spooner et al. vs. Pacifica Foundation, Application for Leave to Sue in Quo Warranto" (no date): home.pon.net/wildrose/agpetition.htm.
14 Carol Spooner, interview with author (December 1, 2002), pp.6-7; "Chronology of a Crisis": www.ominous-valve.com/pac/pacific2.html.
15 KPFA listeners could hear the author's voice in one of those carts, exhorting the subscribers to run and vote.
16 Adrienne Rich, Alice Walker, et al., "An Open Letter to the Board of the Pacifica Foundation and Mary Frances Berry, Chair," *The New York Times* (August 18, 1999): www.radio4all.org/fp/nytimesad.gif.
17 Robert McChesney, *Telecommunications, Mass Media, and Democracy: The Battle for Control of U.S. Broadcasting, 1928-1935* (New York: Oxford University Press, 1994); Edward S. Herman and Noam Chomsky, *Manufacturing Consent: The Political Economy of the Mass Media* (New York: Pantheon Books, 1988); Ben H. Bagdikian, *The Media Monopoly* (Beacon Press, 2000).
18 James Fallows, *Breaking the News: How the Media Undermine American Democracy* (Vintage Books, 1997); Dean Alger, *Megamedia: How Giant Corporations Dominate Mass Media, Distort Competition, and Endanger Democracy*

(Rowman and Littlefield, 1998); David McGowan, *Derailing Democracy: The America the Media Don't Want You to See* (Common Courage Press, 2000).

19 Norman Solomon, *The Habits of Highly Deceptive Media: Decoding Spin and Lies in Mainstream News* (Common Courage Press, 1999); Danny Schechter, *News Dissector* (Akashic Books, 2001).

20 See, on FAIR's Web site, www.fair.org/whats-fair.html#mission and www.fair.org/extra/writers/cohen.html.

21 Jesse Walker, *Rebels in the Air: An Alternative History of Radio in America* (New York: New York University Press, 2001), pp.209-18.

22 Gene Hyde, "Independent Media Centers: Cyber-Subversion and the Alternative Press," *FirstMonday: Peer Reviewed Journal of the Internet*, vol. 7, no. 4 (2002): www.firstmonday.org/issues/issue7_4/hyde/index.html.

23 "IndyMedia Frequently Asked Questions": http://process.indymedia.org/faq.php3.

24 John Whiting, "Pacifica in Vincula" (January 1996): www.radio4all.org/fp/vincula.htm.

25 Ibid.

26 Ibid.

27 Jesse Walker, "With Friends Like These: Why Community Radio Doesn't Need the Corporation for Public Broadcasting" (July 24, 1977, Cato Policy Analysis No. 277): www.cato.org/pubs/pas/pa-277.html.

28 Ibid.

29 Norman Solomon, "'For Sale' signs" (July 29, 1999): www.sfbg.com/kpfa/sale.html.

30 Robert McChesney, interview with David Barsamian, "Media Matters: Monopolies, Pacifica, NPR & PBS" (Boulder, Colorado, November 10-11, 1999): www.radio4all.org/fp/122199mcches-barsam.htm.

31 Ibid.

32 Adrienne Rich, Alice Walker, et al., "An Open Letter to the Board of the Pacifica Foundation and Mary Frances Berry, Chair," *The New York Times* (August 18, 1999): www.radio4all.org/fp/nytimesad.gif.

33 Pete Bramson, interview with author (August 23, 2002), p.12.

34 Bramson, interview with author (August 23, 2002), pp.15-16.

35 Marc Cooper, "Whose Pacifica?" *The Nation* (May 10, 2003): www.thenation.com/doc.mhtml?i=19990510&s=cooper.

36 Ibid.

37 Ibid.

38 Marc Cooper, "Get Real: Listeners Like the New Network, Not the Old One," *LA Weekly* (August 13-19, 1999): www.laweekly.com/ink/99/38/features-cooper.php; Marc Cooper, "What's Mumia Got to Do with It" (February 9, 2000): www.motherjones.com/reality_check/mumia.html.

39 Marc Cooper, "Liberals Stuck in Scold Mode" (October 14, 2001): www.commondreams.org/views01/1014-02.htm.

40 Paz Cohen, "To All News Department Volunteers, 1977," cited in Jno Arquette Degraff, "Radio, Money, and Politics: The Struggle to Establish WPFW-FM, the Pacifica Foundation's Black-Oriented Washington Station" (Ph.D. dissertation, University of Maryland, College Park: 1995), p.113.

41 Marc Cooper, "Pacifica on the Brink" (July 22, 1999): www.thenation.com/doc.mhtml?i=19990809&s=cooper.

42 Marc Cooper, "Get Real."

43 Michael Palmer, quoted in "Freedom's Just Another Word," *The Texas Observer* (August 6, 1999): www.texasobserver.org/showArticle.asp?ArticleID=316.

44 Mary Frances Berry, "KPFA Report to the Listeners w/Mary Frances Berry and Lynn Chadwick," audio cassette (May 5, 1999).

45 See www.imru.org/what.html for the history of IMRU; KPFK Spring 2001 broadcasting schedule (4/4/01). As a frequent listener to KPFK in 2000, I would never have guessed that Beaupre was a winner of the Ruben Salazar award from the California Chicano News Media Association: see "About Jon Beaupre," *Broadcast Voice*: firstbomb.com/bv/jon.htm.

46 Alexander Cockburn, "Pricks Up Your Ears" (July 22, 1999): www.counter-punch.org/pricks.html.

47 Robert McChesney, "From Pacifica to the Atlantic," *The Nation* (October 11, 1999): www.thenation.com/doc.mhtml?i=19991011&s=mcchesney.

48 Judith Coburn, "There's Something About Mary," *Salon* (October 12, 1999): www.salon.com/news/feature/1999/10/12/berry/index2.html.

49 Marc Cooper, "The Pacifica Struggle Continues," *The Nation* (August 19, 1999): www.thenation.com/doc.mhtml?i=19990906&s=exchange.

50 Press release, "16 Radio Stations to Boycott Pacifica Network Programming on October 27" (October 26, 1999): www.radio4all.org/fp/102799boycott.htm; "A Day Without Pacifica," recollection of author.

51 Norman Stockwell, letter to Lynn Chadwick, November 18, 1999.

52 Dan Coughlin, interview with author (November 7, 2002), pp.1-4.

53 Dan Coughlin, interview with author (November 7, 2002), p.5; Pat Scott, interview with author (January 31, 2003), p.21; Amy Goodman, interview with author (August 15, 2003), p.18.

54 Ella Taylor, "Family Feud: The Left Eats Its Own at KPFK" (March 22-28, 2002): www.laweekly.com/printme.php3?@eid=33358.

55 "Debate on Zimbabwe," *Democracy Now!* (April 25, 2000): www.democracynow.org/article.pl?sid=03/04/07/0230232&mode=thread&tid=5; "The Green Threat? Debate Between Toby Moffett and Barbara Ehrenreich on the Nader Candidacy," *Democracy Now!* (October 6,

2000): www.democracynow.org/article.pl?sid=03/04/07/0243246&mode= thread&tid=5.

56 Dan Coughlin, interview with author (November 7, 2002), p.7.

57 Ibid.

58 FAIR news release, "CounterSpin Once Again Censored by a Pacifica Station" (November 10, 1999): www.savepacifica.net/991110_press.html.

59 "Dan Coughlin's 10/27/99 Report re: Affiliates": www.savepacifica.net/991027_coughlin.html.

60 Dan Coughlin, interview with author (November 7, 2002), p.16.

61 Amy Goodman, Verna Avery Brown, et al., "To Pacifica Board Members, November 4, 1999" and "PACIFICA FOUNDATION NEWS RELEASE, For Immediate Release: November 3, 1999": www.savepacifica.net/19991110_coughlin.html.

62 "PACIFICA FOUNDATION NEWS RELEASE, For Immediate Release: November 3, 1999"; "Letter of Ralph Engelman to Pacifica Board Chair Mary Frances Berry and Other Board Members" (no date); letter from Nan Rubin, November 6, 1999, cited in "Response to Removal of Dan Coughlin as News Director at PNN": www.savepacifica.net/19991110_coughlin.html.

63 Amy Goodman, Verna Avery Brown, et al, "To Pacifica Board Members, November 4, 1999."

64 Steve Behrens, "Did Coughlin Lose His Job for Breaking the 'Dirty Laundry Rule'? Staffers Protest Pacifica Transfer of News Chief" (November 15, 1999): www.current.org/rad/rad921p.html.

65 Verna Avery Brown, interview with author (October 2002), p.13.

66 "Pacifica Network Crisis Spreads: Award-winning Journalist Is Banned from KPFK for Exercising Free Speech Rights," Online Journal (September 2, 1999): www.victorian.fortunecity.com/brambles/499/KPFA_Pacifica/Urevich/urevich. html. Apparently the piece angered Schubb because, despite his having asked not to be quoted, Urevich paraphrased his remarks for the article.

67 Aaron Glantz, interview with author (October 29, 2001), pp.2-3.

68 Ibid.

69 "Letter to Pacifica Management from Pacifica Reporters Against Censorship" (January 24, 2000): www.fsrn.org/letter_to_management.html.

70 Steve Behrens, "Pacifica Moves to D.C.; Anchor Leaves in Dispute," Current (January 24, 2000): www.current.org/rad/rad002p.htm.

71 Kellia Ramares, "Berkeley Police Chief Issues Stinging Rebuke of Chadwick and Pacifica," Online Journal (September 19, 1999): www.victorian.fortunecity.com/brambles/499/KPFA_Pacifica/PoliceChief/ policechief.html.

72 "Stringers Call Three-Month Strike Against Newscast" (February 7, 2000): www.current.org/rad/rad002p.html.

73 David Giovanoni, "The Pacifica State" (February 25, 2000), p.1.
74 See http://web.archive.org/web/20000304113855/http://www.pacifica.org/.
75 Saul Landau, Paul Baran, and Richard Brody, "Panel Discussion on Cuba, Moderated by Elsa Knight Thompson," audio tape (Los Angeles: Pacifica Radio Archives, 1962). For a detailed description of the battle Pacifica fought with the SISS, FBI, and FCC in 1962 and 1963 see Matthew Lasar, *Pacifica Radio: The Rise of an Alternative Network* (Philadelphia: Temple University Press, 2000), chap.10.
76 Saul Landau and Jack Willis, "Paul Jacobs and the Nuclear Gang," *Link TV*: www.worldlinktv.com/programming/programDescription.php4?tz=0&code =paul.
77 "Pacifica History: Highlights of Pacifica Radio's 50 Year History of Radio Broadcasting": www.pacificaradioarchives.org/learn/history.php, under 1976; John Dinges and Saul Landau, *Assassination on Embassy Row* (New York: Pantheon Books, 1980).
78 Saul Landau, *The Uncompromising Revolution*, video documentary (Cinema Guild, 1976).
79 Saul Landau, *Red Hot Radio: Sex, Violence, and Politics at the End of the American Century* (Monroe, ME: Common Courage Press, 1998).
80 Saul Landau et al., "An Appeal to All Progressives! Stop the Pacifica Bashing!" *MoJoWire Newswire* (February 2000): www.motherjones.com/news_wire/pacifica_letter.html.
81 Ibid.
82 Chart of stringer contributions to *PNN* since July of 1999, Free Speech Radio News spreadsheet document in possession of author.
83 Ed Herman, "Letter to Saul Landau" (February 22, 2000): www.fsrn.org/landau_herman.html.
84 "Progressives Respond to Saul Landau's Letter" (February 25, 2000): www.fsrn.org/landau_response2.html.
85 Mary Frances Berry in Pacifica Foundation Board of Directors Meeting, Volume II, February 27, 2000, p.171.
86 Pam Sqyres, "New Storm over Pacifica," *Mother Jones* (February 25, 2000): motherjones.com/news_wire/pacifica_letter.html.
87 Jim Curtis, "A Short and Biased History of North Bay for KPFA," unpublished manuscript, May 22, 2005.
88 Marc Cooper, "Get Real."

CHAPTER 7

Revolution, 2000-2001

The second worst thing that could possibly happen has happened. We won.

SHERRY GENDELMAN

As the spring of 2000 arrived, Pacifica's protestors saw a long, difficult road ahead of them. "It's like Pacifica's board of directors are the Israelis and we're the rock-throwing Palestinians," one prominent dissident confided to me in all seriousness at about this time.[1] But in fact this media Intifada had gained considerable ground. *The New York Times* no longer declared that Pacifica was "dancing towards the mainstream" or "ruffling left-wing feathers" in pursuit of progress. Instead, headlines chronicled a relentless stream of scandals and crises. Meanwhile, the network's governors and the growing dissident community played roles that would inevitably lead to the downfall of the former within a relatively short time. Pacifica's national management responded rigidly and punitively to all acts of defiance. In response, the Free Pacifica movement mobilized over every outrage, real or perceived. As the network's top brass continued to jettison people from the organization, they added to the critical mass of exiles ready and willing to rock the boat until its officers jumped out or sued for peace. At the same time, in their efforts to understand the Pacifica crisis the general public increasingly embraced the democracy narrative. As a result of these dynamics, by late 2002 the Pacifica network stood poised to become a truly democratic organization.

Hitting Foggy Bottom

Shaken by the events of the past year, both Lynn Chadwick and Mary Frances Berry disclosed at the February 2000 board meeting that they planned to leave the Pacifica organization. Berry announced that she would not remain for another three-year term. She also told board members that Chadwick would resign as executive director on March 1, to be replaced by Bessie Wash, former general manager of WPFW.[2]

But no one had any illusions that these departures would bring peace. The board majority – Berry's allies – set themselves to the task of replacing Berry and adding new board members. They ran roughshod over anything remotely resembling democratic procedure. The board had polarized over the crisis in Berkeley and Dan Coughlin's reassignment. Four members – two from Berkeley, one from Los Angeles, and another from Washington, D.C. – were now openly critical of Pacifica's actions. Several Berry allies had recently quit, one offering a parting shot at the board dissidents. "I am particularly concerned about the number of Governing Board members who seem confused about their roles and pressured by their fear of criticism from the great Northern California E-mail machine," June Makela wrote in a bitter resignation statement read at the meeting.[3]

Following Makela's screed, Berry moved quickly and aggressively to place her loyalists at the head of the organization. On February 27, board member and Berry ally Frank Millspaugh, a former WBAI manager, nominated David Acosta from Houston as chair of Pacifica, and Ken Ford as vice chair. It was Acosta whom Berkeley board member Pete Bramson said had proposed taking out a five-million-dollar loan on the sale of KPFA. Ford came from WPFW's local advisory board and was a staunch Berry supporter.

Tomas Moran, dissident board member from the San Francisco Bay Area, asked for a point of order. "I didn't know that there was an election happening today," Moran said.

"It says elections on the agenda," Berry replied.

"I thought it was elections of new Members of the new board," Moran explained.

"Does anybody else have any comments?" Berry asked, then called for a vote.

"We say no," someone in the audience cracked.

"Could we have order in the room please?" Berry demanded.[4]

A majority quickly elected Acosta and Ford. Berry moved on to board member nominations. There were five, she explained: Leslie Cagan and Beth Lyons from New York City, Bertram Lee and John Murdock from Washington, D.C., and Valerie Chambers from Houston.

Moran protested again.

"Madam chair, " he began, "the process to announce to everybody the fact that there are openings on the Board, the method for which nominations are received far and wide from a variety of sources, and the process for all board members to be notified in advance and to receive CVs and other material in advance and a report in advance from those who have maybe personally interviewed the candidates is essential in electing people to the Board."

In other words, none of this had taken place. Undaunted, Berry looked around the room. "Any other comments from anyone?" she asked. With that, the majority voted in five more members.[5]

The introduction of Bertram Lee and John Murdock disquieted even Pacifica's apologists. A former co-owner of the Denver Nuggets baseball team, Lee had a solid reputation as a reckless entrepreneur with a slew of burned bridges behind him. "His landlord is trying to evict him from his $4,750-a-month Foggy Bottom apartment for delinquent rent and bounced checks," began a 1999 profile on Lee in the *Washington Post*. "He acknowledges he's behind on child-support payments to his ex-wife. He is under court order to pay more than $100,000 to a former business partner, and he briefly filed for personal bankruptcy last year."[6] Even more disturbing was Lee's management of radio station WKYS in Washington, D.C., detailed in another *Washington Post* piece. NBC had transferred the station to Lee and several other investors under a federal program which gave tax breaks to corporations that sold broadcast media to minority owners. Since NBC stood to save about fifteen million dollars in taxes as a result of the sale, they also lent Lee's firm ten million dollars.[7]

That money quickly went up in smoke. The station's top on-air host took a job at another station, and WKYS's Arbitron ratings went into free-fall. In 1994 Lee sold WKYS for $8,500,000 less than the purchase price. Lee and another partner received $100,000 in cash each under agreements that barred them from working for any other black-oriented radio station in the Washington, D.C., area for two years.[8] Several months after Lee's appointment to the Pacifica board, the mayor of Washington, D.C., removed him from the board of the corporation that ran District of Columbia General Hospital. Auditors revealed that the hemorrhaging health-care institution had a cash deficit of $90,000,000. They recommended laying off almost 300 of its 2,000 employees and overhauling the hospital's top management.[9]

Attorney John Murdock presented prospects worrisome to Pacifica activists for different reasons. He had no trail of collapsed business deals, just a job with Epstein Becker and Green, a Washington, D.C., management law firm whose Web site boasted that its attorneys helped companies maintain a "union free workplace." Epstein represented management in every variety of employer bias case, from accusations of race or gender discrimination to charges of violating the Americans with Disabilities Act (ADA). In the realm of workplace safety, the outfit boasted that it defended managers against "complaints of retaliation and whistle-blowing violations filed with federal and state OSHA offices."[10] In short, Murdock worked for a company that worked for what the traditional Pacifica radio perspective clearly understood as the Bad Guys.

These appointments therefore immediately sent up widespread alarums. "Pacifica Foundation Poised to Add Controversial DC

Businessman Bertram Lee Sr. to Its Board of Directors," ran a press release from San Francisco's Media Alliance just before Lee's nomination.[11] His experience in buying and selling a radio station raised plenty of red flags. For the next year, references to the "union free workplace" Murdock's employer promised would become a staple of Free Pacifica literature. Pacificans across the country read the news of these appointments and scratched their heads. Why would Berry, they wondered, recruit such people to the governing board? Most arrived at two conclusions: to help Pacifica fight the lawsuits, and to facilitate selling a radio station.

The second conclusion was plausible, the first quickly confirmed. Soon Pacifica would hire Epstein Becker and Green to defend the foundation in court. But dissidents refused to see, much less acknowledge, that other factors doubtless also played a role in their recruitment. Both Lee and Murdock were African-American men with close ties to black philanthropy and the non-profit sector. Lee had a long record of progressive international and domestic activism. In the mid-1980s he organized Nelson Mandela's Democracy Now tour, in which the anti-apartheid leader traveled the U.S. raising money for voter registration in South Africa. Lee also helped run the Congressional Black Caucus Foundation and the Martin Luther King, Jr., Center for Nonviolent Change.[12] As an attorney for Epstein Becker and Green, Murdock did not bust unions or help employers discriminate against people in wheelchairs. He represented HMOs and rehabilitation centers that had gotten into trouble with Medicare or some other federal agency.[13] Clearly Murdock and Lee had joined Pacifica as part of the board majority that had supported the shutdown of KPFA in 1999. But the tendency of Pacifica's white activists to see these two individuals in entirely mono-dimensional terms exacerbated ethnic tensions already festering throughout the network, especially at WPFW. "Heterosexual Black males are an endangered species inside Pacifica," one former Pacifica staffer bitterly told Askia Muhammad for an article titled "Are Anti-Pacifica Radio Protesters Racists?"[14]

Murdock's and Lee's appointments had also been part of a

compromise. WBAI LAB members had strongly lobbied for the appointment of social activist Leslie Cagan to the board. At first Berry resisted, then WPFW representative Rob Robinson brokered a deal: Cagan for Murdock and Lee. Perhaps to appease the New York station staff, who had yet to stage a revolt against Pacifica, Berry went along.[15] In retrospect it seems she should have trusted her first instincts.

Two years after her appointment to Pacifica's board, Chris Hedges of *The New York Times* profiled Leslie Cagan, calling her "one of the grandes dames of the country's progressive movement." Cagan attended New York University in the late 1960s and did not drop out only because that would have made it "harder to organize on campus," as she told Hedges. After taking a degree in art history, she went on to run congressional campaigns and to manage a drive to normalize relations with Cuba. She also served as key organizer for the massive 1982 demonstration at the Second Session on Nuclear Disarmament at the United Nations.[16] As central to the American Left as anyone, Cagan had survived endless factional and ideological wars with her equilibrium and reputation intact. She was uniquely qualified to provide leadership in the worst crisis Pacifica's governing board ever faced.

That crisis quickly escalated after her arrival. Following Carol Spooner's class action lawsuit, two more governing board members sued the Pacifica Foundation in September. The action against the Pacifica board by Rob Robinson of WPFW and Rabbi Aaron Kriegel of KPFK listed a veritable encyclopedia of irregularities. The executive committee of the Pacifica board did not give notice of their meetings to other board members, the plaintiffs charged, nor did they produce minutes of their deliberations. Certain board members were allowed to stay on beyond their terms, depending on their loyalty to the board majority. The executive committee did not include other board members in deliberations over key staff hires. Robinson and Kriegel's lawsuit listed 98 factual allegations against Pacifica, many of them pointing to arbitrary actions taken by the board's chair, Mary Frances Berry.[17] Now Acosta and Ford faced three procedural lawsuits and the departure of the powerful figure holding their narrow majority together.

Sensing the tenuousness of their grip upon the organization, the Pacifica national board searched for legal exit strategies. Among various options, Pacifica's new executive director explored setting up a foundation in Washington, D.C., and merging the California corporation into it. But Pacifica's regular attorneys identified too many obstacles blocking the path of this legal maneuver. The merger would require the approval of California's attorney general, not likely since Carol Spooner's lawsuit had won relator status. The results of the lawsuits would attach themselves to the D.C. corporation anyway. And, of course, the move would raise more public suspicions. "[M]erging CA Pacifica into DC Pacifica could complicate the litigation and lead to accusations that Pacifica was trying to circumvent California requirements," the foundation's lawyers warned.[18]

In truth, there was no back door through which they could escape. Meanwhile, dissident forces began to reconstruct the organization even before winning control of the national board.

Let's Put on a Show!

As Berry's allies struggled to maintain their majority on the national board, KPFA's local advisory board began democratizing itself. Deliberations for creating a local board elected by paid staff, station volunteers, and listener-subscribers began at the start of the year 2000. The LAB authorized a plan in February. By August, two dozen candidates had obtained the requisite ten nomination signatures they needed from other KPFA listener-sponsors to run. The election was held in October and 2,500 people voted. The slate of democratically selected advisory board members were seated in November.[19]

The Pacifica board majority and staff watched this development with apprehension; the move obviously set an example for the rest of the organization. Key players could not agree on how to respond. Pacifica attorneys considered sending the KPFA LAB a "cease and desist" letter, then decided against it. Attorney John Crigler worried "about the PR fallout that could result from saying Pacifica's policies prohibit the use of democratic elections. That assertion can easily be used to support the conclusion that Pacifica is constitutionally undemocratic."[20] Some board members wanted to dismantle all of the network's current LABs and replace them with new appointees. Mark Schubb of KPFK supported this suggestion.[21] But even board member Michael Palmer, advocate of a station sale, saw some obvious problems with it. "[Q]ualified LAB replacements," he wrote in October, "would be hesitant to come join without recognized authority to perform as a LAB, and in the case of the Bay Area, some way of deflecting the harassment that would ultimately reach their doorsteps if they were to assume LAB membership."[22]

At the same time the network's striking stringers boldly moved beyond withholding their labor. On February 11, 2000, they broadcast the first edition of *Free Speech Radio News* (*FSRN*) at 3:30 p.m. on KPFA. Although the half-hour newscast only ran once a week at first, the fifteen affiliate stations that had staged "A Day Without Pacifica" quickly picked up the production. *FSRN* made that easy. In addition to uploading the broadcast onto the National Public Radio satellite, they turned each half-hour edition into digital audio and put it on their Web site, www.fsrn.org, for download. Stringers in Europe, India, and the Middle East began contributing stories. The edition of February 25 included a dispatch from Kosovo produced by former *PNN* stringer Sputnik Kalambi, news of a riot at California's Pelican Bay prison, and a report on the arrest of 50 University of Wisconsin students protesting sweatshop labor.

By March, twenty-two community radio stations ran the program. Almost 100 academics signed a petition supporting the strike and refusing to be interviewed by *Pacifica Network News*. California's Alameda County and Santa Cruz labor councils endorsed *FSRN*. In April the stringers voted to continue their action for another three months, but it was obvious that it had grown into something far more sophisticated than a walkout, and a lot more fun. "It really was like a kind of a Judy Garland, Mickey Rooney 'Let's Put on a Show' kind of thing," WBAI's Eileen Sutton recalled.

"I mean, it was that kind of 'Let's, let's just do this! We're going to do a strike cast!' You know, 'What does that mean? Who cares? Let's raise money. We're all reporters, so let's just do it.'"[23]

Amy Goodman constantly maneuvered through the crossfire between Pacifica's dissidents and its governors. Even *PNN* reporters who remained loyal to the news service worked under constant suspicion and interference from the Pacifica national office. "This causes *PNN* staff to spend time explaining this situation and reduces their productivity on the show," one Pacifica administrator complained. "We cannot tolerate Foundation Staff members preventing other Foundation Staff members from doing their job."[24] Pacifica management now demanded strict obedience from everyone, and especially from Goodman, whose relationship with the foundation had deteriorated after the reassignment of Dan Coughlin.

In search of an enforcer, Wash appointed as acting national program director the man who called the cops on KPFA. Garland Ganter did not hesitate to trust his punitive instincts regarding Goodman. On August 18, 2000, Goodman decided to liven up her coverage of the Republican National Convention in Philadelphia by inviting famed consumer advocate and Green Party presidential candidate Ralph Nader into the convention. To secure his entrance she gave Nader a press pass to the convention hall. Soon Nader was surrounded by reporters asking him questions, the impromptu press conference covered by *Democracy Now!*. Ganter was not impressed. Not only did he reprimand Goodman for the stunt, he revoked her press credentials.[25] Mary Frances Berry denounced Goodman's action at the next national board meeting and refused to support a resolution proposed by Leslie Cagan commending *Democracy Now!*.[26]

Matters only got worse when Pacifica hired a permanent national program director. Steven Yasko, former program operations manager for National Public Radio, took the position.[27] The sparks started flying almost immediately. The first issue was the demand that Goodman produce pieces for *PNN*. On Friday, September 8,

2000, Cuban president Fidel Castro came to New York City to address a United Nations conference. That day Castro also spoke for four hours at Manhattan's famous Riverside Church in Harlem, where Martin Luther King, Jr., had disclosed his opposition to the Vietnam war.[28] Tensions quickly flared across the network over whether Pacifica would broadcast the speech nationally and, if so, who would provide the coverage, WBAI or a reporter from *PNN*. Hovering over this flap were strong differences about the Castro regime. WBAI's Bernard White distrusted *PNN's* perspective on Cuba, calling its coverage "anti-Castro, anti-Leftist actually." By the time of the event, *PNN* had not obtained a press pass.[29] Yasko sent a communiqué to Goodman, who had already broadcast portions of the address on *Democracy Now!*: "You are instructed to provide a piece on the Castro speech for the Tuesday, September 12, 2000 broadcast of *PNN*," he demanded in an email message. "This is non negotiable and the piece is to be here per instructions..." Yasko sent the email at 2:30 in the afternoon on Monday, September 11. Goodman replied twelve hours later. "It's 2:30 am," she began. "The problem is I have to be back at 6am to prepare for the morning show DN and I haven't finished the *Pacifica Evening News* piece yet. This morning (mon) I came in at 5:30 to prepare the Castro show for today's (monday's) DN," She was exhausted, Goodman explained, and wanted to go home soon. "You said if I don't get the piece in for the evening news, you will consider it insubordination. What do you suggest? Amy."[30]

It went downhill from there. When on October 4 Goodman complained to Yasko about Pacifica's increasingly dysfunctional satellite system, the former apparently lost his temper. Dan Coughlin, still on salary in some indeterminate position, overheard the speakerphone fight and sent an email of protest. "Steve, I was appalled to hear you shouting at Amy during your conversation with her this afternoon," he wrote in a message cc'ed to Bessie Wash. "What kind of behavior is this?? Your aggressive manner, ugly tone, and yelling was shocking and upsetting for those of us in the *Democracy Now!* office." Coughlin characterized the exchange as "just the latest in a series of abusive actions by you against Amy. . . . I have advised Amy NOT to talk with you any more until the matter of your ugly and unprofessional behavior is resolved."[31]

The next day Yasko sent a message to Pacifica executive director Wash. "Dan really shouldn't piss me off," Yasko's email began.

I'm going up tomorrow to give Amy her letter, pending final review with Larry [probably Pacifica personnel lawyer Larry Drapkin]. But first I'm going to confuse her by seeing Dan first.

Ken is going to call Dan today and tell him that he is entitled to 48 days of severance and three weeks of notice (he started in 96, I checked with Lucy on the dates) and that is a good deal given the fact that everyone is unclear about weather [*sic*] he is in or out of the bargaining unit. . . .

If Dan doesn't agree. I will tell him I've changed my name to Monty Hall and maybe he shouldn't risk finding out what is behind door number 2. I'll just let him know I've been reading the union agreement about our obligations. . . .

Then I'll sneak out of the station, go have *2* glasses of wine and waltz my butt in for round two with Amy.

If you don't agree, let me know. I hope I made this entertaining enough that it made you feel better. Don't stress on this. I know I have your backing and I just want to get specifics on you for documentation. Don't call or write back unless there are significant things I don't know about that would affect this.

You stay home. Lights out. All Phones turned off. All radio turned off. Turn on Queen Latifah, Rosie and Oprah, open up a Martel and relax.[32]

Shortly after that, Amy Goodman got Yasko's letter, at which point she decided that she had had enough. On October 18 Goodman composed a public reply to Pacifica's memorandum, which she then sent to the Institute for Public Accuracy, a progressive media watchdog group in Washington, D.C. IPA's Sam Husseini distributed the response over the Internet. *Democracy Now!* was,

Goodman charged, being "subjected to a withering assault by Pacifica management. The motivation is blatantly political. *Democracy Now!* is a hard[-]hitting grassroots program that is not afraid of tackling controversial issues day after day in the Pacifica tradition."[33] Goodman accused Pacifica of trying to censor her for her critical coverage of the Democratic Party and for "giving voice to a growing grassroots movement that fundamentally challenges the status-quo. "On September 14, Goodman disclosed, Yasko had summoned her to a Pacifica general managers meeting. "KPFK Manager Mark Schubb expressed his repeated criticism that audiences don't want to hear graphic details of police brutality before breakfast," her memo continued, "or as he said last year 'before I have my coffee.' He criticized our coverage of Mumia Abu-Jamal, East Timor and questioned why I asked Spike Lee about his affiliation with Nike. Pacifica's Chief Financial Officer weighed in with her criticism of American prisoner Lori Berenson in Peru (we had just aired an exclusive interview with her that received widespread national press.) After the meeting, Yasko took me into the hotel lobby and shouted, 'I am your boss! I am your boss!'"

Yasko had placed onerous demands on *Democracy Now!*, the statement charged. These included regularly providing his office with a list of possible shows for the coming week, three clearly determined in advance. Yasko also wanted to impose two producers of his choice on the program, Goodman claimed, and to prohibit *Democracy Now!* from using volunteers. In addition, Pacifica now insisted that she clear all speaking engagements in advance with foundation officials, "an outrageous intrusion into my personal life and an illegal attempt to control my right of free speech." Goodman appealed to the Pacifica community to demand that Yasko "cease his harassment and retaliation" against her. "We are not NPR. We are not US government media. We are not the corporate media," she concluded. "We are *Democracy Now!* The Exception to the Rulers."[34]

Frank Ahrens, media reporter for the *Washington Post*, included an item about the flap in his regular column for October 31. He wrote skeptically of Goodman's claims, especially her insistence that she could not book guests a week in advance. "That, at least, seems like a reasonable rule," Ahrens wrote, and wondered why Goodman had not provided the public with a full copy of the letter that she denounced. On the other hand, the reporter got Yasko to admit that he had indeed shouted at Goodman that he was her boss.[35] He may as well have used a megaphone for all the good it would have done. Pacifica's latest national program director had no real authority over the woman who had become the voice of Pacifica radio. Yasko and Wash needed Goodman much more than she needed them. As long as they peacefully coexisted with the program, they could refute the charge that Pacifica wanted to trim the network's radical sails. Now that last ideological lifeboat was sinking fast, cheerfully escorted into the deep by prestigious dissidents like Ed Herman. Pacifica board apologists cited *Democracy Now!'s* "continued presence as showing the management's acceptance of a leftist and left news program," observed Herman in an article for Z magazine. Where were their voices now that she was under attack? he asked. Saul Landau's silence and that of "the Landau statement signers at the Institute for Policy Studies and *The Nation* is striking."[36]

Goodman's troubles also created new dissidents. Even after the Battle of Berkeley, media critic Danny Schechter accused Pacifica activists of myopia. Now he sounded like a member of Take Back KPFA, praising *Democracy Now!* in an editorial for his Web magazine *MediaChannel.* "If you have ever heard it, and want to save it, then it's time to speak out," Schechter concluded. The piece concluded by offering readers the email addresses of prominent Pacifica board members.[37]

But the Yasko fight had its most serious impact on WBAI, where Goodman and her staff produced *Democracy Now!*. Even before her disclosures the station had stood at the brink of a meltdown.

It's Just Me

In the autumn of 2000, relations between the senior staff of WBAI and Pacifica went from bad to worse. First came the tussle over the Castro speech, then a brief firefight over WBAI's coverage of a

Palestinian Right-of-Return rally staged in Washington, D.C. Five days after Castro's appearance, a contingent of activists marched on the nation's capital demanding the right of Palestinian refugees to repatriate to all areas of Israel from which they had been displaced. WBAI producer Barbara Nimri Aziz hosted the September 16 event from the station's studios, while on-the-scene reporters interviewed demonstrators from D.C.[38]

Bernard White had flown to San Diego to attend a community radio conference during the broadcast. According to White, Steve Yasko, also at the gathering, confronted him shortly after the program, demanding to know whether WBAI had received any money to broadcast the Palestinian rally. No, White replied. During the course of the conversation Yasko disclosed that someone from the Corporation for Public Broadcasting had complained about the coverage. Later that night White also received a call from Bessie Wash. She requested a report on the event and WBAI's coverage of it. White refused, insisting that he answered directly to WBAI general manager Valerie Van Isler.[39] According to Van Isler, Wash then called her and demanded a written statement. Van Isler complied, but relations between Pacifica and WBAI management, already damaged by the Castro speech fight, continued to sour.[40]

Once Goodman had gone public about her conflicts with Yasko, her colleagues Van Isler and White rallied to her defense. But not everyone at WBAI shared their sympathies. In contrast to KPFA, where relative comity existed among staff, serious rivalries plagued the internal life of Pacifica's New York frequency, exacerbated by the process by which Van Isler had chosen the station's latest program director.

On March 23, 1999, the Pacifica community had learned that Samori Marksman had died of a heart attack in his sleep. He was 51 years old. The Cuban government sent its regrets. Upon receiving the news, Janet Jagan, president of Guyana, ordered her cabinet meeting to recess. Nine days later, 3,000 people mourned Marksman's untimely passing at the Cathedral of St. John the Divine. The station produced a three-hour memorial for him.[41] But over these impressive ceremonies loomed an obvious and difficult question. Who would fill Samori Marksman's shoes? Van Isler had kept out of programming decisions for the most part, leaving them to her now deceased colleague. Marksman's replacement would obviously wield a great deal of power at the station.[42]

To deal with the task, WBAI formed a hiring committee of 11 people – paid and unpaid staff, management, and representatives from the Pacifica governing board and WBAI's local advisory board. They announced the position, collected about 30 resumes, and quickly narrowed the search down to a handful of candidates, prominent among them Laura Flanders, host of FAIR's program *CounterSpin*, Bernard White, now serving as interim program director, and afternoon WBAI talk show host Utrice Leid.[43]

A native of Trinidad, Leid arrived at WBAI every weekday with "a big booming voice and big earrings of silver and onyx that match the heavy ring on her finger," as a reporter described her. She was 45 when she applied for the job. In recent years she had worked as a receptionist for the *Amsterdam News* in Harlem, started her own black-oriented news service, then served as managing editor for *The City Sun*, a black-owned newspaper in Brooklyn. Leid had been at WBAI since 1993.[44] Her drive-time show *TalkBack!* had a large following, and she made no secret of her ambitions. "I look forward to being tested," Leid boasted in an interview. "In every moment that I've been tested, I've found that I've been equal or even superior to the task."[45]

By the late 1990s a subtle rivalry had set in between Leid and Bernard White that had its roots in a difference in political style. The New York journalist Jim Sleeper portrays black Harlem and black Brooklyn in the 1980s and 1990s as regional competitors – the former community more often seeking coalitions with progressive whites, the latter favoring go-it-alone strategies exemplified by Leid's *City Sun*. At WBAI, White and Leid tended to parallel that division. White worked closely with Amy Goodman to bring a wide variety of voices to WBAI's morning air. In contrast, Leid borrowed from the station's free-form tradition; her afternoon show *TalkBack!*

tended to function more as a launching pad for her own opinions. They, in turn, reflected the *City Sun's* editorial page, which brought "aggressiveness to the coverage of politics and racial issues," as one study of New York race relations politely put it, "that had long been missing from the *Amsterdam News*" of Harlem.[46]

The WBAI program director hiring committee interviewed all three candidates. After meeting with White they rejected his application. Then the committee interviewed Flanders and Leid. Finally they decided, by six to four with one abstention, to recommend Leid for the position. Van Isler took the matter under advisement. Months later, to almost everyone's dismay, she hired Bernard White for the job. The decision astonished even LAB member Miguel Maldonado, White's only supporter on the hiring committee. "I couldn't believe it," he later recalled.[47] But Van Isler remained adamant. "A general manager does not have to accept every recommendation," she later insisted, "and has the authority and the responsibility to review the recommendations and act on them or not act on them."[48]

Van Isler's decision to buck the recommendation of her own hiring committee compromised her already shaky tenure at WBAI. Although she had strong backers at the station, she also had plenty of detractors. Staff member Paul DeRienzo's impression of Van Isler was harsh, but not unique to him. "She was impenetrable as a personality; in fact it was as if she had no personality at all. In two decades I cannot remember seeing Valerie laugh or smile; she was totally humorless," he recalled. "Everybody knew she was in over her head and unable to manage WBAI, but her old-time radical friends on the Local Advisory Board (LAB) supported her anyway."[49] In fact, even some LAB members called for her removal. It appears that Van Isler maintained her authority at WBAI at least in part by leaving the premises as infrequently as possible. In a 1994 memorandum to David Salniker, Samori Marksman described Van Isler as "one of the most dedicated workers on this planet," but asked Pacifica to place her on mandatory three-month leave.[50]

Meanwhile Leid's fans raised hell over the decision to hire White, the chorus of protests led by black nationalist attorney Alton Maddox. This was not surprising. In the late 1980s Leid had championed one of Maddox's most controversial cases, that of Tawana Brawley, a black teenager whose family in 1987 charged four white police officers with raping and assaulting her. Ten years later, long after prominent journalists declared the campaign a hoax, Leid still defended Maddox, now facing charges of defamation that stemmed from the case.[51] In April of 2000, shortly after White's hiring as permanent program director, Maddox and Leid appeared at a community gathering to discuss the situation at WBAI. "We live in a morontocracy," Maddox declared in a long, rambling speech. "Morons rise to the top in our community. . . . And we try to present ourselves in a self-fulfilling prophecy of what white folks have said about us. And so it was not surprising to me that when the job of program director at WBAI came up, that the best and the brightest would not be chosen." Maddox called for a boycott of WBAI. Leid left it up to the audience. "If you wish to express your outrage . . . please feel free to do so," she declared. "I know for a fact that without black support the station would not survive. It hurts all the more that the general manager titularly is black, but these again are points of contradiction. Not everything black is beautiful."[52]

This was the situation that Van Isler faced as she came to work on November 28, 2000, for a meeting with Bessie Wash. WBAI's general manager expected a performance review. Instead Wash offered her a position in Washington, D.C., with the foundation. When Van Isler declined the job, Pacifica's executive director warned her that she had until the end of December to reconsider or be fired.[53] Van Isler's allies at WBAI, Bernard White prominent among them, immediately denounced her impending dismissal, insisting that it compromised the station's independence and credibility. The action damaged "all of the hard-earned goodwill and positive energy that we have built up with our listenership over the last several months," a memo from WBAI's "management team," protested, making ominous references to the KPFA crisis. "As a result of what took place in Berkeley, we began to lose membership (and income). Our listeners began to lose faith in Pacifica. It was the efforts of this management team that promised to repair that damage by renewing the trust that was lost through no fault of our own." Long-standing critics of Pacifica such as FAIR quickly equated WBAI's management shakedown with KPFA's. "Pacifica's latest move is reminiscent of the 1999 removal of general manager Nicole Sawaya from Pacifica's KPFA-Berkeley," FAIR declared in a press release.[54]

But the KPFA analogy only went so far. White, Van Isler, and their allies at WBAI were in a far more vulnerable position than the staff at their sister station in Berkeley. KPFA had been able to resist Lynn Chadwick's attempt to restructure the station in large part because the frequency's middle management remained solidly opposed to her intrusions even after Sawaya's ouster. But WBAI middle management was a shambles. Not only had the New York station's dominant personality, Samori Marksman, recently died, but so had WBAI's longtime operations director, Paul Wunder. Months after Van Isler's decision to make White permanent program director, key WBAI staff and local advisory board personnel were still furious about the move. So were WBAI's dissidents. By 2000 the listener-activist group Save Our Station had merged with KPFA's Center for a Democratic Pacifica (CDP) to create CDP-New York. Most CDP-New Yorkers distrusted White, to put it mildly. "During this year of crisis at Pacifica, Bernard's public comments on the National Board's actions have been curiously absent," declared a CDP-NY editorial written shortly after White's hire as program director. "This silence had the effect, if not the intent, [of making it] clear to Pacifica management that Mr. White would not rock the boat. Indeed, Mr. White has actively cooperated with the Pacifica National Board by his conspicuous silence on anything critical of his employers. This is in sharp contrast to others at WBAI, such as Utrice Leid of 'Talkback', or Paul DeRienzo and Joan Moossy of 'Let 'em Talk.'"[55]

On top of all this, WBAI suffered from an internal culture of race-baiting exemplified by Leid's crack about Van Isler's "titular" blackness. In short, the station must have appeared to the Pacifica national office as a veritable smorgasbord of opportunists ready to sell one another out. All Bessie Wash had to do was choose which to put on her plate, a task she appeared to have completed 48 hours before Christmas.

At 1:48 a.m. on Saturday, December 23, shortly before Bernard White and his colleagues had scheduled a teach-in on the crisis at the station, WBAI's night-owl audience heard the voice of Utrice Leid. "We interrupt this program," she began, laughing and joking with the hosts of the station's regularly scheduled music show. "I understand that you are getting a couple of calls and it is appropriate that we should break something on this show: 'This just in.' I want to say that there has been a change in management. I'm delighted to say that I've been named the interim station manager at WBAI. And I'm hoping that in the coming weeks as we face a tough hill to climb that we will find the energy and the mutual respect and all the good things that we can summon up within ourselves to meet the challenges ahead and will do that. In the meantime there is no coup. Just me. Just me. And we are doing some changes. Everything remains the same. All programs will continue as always. . . . No swat team is here. Nobody is being patted down. No metal detectors or anything like that. We're just making a change and we'll be ok.... No changes in programming," Leid reiterated. "No people need to worry about anything. There's nothing going to happen. It's just simply a change in administration."[56]

About five hours later, at 7 a.m., a ringing doorbell awakened Bernard White, the first person to learn that nothing was not going to happen. He rose to meet a messenger bearing two checks and a letter from Bessie Wash. He had been fired as WBAI's program director, the letter explained. If he showed up at the station he would be arrested. Another messenger brought the same news to Sharan Harper, executive producer of *Wake-Up Call*. The next day staff and volunteers went down to WBAI and discovered armed guards controlling studio access. The guards told several more staff to leave the premises. No SWAT team may have accompanied Leid to WBAI that night, but the guards did, as she changed the locks at the station's Wall Street offices.[57]

The Christmas Coup, as activists quickly dubbed Leid's takeover, showed that Pacifica had learned something since its awkward attempt to clobber KPFA in 1999. Pacifica's executive director and WBAI's new general manager cleverly picked the holiday season to make their move, a time when most station supporters were preoccupied with family matters. And it appears that Wash gave more thought than had Lynn Chadwick as to who would replace the woman she had ousted.

But Wash's strategy had one fatal flaw. Valerie Van Isler's successor did not seem to grasp that her new job as manager might mean she would have tone down her role as a talk-show host. Leid returned to her regular program, *TalkBack!*, on Monday, January 1, 2001. Callers immediately demanded an explanation for her actions. She was happy to comply, and at great length. Van Isler's, White's, and Harper's firings were necessary, Leid explained, because of the machinations of a "Svengali" at WBAI. "It is about an individual who is out of control, and has been for years at this station, and whose actions have now resulted in the termination of Bernard White and Sharan Harper," she declared, "I am saying that our problems started with one individual ... but no one for some reason has been able to confront that individual squarely and say, 'You are largely the reason we are in this mess.'"[58]

Everyone suspected, or thought that they knew, who the "you" was – Amy Goodman. With that announcement WBAI descended into bedlam, the rest of the network following shortly thereafter.

Another Part of Your Army?

By mid-January the freezing cold streets outside WBAI's Wall Street headquarters, just 100 feet from the East River, had become backdrop to an endless procession of demonstrations, impromptu meetings, and picket lines protesting Leid's coup. In the middle of the holiday season, over 1,000 WBAI supporters packed a union hall in lower Manhattan to strategize resistance to the takeover.[59] On

January 6, 2001, about 500 people rallied in front of the station with placards that read "Democratize WBAI! Rehire Fired Producers!" "Despotism Won't Fly at WBAI," and "Pacifica: No to the Climate of Fear at WBAI!"[60]

As the new year began, confrontations between the Leid administration and WBAI activists took place almost daily, the first sparked by the local advisory board's attempt to hold its next regularly scheduled meeting at the station. About 50 people showed up for the January 23 evening gathering. Leid refused to allow the board to assemble at WBAI if it opened the event to the public (which was the original point of local advisory boards). In response, about 20 board members, legal observers, reporters, and listeners rode up to the tenth floor of 120 Wall Street, home to the WBAI studios. There they found Leid standing at the entrance with security guards. A tense standoff ensued. LAB supporters began chanting, "Whose station? Our station!" Several women in wheelchairs got into an argument with WBAI's new general manager. About 20 police officers rushed to the scene and attempted to disperse the crowd, nine of whom refused to leave and were promptly arrested for trespassing.[61]

WBAI's travails for the next six months can be summarized as follows: by the late summer of 2001, Utrice Leid and her new management team had tanked just about everyone who either denounced the Christmas Coup over the station's airwaves or openly expressed any misgivings about her regime. "A purge of dissidents at listener-sponsored WBAI/99.5 FM appears to be almost complete," concluded a reporter for *New York Newsday* in early August. "24 staffers and volunteers, including the most vocal opponents of station management, have been fired or banned." WBAI programmer Bob Lederer's experience was typical. Station management banned him from the station on Monday, August 6. Leid then presented Kathy Davis, co-host of Lederer's show *Health Action*, with a set of boilerplate threats. "If the program in any way strays from its mission with the intent to inspire listeners to go against the will of current management, and if you as host do the same, the program will be cancelled and you will be off the air," directive number two read. "You will receive no further warning about this."[62]

Only one prominent on-air personality critical of the new regime had survived up to this point, and for her WBAI became a veritable gauntlet. In addition to hosting *Democracy Now!* Amy Goodman co-hosted *Wake-Up Call* with Bernard White. With the latter's ouster, Leid assigned her likely Svengali a new partner. African-American programmer Clayton Riley had a smooth voice and a quick temper that he kept in good practice on and off WBAI's airwaves. Race relations on *Wake-Up Call* slowly deteriorated for the next two weeks, bottoming out on February 6 after a set of very nasty on-air exchanges between Riley and listeners at around 7 a.m. One listener called for subscribers to boycott WBAI's next pledge marathon, instead putting the money in an escrow fund. "You mean a Jim Crow fund," Riley laughed, then lectured his audience. "This is typical of the kind of attitude that says 'You can tell me, because of who you are and who you view me to be.' You can make these kind of demands. It sort of sounds to me like somebody saying 'Boy! You tell me what I want to know. You know you smear Amy Goodman not too many years ago we would have had you swinging from a tree for talking to her like that.' That's what I'm hearing."[63]

After this exchange Amy Goodman came on to do the news. The two took more phone-ins, the next from a racist crank caller. "Nigger in the woodpile!" he shouted, then hung up.

"Another part of your army I guess, Amy?" Riley quickly said.

"Clayton, I thought you'd apologize for saying that," Goodman responded.

"Well, why don't you apologize for these people calling in support of you saying things like that?" Riley demanded. "Have you ever apologized?"

"I condemn when anyone uses a term like that," she replied.

"No you don't. You didn't condemn it just now."

"Yes I do."

"Now you are! . . . you didn't say a word, Amy, you didn't open your mouth."[64]

That, of course, would have been difficult for Goodman to do. Aside from the fact that the caller had not disclosed in whose support, if anyone's, he had made his racist crack, Riley attached it to Goodman before she had a chance to speak. After a few more calls, Robert Knight came into the studio to report the news. "Good morning, Robert," Goodman said with relief in her voice. "Good morning," Knight responded. "People who say 'nigger' are not Amy's people," he gallantly declared.

"How do you know that, Robert?" Riley asked. "How can you be so sure?"

Sensing that the situation had reached the brink of disaster, the studio board operator switched to jazz. The conversation continued off the air, although the studio air-check recording device continued to run. In the transition Goodman thought she heard Riley say something under his breath.

"Clayton, did you just call me a white bitch?" she inquired.

"I don't think so," Riley replied.

"Clayton, I want an apology," Goodman continued. She repeated the request three times.

"Are you demanding one?" Riley responded. "Is this your plantation personality to say, 'Nigger, I want an apology'?"

"She didn't say that!" Knight interjected.

"Did you hear me use your name?" Riley asked Goodman. "Maybe I was talking about 'her,' maybe I was talking about him. Maybe I was talking about somebody who was out in the reception area. I didn't use your name. I'm not that stupid. I know you're used to using, dealing with your 'Nubians' in here, I'm not one of them. You know – you, this slave, and the rest of your 'Nubians.'"

Knight, who was also black, got the inference. "'Slave'?" he shouted. "You call me a 'slave'?"[65]

Even before this horrendous exchange – the recording of which activists obtained, digitized, and put up on the Web – the Goodman/White camp realized that they were slowly being driven out of WBAI. Pacifica management had time on its side. All they had to do was keep up the pressure and pick their opponents off one at a time. If the Goodman/White faction wanted to roll back the Leid regime, they would have to escalate the fight beyond a struggle for control of one radio station. The Battle of Berkeley illustrated the limits of that approach. The KPFA community had repelled Pacifica's intrusions in 1999, but the governing board's hostile majority remained intact.

In addition, Van Isler's and White's tenure at WBAI had always been shaky. While the way Pacifica had driven Van Isler and White from their jobs appalled most WBAI activists, few dissidents had any illusions about the pair. Both had supported the Pacifica board for the most part. Van Isler had defied anything resembling institutional democracy by picking her hiring committee's last choice for program director. And one could hardly characterize the installation of Utrice Leid – who often questioned whether African-Americans should support the Democratic Party on her show *TalkBack!* – as a step toward "mainstreaming" the station. In fact, shortly after Goodman's fight with Yasko, Leid had appeared at a brief demonstration outside the station in support of *Democracy Now!!*[66] WBAI's new general manager may have been, as many thought, a race-baiting opportunist, but she was no NPR clone. If the New York station's fired and banned wanted to retake 99.5 FM, they would have to frame their struggle in much larger terms.

Fortunately, by early 2001 a critical mass of individuals throughout and around the network had come to a consensus about Pacifica's future, best summarized by Robert McChesney in *The Nation*. "Revise the legal structure of Pacifica so that it better reflects the actual nature of the five stations and how they do operate, and should operate," McChesney argued. "Give the staff and listeners more formal power."[67] Six members of the eighteen-member national board now functioned as a dissident opposition. FAIR had proposed a transitional slate of twelve noted progressive figures to replace the present board.[68] As had KPFA listeners in 1999, WBAI subscribers throughout the New York tri-state region were mobilizing against the Christmas Coup, holding public meetings as far west as South Orange, New Jersey.[69]

But the Free Pacifica movement remained a disparate array of revolutionaries. Although their principals frequently met with each other, they had yet to join forces in any deliberate fashion. Such coordination would require the intervention of someone within Pacifica who understood the network's resources and had the organizing skills to exploit them. Until now, that person had not appeared on the scene.

"Grand Theft Radio"

Juan Gonzalez had co-hosted *Democracy Now!* since the program's inauguration in 1996. He generally appeared on the show several times a week, taking a break from his regular job as a columnist for the *New York Daily News*. Born in Ponce, Puerto Rico, Gonzalez grew up in East Harlem, studied at Columbia University, and participated in the student strike of 1968. After that he helped found the Young Lords, a Puerto Rican activist group modeled on the Black Panthers.[70] In 1990, after Gonzalez took a position with the *New York Daily News*, its owner, the *Chicago Tribune*, forced a strike on the paper's 2,500 employees. Management representatives met with African-American churches in New York, trying to convince them that the *Daily News's* unions excluded blacks. Gonzalez participated in a union-sponsored "corporate campaign" to counter this propaganda offensive. After a long struggle the strikers won, in large part because they convinced the *Daily News's* black readers not to buy the paper during the walkout.[71]

On January 30 Pacifica listeners heard Amy Goodman welcome Gonzalez to the latest edition of *Democracy Now!* "I have an important announcement for folks," Gonzalez began, and asked his listeners to get a pencil and paper. Without explaining what it was for, he gave out a telephone number, then an email address, pacifica campaign@yahoo.com. Then came the disclosure. "I am resigning today, effective immediately, from *Democracy Now!*," he explained. "Because I've decided that the current management situation at Pacifica has become intolerable. And despite my hope that the

majority of the Pacifica Foundation's board of directors would come
to its senses, the situation has only gotten worse.... Quite simply I've
come to the conclusion that the Pacifica board has been hijacked by
a small clique that has more in common with modern-day corporate
vultures than with working class America." The board illegally
changed the foundation's bylaws, Gonzalez continued, and sought to
crush dissent at KPFA, *PNN*, *Democracy Now!*, and WBAI.

"Finally, Amy," Gonzalez concluded, "I've got to tell you that the
consistent attacks on you, the most important public face of Pacifica,
have so poisoned the atmosphere at Pacifica that it has become
increasingly difficult for many people of conscience to continue
working here." Gonzalez announced that he was starting a national
corporate campaign to force the Pacifica board majority to resign.
He asked for Pacifica listeners to withhold donations to the foundation and its radio stations and to give their money to the lawsuits
instead.

Goodman made sounds as though she wanted to speak, but
Gonzalez stopped her. "I know you can't say anything, Amy, because
of the gag rule at this station, as there are at many Pacifica stations
right now," he concluded. "That's why I felt it important to resign as
I make this statement. But my best wishes to you and all the other
people still working at Pacifica. Don't worry, the network will be
rescued soon."[72]

Pacifica listeners heard Gonzalez's announcement on at least two
of the network's five stations (WPFW quickly drowned his comments
out with jazz). Dozens of independent community stations broadcast
it uncensored. Gonzalez's call for a boycott came just as KPFK in Los
Angeles completed a ten-day fund drive. "I thought it was a really
cheap shot for somebody who decided not to work there anymore,"
KPFK manager Mark Schubb told the *Los Angeles Times* in response
to what he heard. "[Gonzalez is] a fine journalist, but on this one he's
wrong."[73] Hundreds of Pacifica activists across the network thought
otherwise. They rushed to Gonzalez's new Web site, www.pacifica-
campaign.org, to volunteer for the cause. The Pacifica Campaign
would tap into their rage and direct it, with a vengeance, toward the

Pacifica national board.

"GRAND THEFT RADIO – WHY ARE CORPORATE VULTURES POUNCING ON PACIFICA?" asked the headline for a Pacifica Campaign flyer released shortly after Gonzalez's announcement. "Half a century ago, journalist Lew Hill had a bright idea: listener-supported, community radio that would provide a forum for free expression and dissenting views," the leaflet continued. "Today, there are very few independent, locally-oriented stations left – and Hill's legacy is under siege. Extraordinary programs like Amy Goodman's *'Democracy Now!'* have been placed at risk by corporate predators whose motto seems to be 'Democracy No!'" The handout depicted the Pacifica board majority as a veritable rogue's gallery of opportunists – each with his or her own mug shot – waiting for their chance to sell a Pacifica station. "The 'Christmas Coup' at WBAI reveals Pacifica's ruthlessness and utter disregard for the democratic process," the document continued, then listed the names and email addresses of Pacifica board members.

The leaflet contextualized the struggle to reclaim WBAI within the democracy narrative and tapped into the progressive public's enormous anxiety about the inaccessibility of media. "With stations all over the country becoming more standardized and 'formatted' every day, those that offer non-conformist news and opinion are an endangered species," the text concluded. "Already, Pacifica's WPFW in Washington and KPFT in Houston have gone virtually all-music, with only a few minutes a day of news and public affairs. Will you help rescue free-speech radio from the corporate vultures?"[74]

Most progressive New York journalists embraced this stance after the Christmas Coup. "Fish Rots from the Head – Pacifica Falls into Corporate Hands," ran the headline for *Village Voice* media writer Cynthia Cott's January 17 edition of "Press Clips."[75] "WBAI Fights Management's Move to Turn the Station into NPR Lite," ran a longer *Voice* feature on the struggle.[76] "This Just In: We're Fired," *Time* columnist Steve Lopez titled his story on the WBAI fight. "A Hostile Takeover Rocks Radio's Voice on the Left."[77]

Utrice Leid and her supporters played into this script with guile-less gusto. On March 5 WBAI programmer Ken Nash invited U.S. Congressmember Major Owens to speak on Nash's labor show *Building Bridges*. Until recently Nash had co-hosted the program with his colleague Mimi Rosenberg, but Leid had fired her for "reprehensible behavior," as WBAI's manager later told a reporter. Apparently Owens's comments, directed toward the situation at WBAI, displeased Leid. She entered the studio while Owens was speaking and demanded access to the microphone. Versions differ on what happened next. Leid claimed that Nash "elbowed her neck and shouted her off the microphone." The studio board operator then switched to jazz (apparently Pacifica's favorite censorship music) and Owens hung up. Nash insisted that he never touched Leid, who simply cut off his mike.[78]

What mattered, of course, was how Owens felt about the inter-view, and he took it quite badly. The Congressmember did not experience himself as having hung up on WBAI, he declared in a speech made three days later on the floor of the House of Representatives. "Mr. Speaker, tyrants in control of totalitarian countries like China, Serbia, and Iraq consider control of the airwaves an absolute necessity," Owens began. "They ruthlessly enforce censorship of a kind few of us in America can imagine. On last Monday, however, I had the weird and frightening experience of being gagged by a radio station manager in my own home city of New York." Owens explained that he was frustrated by the limited number of venues for free speech in the city, citing five Haitian low-power radio stations that had recently been shut down. "The situation at WBAI has implications far beyond this one station," he continued. "Freedom of speech over the airwaves via radio, broad-cast television, and cable television is presently quite limited for the majority of Americans." His treatment on WBAI's airwaves confirmed his worst fears for the future of the station. "There are those who see profits being made via WBAI and other Pacifica stations," the Congressmember warned. "Some of the persons who have recently been appointed to the Pacifica Board represent such powerful commercial interests. In my opinion, WBAI is an endangered station as long as such business predators are on the Pacifica Board." With that, Owens quickly scheduled a congressional hearing on the media and the Pacifica crisis.[79]

At least one journalist sensed that the WBAI crisis might be a little more complex than a fight between corporate interests and the people. In June, Benjamin Soskis, reporter for *The New Republic*, decided to write a story on the struggle, which he found unfathomable. How could WBAI's protestors accuse the station of going corporate, Soskis wondered, when its new general manager, Utrice Leid, "earned her love beads as a host of a popular wbai afternoon talk show"? But while Soskis experienced the protesters as myopic and self-righteous, he declared them "models of sanity compared to Leid." Indeed, by the summer of 2001 it appeared to many that she had elevated race-baiting to a new plateau of goofiness, insisting that the protests had their roots in "white supremacist ideology" and "white resentment of Pacifica being in the hands of a capable black woman," Bessie Wash. "It's about the will of the European to dominate," Leid declared over the station's airwaves, "and some folks simply can't get over it!" Like a tourist in some strange locale, Soskis scratched his head over what he was seeing and hearing. "Leid's allegations ignore a few small facts," he observed, "for instance, that both Van Isler (the ousted general manager) and White (the axed program director), are black, and half of the dismissed WBAI staffers are minorities" – not to mention the treatment of Major Owens, a member of the Congressional Black Caucus.

But in his search for a larger explanation for the fight, Soskis could not get past his own contempt for the Pacifica community. The contradictions he identified were no surprise, he concluded, since "on the far left, using microscopic ideological differences as an occasion to label your opponents as racists, McCarthyites, Stalinists, or Nazis is a venerable tradition."[80] Although a sharp observer, Soskis could not see the bigger picture. The WBAI struggle had become a proxy battle in a larger war to democratize Pacifica radio. White and his supporters now embraced democracy because, like the KPFA staff in 1999, they feared Pacifica's governors more than the network's listener-subscribers. And WBAI's long-standing dissidents now backed them not because the "fired and banned" – as WBAI's ousted staff were known – had evinced respect for democratic process, but because an overthrown national board represented their only chance to win formal power for the network's listeners. In the grand old Leninist tradition, Pacifica's grassroots revolutionaries supported the White/Van Isler regime the way a rope supports a hanging man. And the general progressive public easily read the Pacifica crisis just as the Pacifica Campaign read it: as a metaphor for the larger crisis facing American telecommunications. If they could not figure out how to democratize the rest of the media, at least they could do it at Pacifica radio.

The only alternate understanding of the crisis available to the public, the relevance narrative, dropped dead with the appointment of Utrice Leid as general manager of WBAI. Marc Cooper and his supporters could no longer make a case for Pacifica's *Le Monde* future when Alton Maddox's preferred talk show host reigned over the network's New York station, ranting about titular black people. On July 9, 2001, *The Nation's* Web site posted a long document titled "Pacifica Myths and Realities," signed by "KPFK-LA Management," which probably meant Mark Schubb and possibly Cooper (or the "Marks brothers" as KPFK dissidents now called them). This "true/false" style essay attempted to refute dissident claims of corporate influence on Pacifica's board, plans to sell a radio station, and moves toward more mainstream programming, but the statement articulated no broad vision for Pacifica à la Cooper's 1999 *Nation* editorial. Instead it fought over details, and in the realm of details the dissidents ruled. Lyn Gerry quickly composed a long reply to "Myths and Realities" which *The Nation* posted as well.[81]

Meanwhile Amy Goodman doggedly marched into the ogre's den every day to produce and host *Democracy Now!*. A month after her dressing-down from Clayton Riley, WBAI management fired her from *Wake-Up Call*.[82] By early spring Goodman concluded *Democracy*

Now! with a consistent farewell: "from the embattled studios of WBAI, from the studios of the banned and the fired." This sign-off drove Pacifica management and their supporters crazy. While the Pacifica campaign pushed its boycott, all 5 Pacifica stations and 65 affiliates heard Goodman's quotidian reminder that the network was in turmoil. Seventeen members of the KPFK staff signed a statement demanding that she stop.[83] On March 26, Bessie Wash could endure it no longer. As Goodman interviewed novelist Alice Walker on *Democracy Now!*, Wash had satellite engineers stop the show so that Wash could speak live over their voices. "This is Bessie Wash, executive director of the Pacifica Foundation," she began. "It is necessary that I interrupt your regularly scheduled program to speak to those that are being misled by a small group of individuals." Wash went on to tell *Democracy Now!'s* startled audience that on the previous Friday an "anti-Pacifica" protestor had physically attacked a KPFT employee during a fund-raising event. The attack came just two weeks, Wash charged, after WBAI's general manager, "also a female," was assaulted while trying to interview a Congressmember. "We have thus far tolerated the slander, lies, false accusations, attempts to disrupt daily operations and the strategic effort to create an atmosphere of crisis at Pacifica," Wash concluded. "However, any and all participants that are engaged in violence and threats will be prosecuted to the full extent of the law."[84]

Pacifica then submitted charges against the KPFT protestor, one Edwin Johnston, in both Harris County Municipal and Superior Court. A declaration filed by Pacifica attorneys alleged that Johnston had attacked Ganter and his wife, KPFT development director Molly O'Brien, during the KPFT lawn party.[85] Johnston told the court that during the event O'Brien had snatched a handful of leaflets from one of the protestors. When Johnston approached her to get them back, Ganter and another man seized Johnston, punched him, and dragged him to the ground. Both courts dismissed all charges against Johnston in July and August. He put the legal documents up on a Web site celebrating his victory. The site opened with a photograph of him at the rally cheerfully holding a placard. "Smile if you HONK Garland!" it read. Bright red headlines limned the photo: "Charge #1 Dismissed! Charge #2 Dismissed! Game Over! Play Again?"[86]

By then relations between WBAI and *Democracy Now!* had reached the breaking point. Kris Abrams, producer of *Democracy Now!*, filed a complaint with Pacifica's staff union charging that on August 10 Goodman and Abrams arrived at WBAI to find the station's new public affairs director, Djabel Faye, and morning show host, Marjorie Moore, rummaging through the personal belongings of Bernard White. According to the statement, Goodman protested, left the scene, and returned with a camera. She began taking photos of White's possessions strewn across the floor. Utrice Leid entered the corridor and grabbed the camera. Goodman followed Leid to her office and demanded it back. Leid put her hands on Goodman's shoulders and tried to push her out.

"[T]hey shouldn't be going through and reading his personal papers," Goodman protested to Leid.

"And how do you know that's what they were doing?" Leid asked.

Goodman insisted she had witnessed it.

"Oh," Leid allegedly replied, "just like you witnessed a massacre in East Timor?"[87]

Seven days later Goodman, Kris Abrams, and Brad Simpson of *Democracy Now!* sent an email communiqué to Bessie Wash. The situation at WBAI had become intolerable, they charged. On Monday, August 13, no sooner did the three arrive for work than two WBAI staff members started yelling at Goodman. When she tried to escape to her office, one used the station master key to open the door and continue his harangue. The email made further accusations regarding Clayton Riley's behavior, that he had "assaulted [Robert] Knight in Utrice Leid's office, while she looked on. Riley has also threatened to pay a hitman $400 to break the legs of *Democracy Now!* engineer Anthony Sloan," the email charged. "He has screamed obscenities at former *Democracy Now!* producer Terry Allen. In each case we informed WBAI, Pacifica management about these incidents. Management never responded."[88]

Democracy Now! staff proposed an interim solution. They would produce the program at an outside studio, Downtown Community Television (DCTV) near the World Trade Center. "Our safety is non-negotiable," Goodman, Abrams, and Simpson concluded. "We hope you agree."[89]

With that, the trio fled WBAI and set up shop at DCTV. In response, the Pacifica national office stopped running *Democracy Now!* through its satellite system and instructed its five radio stations not to broadcast the program. Perhaps Bessie Wash thought that in so doing she had rid herself of a nuisance. In reality, she had handed her opponents an enormous tactical and ideological victory. East Timorese Nobel Peace Prize winner José Ramos-Horta quickly issued a statement in Goodman's defense. Jesse Jackson and actor Danny Glover, attending the UN World Conference on Racism in Durban, South Africa, angrily denounced Pacifica's refusal to air *Democracy Now!'s* live coverage of the event. "Who knows whom Goodman interviewed this morning," wrote syndicated columnist Laura Flanders, now a talk show host for *Working Assets* radio. "I couldn't hear the show, and neither could my fellow listeners at more than thirty stations around the USA. Why? Because the people who've hijacked Pacifica – the people's network, the network I've helped sustain for years with my work, love and, yes, my cash – refused to air the show." And while managements at WBAI, WPFW, KPFT, and KPFK complied with Pacifica's orders, KPFA staff defiantly kept *Democracy Now!* on the station's schedule.[90]

Pacifica's five dissident board members quickly pushed for a national board resolution in support of *Democracy Now!* Six months earlier it would have easily gone down to defeat, but the impact of the Pacifica Campaign on the board was now apparent. Since its inauguration in January, the Campaign had coordinated dozens of demonstrations and email and fax blitzes on the workplaces of key players on the national board majority. "Smart mobs," one writer would later call such small, technologically sophisticated armies.[91] On July 10 the Campaign scheduled a "national day of action" to "get Ken Ford off our board!" Protestors in New York and the Bay

Area picketed his employer, the National Association of Home Builders (NAHB). Progressive Portal, a fax- and email-generating Web site, enabled 500 dissidents to send approximately 200,000 messages to Ford's colleagues demanding his resignation.[92] Pacifica Campaigners rented a boat to shadow an NAHB New York Harbor yacht event, holding up signs demanding Ford's resignation.[93] Ford responded by threatening to call in the FBI, a move that alarmed only those Pacificans who knew of the agency's history of harassing and infiltrating the organization.[94] Demonstrators went so far as to picket the home of board member Andrea Cisco, a move that made even some dissidents wince. Twenty-five protestors stood outside her New York residence chanting, "Andrea Cisco, you can't hide. We charge you with radio-cide!" and "Hey hey, ho ho, the corporate gang has got to go!" On July 17 Cisco resigned, the latest of five board members to jump ship, including David Acosta and station sale advocate Michael Palmer.[95]

And so Pacifica's dissident board members found themselves, for the first time, in a good position to win a victory at a board meeting. In late August the board, by a vote of six to five, authorized sending a letter to Bessie Wash ordering her to reinstate *Democracy Now!*. The move received the support of one member of the Acosta/Ford board majority, Valrie Chambers of Houston.[96] But the Pacifica national office ignored the directive, perhaps out of spite, perhaps because Wash had just lost her latest national program director. In early September activists discovered that Steve Yasko managed a personal Web site under his nom de plume "Mike Billt." The site included a link to a porn page, and the guestbook section of the site included a meditation about Amy Goodman with a rather suggestive opening. "I've got a little exercise for you to do, Mike," a message from the "WBAI Good Fairy" began. "Why not imagine that Amy Goodman is a 6'3" muscular jock with six pack and a 'Heavy Package' that needs some attention? Would you just be sitting there across the table staring her down? Or would you be UNDER the table while Amy . . ." The text quickly made the rounds over the Internet. Goodman's lawyer brought the matter to the attention of Pacifica's attorneys, charging that Yasko's "obvious association with misogyny and sexism" fit an overall pattern of harassment. Yasko resigned after the revelation, but had anyone bothered to read the WBAI Good Fairy's message in its entirety, they would have noticed that the statement praised Goodman and denounced Yasko's tenure. "The morning shows that replaced the former *Wake Up Call* are by ANY standard a total disaster," it concluded. "And YOU as director of NATIONAL programming have made no constructive contribution to the ONE national show that works in your network."[97]

It did not matter. Nothing had to make immediate sense any more in this protracted institutional slugfest. The end target was the Pacifica national board, and it was crumbling fast. KPFK's Marc Cooper read the graffiti on the wall and issued a public statement over the Internet. Cooper had denounced the firing of Nicole Sawaya, but he had also criticized KPFA for airing its dirty laundry. "One hundred days later, I was proven correct when the station descended into chaos," he declared. It had all gone downhill from there. "The current fight is between two entrenched bureaucracies – one at the national level, and a collection of similar entities at the local level. There's plenty of hot air being blasted around about democracy, community, representation, etc. But no one is talking about how to produce thoughtful, responsive, agile, intelligent radio and how to bring Pacifica's mission to a wider audience."

"Meanwhile," Cooper continued, "the dissidents could not get their story straight."

> Read through their blizzard of websites over the last two years, and the "issue" keeps moving around: First it was Pacifica's firing of KPFA Manager Sawaya; then it was "governance" and the local boards – no, the national board – then it was the Democrats taking over, or was it the corporatists and the commercializers; then, briefly, it was the FBI; soon after, Pacifica's supposed plan to move out of California; promptly, it morphed into a "strike," against *PNN*; and then recently the dastardly "Christmas Coup," which lasted only until the issue shifted to the National Association of Homebuilders. As I write, the new flavor of the week is *Democracy Now!*

Like Benjamin Soskis, Cooper was half right. A battle between the Pacifica bureaucracy and the staffs of two of its radio stations, WBAI and KPFA, represented the backbone of the crisis. Both of these local bureaucracies had, until 1999-2000, to varying degrees supported Pacifica and its plans to streamline the organization. But since the summer the situation had morphed into something far more serious than an institutional stalemate. KPFA's and WBAI's renegade staffs, as well as the staff of *Democracy Now!*, had put themselves at the forefront of forces that had been churning on the ground floor of the organization for years – listeners, volunteers, and activists who, for a variety of reasons, had always opposed Pacifica's plans to remake the institution. All of these tendencies now coalesced in pursuit of a single remedy: a truly democratic system of governance for Pacifica, a cure that KPFA and WBAI staffs hoped would allow them to defend themselves and that the foundation's activists hoped would allow them real input into the organization's future. At any given moment one could find someone within the network who sincerely cared about each of the issues Cooper derisively described. At the same time they all functioned as proxy issues, a matrix of grievances now presented in the service of one goal, the overthrow and democratic transformation of the Pacifica national board. A social revolution was in process at Pacifica radio, a transfer of political power from the top of the organization to the bottom, a correction of the structural flaw that Lewis Hill had written into the foundation's bylaws – his omission of any formal role for listener-subscribers in governance.

Cooper would have none of it. "For my part, I now have absolutely no interest in the actual denouement of this tiresome remake of yet another Friday the 13," he wrote. "I don't think it matters very much to journalism, the so-called left or what's left of Pacifica's listenership. The historic project of Pacifica Radio as it was conceived and nurtured over several decades is now dead. Bessie Wash, Amy Goodman, Utrice Leid, Juan Gonzalez, Dennis Bernstein, FAIR, John Murdoch and Leslie Cagan alike will serve as pallbearers."[98]

It was September 10, 2001.

God Bless Pacifica

The next morning, WBAI's Robert Knight lay on his bed and stared at the ceiling of his apartment. Knight lived on the 32nd floor of a huge apartment complex in lower Manhattan, right off the East River. From his spacious living room window he could see the Bronx, Queens, and the United Nations building nearby. From his bedroom he could survey the entire Manhattan skyscraper line from Battery Park to the Empire State Building – far beyond, in fact, thanks to a small collection of telescopes. As Knight lay there, the radio chattered in the background. He was in a bad mood, having gotten little sleep that night. Knight rose, checked the news on his computer, and tuned the radio to WBAI, from which he had recently been fired by Utrice Leid. Listening to the station put him in a worse mood. Bleary-eyed, he went back to bed.

Then he noticed the plane. "I could see the wings and all different parts of it," Knight recalled. It flew at a disturbingly low altitude right over a densely populated area of Manhattan. "You never see planes there," he later explained, "because the Federal Aviation Administration has rules that traffic has to fly over the Hudson River and sort of avoid the center of Manhattan." Still half asleep, Knight puzzled over what he had observed. "It's like when Niagara Falls freezes. You know that there's an anomaly."

Then the radio announced that the World Trade Center had been hit. He rushed to the window, and, there, to his horror, stood the northern tower in flames. Knight immediately turned on his satellite cable TV and his computer and grabbed a long telescope. He pointed it the building. "You could see the black smoke coming out of the impact zone of the plane," Knight remembered, but having covered many fires as a reporter, this blaze struck him as different. "I could see it burning in places where it should not be burning. I could see it burning ten and fifteen stories above and below – little pockets of flame."

Suddenly the second tower exploded. Knight jumped back and

desperately scoured the radio dial for news. Two planes had hit the complex, en route from Boston and headed to California, one commercial station reporter explained. "There must be some kind of navigational error that's drawing the planes to this place," the announcer speculated. Knight shuddered. No, he felt sure, this was no error. "I knew that this was a maximal bomb" – two gigantic bullets filled with high-density kerosene jet fuel.

The telephone rang. KPFA's Dennis Bernstein and *Democracy Now!* wanted Knight to go live with a report. And so Knight narrated the September 11th attacks from the vantage point of his apartment. Armed with his telescopes, he described the collapse of the buildings, smoke cascading into the sky, thousands of New Yorkers fleeing Manhattan on foot via bridges, soot and debris floating up the East River, the FDR Drive cleared for ambulances, and, to his dismay, the paucity of them as it became all too clear that most casualties caused by the terrorist act would be fatal.[99]

WBAI went off the air for some days after the attack on the World Trade Center. When it returned to functionality, to the anger of listeners the station aired healing prayers and dirges and eschewed on-air discussion about the disaster.[100] Meanwhile, Amy Goodman broadcast daily reports on the crisis in lower Manhattan, sometimes staying on satellite for hours. Four of the network's five radio stations idiotically obeyed Pacifica's orders not to run her reports. KPFA kept Goodman on the air, even though staff feared that Pacifica might try another assault on the station's transmitter.

Pacifica management's war with its signature national program alienated a huge chunk of the progressive Left. Dissidents staged continual demonstrations, picket lines, teach-ins, and fax and email blitzes against individuals on the national board. A member of the New York City Council submitted a resolution calling for WBAI to rehire all its fired and banned programmers; 17 of her colleagues quickly co-sponsored the bill. The New York Central Labor Council, the New York Taxi Workers' Alliance, and the City University Professional Staff Congress endorsed a march protesting the Christmas Coup.[101] California state senator John Burton threatened

Pacifica with new legislative hearings on the crisis.[102] Privately key Pacifica funders wrote to give vent to their alarm. "I wish to express my very serious concern over reports that Amy Goodman and 'Democracy Now' are under serious pressure from Pacifica to 'soften' coverage and that Ms. Goodman has been deprived of resources and even threatened with termination," wrote Gregory MacArthur, whose J. Roderick MacArthur Foundation had given thousands of dollars to WBAI.[103]

Meanwhile *Free Speech Radio News* began to edge out *PNN*. The Pacifica Campaign, flooded with contributions, made a strategic decision to bankroll the fledgling news service, allowing it to run on a daily basis.[104] By May 2001, 47 community radio stations ran *FSRN*, now hosted by Verna Avery-Brown.[105] *PNN* staff, short on stringers, increasingly relied on an outside contractor, Feature News Service, which also provided content for commercial radio, including *Fox News*. The move made excellent dissident propaganda. Here was yet more evidence of the mainstreaming of Pacifica radio. "By increasingly contracting out its news reporting to FSN, Pacifica Network News is losing its very reason for being," a *FSRN* staff member charged, "providing independent reports from around the world, which draw on unique news sources rooted in movements for social change."[106]

In response to this onslaught, Pacifica spent practically every cent it had on lawyers, private investigators, and public relations firms. It needed the attorneys more than ever because, despite the foundation's best efforts to bottle up the lawsuits in slow-moving federal courts, the dissidents' scrappy street lawyers had gotten federal judges to bounce them back to Alameda County. Suddenly Pacifica faced a long, expensive jury trial. Perhaps sensing the national office's inexperience with a crisis of this magnitude, the institution's hired defenders feasted on the foundation's exchequer. By the end of the year board member John Murdock's Epstein Becker and Green had worked Pacifica to the tune of over $1,200,000 in billable hours. Wash then fired Epstein Becker and turned to the law firm of Williams and Connelly, staffed by none other than President Bill

Clinton's Special Counsel Gregory B. Craig. Williams and Connelly billed Pacifica for almost $500,000.[107] Mitchell Silverberg, brought in to manage the *Democracy Now!* war, handed Pacifica an invoice for about the same. Two more legal outfits ran up bills of $250,000 each.[108]

The lawyers also brought in a private investigation agency to dig up information on the dissidents. By October of 2001, Decision Strategies, working with Williams and Connolly, had run up expenses and fees for Pacifica to the tune of $214,505.16. If their list of itemized activities from September 4 through October 15 was representative of their work, they earned this sum primarily by paying operatives to sit at their computers and look at Pacifica dissident Web sites and newsgroup lists at from $70 to $280 dollars an hour. "09/19/01 JPF Monitor hotline; Monitor newsgroup postings/Internet site; Listen to Pacifica Board of Directors Meeting," ran a typical entry.[109]

Finally, since by the summer of 2001 practically no one on the Left would defend Pacifica, the foundation placed on retainer the public relations firm of Westhill Partners. On August 8, 2001, Westhill gave a Powerpoint presentation of their strategy for Pacifica. The slides mapped out a regimen with counterinsurgency rhetoric and mediocre slogans. "PHASE TWO: *Neutralize Dissenters*," read one section. "Pacifica will not waiver [*sic*] from serving the public and not the interests of a few misguided individuals." Key op-ed pieces would be placed in the outlets' "five major markets." Videos, press materials, and a national newsletter would be produced. Westhill also recommended that the foundation obtain the assistance of a group of "high profile individuals" to serve as "third party spokespeople." The firm presented their own list of "possible candidates," including trial lawyer Alan Dershowitz, former Texas governor Ann Richards, civil liberties attorney Floyd Abrams, former Berkeley congressman Ron Dellums, and former United States presidents Jimmy Carter and Bill Clinton.[110] For the dispensation of this wisdom Westhill Partners presented Pacifica with an invoice for $446,957.111.

The Pacifica national office made payments for these services by sucking the network's radio stations dry. The foundation's finances operated on a "lockbox" system, in which Pacifica's five frequencies forfeited their income to special accounts managed by the national office's financial division. The executive director then distributed this income back to the five stations and the national programming department using station "lockbox" checks. Now the money went to lawyers instead. On July 31, 2001, for example, Pacifica paid Williams and Connolly with checks marked "WBAI Lockbox," "KPFK Lockbox," and "WPFW Lockbox," for $5,000, $15,000, and $30,000, respectively.[112]

Then there was the budget of the Pacifica National Office. In July of 2000 a Pacifica administrative assistant managed to spend almost $9,000 on caterers for a single administrative council dinner complete with bartender and butlered hors d'oeuvres.[113] Pacifica Foundation American Express records indicated that by June 30, 2001, Wash had racked up $196,320.78 in credit card expenses: about $60,000 for lodging, over $20,000 for retail, over $50,000 for plane tickets, and $56,000 for a category titled "other." The previous year records indicate that Wash had incurred over $109,000 and $107,000 in two separate American Express accounts, the second including over $30,000 in "retail" category bills. Garland Ganter of KPFT's record indicated a $71,000 expenditure for the year 2000, including over $22,000 in retail purchases and $10,000 for "other."[114]

And so by late 2001 station managements and staffs noticed that Pacifica was no longer paying their operating expenses with any consistency. Ironically, while the Pacifica boycott had little impact on KPFK's finances, Pacifica's spending did. On October 17, 2001, KPFK staff sent a desperate message to the Pacifica national board. "Employees owed as much as $1200 are simply ignored," programmers disclosed. "We can no longer use Fed Ex, pick up parts for repairs and installations, or go to Staples for copy paper. We have no petty cash. Our phones have come within one hour of shut-off. Our new antenna cannot be installed because it cannot be delivered because of unpaid transfer and storage bills."[115] California Assemblymember Jackie Goldberg wrote to Pacifica on behalf of KPFA. "I have received information indicating that KPFA's bills are regularly unpaid or paid late," Goldberg charged, "station funds in its lockbox account have been depleted, and business staff at the local station have been unable to gain access to basic station financial information."[116]

In the face of this rapidly deteriorating situation, Wash and the majority on the Pacifica board made one last desperate attempt to hold onto power. Bessie Wash promoted Utrice Leid to national program director. On September 19, board vice chair Ken Ford barely managed to secure the appointment of five more members over the objections of the dissident minority. The new board members included former Washington, D.C., mayor Marion Barry and activist comedian Dick Gregory. They then elected as chair former Los Angeles City Councilmember Robert Farrell.[117]

Farrell made various gestures toward reconciliation. He issued a public "peace initiative" that asked the Pacifica Campaign to suspend its activities, urged the dissidents to suspend their lawsuits, and encouraged Amy Goodman to "come back to a supportive Pacifica." The declaration's conclusion suggested the extent to which the events of September 11 and the enormous patriotic backlash that followed it had traumatized the left. "God Bless Pacifica, God Bless America," his statement concluded.[118] But, like Saul Landau's appeal, Farrell's gesture offered the rebellion's principals nothing while urging them to stand down. Faced with an expensive lawsuit trial, a bankrupt national office, and a veritable army of boycotters, demonstrators, and Internet warriors, Farrell and his allies did what Pacifica should have done two years earlier. They surrendered. On Wednesday, December 12, 2001, representatives of defendants and plaintiffs in all three bylaws lawsuits signed a settlement that would commit an interim board to creating a democratic structure for the Pacifica Foundation.[119]

Suddenly the Free Pacifica movement had inherited a network in complete chaos and millions of dollars in debt – most of it to lawyers.

Sherry Gendelman, former chair of KPFA's local advisory board and a plaintiff in the Adelson suit, called me a few hours after the settlement document had been approved. "Matthew, the second worst thing that could possibly happen has happened," she said. "We won."[120]

Endnotes

1 Recollection of author.
2 Steve Behrens, "Turnover but No Retreat at Pacifica," *Current* (March 6, 2000): www.current.org/rad/rad004p.htm.
3 Pacifica Foundation Board of Directors Meeting, on the Date of Sunday, February 27, 2000, p.177.
4 Ibid, pp.169-70.
5 Ibid., p.181.
6 Eric Lipton, "Entrepreneur's Personal Finances Imperil Baseball Bid," *Washington Post* (April 2, 1999), Metro, p.B1.
7 Jerry Knight, *Washington Post*, "NBC to Forgive Loan to Firm Owned by Brown, Others" (February 25, 1995), p.C01.
8 Ibid.
9 Avram Goldstein, "Board for D.C. General Overhauled," *Washington Post* (June 5, 2000), p.A01.
10 "Practice Areas: Labor & Employment, Traditional Labor Law": www.ebglaw.com/prac_41.htm; "Labor and Employment: Employment Discrimination Law": www.ebglaw.com/prac_42.htm; "Labor and Employment: Occupational and Safety Health Law": www.ebglaw.com/prac_51.htm.
11 "Pacifica Foundation Poised to Add Controversial DC Businessman Bertram Lee Sr. to Its Board of Directors," Media Alliance press release (February 25, 2000).
12 Knight, "NBC to Forgive Loan to Firm Owned by Brown, Others"; "John Hope Franklin Is the Charter Day 2001 Speaker," *Howard University News Briefs*:www.howard.edu/newsevents/Capstone/2000/Feb.2001/fnews4.htm. Ironically, when Lee died in 2003, Pacifica's Web site, now run by former dissidents, eulogized him. See "Bertram Lee Jr.: A Life Well Lived": www.pacifica.org/news/031007_BertLee.html.
13 Biography of John Murdock, *Epstein Becker & Green*: www.ebglaw.com/atty_bio_59.htm.
14 Askia Muhammad, "Are Anti-Pacifica Radio Protesters Racists?" *Black Journalism Review* (Autumn 1999): www.blackjournalism.com/racismat.htm.

15 Judith Scherr, "Meeting Frustrates Local Rep," *Berkeley Daily Planet* (February 29, 2000), p.1.
16 Chris Hedges, "A Longtime Activist Escalating the Peace," *The New York Times* (February 4, 2003), p.B2.
17 In the Superior Court of the State of California Alameda County, *Robert Robinson, Rabbi Aaron Kriegel vs. The Pacifica Foundation*, Case No. 831286-0, September 19, 2000, pp.10-19.
18 Adam Brownstein, letter to John Crigler, "Re: Pacifica Foundation: Incorporation of a D.C. Non-Profit Corp. & Merger of the Existing California Corporation Into It" (June 23, 2000), *Pacifica National Office Papers (PNOP)*, Box 181.
19 "2/22/00 Draft Proposal for KPFA Elections, KPFA LAB Election Project": www.ringnebula.com/folio/Issue-5/Draft%20Proposal%20for%20KPFA%20 Elections%2002-22-00.htm; KPFA Local Advisory Board Minutes, Wednesday, October 11, 2000: www.cfdp.info/CdP%20and%20Other%20Meetings/1011_lab.htm.
20 John Crigler, email to Jim Peterson, September 12, 2000, *PNOP*, Box 181.
21 Mark Schubb, Administrative Council Meeting, March 2, 2001, *PNOP*, Box 181.
22 Michael Palmer, letter to Bessie Wash (October 12, 2000), *PNOP*, Box 181.
23 "Progressive Academics Support the Strike" (February 7, 2000), "First Installment of Free Speech Radio Debuts" (February 11, 2000), and "South Bay AFL-CIO Endorses Strike" (February 11, 2000), LL ON *FSRN/PRAC Archive for the Year 2000*: www.fsrn.org/archive2000.html; Eileen Sutton, interview with author (November 7, 2001), p.13.
24 SYPacifica [possibly Steve Yasko] to JSPacifica, subj: Re: Administrative Council Meeting, email, January 30, 2001, *PNOP*, Box 181.
25 Matt Martin, "PACIFICA RADIO DENIES DEMOCRACY NOW! PRESS PASSES AT THE D.N.C.," *Free Speech Radio News* (August 18, 2000), transcript.
26 Mary Frances Berry, quoted in PACIFICA Foundation Board of Directors Meeting, Taken on the Date of: Sunday, September 17, 2000: www.ringnebula.com/PNB/PNB_2000_0917.htm.
27 Brennen Jensen, "Radio Active, Will New Sounds Awaken Towson University's Slumbering Radio Station?" *Baltimore City Paper Online* (January 15-21, 2003): www.citypaper.com/2003-01-15/mobs.html.
28 Paul Siegel, "Castro Speaks to Thousands in Harlem" (October 2000): www.socialistaction.org/news/200010/castro.html.
29 Bernard White, interview with author (November 1, 2002), p.11.
30 SYPACIFICA to amyg@pacifica.org, subj: RE: Castro piece, email (September 11, 2000), and amyg@pacifica.org to SYPACIFICA, subj: too much, *PNOP*, Box 181.

31 danc@igc.org to sypacifica@aol.com, Subj: Abuse and Harassment of Amy Goodman, email (October 5, 2000), p.1, *PNOP*, Box 181.

32 SYPACIFICA to BMWPacifica, Subj: so here is my NYC plan, email (October 5, 2000), p.1. *PNOP*, Box 181.

33 "To: Pacifica Executive Director Bessie Wash and Board of Directors, From: Amy Goodman," (October 18, 2000): www.savepacifica.net/20001019_amyletter.html.

34 Ibid.

35 Frank Ahrens, "Pacifica Battles Show Host for Control," *Washington Post* (October 31, 2000), p.C01.

36 Ed Herman, "Endgame at Pacifica? The Washington Management Targets Amy Goodman (with a Call to Action)," *ZNet* (no date): www.zmag.org/CrisesCurEvts/Pacifica/endgame.htm.

37 Danny Schechter, "Saving Amy: The Exception to the Rulers" (October 27, 2000): www.mediachannel.org/views/dissector/amy.shtml.

38 "September 16, 2000: Listen to Live Webcast of Right of Return Rally": www.abunimah.org/features/000914rorwebcast.html.

39 Bernard White, interview with author (November 1, 2002), p. 21.

40 Valerie Van Isler, interview with author (November 3, 2002), p. 12.

41 "Tribute to Samori Marksman," *Democracy Now!* (April 1, 1999), radio broadcast; Alexander Cockburn, "Rebellion at Pacifica," *The Nation* (April 8, 1999):www.thenation.com/doc.mhtml%3Fi=19990426&s=cockburn.

42 Paul DeRienzo, "Perspectives on WBAI – The Decline & Fall of Pacifica: Part 2," *GNN: The Gary Null Network* (no date): www.garynull.com/Issues/WBAI/DeRienzo2.aspx.

43 Miguel Maldonado, interview with author (March 8, 2002), p.3.

44 Lunda Richardson, "A New Boss at an Old Voice of the Left," *The New York Times* (January 27, 2001), p.B2.

45 Ibid.

46 Jim Sleeper, *The Closest of Strangers: Liberalism and the Politics of Race in New York* (New York: W.W. Norton, 1990), pp.56-61, 292-93; Robert D. McFadden, E.R. Shipp, et al., *Outrage: The Story Behind the Tawana Brawley Case* (New York: Bantam, 1990), p.318.

47 Miguel Maldonado, interview with author (March 8, 2002), p.3.

48 Valerie Van Isler, interview with author (November 3, 2002), p.20.

49 Paul DeRienzo, "The Decline & Fall of Pacifica: Part 1, What's the Future of Pacifica?" *GNN: The Gary Null Network* (no date): www.garynull.com/Issues/WBAI/DeRienzo1.aspx.

50 Ibid.; Samori Marksman, memo to David Salniker, February 21, 1994, 2, *PNOP*, Box 181.

51 Utrice Leid and E.R. Shipp, "Brawley," *Democracy Now!* (December 23, 1997):

http://www.democracynow.org/article.pl?sid=03/04/07/0331210&mode=thre ad&tid=5. For Leid's earlier involvement in the Brawley debacle see Robert D. McFadden, E.R. Shipp, et al., *Outrage*, pp.318-19.

52 "Leid, Maddox and the Battle for Absolute Control of WBAI," *As Info Radio Project* (April 2000): www.radio4all.net/proginfo.php?id=2547.

53 Jayson Blair, "Hundreds Protest Firings at WBAI FM," The New York Times (January 7, 2001), p. 23; Jayson Blair, "Pacifica Foundation Locks WBAI Station Manager Out of Office," *The New York Times* (December 28, 2000), p. B1; Janny Scott, "A Voice of Protest Rises for Itself," *The New York Times* (December 23, 2000), p.B1.

54 FAIR Press Release, "MEDIA ADVISORY: PACIFICA MANAGEMENT MOVES TO UNDERMINE WBAI'S INDEPENDENCE" (December 1, 2000); "To: Bessie Wash, Executive Director, Pacifica Foundation, From: WBAI Management Team, Re: Actions Proposed Against Station Manager" (November 30, 2000): www.savepacifica.net/20001201_wbai.html.

55 CDP-NY, "WBAI General Manager's Van Isler Overrules Selection Committee in WBAI PD Hire" (no date): www.ringnebula.com/folio/Issue-8/K-WBAI_PD_Hire_0720.htm.

56 Utrice Leid, "We Interrupt This Program," *As-Info Radio Project* (December 23, 2000): www.radio4all.net/proginfo.php?id=2432.

57 Stephanie Lash, "Firings Strengthen Pacifica Control of New York Outlet," *Current* (January 15, 2001): www.current.org/rad/rad0101wbai.html.

58 Ibid.

59 Eileen Sutton, "Huge NY Meeting to Support WBAI While Pacifica Management Continues Purges Inside Station," press release (December 29, 2000): www.savepacifica.net/20001229_wbai.html.

60 See "WBAI Rally": http://revolutionarywebdesign.com/wbai/jan6/index.htm.

61 Paul DeRienzo, "Perspectives on WBAI, The Decline & Fall of Pacifica: Part 2"; Karen Frillmann, press release, "FOR IMMEDIATE RELEASE: WBAI LOCAL ADVISORY BOARD SET TO CHALLENGE BAN ON MEETING; ARRESTS EXPECTED" (January 23, 2001): www.savepacifica.net/20010123_press.html; Eileen Sutton, "Report on WBAI LAB Meeting, 1/23/01": www.savepacifica.net/20010123_wbai_lab_arrests.html.

62 Kathy Davis & I Removed from Health Action; I'm Banned, email by Bob Lederer (August 7, 2001), see www.2600.com/news/view/article/637.

63 "OFF-AIR TAPE SHOWS NATURE OF CONFLICT AT WBAI," *2600 News* (February 6, 2001): www.2600.com/news/view/article/679.

64 Ibid.

65 Ibid.

66 Rita Lasar, interview with author (November 3, 2002), p.1.

67 Robert McChesney, "Pacifica-A Way Out," *The Nation* (January 25, 2001): www.thenation.com/doc.mhtml%3Fi=20010212&s=mcchesney.

68 "Prominent Progressives Suggest New Board Members for Pacifica," FAIR
    press release (October 28, 1999): www.fair.org/press-releases/pacifica-
    proposal.html.
69 "WBAI LISTENERS ORGANIZING IN NEW JERSEY; SOUTH ORANGE
    MEETING FEBRUARY 4," press release, no date
    www.savepacifica.net/20010130_wbai_jersey.html.
70 David Barsamian, "Juan Gonzalez: The Progressive Interview," *The
    Progressive* (April 2000): www.progressive.org/int0700.htm.
71 Louis Proyect, "Report on WBAI Rally" (January 6, 2001): www.mail-
    archive.com/marxism@lists.panix.com/msg17103.html.
72 Juan Gonzalez, resignation statement on *Democracy Now!* (January 30,
    2001), audio file.
73 Steve Carney, "Turmoil Continues to Rock Pacifica Stations," *Los Angeles
    Times* (February 9, 2001).
74 "Grand Theft Radio: Why Are Corporate Vultures Pouncing on Pacifica?"
    Pacifica Campaign leaflet, 2001 (no date but distributed in February).
75 Cynthia Cotts, "Fish Rots from the Head-Pacifica Falls into Corporate
    Hands," *Village Voice* (January 17-23, 2001):
    www.villagevoice.com/issues/0103/cotts.php.
76 "WBAI Fights Management's Move to Turn the Station into NPR Lite:
    Morning Sedition," *Village Voice* (January 17-23, 2001):
    www.villagevoice.com/issues/0103/sadasivam.php.
77 Steve Lopez, "This Just In: We're Fired: A Hostile Takeover Rocks Radio's
    Voice of the Left," *Time* (January 29, 2001), p.6.
78 Frank Ahrens, "Pacifica Radio Airs Its Troubles at Hill Forum," *Washington
    Post* (May 16, 2001); Ken Nash, "Letter to Frank Ahrens" (May 18, 2001):
    http://www.savepacifica.net/media/20010518_nash.html.
79 Major Owens, "Radio Free Speech Is Being Denied in New York City,"
    address before the United States House of Representatives, (March 8,
    2001): www.radio4all.org/freepacifica/xmas/0308owens_speech.html;
    "Congressional Caucus to Host Pacifica Hearings," press release (May 6,
    2001): www.savepacifica.net/20010506_congress_hearings.html. This was
    the first time that Owens had taken a principled stand against a race-
    baiting individual or regime. In the 1970s at a closed meeting a Harlem
    activist referred to New York City Council Chair Carol Bellamy as a "white
    bitch." Owens sprang to his feet. "We won't have that kind of talk in this
    room!" he declared. "The real test of what we are is what we say when
    we're among ourselves!" See Sleeper, *The Closest of Strangers*, p.282.
80 Benjamin Soskis, "Static," *The New Republic* (July 9 and 16, 2001), 19-21.
81 KPFK-LA Management, "Pacifica Myths and Realities," *The Nation* (July 9,
    2001): www.thenation.com/doc.mhtml?i=20010716&c=1&s=kpfkla2001;
    Lyn Gerry, "Pacifica Management's Lies and Misrepresentations," *The

Nation (May 24, 2001): www.thenation.com/doc.mhtml%3Fi=20010604&s= gerry20010524.

82 Eileen Sutton, "Amy Goodman Officially Fired from WBAI's Wake-Up Call," press release (March 14, 2001): www.savepacifica.net/20010314_goodman.html.

83 Joe Domanick, Beto Arcos, Jon Wiener, Robert Mora, Yatrika Shah-Rais, Marc Cooper, Sergio Mielniczenko, Susan Weissman, John Retsk, Jay Kagelman, Art Gould, Barbara Osborn, John Beaupre, Barry Smolin, Hector Resendez, Earl Ofari Hutchinson, and Simeon Pillich, "To: Amy Goodman, From: The On-Air Programmers of KPFK, Re: Up-Coming Summer Fund Drive," email (May 15, 2001): www.peak.org/mailing-list/archive/grc/msg01084.html.

84 Bessie Wash quoted in rebroadcast of speech on the *KPFA Evening News* (March 26, 2001): www.savepacifica.net/media/20010326_kpfanews.ram.

85 "Declaration of Garland Ganter in Opposition to Order to Show Cause re: Preliminary Injunction," Alameda Superior Court (April 10, 2001), Case No. 831252-3.

86 "Declaration of Edwin Johnston in Support of Plaintiffs' Motion for Preliminary Injunction" (April 2001); Case # 1052483, Harris County Municipal Court, (August 29, 2001); Case # A1614058-4-2, Harris County Superior Court (July 16, 2001). See "Violence from KPFT": www.hal-pc.org/~edi/kpft.html.

87 Kris Abrams, email to Kim Roberts, AFTRA, Bessie Wash; Executive Director, Pacifica Foundation, Re: events at WBAI (August 10, 2001), *PNOP*, Box 181.

88 Amy Goodman, email to Pacifica national board members, Subject: Safety (August 20, 2001), *PNOP*, Box 181.

89 Ibid.

90 Laura Flanders, "I Want My Democracy Now!" *Working for Change* (August 14, 2001): www.workingforchange.com/article.cfm?ItemID=11741; Media Alliance, "Jesse Jackson, Actor Danny Glover Call on Pacifica to Stop Blocking Broadcasts" (September 5, 2001), press release; "Statement by José Ramos-Horta on Amy Goodman and Santa Cruz Massacre" (September 3, 2001): www.etan.org/news/2001a/09hortadn.htm.

91 Howard Rheingold, *Smart Mobs: The Next Social Revolution* (Perseus Publishing, 2002).

92 Pacifica Campaign, "Get Ken Ford Off Our Board!" (July 9, 2001), press release: www.progressiveportal.org/pacifica/letters1.html.

93 Mike Janssen, "As Foes Slam Pacifica, Their Targets Cry Foul," *Current* (August 20, 2001): www.current.org/radio/radio0115p.html.

94 The author was particularly concerned about this development: see From: Leslie Cagan, Tomas Moran, Rob Robinson, Pete Bramson and Rabbi

Aaron Kreigel, Memo to Members of the Pacifica National Board" (July 3, 2001), and Matthew Lasar, "An Open Letter to Ken Ford; Re: the Federal Bureau of Investigation" (June 23, 2001): www.savepacifica.net/20010703_fbi.html.

95   Benjamin Soskis, "Static," *The New Republic*, 19-21; "Chronology of a Crisis" (July 17, 2001): www.ominous-valve.com/pac/pacific2.html; Save Pacifica, "Two More Pacifica Board Members Resign, Including Chair David Acosta!" (June 13, 2001), press release. I took part in various free Pacifica protests, but I drew the line at picketing people's homes.

96   "National Board Votes by Slim Margin to Support Democracy Now!" (September 2, 2001), press release.

97   "Pacifica Elects Dick Gregory, Marion Barry to Board; Yasko quits" *Current* (August 20, 2001): www.current.org/radio/radio0115p.html; Richard A. Levy, letter to Gregory B. Craig (September 5, 2001), pp.1-2, with fax documents, pp.5-7, *PNOP*, Box 181.

98   Marc Cooper, "Public Statement on Pacifica," *The Nation* (October 3, 2001): www.thenation.com/doc.mhtml%3Fi=20011015&s=cooper20011003.

99   Robert Knight, interview with author (November 8, 2001), pp.7-8.

100 Chris Thompson, "The Battle for KPFA and the Soul of Pacifica Is Over," *East Bay Express* (January 9, 2002), p.21.

101 David Hinckley, "City Council Panel Tackles WBAI Case," *New York Daily News* (May 7, 2001); Keith Crandell, "WBAI's Loyal Listeners Step Up Their Protests," *Downtown Express* (May 8-21, 2001), p.5.

102 John Burton, letter to David Acosta (June 1, 2001), p.1, in possession of author.

103 Gregory MacArthur, letter to David Acosta (November 3, 2000), 1, *PNOP*, Box 181.

104 Aaron Glantz, interview with author (October 29, 2001), p.5

105 "Free Speech Radio News Goes Daily" (May 9, 2001), press release: www.fsrn.org/20010510_daily.html.

106 Vanessa Tait, "Feature Story News: Is It Pacifica or Is It Fox?" *FSRN* (February 2000): www.fsrn.org/fsn.html.

107 Resume, Gregory B. Craig, *PNOP*, Box 181.

108 Kimerling, Magulies & Wisdom, Ltd. Audit of Pacifica, Statement of Professional Fees by Firm, October 1, 1999, to December 31, 2001, February 5, 2002, p.19; possession of author.

109 Decision Strategies, Description of Services, Inv. #2572-001-08, October 30, 2001, 4, *PNOP*, Box 181.

110 The Pacifica Foundation, Strategic Recommendations, August 8, 2001, Westhill Partners Powerpoint presentation, *PNOP*, Box 181.

111 Kimerling . . . Statement of Professional Fees, p.19.

112 Pacifica – WPFW Lockbox, 00013203, Pacifica – KPFK Lockbox, 00014672,

Pacifica – WPFW Lockbox, 00009823, *PNOP*, Box 181.

113 RSVP Catering company schedule and invoices for Friday, June 9, 2000, *PNOP*, Box 181.

114 American Express Small Business Services, The Corporate Platinum Card Quarterly Management Reports, for quarters 12/31/00 and 06/30/01, *PNOP*, Box 181.

115 Betos Arcos, Dan Pavlish, Jeff Kaufman, Jon Beaupre, unintelligible signature, Danielle Moroson, Marc Cooper, and Keola Kama, email to the Pacifica National Board, October 17, 2001, *PNOP*, Box 181.

116 Jackie Goldberg, letter to Robert Farrell, October 16, 2001, 1, *PNOP*, Box 181.

117 "Pacifica Elects Dick Gregory, Marion Barry to Board; Yasko Quits," *Current* (September 24, 2001): www.current.org/radio/radio0115p.html.

118 Robert Farrell, text of peace initiative, September 27, 2001; possession of author.

119 Carol Spooner et al., "SETTLEMENT AGREEMENT" (December 12, 2001): www.savepacifica.net/settlement.html.

120 Recollection of author.

CHAPTER 8

Frequently Asked Questions

You gotta wonder: what the hell was this fight about, anyway?
CHRIS THOMPSON

The settlement of December 12, 2001, set up an interim board of directors for Pacifica, which network activists immediately dubbed the iPNB. On the iPNB sat five members of the old guard, five dissident board members, and five members selected by each of the network's local advisory boards. This gave the reformers roughly two-thirds majority in decision-making. The agreement committed the group to the task of rewriting the foundation's bylaws, using KPFA's listener-subscriber-elected model as a starting point. Any section of the bylaws involving the network's local advisory boards had to be approved by three of the foundation's five LABs.[1]

The iPNB quickly elected a new slate of officers, with Leslie Cagan as chair. Once installed, the board voted to restore *Democracy Now!* to the airwaves. This proved easier to decree than to enforce. Utrice Leid resigned as Pacifica national program director on the day of the settlement, but WBAI remained in the hands of staff who had supported her and Bessie Wash. On January 7, 2002, Amy Goodman decided to conduct a live program about why WBAI had yet to broadcast her show. Cagan, Juan Gonzalez, and filmmaker Michael Moore joined Goodman in her downtown studio. While thousands listened, they picked up the telephone, called WBAI's receptionist, Fred Kuhn, and ad-libbed a Pacifica version of Abbot and Costello's legendary routine *Who's on First?*

"Hello!" Goodman said over the airwaves. "Is this Fred?"

"Yes," Fred replied.

"Hi Fred," Goodman continued. "We've got someone on the line for you."

Michael Moore took the telephone. "Fred. This [is] Michael Moore."

"Yes Michael," Fred replied.

"How are you doing Fred? You're in the studio at WBAI?"

"I'm in the front switchboard," Fred explained.

"Hey, listen man," Moore continued. "I told a lot of people that I was going to be on 'BAI this morning, on *Democracy Now!* . . ."

Fred disclosed that he had heard on WBAI that the show would be broadcast at some point during the day.

". . . you won't put it on live?" Moore asked.

"Well it's not on live," Fred responded. "That's all I can tell you."

With that, Fred fled to find the station's public affairs director, Djabel Faye, who picked up the line, apparently unaware that the conversation was being broadcast live.

"Hello," Faye said.

"Djabel, it's Michael Moore," Moore began.

"Hey, how you doing man?" Faye replied.

"Good. Hey I'm on this show *Democracy Now!* And, like, people in New York aren't able to pick it up on WBAI and it's supposed to be on. . . ."

"Who told you that it was supposed to be on?" Faye asked.

"Well, I read about this board meeting or something, that the Pacifica board ordered it on to all the stations?" Moore asked.

"Well, I personally also read it from the outside but the truth is that there has not been one single written paper from Pacifica [the executive director] that would urge us to play."

"You didn't get the memo then?" Moore asked.

"No," Faye insisted.

Moore asked Faye for WBAI's fax number so that he could send the board's memo regarding reinstatement of *Democracy Now!*

"No, no, we got a memo from Leslie Cagan but we're waiting for something from Pacifica, not from Leslie Cagan," Faye continued.

"But she's the president of the board," Moore replied.

"Well maybe she should order Pacifica to send us a memo," Faye explained. ". . . If you want me to talk or listen to you, you have to show a little bit of respect. What I'm telling you is simple. You want some information? You are telling me Leslie Cagan wrote a memo. I'm saying the memo is not enough for us to put *Democracy Now!* on the air."

Leslie Cagan took the telephone. "My understanding was that our acting executive director of the Pacifica foundation did have communication with each of the five station managers and that all the station managers knew that this was the decision of the board," she said.

As Faye reiterated that the lack of a piece of paper prevented him from broadcasting the program, Goodman introduced Dick Gregory, comedian and Pacifica board member, to the discussion.

"Dick are you there?" Goodman asked.

"Good morning," Gregory declared. "God bless you."

"Who is Dick Gregory . . . wait a minute?" Faye asked. "Is this a meeting, or what?"

"No, this is *Democracy Now!*" Goodman declared. Within a few days the program broadcast again on WBAI.[2]

A week later Cagan sent another memo to the building security manager at 120 Wall Street, authorizing entry and access for the nearly sixty people who had been fired, banned, or barred in some context from WBAI over the preceding 12 months.[3] Welcoming them back to their jobs was the network's new executive director, none other than Dan Coughlin, who presided over a management overhaul at the five Pacifica stations. Garland Ganter resigned his post as general manager of KPFT and was replaced by longtime Houston activist Duane Bradley. Lou Hankins had taken the position of WPFW general manager after Bessie Wash's promotion.

Pacifica quickly replaced him with former *Julianne Malveaux Show* producer Tony Regusters. KPFK's Mark Schubb went on leave after the settlement. He never returned. Pacifica put Los Angeles talent agent Steven Starr in his place.[4] A furious Marc Cooper refused to ask listeners for money during the next subscriber marathon. Starr suspended his drive-time show. Cooper opted to move on. "For those of you who have expressed concern about my future, let me re-assure you that under present conditions, leaving KPFK is only a liberation," he wrote in a public email message. Cooper's satellite show *Radio Nation* continued to broadcast at the station.[5]

Pacifica put WBAI's ousted general manager, Valerie Van Isler, back at her desk. But all these moves, even Van Isler's restoration, were made on an interim basis. Hundreds of activists formed hiring committees to seek out the network's next generation of permanent managers, including a new boss for Pacifica's New York frequency. The next Pacifica national board meeting, held in January 2001, said worlds about who had taken control of Pacifica radio. Rather than assembling in a hotel conference room, the iPNB gathered in the cavernous, wood-floored hall of New York's hotel workers union; a subscribers group sold organic cookies in the lobby. Under the previous regime, public comments were restricted to the end of the meeting; now listener feedback panels preceded each two-hour section of the conference. "Now we have some power here," WPFW activist Frank Wagner told *Current* magazine. "It's really encouraging."[6]

Pacificans found the organization's financial situation less encouraging. Coughlin hired an accounting firm to audit the network. In early February the auditors disclosed that Pacifica faced a deficit of over six million dollars, a loss incurred over the past 15 months, much of it owed to law firms, public relations companies, and private investigation agencies. Suddenly the reformers faced a painful irony – they would have to pay back all the money the previous regime had spent to fight them, and quickly, before creditors forced the foundation into bankruptcy. Among other recommendations, the auditing firm urged Pacifica to eliminate its national programming division, which included the *Pacifica Network News (PNN)* but did not include *Democracy Now!* Coughlin followed the advice, a move *PNN* staff understandably interpreted as payback. "Part of it is personal," regular *PNN* reporter Don Rush told a journalist following the elimination of his job. "Once their side won, we would be the people to go." But in 2002 *PNN's* national programming division had run a deficit of almost a million dollars for a service which, in truth, generated very little listener loyalty to the network. In early 2000 Bessie Wash attempted to solicit funding for *PNN* and *Democracy Now!* from the Solidago Foundation. "The work of the Pacifica Network News is not of primary interest to the Foundation as it does not offer a strong vehicle for grassroots voices," came a Solidago officer's reply. "It also is not a program that our grantees listen to. The 'buzz' around *Democracy Now!* among both grassroots activists and funders is extraordinary. So I thought it would be important for you to understand that *Democracy Now!* and only *Democracy Now!* is our funding priority."[7]

It would take the national office several years to pay back most of the debt that Pacifica owed. Meanwhile, the organization's activists began the slow, complicated work of democratizing the foundation's bylaws. A reader who has come this far has followed more Pacifica fights than any innocent person should endure. The bylaws debate will therefore be described in brief. Almost everyone agreed that the network's listener-subscribers should elect their respective local advisory board delegates and that those delegates should subsequently elect directors to the national board. A contingent within the organization called for gender and ethnic representation goals to be set for all local advisory board elections. Their "Draft A" model proposed extending elections if the process did not meet those goals and appointing minority members if necessary.[8] But others feared that this regimen would expose the foundation to lawsuits. Ultimately three out of five of the network's LABs narrowly approved Draft B – bylaws that authorized the foundation's 90,000 listener-subscribers and 700 paid staff and volunteers to elect their LABs, but did not include demographically based diversity goals.[9]

Needless to say, the debate, which took place over about 18 months, got very nasty on occasion, especially after the judge who had presided over the settlement approved the process by which Pacifica approved Draft B. "At the core of this, these white people on the Pacifica board felt that black folks, that niggers, came in and messed up their nice, laid back foundation," one diversity goals advocate bitterly concluded over WBAI's airwaves. "And they [white people] wanted to take it back, take it back to the bosom of Berkeley, where we can become a lily white organization again."[10] As this quote suggests, the bylaws writing process had the potential to go quite badly. Fortunately, the new Pacifica board abolished the gag rule. Programmers were not fired for expressing their perspective on the bylaws question over the airwaves. No station fell apart over the debate. In September 2003 Pacifica opened nominations for local board delegates. Candidates began to throw their hats into the ring, including those who had opposed the bylaws under which they now ran.

The cheering and booing had ended. The headlines vanished. The Pacifica crisis was over, at least for the general public. Still, a few journalists stood at the tail end of the drama and scratched their heads. "You gotta wonder," Chris Thompson, reporter for Berkeley's *East Bay Express*, asked his readers in January 2002, "what the hell was this fight about, anyway?"[11]

Did Pacifica's leaders cause the organization's crisis by trying to move the network toward the corporate sector and the Democratic Party?

Dissidents repeatedly leveled this charge against the foundation, particularly during the late stages of the Pacifica crisis (1999-2001). A "sneak attack" by "corporate and Democratic infiltrators," an activist labeled Utrice Leid's takeover. "Pacifica, at present, isn't beholden to the Democratic Party," Geov Parrish wrote in August of 2001, "it is the Democratic Party, appealing to listeners by positioning itself imperceptibly to the left of the Republican NPR."[12]

But it is difficult to assemble a consistent pattern of evidence supporting the conclusion that the complex coalition which supported Mary Frances Berry from the late-1990s through 2001 gave its allegiance to and drew its strength solely from the corporate sector and the Democratic Party.

Certainly elements from the Democratic Party played a crucial role in Pacifica's civil war. Free Pacifica activists often cited Berry's close ties to the Clinton administration, but such alliances were nothing new for Pacifica. They went back to the 1960s, when Harold Winkler, former director of *Time* magazine founder Henry Luce's Council for Democracy, served as president of the Pacifica board, and Hallock Hoffman, son of Paul Hoffman, president of the Ford Foundation and co-executor of the Marshall Plan, served as his successor.[13] Pacifica had always worked with Democrats and prominent liberals from the corporate sector, among them Louis Schweitzer, the Kimberley-Clark Corporation executive who gave WBAI to the institution. Such individuals had always played a role in Pacifica governance, had always expressed some discomfort with Pacifica programming, and had always been charged with attempting to interfere with the organization's radical mission.[14]

The Pacifica Campaign often characterized members of the Pacifica board circa 2001 as corporate infiltrators. But a closer look at their biographies indicates a more complex cast of characters. Berry ally David Acosta, for example, worked as an independent accountant for Houston-based popular musicians, among them South Park Mexican, Norma Zenteno, Raul Rekow from Santana, Grupo Ka-che, and Mango Punch. Until recently Acosta himself belonged to a band, Sol y Luna, which in 1994 the alternative weekly *Houston Press* called the city's best Latin ensemble. WBAI's Frank Millspaugh, another Berry supporter, served as general manager of WBAI during the free-form era of the late 1960s and early 1970s. Many of the African-American members on the board who supported Berry did labor in the corporate sector, but, as in the case of Bertram Lee, they also had long histories of progressive, grass-roots, philanthropic work.[15] Dave Fertig, a dissident board member from Los Angeles who participated in the settlement of 2001, later provided an unflattering description of their objectives:

The Berry board wanted to use Pacifica to advance their political voice, which they naturally saw as the wisest voice. Also it was their clique and social milieu, a predominantly black, urban, and East-Coast/Southern BUPpie/Black Bourgeois that arose from the institutionalized wreckage of the now calcified and pilfered anti-poverty programs and the wistful, almost-geriatric freedom-rider/civil rights movement. The former dashiki-wearing, meeting-disrupting street radical Marion Barry was now a muni bonds broker, former CP paper-peddler Bert Lee was now a media magnate and Nike factory owner (in South Africa), etc., etc. They knew what they wanted from Pacifica, and it wasn't just an open debate on the air, it was promotion of their social and political views, their programs, their friends and their businesses, which were tightly interwoven and economically interdependent.[16]

Dissidents constantly pointed to Pacifica's attacks on Amy Goodman as evidence of the leadership's desire to rein her in. But Steve Yasko's and Garland Ganter's behavior toward Goodman seemed to derive less from a desire to influence her politics than from a wish to demonstrate to the Pacifica national office that they were managing her and thereby justifying their salaries. In fact, a noticeable *lack* of interest in political content and an increased concern with exercising personal authority characterized much of the behavior of Pacifica top management from the mid-1990s onward. Although Goodman charged that Yasko, Mark Schubb, and others wanted her to tone down her politics, criticisms that *Democracy Now!'s* broadcasts suffered from stridency and even political naiveté came from its supporters as well.[17] It appears that much of the fighting over Goodman and *Democracy Now!* emanated from honest disagreements within the Left about politics and presentation.

Writers such as Alexander Cockburn frequently referred to the influence of the Corporation for Public Broadcasting, especially in regard to the February 1999 bylaws changes that turned Pacifica's governing board into a self-appointing body. But the motivation for that move came primarily from the Pacifica national office seeking a more manageable board. Although dissidents often referred ominously to CPB executives Robert Coonrod and Richard Madden's former employment with the Voice of America as the reason for their intervention, another reading of that chapter of CPB/Pacifica history is equally plausible. After the KPFK "Afrikan Mental Liberation Weekend" debacle of 1993, CPB bureaucrats smiled upon a more centralized system of governance at Pacifica that would prevent its five stations from broadcasting fare that the Republicans could use to attack public radio and even the CPB itself. I asked Jeannie Bunton, the CPB's director of communications, whether that might have been the CPB's motive. "No," came her ambiguous reply. "How the Pacifica Foundation's network model is structured is not of concern to CPB, provided that its governance is in compliance with Federal Regulations and our own internal policies." But some Pacifica board members clearly perceived the structural changes the CPB recommended in response to Pacifica's inquiries as a response to right-wing pressure attacks on both the CPB and Pacifica. "We were getting a lot of heat," board member Ken Ford later explained, citing Republican attacks from Congress regarding CPB support of Pacifica. "CPB got concerned because they wanted to stay in business. There are other stations and why is Pacifica giving them a lot of headaches through the Congress? So [they] were accused indirectly of taking favorites with Pacifica and they would have to treat Pacifica with full accord with the laws."[18] In other words, CPB policies toward Pacifica during this period may have stemmed primarily from defensive motives.

Finally, many Pacifica programmers who chose to ally themselves implicitly or explicitly with the Berry board could not accurately be described as mainstream, Democratic Party-based journalists. Both Marc Cooper and Saul Landau publicly endorsed the presidential candidacy of Ralph Nader in 2000. "My only personal regret is that I had but one ballot to cast for Ralph," Cooper declared in *Mother Jones* magazine after the election. KPFK broadcast Nader's Los Angeles election night rally live over the station's airwaves.[19] Utrice Leid's WBAI continued to air the daily programs of health activist Gary Null, who questioned whether HIV causes AIDS or is the sole cause.[20] Author Jim Marrs made appearances on the station during the Leid months. As WBAI dissidents noted, his book *Rule by Secrecy: The Hidden History That Connects the Trilateral Commission, the Freemasons, and the Great Pyramids* contended that even if anti-Semitic Czarist writers faked the Protocols of the Elders of Zion, its warnings were still "prophetic."[21] Ralph Schoenman, author of *The Hidden History of Zionism*, also made fundraising appearances during Leid's October 2001 marathon.[22] Whatever one thought about such fare, it could hardly be described as pandering to the Beltway.

Did Pat Scott's Pacifica try to "NPRize" the network, as dissidents argued?

From the mid-1980s onward, Pacifica did indeed adopt programming and organizational and analytic techniques from commercial and public broadcasting. Pacifica stations embraced strip-programming schedules. Managements evaluated station performance through Arbitron ratings. They replaced volunteer on-air hosts with paid broadcasters. They incorporated more satellite-distributed fare into their schedules. Although Pacifica refused to accept corporate underwriting for programs long after most public broadcasters embraced the practice, as noted earlier, the board in 1989 established a policy of leniency with regard to these rules at both cash-poor KPFT and WPFW. As a result, KPFT broadcast BBC's *The World*, a program underwritten by the pharmaceutical company Merck.[23]

Some of these practices clearly compromised Pacifica's historic commitment to broadcasting free of commercial influence. But many had broad support within the progressive media community and among Pacifica listeners and programmers.

As this study has shown, many progressive journalists applauded Pat Scott's efforts in the mid-1990s to increase Pacifica's audience by centralizing and professionalizing the institution. After the Battle of Berkeley in 1999, longtime Free Pacifica activists often confronted the paid staff of KPFA, now committed to democratizing the organization. "Where were you when the Scott regime purged grassroots voices throughout the network?" they demanded. It was a good question. The honest answer was that they, and a large portion of the organization's listener-subscribers, had supported these "house-cleanings," as Alexander Cockburn sympathetically described them in 1997. Progressive journalists writing for Berkeley's *East Bay Express*, Los Angeles's *LA Weekly*, and the *Houston Press* had all offered positive representations of the changes taking place throughout the network during and even after the Pat Scott period. Even progressives who opposed Saul Landau's intervention in 2000 paid a backhanded compliment to the Scott regime in their public response. "If [Landau's] 'Appeal' were written a couple of years ago, when criticism of the network's leadership seemed more alarmist and exaggerated, it might have been defensible," declared nearly sixty prominent leftists in their answer to Landau's "Stop the Pacifica Bashing!" petition.[24]

The Free Pacifica movement often pointed to the music-heavy formats of KPFT in Houston and WPFW in Washington, D.C., as evidence of an attempt to depoliticize the organization. But for different reasons both stations broadcast to extremely challenging environments which required some degree of strategic adaptation. The multilingual format experiments of KPFT senior staffers Larry Yurdin, Ray Hill, and Rafael Renteria in the 1970s and early 1980s should be hailed as unique moments in the history of broadcasting. Unfortunately, few Houstonians tuned in to appreciate them at the time. Renteria later acknowledged the limits of KPFT's multilingual experiment. "With respect to the hodgepodge nature of that kind of programming, I think that's a legitimate criticism, that it doesn't pay attention to the way that people listen to radio," he later commented. "I don't object to strip programming. I object to programming that isn't mission driven."[25] Ray Hill went further, praising his managerial successor, Jean Palmquist, for undoing much of what he accomplished during his tenure. "The first thing Jean did was start putting some structure and some discipline, some bureaucracy in the station," Hill recalled. "Everybody in the station absolutely hated her. I loved her because I thought she was doing what needed to be done to clean up after me. And then Jean started cutting down on the languages. Well, hell, by that time, by the time Jean got there, we were broadcasting in fourteen languages. And so she started trimming that down to size and did a remarkable job."[26] As late as the summer of 2004, despite the ouster of Garland Ganter at KPFT, the station continued to broadcast underwritten satellite programs such as the *BBC World Service* and *World Café*.[27] To describe the process Pacifica underwent in the late 1980s and early 1990s as "NPRization" caricatures rather than analyzes the enormous problems the organization faced and its responses to those challenges.

If Mary Frances Berry's Pacifica had stopped the Free Pacifica movement from democratizing the network, would the Pacifica National Board have sold WBAI or KPFA?

The evidence suggests to this historian that while players on Mary Frances Berry's board publicly denied interest in selling a station, privately they continued to pursue the idea.

No sooner did the Pacifica board turn itself into a self-appointing body in February of 1999 than the cat began popping its head out of the bag regarding a station sale. "Things could happen, but that is not at all on the agenda here," Lynn Chadwick told *Current* magazine. "These stations are what we are all about, they're our most valuable asset. There have been conversations at odd times . . . but the organization is financially stable right now. . . ."[28] Of course Chadwick's comment raised the question of what Pacifica might do if its key officers declared the organization financially *un*stable, the position taken by board member Michael Palmer in his famous email to Berry proposing the sale of KPFA and/or WBAI. "My feeling is that we are experiencing a slow financial death which is having the normal emotional outbursts commensurate with such a disease," Palmer wrote on July 13, 1999. "This board needs to be educated, quickly, and to take action that will be far more controversial than the KPFA situation. How can we get there?"[29]

Apparently this was not the first time Palmer had raised the issue.

"From day one, all he's talked about is selling one of the frequencies," charged Nan Rubin, former WBAI LAB chair, during the Battle of Berkeley. "The rest of the board couldn't shut him up. And that other guy from Houston, David Acosta? He's just as bad." By late July a critical mass of board members seems to have become educated, Palmer style. Charles Burress of the *San Francisco Chronicle* reported on July 28 that Pacifica's seven-member executive committee would soon vote on a sale, and that a majority of the committee appeared ready to approve the idea.[30] A day later Bay Area board member Pete Bramson publicly charged that the board's executive committee was considering taking out a loan against the value of KPFA's license.[31] The public disclosure of this plan seemed to cool some key board members on the idea, but not all of them. Berry told the *Chronicle* that it was difficult to persuade some executive committee members to permit the KPFA staff to return. This was confirmed by Michael Fineman, whose crisis public relations management team had by then been hired to represent Pacifica.[32] "Some board members advocated less conciliatory alternatives," Fineman later disclosed in a report on his firm's work for the foundation, although he would not detail what those alternatives were. Neither would their advocates, since Fineman wisely counseled the board to leave the talking up to Chadwick and Berry.[33]

But even after Berry publicly insisted that the board had rejected a station sale, she hinted that she would not take a buyer's quote from the Berkeley City Council as an insult.[34] Nor did the issue go away upon resumption of normal operation at KPFA. In late August of 1999 WBAI programmer Mimi Rosenberg stopped at her station to drop off a tape. There she discovered Pacifica's chair holding an impromptu meeting with the staff. What Berry allegedly said so shocked her that she immediately called KPFA and consented to an interview over the station's airwaves. According to Rosenberg, Berry asked the WBAI staff "how we would feel if numerous stations of a smaller nature were purchased and there was a voice given in Atlanta and throughout the south, etc. versus the maintenance of the signal the frequency, the license in California."[35] Her interviewer asked if Rosenberg interpreted this as a proposal to sell the Berkeley station. "I would take it as a signal that KPFA is in grave jeopardy," Rosenberg replied. "[Berry's] antipathy to KPFA is such that she was certainly fielding the issue of a sale."[36] Journalist Judith Coburn of Salon found another WBAI staff member who anonymously confirmed that Berry proposed selling KPFA and purchasing a string of radio stations in the South – "A kind of black NPR."[37] Berry angrily denied that she had made such a suggestion. "They said I was a fascist, a CIA agent, a black bitch. They said I was going to sell Pacifica and buy some black stations in the South. Because that's what black people do," she told a reporter.[38]

Dissidents indeed called Mary Frances Berry many inappropriate things during the Pacifica crisis, but no one suggested that black people have an inherent taste for selling radio stations, least of all WBAI's African-American morning show host Bernard White. He also heard Berry's comments at the meeting. "She said that one of the things that the national board was considering was the purchase of some stations in the Midwest, some smaller stations in the Midwest and in the South," White recalled. "And that the question was where would the money come from to purchase the stations given the high cost of stations at this time. She said through the sale of one of the radio stations, through the possible sale."[39]

Although Pacifica repeatedly promised publicly not to sell a station, hints of alternate plans periodically surfaced like institutional Freudian slips. In January of 2001 board member John Murdock proposed new bylaws for the organization that would have authorized the board's executive committee to deal with Pacifica's assets as long as the action did not include "the sale, transfer or other disposition of substantially all of the assets or property of the Foundation." As activists noted, the language did not forbid the cashing in on "substantially some" of the network, such as KPFA or WBAI. The bylaws also allowed board members "to receive reasonable compensation for services rendered to the Foundation in a professional capacity."[40] On October 23, 2001, the *San Francisco Examiner* interviewed board member Ken Ford. According to the article, Ford insisted that Pacifica had no intention of selling a station, but he was quoted as saying, "KPFA in Berkeley and WBAI in New York are in the broadcast band reserved for commercial stations. I've been told non-commercial licenses sell for $30 to $40 million and commercial licenses sell for $150 to $250 million each. Think of what we could do with the difference! Let's parley these commercial licenses into more stations around the country. To me that's just common sense."[41] Pacifica quickly issued a press release in which Ford claimed that he had been misunderstood, that he had paraphrased the ideas of another board member (possibly Michael Palmer).[42] The board had decided that no stations were for sale, the release reiterated. Indeed, Pacifica's FCC lawyer John Crigler received strict instructions from Lynn Chadwick to tell anyone who called expressing interest in buying a Pacifica station that none were for sale.[43]

But that is apparently not what Patrick M. Clawson of Radio America heard when he called Pacifica on October 29, 2001, proposing to buy WPFW for the non-profit talk-radio distribution network, "driven by its commitment to traditional American values, limited government and the free market," according to its Web site.[44] "This letter follows up on telephone conversations I had this morning with Mr. Ford and Ms. Meredith [Pacifica's assistant executive director] concerning news reports that the Pacifica Foundation is experiencing financial difficulties and may consider selling some or all of its radio stations," Clawson's letter of that date addressed to the Pacifica national office began. He also proposed buying WPFW or other Pacifica stations, leasing WPFW through a local marketing agreement, or leasing airtime on WPFW or other Pacifica stations. "Please contact me immediately so we may discuss the mechanics of making a formal offer and presentation to the Board of Directors for consideration at its next meeting."[45]

I found Clawson's communication while going through Pacifica's papers after the iPNB settlement had been reached, and I immediately called him. Clawson expressed great frustration that after their discussions, neither Meredith nor Ford followed up on his

proposals. "Just another example of Pacifica's lack of profession-
alism," Clawson told me bitterly. In my interview with board
member Ken Ford, Ford acknowledged that he had spoken with
Clawson and had offered what could be described as halfhearted
encouragement. "[M]y comment to the gentleman was: (1) I suggest
you send letters to the other people on the board and (2) there's no
way in hell they're going to sell you this station [WPFW]," Ford later
recalled.[46] Unfortunately for Radio America's hopes for a possible
partnership with Pacifica, Ford resigned from the board several days
after Clawson sent his letter, and Meredith was soon to follow.[47] Even
after the settlement, Berry ally Bertram Lee, now sitting on the
iPNB as one of the members of the former Berry majority, told
board members at a retreat that while he regarded the station sale
question as moot, it still seemed to him a good idea.[48]

In fairness, it must be said that it was. Selling a Pacifica station
would have generated millions of dollars for the foundation,
allowing the network to at least double its broadcasting reach
around the United States. Ford later insisted that the board had
never seriously considered selling KPFA during the Battle of
Berkeley in 1999, and that the board discussions about a sale that
took place were spoken in frustrated jest. "And the issue there was
like, when you've got a kid that misbehaves, you want to get rid of
them," Ford later recalled. "People say 'I want to kill this kid.' But
they love them. So you just say it out of frustration and you move
on."[49]

But even Ford and another board member had advocated what
he called a station "swap" but in fact involved a station sale. Pacifica
would have sold WBAI, a commercial license worth perhaps as
much as two hundred million dollars, and purchased a license on
the educational section of the FM bandwidth in Long Island for a
lower price. The monetary difference pocketed would have been
substantial. "We could have made, estimates were I guess around
anything between twenty and thirty million dollars we would have
netted off the transfer," Ford later explained. "That would have
bought us two or three more licenses, possibly one in Detroit or

Chicago, Atlanta, and another part of the country. We could have had almost double our entree into the masses."[50] This proposal may very well have been what Berry was talking about in her meeting at WBAI in the late summer of 1999.

Had Pacifica's directors by that year not cut off everyone but themselves from a formal say in the foundation's governance, and had they publicly advocated station sale proposals rather than letting the subject slip out via Michael Palmer's accidentally disclosed email, the recent history of Pacifica radio might have evolved very differently. But Pacifica's leaders had become obsessed with freeing themselves from any binding accountability to the rest of the organization, going so far as to explore the legality of creating a new foundation and merging Pacifica into it.[51] Having opted to rule by secrecy and fiat, their whispered discussions about "swaps" and sales could only appear to others as plots to further wrest the organization's assets from Pacifica's listener-subscribers and staff, and they might have been just that.

Thankfully, we will never know for sure what the Berry regime might have done with the network's assets had they won the Pacifica struggle. What I personally found galling was the extent to which Berry's apologists urged the Left to accept the Pacifica board's word on the matter without skepticism. "[T]he Pacifica National Board has passed multiple unanimous motions declaring that no station is for sale," assured KPFK management in a July 9, 2001, statement published on *The Nation* magazine's Web site, as if because a group of public officials say something everyone knows it must be true.[52] Apparently the financial liquidation of KPFA or WBAI by a board without any accountability to the public was a chance some progressives were willing to take. It was, understandably, not a chance that KPFA's or WBAI's grassroots supporters were willing to take for themselves. "I didn't believe that Pacifica's behavior stemmed from a right-wing plot to take over the network," later commented KPFA local advisory board chair Sherry Gendelman. "But I did think that the final configuration of the old Pacifica board had on it individuals who joined to profit off of the astonishing value of the Pacifica stations since the passage of the Telecommunications Act of 1996."[53]

Did ethnic tensions within Pacifica precipitate the crisis of the late 1990s?

While ethnic antagonisms have played a significant role in the life of Pacifica radio for many years, they did not initiate the organization's troubles during this period.

Divisions over "racial" and ethnic issues have plagued the American Left since the decline of the civil rights coalition after the passage of the Voting Rights Act in 1965.[54] These tensions played themselves out regularly at Pacifica radio. In the 1970s, black, Latino, and Asian programmers often charged white managers and governors at Pacifica with refusing to adequately open up the network's resources to them, or with displaying various forms of insensitivity to minorities. Managers countercharged that minority programmers sought, not to integrate their broadcasting projects into the life of Pacifica, but to create entirely separate enclaves, unaccountable to the rest of the organization.

This dilemma played itself out very dramatically at KPFA in the 1970s. But by the late 1980s, most minority managers at Pacifica had abandoned the Third World enclave strategies characteristic of the "community radio" era described in Chapter 3. Indeed, as outlined in Chapter 5, some of the strongest advocates of strip programming in the 1980s and 1990s, Pat Scott prominent among them, approved of schedules that swept away many of the minority activist programs inaugurated in the 1970s.

During the crisis of the late 1990s, Pacifica management often claimed that the network's dissident groups were simply white listeners and programmers resistant to their plans for bigger and more diverse audiences. Programmers countercharged that Pacifica had cancelled various minority activist programs founded in the 1970s, especially at KPFK, KPFA, and KPFT. Mary Frances Berry and her allies correctly observed that KPFA's audience was predominantly white (although it is less so now than it was in the 1990s). But during this period Pacifica management never explained, much less demonstrated, *how* they planned to make the networks' West Coast audience more diverse. A limited rhetoric rather than proven practice was all that supported their claims to want to diversify the institution.

Once Pacifica shut KPFA down in the summer of 1999, whatever civility existed around this issue dissolved into a verbal free-for-all of race-carding, race-baiting, and racism. Pacifica employees were sometimes called "nigger bitch" and "house nigger" during verbal confrontations.[55] Polite and reasonable white dissidents regularly heard Pacifica leaders and their staff allies intimate or boldly claim that racism and white supremacy motivated their concerns. As Mary Frances Berry and some of her fellow board members were black, and many of KPFA's dissidents were white, long-suppressed fears were now expressed openly. "[T]here certainly was a presumption which was spoken aloud, that you had a group of black people who were running the organization and they wanted to go off and do something that was going to be more directed towards what those folks thought black people wanted," African-American board member John Murdock later commented. "And that was said more than a few times."[56]

Besieged with hostile emails, Pacifica board member Ken Ford, also African-American, came away from the battle with a bitter taste regarding the American Left. "I've been in places where I have been called a lot of negative things – in the South, and even in Chicago," he later recalled. "But a lot of people that I found in California on the Left, they were some of the most hardened racists, and they were hypocrites to be that way."[57]

But Murdock left his stint at Pacifica with a different impression. "For me personally, there were some instances where race clearly had something to do [with the situation]," he later explained. "I don't think that for most of the people, no matter what their views, who were involved, who sent me emails, I don't think that most of them they even knew that I was black. I don't think for most of them it mattered. I got a couple of things that were threatening and way out of line, and that was a problem. But it would not be fair to people who emailed me and didn't know me and oftentimes said things that were informed, to assume that they did it based on race."[58] Although the Pacifica crisis of the 1990s greatly exacerbated the network's perennial tensions around "race" and ethnicity, these tensions alone did not cause the institution's civil war.

Why did the Pacifica network experience a social explosion from 1999 through 2002? And why did the network's crisis spread out into so much of U.S. civil society?

We can best understand Pacifica radio's history as two stories moving through time, constantly influencing each other. The first story focuses on the organization's internal life – always contradictory, volatile, and unstable. The second story tracks Pacifica's ever shifting external environment – government regulation of broadcasting, changes in media, and ways that people who paid attention to Pacifica defined the network's purpose. The Pacifica Foundation's attempts to recreate the organization in the late 1980s and 1990s would have caused trouble under any circumstances. But Pacifica's external environment made the situation much more challenging. A historical understanding of Pacifica's public crisis in the late 1990s begins with Pacifica's internal story, and specifically with the contradictions Pacifica's founders structured into the organization in the 1940s and 1950s.

Lewis Hill and his fellow conscientious objectors came out of the Second World War determined to use radio to bring their radical ideas to a mass medium. They wanted to break through the marginality to which pacifism had been confined during the war. Hill saw listener-supported, noncommercial radio as essential to this task, since it would keep the content of his radio station free from the influence of advertisers, who would inevitably pressure the station to tone down its politics. But in mapping out an internal structure for his foundation, Hill also saw his future radio station's listener-subscribers as a potential source of unwanted pressure. He and his fellow pacifists had every reason to fear that if they shared political power with KPFA's listeners, they ran the risk of being voted out of office, just as they had been pushed underground during the overwhelmingly popular Second World War. Hence Hill created a structure that gave the franchise to the foundation's staff but shut out KPFA's listener-subscribers from any formal role in governance. The staff, not the listeners, would choose the foundation's board of directors. As time progressed, Hill came to distrust even staff presence on the board. By the early 1960s, a conventional, self-appointed board of directors governed Pacifica's three radio stations as nonprofit overseer.

This structure served short-term objectives but hurt the organization in the long run. It minimized Hill's and his successor's risk of losing political power within the institution, but it denied subsequent Pacifica boards any semblance of legitimacy. Without an elective mandate and a monetary endowment to dispense, real power within Pacifica quickly fell to the network's one, then three, then five radio station staffs. They, not the board, tended to dictate policy throughout Pacifica. In order to mediate the tensions generated by the disenfranchisement of the organization's actual philanthropists – the foundation's listener-subscribers – Pacifica station staffs developed a rhetoric of moral ownership for use during marathons and pledge drives. WBAI/KPFA/KPFK was "your radio station," listeners constantly heard staff tell them over the airwaves. Generation after generation of Pacificans drew upon this rhetoric, rarely questioning its logic. "[W]e passionately believe in Lou Hill's anti-war vision of social-justice, and of a radio station answerable to no one other than its own listener-sponsors," a dozen members of KPFK's staff declared in a public statement in 2001.[59] In reality the opposite condition prevailed. KPFK, like the other four Pacifica stations, answered legally to the FCC, the CPB, the IRS, and the Pacifica national board – in other words, everyone but the frequency's listener-subscribers, a situation those listener-subscribers noticed and protested with regularity through the station's history.

The rhetoric of moral ownership smoothed over this contradiction embedded in the organization's governance, that Pacifica's listener-subscribers lacked any legal control over an institution that depended almost entirely on them for funding and operation. But that rhetoric did little to create a stratum of leadership within the institution that most Pacificans saw as legitimate. A system of anarcho-feudalism gradually dispersed throughout Pacifica. By the late 1970s the "network" functioned as five poverty-stricken bureaucracies whose local and regional ties far outweighed any sense of obligation to Pacifica's national board or its tiny national office. In fact, the creators of Pacifica's second radio station, KPFK, did not even want to join the foundation. When Louis Schweitzer gave WBAI to Pacifica, the frequency already had a format and staff. KPFT's founders affiliated in part because they thought Pacifica's non-profit status would smooth over their license acquisition process. Some WPFW staff members regarded Pacifica as a white supremacist tyrant, even when the chair of the board and the executive director were black.

These five bureaucracies tolerated Pacifica's top-down legal system as long as foundation officials refrained from interference with their regional power structures. When they did interfere, in the 1970s, provincial revolts such as the KPFA and WBAI strikes of that period quickly followed. In response, the foundation developed a national board system that mirrored the institution's feudal political economy. Each of the network's five self-appointed, non-listener-subscriber-elected local advisory boards appointed their own members to the national board. This is what the organization's activists experienced as the "democracy" that Mary Frances Berry's Pacifica stole from them in February of 1999.

With the election of Ronald Reagan in 1980 and the consequent shift of American politics and culture to the Right, media-conscious individuals on the Left looked to Pacifica radio to construct a credible national broadcasting response. But while Pacifica superficially appeared the perfect candidate for a makeover into the electronic newspaper of the American Left, it was anything but the appropriate institution for the job. By the mid-1990s the evisceration of local access in both commercial and "public" radio in the

United States had turned Pacifica into a "contained" network, something close to the equivalent of five Indian reservations for people who wanted to hear and produce local-access noncommercial radio. In practice, "community radio" at Pacifica meant radio for people with few better places to go, a situation which turned all five stations into personnel management nightmares. The first attempts in the early 1980s to create a truly unified mission for Pacifica and to rethink the organization as a network rather than a five-station confederacy quickly collapsed, most spectacularly at KPFK in Los Angeles.

The experiences Pacifica underwent at KPFK and nationally between 1980 and 1984 should have raised warning flags about the institution's adaptability. But the widely perceived necessity of building a media response to Reaganism generated a steady stream of candidates ready and willing to step repeatedly into the breach. These women and men took on the thankless tasks of restructuring the balkanized, fragmented broadcasting schedules at individual Pacifica frequencies, running capital campaigns for better equipment and new station homes, and building the institutional consensus necessary to clear the way for national programming. Under the administrations of David Salniker and Pat Scott, they achieved successes, most notably in the inauguration of *Democracy Now!*

The reconstruction of the organization, however, came with a significant internal price tag. Scott and Salniker's reforms in the late 1980s and 1990s resulted in the dislocation of hundreds of programmers who, thanks to the containment of the organization, had no equivalent venues to which to transfer their broadcasting activities. These exiles and their small, passionate followings gradually mobilized to fight their way back into the institution, using the Internet as their primary means of communication and organizing. In response, Pacifica developed a managerial culture of toughness. Station managers, program directors, and the foundation administrators began to resemble club bouncers, ready to get verbal and in some instances physical with anyone who stood in their way. But while this cadre of staff could manage Pacifica's core structural problem – an oversupply of constituents combined with an under-supply of space – they could not eliminate it. Nor could their efforts compensate for the fact that the national board still enjoyed no endowment or real legitimacy. Personally exhausted, the main figures in the Scott regime, including Scott herself, fled the organization in 1998, leaving it in the hands of a chair and an executive director who knew how to stand their ground but had little sense of the institution's limits. Anxious to consolidate their authority, they turned the national board into a self-appointing body, removing the only vestige of democratic legitimacy the board enjoyed, its reciprocal relationship with its five local advisory boards. By 1999 Pacifica had become a social explosion waiting to happen.

The firing of KPFA general manager Nicole Sawaya on March 31, 1999, provided the spark that blew up the gasoline can. KPFA's senior staff had for the most part supported the core reforms of the Scott administration – strip programming, increased reliance on satellite fare, and professionalization. But Sawaya's sudden dismissal signaled to the members of the KPFA staff that the process of reform had run amuck. Why would Pacifica dismiss a manager with whom they worked well unless control had become more important than goals? Outraged and fearful of further personnel changes, the staff staged a rebellion, suspending the station's long-standing "gag rule" against on-air discussion of Pacifica's policies in the hope that, as in the KPFA strike of 1974, the Pacifica board would quickly capitulate to their demands.

It was twenty-five years later, however, and Pacifica had ballooned into a sizable bureaucracy, led by an executive director, Lynn Chadwick, who was an old hand at community-radio wars. Both Chadwick and the new chair of Pacifica's board, Mary Frances Berry, clearly saw the crisis at KPFA as a test of their leadership. Their refusal to back down forced the KPFA staff to enter into an alliance with the network's old-guard dissident movement and to open the station's resources to that movement.

Pacifica responded by escalating the crisis, taking actions that tore asunder the carefully constructed web of mystification designed to preserve the organization's fragile internal stability. During the summer of 1999 furious staff, volunteers, and listeners constantly confronted Pacifica with the same question: Who owns KPFA? Tens of thousands of KPFA listeners had for decades been spoon-fed on the rhetoric of moral ownership. KPFA was their radio station, they had been told constantly. Was that still true? Chadwick's and Berry's obstinacy left them no choice but to answer the question honestly. KPFA was not their radio station, they replied to stunned listeners. Pacifica owned the station's license.

I cannot emphasize strongly enough the level of shock with which longtime KPFA listeners received this revelation. Many called me in 1999 pleading that I tell the public what they hoped was "the truth" – that Pacifica did not own KPFA. Further stark evidence of the actual truth came in the form of Pacifica board member Michael Palmer's accidentally disclosed email proposing the sale of KPFA for approximately sixty million dollars. It did not matter that for the next two years Pacifica repeatedly promised not to sell a station. What stunned thousands of Bay Area KPFA supporters was the fact that all the money and work they had given KPFA for years meant nothing. A small group of people completely unaccountable to KPFA's listeners *could* sell "their" station. The rhetoric of moral ownership had been exposed as a fraud. A naked power struggle now ensued in the streets and the courts over who would legally own KPFA – and the rest of the network.

Pacifica's crackdown on KPFA reverberated through the organization like an institutional Rube Goldberg contraption. KPFA staff had run Pacifica's satellite operations. With those responsibilities transferred elsewhere, the network's satellite service deteriorated rapidly. This enraged Pacifica's affiliates, many of whom staged a one-day revolt, refusing to run the *Pacifica Network News*. Their action forced on the network's news director the question of whether to acknowledge the revolt as a news story. When he did, Lynn Chadwick demoted him, polarizing the organization's national programming bureaucracy, especially Amy Goodman and other staff based at WBAI. This exacerbated tensions at the New York station, which further deteriorated throughout 2000, prompting Pacifica to oust the frequency's general manager. The station exploded, then divided. Within months, over a dozen key staff members and their supporters had been fired or banned from WBAI's studios.

Looking in from the outside, or, in the case of Amy Goodman, from the embattled inside, WBAI's Bernard White, Dan Coughlin, Juan Gonzalez, Valerie Van Isler, and their supporters faced a very different situation from that of the KPFA staff. The staff at KPFA had taken back their radio station, then drifted into a stalemate with Pacifica. WBAI's fired and banned could not afford the luxury of stasis. Gonzalez and his faction made a bold decision to tap into the widespread discontent surrounding the network and direct it toward an organized, nonviolent assault on the Pacifica national board. Critics of their efforts cried foul play early and often (while making excuses for or saying nothing about the police-plus-armed-guard shutdown of KPFA in 1999). A paraphrase of a famous presidential quote best summarizes Pacifica's troubles in 2001: Those who made democratic change at Pacifica impossible made the Free Pacifica movement inevitable.

But the movement did not succeed by confrontation alone. Here is where the second story, the external story, came in again. The Free Pacifica movement's rhetoric about a corporate takeover tapped into widespread public anxiety and concern over the turn toward monopoly that broadcasting had taken since the triumph of Reaganism in the early 1980s, made far worse by the Telecommunications Act of 1996. Tens of thousands of Pacifica supporters and sympathizers easily read the Pacifica struggle as a metaphor for that larger crisis. Pacifica's "retooling," *Time* magazine columnist Steve Lopez observed in January of 2001, "comes after a consultant [David Giovanoni] sniffed that Pacifica's impact has gone from 'insignificant to irrelevant.' If they paid this guy 25¢ they were robbed. What's irrelevant is the numbing prattle of indistinguishable loudmouths who populate ratings-drive broadcast media."

"Everything is numbers today," Lopez continued.

The weekend box office. The President's approval ratings. The quarterly profits. For 50 years, there was one place where numbers did not exist as a measure of success or as validation of purpose. Pacifica broadcasting can be tedious at times, with its tie-dyed version of truth and justice. But the voice is indignant, probing and unapologetic, and in the age of mega-media conglomerization, an alternative view is a necessity.[60]

This sentiment, widespread and omnipresent, resolved Pacifica radio's civil war. It convinced thousands of politicians, academics, lawyers, activists, and celebrities to sign partisan statements about an institutional conflict they barely understood. It prompted the Attorney General of California to endorse a class action lawsuit against the head of the U.S. Civil Rights Commission. The Pacifica network became the *no pasaron* line in the fight against media corporatization. Only in this context can we understand why a struggle over 5 out of the nation's over 13,000 radio stations became such a cause.

Does this imply that the Free Pacifica movement saw corporate and mainstream influence where none existed? Of course not. The corporate/mainstream/Democratic Party pressure clearly asserted itself in ad agencies idiotically suggesting that Pacifica retain Jimmy Carter and Bill Clinton as third-party spokespersons; professional audience number crunchers for whom content took a back seat to ratings; and corporate crisis management PR firms hired to spin the armed occupation of KPFA.

A focus on these factors alone, however, loses sight of the origins of the Pacifica crisis – an attempt by the American Left to convert a confederacy of grassroots radio stations into a powerful and unified national voice. This study argues, with the benefit of hindsight, that that effort failed because conditions within and beyond Pacifica made it impossible. Of course none of the historical actors who led and managed Pacifica from the early 1980s onward enjoyed that hindsight. As they continuously banged their heads against the hard wall of reality, they became frustrated and cynical. They lost any sense of the values they sought to promulgate elsewhere – openness, democracy, and free speech. They gradually came to see their own constituents as the enemy and the outside corporate/governmental world as their friend. In the end, they pushed Pacifica's contradictions to the limit and provoked a transformative crisis. A project intended to radicalize America wound up radicalizing itself. As of this writing, Pacifica radio is surely one of the world's most democratic independent media networks.

What does the future look like for Pacifica radio?

Pacifica radio's health and future are intricately tied to external conditions far more than to the nature of its internal structure.

No matter what system of governance Pacifica establishes, and no matter how democratic it remains, the organization will still face external pressures that severely compromise its ability to manage personnel and build consensus about the foundation's programming mission. Monopolized, automated, and preformatted to the millisecond, the AM and FM airwaves beyond Pacifica are less directly accessible to public input in any form than at any time in United States history. This condition will continue to saddle Pacifica with far more programmers and programming visions than the institution can handle, even allowing for the opportunities the Internet now offers programmers. Ironically, Pacifica could democratize itself precisely because, even during the Pat Scott and Lynn Chadwick years, it remained far more open and accessible than most commercial or "public" radio stations. Two examples of less successful attempts to resist corporatization elsewhere illustrate this point and the external dilemma that confronts the Pacifica network.

At the same time that the WBAI crisis erupted in 2001, rumors surfaced that the owners of the *Jewish Daily Forward* planned to sell their talk radio station, WEVD in New York City. Inaugurated in 1927, WEVD's liberal founders named their frequency's call letters after Eugene Victor Debs, five times U.S. presidential candidate and head of the Socialist Party of America. The *Forward* bought the signal in 1931 and offered programs in Yiddish, Polish, and Greek. By the late 1990s management ran WEVD as a talk radio station, among its hosts former New York City Mayor Edward Koch. WEVD usually delivered an annual profit, but the same could not be said for its owner. The *Forward* began posting losses of about two million dollars a year in the 1990s, thanks to a dramatic drop in subscriptions. Not surprisingly, after the passage of the Telecommunications Act of 1996, *Forward* management began thinking about selling the station for its market price, approximately ninety million dollars, enough to keep the newspaper running for decades.[61]

Manhattan postal worker Chuck Zlatkin had listened faithfully to WEVD for years. The rumors of the sale alarmed him. He and a circle of friends called and wrote to WEVD management asking for the truth. They received not a single response. Finally, in August, *Forward* officials confirmed their plan to turn WEVD over to ABC/Disney's ESPN sports radio network. Furious WEVD fans held demonstrations in front of the station. They pleaded with local politicians to protest the move. They raised thousands of dollars to launch a legal challenge to the sale. And, like Pacifica's dissidents, they started their own Web site, www.saveWEVD.com.[62] On Friday, August 31, Zlatkin and his followers held a candlelight vigil outside WEVD's Seventh Avenue offices in Manhattan to mark and protest the station's transition from a liberal news format to 24-hour sports talk. "The Forward Association and the Disney/ABC/ESPN hijackers were placed on notice," *Save WEVD's newsletter* bravely declared the next day. "[D]on't think we're here to sit Shiva. We're here to stand up for what's right!"[63]

But Save WEVD's efforts were of no avail. Unlike Pacifica's stations, WEVD offered no beachheads upon which the troops of democratization could launch a serious attack. WEVD had no federally mandated local advisory board. The law did not require the station's management to hold open meetings and hear the concerns of listeners. Despite the 1934 Communication Act's clear stipulation that the airwaves belong to the public, FCC regulations provided no serious legal roadblocks to a commercial license transfer unpopular with listeners. Nine months later, after the FCC rejected Save WEVD's "Petition to Deny" ABC's license application, the group conceded defeat. "Again, thanks to all who lent support and encouragement through this period of struggle," Zlatkin concluded in one of his last email newsletters. "We live in dire times. Access to information and the ability to express our first amendment rights are under attack each day."[64]

At the same time a tense standoff between minority youth groups and management at hip-hop station KMEL-FM in San Francisco exploded after the firing of David "Davey D" Cook, the frequency's popular deejay. Although management insisted that they let him go in October 2001 because of budget cuts, KMEL fired Cook just after he invited East Bay Congressmember Barbara Lee and popular hip-hop artist Boots Riley onto his show to air their objections to the impending bombing of Afghanistan. Cook also co-hosted the 4:00 p.m. *Hard Knock Radio* strip at KPFA. Within days, spirited picket lines and an email/fax blitz hit the station. "Check your priorities," one community leader warned KMEL management at a demonstration. "Without the community, your station would never have been made."[65]

Anger toward KMEL ("the people's station," as it called itself) had been mounting ever since Clear Channel purchased the frequency's former owner, AM/FM Inc., in 1999. Clear Channel acquired KMEL and 489 more radio signals for twenty-four billion dollars, almost forty-nine million dollars a unit.[66] The transaction completed Clear Channel's 1,200-station empire. Just before the move, KMEL cancelled *Street Soldiers*, an award-winning talk show produced by the Omega Boy's Club and aimed at at-risk inner-city youth.[67] In response, a group of Bay Area African-American leaders announced plans to file a complaint against the merger.[68] Even though KMEL management eventually put *Street Soldiers* back on the air, Cook's 2001 ouster struck a raw nerve in KMEL's estimated 600,000 regular listeners. Unlike *Street Soldiers*, Cook readily raised issues about racism and politics on his show, earning him a large and dedicated youth following.[69]

In response to Cook's firing, the Youth Media Council, a coalition of musicians and organizers, formed the Building a People's Station

Media Campaign to exert influence over KMEL's policies. The group carefully monitored KMEL's air sound for months, then issued a report in the fall of 2002 titled "Is KMEL the People's Station?" The coalition's study came to three general conclusions about KMEL: first, the frequency's management excluded local artists and activists from the station's air sound; second, station staff employed no consistent means of encouraging listener feedback beyond contests and games; and, finally, KMEL talk shows such as *Street Soldiers* emphasized self-help and avoided discussion of collective social change. "Solutions to problems raised in content were limited to individuals making better choices, getting new game plans, and changing personal behavior," the report charged. "Root causes were completely ignored."[70]

The Youth Media Council document then outlined "Six Steps to Accountability at KMEL," including more on-air access to local musicians, an on-air hotline, and, most important, a formal local advisory board "that represents a range of opinions and can truly advocate for the issues and concerns of KMEL's audience, who are overwhelmingly young people of color."[71] The Campaign's organizers shrewdly understood that the first step to more influence over KMEL's programming schedule was to institutionalize their relationship with station management.

On January 6, 2003, a small group of KMEL activist-listeners, all in their teens and twenties, visited KMEL's South of Market San Francisco offices for a conference with station representatives. They entered the first floor, likened by one journalist to "a tiny security bunker with silent music videos flickering on small wall-mounted TVs." Clear Channel executives listened politely while Malkia Cyril of Youth Media Council made the coalition's case. Ever since Clear Channel took over, she charged, "there has been no access to the airwaves for social justice organizations, an imbalance in programming and content, and no avenues for community accountability."[72] The two groups scheduled another session for the following Wednesday. "We're happy to have people come to us with their ideas and suggestions, and the door's always open to that," a Clear

Channel flak told the *San Francisco Chronicle* after the gathering.[73]

But a year after the Youth Media Council's report, KMEL's Web site showed little evidence of a constructive response to the campaign. The site's Community Center page listed no upcoming public meetings with station management. Its community calendar billboarded no social justice-related events. Its music news page featured no section dedicated to the activities of local musicians. Although the Web site included a Love Zone where listeners could call to sign up with a dating service, no page offered a telephone feedback hotline as requested by the council. In fact, the site listed no station telephone numbers at all.[74]

Because of Clear Channel's obstinacy at KMEL, the signal became to Bay Area radio activists a symbol of the rampant media consolidation created by the Telecommunications Act of 1996. The most hopeful sign of resistance to that consolidation came in the form of massive public opposition to Federal Communication Commission proposals to further relax the nation's media ownership rules. In early June of 2003, by a narrow vote of 3 to 2 the commission permitted even more mega-merging, eliminating caps on how much of the national market television and cable networks could control and scotching a rule that barred corporations that owned newspapers in a media market from buying TV or radio stations in the same region. Prior to the vote, hundreds of radio activists gathered in front of KMEL's headquarters to denounce the impending decision. Protest signs read, "Nothing to say, everything to sell!" and "No more Clear Channels!" Nationally 750,000 people from all sides of the political spectrum contacted the FCC in opposition to the proposals, the biggest response in the commission's history. Both the National Rifle Association and the National Organization for Women passed resolutions against further media consolidation, as did Republican Senator Jesse Helms.[75] The extent of public opposition to the measures manifested itself in an unprecedented vote in September by the United States Senate to overturn these two FCC rulings.[76]

But as long as stories like WEVD and KMEL's remain typical, as long as it remains difficult to exercise local influence over the vast majority of the nation's radio stations, listener-activists will flock to the contained world of Pacifica radio. There, to their initial delight, they will discover an openness and a freedom unheard-of in commercial or even "public" broadcasting. Then they will discover something else: throngs of kindred spirits with competing visions for the organization or pieces of it. Many will spend years of their lives fighting over air time deliberately made scarce by political forces dedicated to privatizing and commoditizing public resources, be they national parks, water systems, electric power plants, or radio stations. The real fight now is with those forces.

"Why settle for crumbs from Pacifica's leadership, when the government is quietly doling all the loaves out to a handful of corporate media giants?" asked media historian Robert McChesney shortly after the reopening of KPFA in 1999. "Why let Wall Street and Madison Avenue have unchallenged control over our journalism and culture? The point is not just to democratize the margins but to battle for the very heart and soul of our whole nation."[77] Indeed, for the foreseeable future the health of Pacifica radio depends, not on what happens within its halls, but on what takes place beyond them. What I hope that Pacifica radio's civil war presaged is a much larger revolt against the forces of monopolization that created the environment which provoked the Pacifica crisis. That campaign has already begun, but it could learn a great deal from the creativity and passion Pacifica radio's listeners and staff demonstrated in their bid to "take back," "save," and democratize the five radio stations they loved best. For that remarkable wave of energy to be unleashed on the nation's mainstream broadcasting structure, we must believe in our hearts what founding regulators of U.S. broadcasting told us in their Radio Act of 1927. "Broadcasting stations are licensed to serve the public," they wrote, "and not for the purpose of furthering the private or selfish interests of individuals or groups."[78] Just as KPFA, WBAI, KPFK, WPFW, and KPFT are our radio stations, so are the rest. We need to take them all back.

Endnotes

1 Carol Spooner et al., "SETTLEMENT AGREEMENT" (December 12, 2001), Sections 1(a), 3(b): www.savepacifica.net/settlement.html.

2 This exchange can be found on "Democracy Now! Returns to Pacifica's Airwaves After Five Months in Exile," *Democracy Now!* (January 7, 2002, audio); Fred Kuhn died in April 2005 after a long battle with cancer. See Don Rojas, "WBAI Mourns the Passing of Our Beloved Fred Kuhn" (April 29, 2005): www.wbai.org.

3 Leslie Cagan, letter to Mr. Catano, January 13, 2002, *PNOP*, Box 181.

4 Mike Janssen, "The Outsiders Are Back In; They Applaud as Pacifica Reverses Course," *Current* (January 28, 2002): www.current.org/radio/radio0202pacifica.html.

5 Marc Cooper Show Taken Off KPFK, email from Marc Cooper to KPFK listeners (February 19, 2002).

6 Mike Janssen, "The Outsiders Are Back In," *Current* (January 28, 2002), and "Pacifica Has Replaced Managers at Four of Its Five Radio Stations," *Current* (February 11, 2002): www.current.org/radio/radio0202pacifica.html.

7 Ross Wisdom, CPA, letter to Pacifica Board of Directors, February 9, 2002, p.4; Pacifica Foundation, "Statement of Activities-National October 1, 2000, through September 30, 2001, UNAUDITED-PER UNADJUSTED TRIAL BALANCE" (February 7, 2002), p.16; Susan Douglas, "Is There a Future for Pacifica?" *The Nation* (March 28, 2002): www.thenation.com/doc.mhtml?i=20020415&c=3&s=douglas; Diana Cohn, Senior Program Officer, Solidago Foundation, letter to Bessie Wash, June 22, 2000, p.1. *PNOP*, Box 181.

8 Pacifica By-Laws Drafts, April 2, 2003, Draft A, Article 4, Section 5.

9 Mike Jansen, "Radio That's Representative," *Current* (September 22, 2003): www.current.org/radio/radio0317pacifica.html.

10 Steven Brown, "RACE-BAITING, "WHITE-TRASHING," ANTI-SEMITISM & IMPERMISSIBLE BEHAVIOR AT WBAI," email article (June 23, 2004).

11 Chris Thompson, "War and Peace," *East Bay Express* (January 9-15, 2002), p.15.

12 Lorna Salzman, "WBAI: The Democratic Party's Newest Target," posted January 28, 2001: nyfma.tao.ca/nyfma02681.html; Geov Parrish, "Pacifica Inc.: The Sad, Slippery Slope of the Corporate Hijacking of Community Radio" (August 22. 2001): www.workingforchange.com/article.cfm?ItemID=11787.

13 Hallock Hoffman, interview with author (October 28, 1996), p.1; "Harold Winkler, Ph.D.," from "Vitae and Biographies of Group Members," Group for Academic Freedom papers (Tolman files), 1950-1956, Box 1, Bancroft Library, University of California.

14 Schweitzer was among those who opposed WBAI broadcasting Chris
    Koch's reports from North Vietnam: see Jesse Walker, *Rebels on the Air: An
    Alternative History of Radio in America* (New York: NYU Press, 2001), p.75;
    dissident KPFK general manager Paul Dallas's critical assessment of
    Hoffman can be found in Paul Dallas, *Dallas in Wonderland: The Pacifica
    Approach to Free Radio* (Los Angeles: 1967), p.207.

15 Lauren Kern, "Turning Out the Static," *Houston Press* (April 5, 2001):
    www.houstonpress.com/issues/2001-04-05/feature2.html.

16 Dave Fertig, interview with author (April 12, 2005), p.2.

17 One of the lead plaintiffs in *Adelson v. Pacifica* pointedly questioned a
    Goodman interview with a conspiracy theorist during Pacifica's live
    coverage of the Clinton scandal hearings in the Senate. "There is little
    doubt that Amy Goodman is extremely talented in many areas,"
    commented KPFA local advisory board chair Sherry Gendelman at a 1999
    Pacifica national board meeting. "Political anchoring of a senate impeach-
    ment trial is outside the bounty of her talent": see "Minutes, Pacifica
    Foundation Board of Directors Meeting, February 28, 1999, Berkeley, CA":
    www.pacifica.org/board/transcripts/tran9906.html.

18 Jeannie Bunton, Director of Communications, Corporation for Public
    Broadcasting, email interview with author (February 19, 2004); Ken Ford,
    interview with author (February 22, 2004), p.2.

19 Marc Cooper, "Smash the Nader Backlash!" *Mother Jones* (November 15,
    2000): www.motherjones.com/reality_check/nader_backlash.html. Landau's
    name appears on Nader's citizens committee: see
    www.votenader.org/press/citizens_committee.html.

20 Gary Null's book *AIDS: A Second Opinion* can be found in Web form at
    www.garynull.com/Documents/aids.htm; the 750 page version with James
    Feast was published by Seven Stories Press in 2000; for a review see Peter
    Kurth, "Quack Record," *Salon* (May 21, 2002):
    www.salon.com/books/feature/2002/05/21/null/.

21 Bill Weinberg, "Rule by Idiocy: WBAI Falls for Right-Wing Conspiracy
    Theory" (no date): www.wbaiaction.org/statements/01-07-10jimmarrs.html;
    Jim Marrs, *Rule by Secrecy: The Hidden History That Connects the Trilateral
    Commission, the Freemasons, and the Great Pyramids* (New York: Perennial,
    2000), p.147. Marrs writes, "The Protocols still chills readers with its
    prophetic description of the methodology for tyranny by a few. Its message
    fits quite well with the elitist outlooks of men like Cecil Rhodes and the
    Rothchilds."

22 See Paul DeRienzo, "Steve Yasko and the Adventures of Mike Bilt," from
    Eating Its Own: Report on the Pacifica Crisis (no date),
    http://pdr.autono.net/message2b.html.

23 "KPFT – The Sounds of Texas, Program Schedule" (January 1999).

24 "Progressives Respond to Saul Landau's Letter" (February 25, 2000): www.fsrn.org/landau_response2.html.
25 Rafael Renteria, interview with author (September 22, 2002), p.15.
26 Ray Hill, interview with author (January 15, 2003), p.14.
27 KPFT program schedule, June 13, 2004: www.kpft.org/programs.php.
28 Lynn Chadwick quoted in Jacqueline Conciatore, "Tempers Rise as Pacifica Lets Board Select Its Own Members," *Current* (March 8, 1999) (ellipses in original): www.current.org/rad/rad906p.html.
29 Michael Palmer quoted in "Freedom's Just Another Word," *The Texas Observer* (August 6, 1999): http://www.texasobserver.org/showArticle.asp?ArticleID=316.
30 Charles Burress, "Foundation Denies KPFA to Be Sold," *San Francisco Chronicle* (July 28, 1999), p.A15.
31 Pete Bramson, "Pacifica National Board Member Pete Bramson's Statement at a 7/28/99 Berkeley Press Conference": www.radio4all.org/freepacifica/bramson.htm.
32 Charles Burress, "KPFA Staff Gets Call to Return to Work," *San Francisco Chronicle* (July 29, 1999), p.A8.
33 "Case Study, KPFA Conflict: Pacifica Foundation," Michael Fineman Associates, unpublished manuscript, no date. I appreciate Michael Fineman's willingness to share this document.
34 Jacqueline Conciatore, "Pacifica Opens KPFA's Doors, Staffers Continue Protest" (August 2, 1999): www.current.org/rad/rad914p.html.
35 Kris Welch, Dennis Bernstein, and Mimi Rosenberg, "August 25, 1999 – Transcript, Flashpoints Interview with Mimi Rosenberg, Local Advisory Board Member for WBAI in New York" (August 25, 1999): www.radio4all.org/fp/0825mimi_re_mfb.htm.
36 Ibid.
37 Judith Cockburn, "There's Something About Mary," *Salon* (October 12, 1999): www.salon.com/news/feature/1999/10/12/berry/index2.html.
38 John Dinges, "What's Going On at Pacifica?" *The Nation* (May 1, 2000): www.thenation.com/doc.mhtml?i=20000501&c=7&s=dinges.
39 Bernard White, interview with author (November 1, 2002), p.13.
40 John Murdock, "Re: Proposed Bylaw Revisions" (January 19, 2001): Section 3.16 and Section 4.2, www.savepacifica.net/bylaws_revise.html. When I interviewed John Murdock for this study, he contextualized his executive committee/station sale section of the bylaws as follows: "[W]hen I wrote the language it was actually to indicate, look, the national board cannot go off and sell a station. But one of the things a board has to be careful about because of its fiduciary responsibilities is not in the bylaws to pick out specific issues that might be important today and foreclose the exercise of reasonable judgment. So there was an attempt to sort of say,

'Look, there are limits to what this board can do.' But on the other hand the board's got to have the flexibility to do what boards do, which is to exercise judgment." John Murdock, interview with author (December 30, 2003), p.2.

41 Fred Dodsworth, "New Alarms Sound over KPFA," *San Francisco Examiner* (October 23, 2001).

42 Pacifica press release,"Statement from Pacifica Foundation Vice Chairman Ken Ford" (October 25, 2001).

43 John Crigler, interview with author (October 16, 2002).

44 See http://www.radioamerica.org/, October 18, 2003.

45 Patrick M. Clawson, letter to Robert Farrell, Ken Ford, and Joanne Meredith (October 29, 2001), p.1.

46 Ken Ford, interview with author (February 22, 2004), p.4.

47 Fred Dodsworth, "New Alarms Sound over KPFA," *San Francisco Examiner* (October 23, 2001) (in the Examiner story Ford also compared Pacifica's dissidents to Al Qaeda); Pacifica campaign press release, "Ken Ford Resigns" (November 1, 2001).

48 Pete Bramson, interview with author (August 23, 2002), pp.30-32.

49 Ken Ford, interview with author (February 22, 2004), pp.3-4.

50 Ibid, p.5.

51 Adam Brownstein, letter to John Crigler, "Re: Pacifica Foundation: Incorporation of a D.C. Non-Profit Corp. & Merger of the Existing California Corporation into It," June 23, 2000, *PNOP*, Box 181.

52 KPFK-LA Management, "Pacifica Myths and Realities," *The Nation* (July 9, 2001): www.thenation.com/doc.mhtml%3Fi=20010716&s=kpfkla2001.

53 Sherry Gendelman, interview with author (August 10, 2004), p.1.

54 I put the word "racial" in quotes because I do not believe that "race" exists. There is only one race, the human race. What does exist, unfortunately, is "racism," which is first and foremost a deluded belief in the existence of "races."

55 Askia Mohammed, "Are Anti-Pacifica Radio Protestors Racists?" (Autumn 1999): www.blackjournalism.com/racismat.htm.

56 John Murdock, interview with author (December 30, 2003), p.3.

57 Ken Ford, interview with author (February 22, 2004), p.6.

58 John Murdock, interview with author (December 30, 2003), p.3.

59 Joe Domanick, Beto Arcos, Jon Wiener, Robert Mora, Yatrika Shah-Rais, Marc Cooper, Sergio Mielniczenko, Susan Weissman, John Retsk, Jay Kagelman, Art Gould, Barbara Osborn, John Beaupre, Barry Smolin, Hector Resendez, Earl Ofari Hutchinson, and Simeon Pillich, "To: Amy Goodman, From: The On-Air Programmers of KPFK, Re: Up-Coming Summer Fund Drive," (May 15, 2001): www.peak.org/mailing-list/archive/grc/msg01084.html.

60 Steve Lopez, "This Just In: We're Fired," *Time* (January 29, 2001), p.6.
61 Jayson Blair, "Liberal Radio Mainstay May Sell to Make Way for ESPN," *The New York Times* (June 26, 2001), p.9.
62 "Legal Challenge," Save WEVD Newsletter (August 23, 2001), email.
63 "End of an Era," *Save WEVD Newsletter* (August 29, 2001), email; "Candlelight Vigil: A Bittersweet Blast," *Save WEVD Newsletter* (September 3, 2001), email.
64 Chuck Slatkin, "Dear Friends and Supporters," *Save WEVD Newsletter* (March 8, 2003), email.
65 Jeff Chang, "Urban Radio Rage," *San Francisco Bay Guardian* (January 22, 2003): www.sfbg.com/37/18/cover_kmel.html.
66 Ibid; "In the Matter of the Applications of Shareholders of AMFM, Inc. (Transferor) and Clear Channel Communications, Inc. (Transferee)," File Nos. BTC/BTCH/BTCFTB/BTCFT-19991116AJP-BDH, (September 1, 2000), p.2; Benny Evangelista, "Radio Titans to Combine," *San Francisco Chronicle* (October 5, 1999), p.C1.
67 Sam Whiting, "KMEL Axes Call-in Show for Youth: `Street Soldiers' Survives in Syndication But Not in S.F.," *San Francisco Chronicle* (July 21, 1999), p.B-1.
68 Venise Wagner, "Bay Area Group Opposes Merger of Radio Firms," *San Francisco Examiner* (October 26, 1999), p.A-1.
69 Neva Chonin, "KMEL Lets Davey D Go," *San Francisco Chronicle* (October 14, 1999), p.62.
70 "Is KMEL the People's Station? A Community Assessment of 106.1 KMEL" (Oakland, CA: Youth Media Council, Fall 2002), p.9.
71 Ibid., p.11.
72 Jeff Chang, "Urban Radio Rage."
73 Neva Chonin, "KMEL Tunes into Cry for Community Input," *San Francisco Chronicle* (January 26, 2003), p.29.
74 Author's perusal of KMEL's Web site, http://www.kmel.com, on October 20, 2003.
75 Verne Kopytoff, "S.F. Picketers Protest Vote on New FCC Rules: Plan to Relax Monopoly Restrictions Draws Fire," *San Francisco Chronicle* (May 30, 2003), p.B-1.
76 Edward Epstein, "Senate Votes to Block New FCC Rules: They Would Let Media Firms Consolidate More," *San Francisco Chronicle* (September 17, 2003), p.A-1.
77 Robert McChesney, "From Pacifica to the Atlantic" (September 23, 1999): www.thenation.com/doc.mhtml%3Fi=19991011&s=mcchesney.
78 Institute for American Democracy, *How to Combat Air Pollution: A Manual on the FCC's Fairness Doctrine* (Washington: D.C.: Institute for American Democracy), p.4.

INDEX

Acknowledgments

It was hard to write *Uneasy Listening*. As I sat at my computer, I often imagined about 5,000 people involved with Pacifica Radio looking over my shoulder, screaming "How dare you say that about me?" in my ear. Doubtless there will indeed be some yelling now the book is out. But, despite my paranoia, I received much support from many Pacificans and friends. I hope that I have remembered and acknowledged all their kind efforts here.

As I began working on the manuscript, people gave me advice about where to get funding. I liked Barbara Lubin's advice best. "Matthew, how about I do a big mass mailing for you," she suggested, "which will raise you some money?" All I had to do to take this excellent advice was let Barbara her work her magic, raising a generous sum from Pacifica listeners. Barbara and her husband Howard Levine paid all the expenses for the mailing. I am very grateful to them, and to Hari Dillon of the Vanguard Foundation, which provided fiscal sponsorship for the project. Almost 150 people donated money to the cause of this book. Their names can be found at the end of the Acknowledgments in alphabetical order. Special thanks go to Scott Atthome, Bonnie Borenstein, Stephen Brown, Peter Coyote, David Barton Flynn, Edward Herman, Hannah Kranzberg, Patricia Thomas, Jerry F. Schimmel, Veronica Selver, and Robbie Osman. Thanks as well to the people who endorsed the mailer's fund-raising appeal: David Adelson, Larry Bensky, Lauren Coodley, Barbara Epstein, Sherry Gendelman, Ed Herman, Sam Husseini, Robert Knight, Robert McChesney, Veronica Selver, Carol Spooner, and Robbie Osman. Carol Spooner did some fund-raising on her own.

Shortly after the mailer went out, envelopes with checks began arriving at my door. One came with an offer. Ann Irving volunteered to transcribe all my oral history interviews, and she did. She transcribed over fifty interviews, an enormous amount of work. Without her dedicated assistance, I never would have completed this book. My luck continued when my good friend Jane-Ellen Long, legendary editor, UNIX aficionado, and Victorian scholar of Berkeley, agreed to edit the manuscript. And my fortune peaked when, after a long and frustrating search for a publisher, Bob Biderman of Black Apollo Press saw promise in my project and committed to its completion.

When I ran out of money (which happened frequently), Sherry Gendelman, long involved in Pacifica governance, came to the rescue. She organized a fund-raiser which brought in additional funds. Former KPFA station manager Jim Bennett generously agreed to let KPFA host the event, and at it both Amy Goodman and Nicole Sawaya spoke eloquently on my behalf. In addition to raising money, Sherry patiently listened to me whine about how hard my life is at least once a week during the course of the project, which is as good as dollars as far as I'm concerned. I also admire Sherry for her work as a lawyer, activist, and fashion goddess.

Probably my most pleasant two weeks working on this manuscript were spent at the gorgeous Mesa Refuge writers retreat at Point Reyes Station in northern California. I am very grateful to Mesa Refuge for putting me up there. I am especially beholden to Lauren Coodley, who encouraged me to apply to the program and endorsed my application. When I returned from Mesa, trusted friends read various drafts of this work and made excellent observations. Thanks to Sherry Gendelman, Ann Irving, Jane-Ellen Long, Bob Mason, Veronica Selver, and Sharon Wood for performing this task.

Over the past few years I have been fortunate to have the opportunity to teach United States history at the University of California at Santa Cruz. The pleasure of working there has been made even greater by the encouragement and support I have received from my friends Meg Lilienthal and Buchanan Sharp, from history department chair Lynn Westerkamp, and from Alan Christy, Mark Cioc, Dana Frank, Lisbeth Hass, Alice Yang Murray, and Bruce Thompson.

I interviewed many people for this book. The winners in this story – those who called for the democratization of Pacifica and eventually got what they wanted – were happy to speak with me. Not surprisingly, those who opposed this agenda, or at least had very public questions about it, were much less enthusiastic about my invitations to dialogue. I regret that I could not convince former KPFK talk show host Marc Cooper, former KPFK general manager Mark Schubb, former executive directors Lynn Chadwick and Bessie Wash, and former Chair Mary Frances Berry, among others, to agree to an interview. Thus I am particularly grateful to former executive director Pat Scott and former Pacifica national board members John Murdock and Ken Ford for talking with me. And I thank Nalini Lasiewicz for helping me to get in touch with them, as well as for sharing her perspective on Pacifica. Extra thanks to Dan Coughlin, executive director of the Pacifica Foundation, for letting me rummage through the latest Pacifica files in Washington, D.C., and for giving me permission to use what I found. And double extra thanks to Emilie Stolzfus and Eugene Stevanus for sharing their wonderful D.C. home with me for five weeks while I worked.

When my first book, *Pacifica Radio: The Rise of an Alternative Network*, was published in 1999, WBAI's legendary program director Samori Marksman invited me to the station for an interview. It was February 28 of that year. Pacifica was about to explode. Just before we went live, Marksman gave me his candid assessment of my writing. "The problem with this book," he explained, "is that it does not deal with race at Pacifica radio." I had to admit that he was right. I made a mental note to call him back for further discussion about that aspect of the organization. Two weeks later, however, Marksman died of a heart attack in his sleep. Upon hearing this awful news, I promised myself that if I ever wrote a second volume on the later years of Pacifica, I would take Marksman's criticism seriously and grapple with the problem of ethnic conflict within the organization.

I cannot say whether Marksman would agree with the conclusions to which I have come regarding this matter, but I thank him for challenging me on this issue.

Just as I began this project, a terrible crime transformed the United States, the world, and my family. Among the approximately 3,000 people who died in terrorist attacks of September 11 was Avrame Zelmanowitz, my maternal uncle, who remained in one of the World Trade Center towers because he did not want to leave a disabled co-worker behind. When President Bush commemorated Avrame's sacrifice several days later, my mother, Rita Lasar, still reeling from the murder of her brother, appealed to the nation not to mindlessly rush to war. She also promised to devote the rest of her life to peace. "I will stay behind, just as my dear brother Avrame did," she declared. "I will stay behind and ask America not to do something we can't take back."[1] Since then the United States has done many things which, unfortunately, cannot be taken back. But I draw solace and inspiration from my mother's commitment, and from the organization to which she, I, and my brother Raphael, belong along with over one hundred other 9/11 bereaved-September Eleventh Families for Peaceful Tomorrows.

Gratitude must also be expressed to all my friends for listening to endless tales of Pacifica madness and for keeping me company over the years, especially to Cappy Coates, Gary Coates, Ilana DeBare, Julia Hutton, Deborah Kaufman, Mimi Lyons, Bob Mason, Jenny McChesney, Ken Rosenberg, Sam Schuchat, Veronica Selver, Alan Snitow, Tamara Thompson, and Louis J. Vandenberg.

My partner, Sharon Wood, supported this project from its beginning, celebrating its high and enduring its low moments with the patience and love she has always given me. A documentary filmmaker, she possesses an understanding of history, culture, and world affairs that takes my breath away. *Uneasy Listening* is dedicated to Sharon and to her finest creation, Jake Chapnick – he off to college this year.

The Donors

Thanks to Benjamin Frankel Adam, Eric C. Aker, Mike Alcalay, Aileen Alfandary, Joan Kramer Allen, Anne Aminos, Clifton Amsbury, Scott Atthome and Patricia Thomas, Nicolette Ausschnitt, Joanne Banko, Edward C. Barber, Jaqueline M.T. Becker, Charles A. Beebe, Howard Bern, William F. Berreyesa, John W Betts, Martin Bigos, Max Blanchet, Bonnie Borenstein, Tim Boyle, Madeleine T. Bratt, David and Lorie Brillinger, Elizabeth Brown, Douglas P. Brozell, Virginia R. Bruno, Elaine L. Bundesen, H. Bruce Byson, Gail Calvello, Bonnie Jean Campbell, Bruce L. Campbell, Sheila Carillo, Harold Carlstad, Douglas and Ann Christensen, Esther T. Clanon, Gladys L. Clark, Howard Jerome Cohen, Marie Cohen, Juanita C. Contreras, Michael Couzens, Peter Coyote, Alex Craig, Colette Crutcher, Virginia Davis, Edward S. Dean, Rick DeCost, Maya del Mar, Lloyd K. Dennis, Barbara Deutsch, William C. Dietrich, Earl and Evelyn P. Dolven, Park A. Donald, David Dresser, E.M. Duarte, Robert Dunn, Joseph Eckerle, H.B. Eckman, Robin Ely, Barbara Epstein, Sallyanne Ericksen, E. Sutter Eugene, Norbert K. Farrell Jr., Phillip Farrocco, Edith W. Feldman, Dave R. Fertig, Jonathan Fisher, G. Gibson Fleming, Jack Wayne Fleming, David Barton Flynn, Michael Freed, Daniel K. Freudenthal, Lottie R. Fryer, Evelyn S. Fujimoto, Jane P. Futcher, Kathleen Jill Gallagher, Marilyn Garrett, David F. Gassman, Anthony Gatchalian, Stephanie Chloe Georgieff, Deborah Gerson, Adi Gevins, Richard H. Goodwin, John H. Gossard, Ruth T. Gray, Santiago S. Guevara, Margaret C. Guichard, Bruce Gurganus, Barbara Haber, William W. Haible, Michael B Hall, Gregory Jay Haney, Bradley Harger, Reza Hariri, Roger D. Harris, Obo D. Help, Patricia Hendricks, Khati Hendry, Edward Herman, Scott Hill, Morris W. Hirsch, Bernhard M. Hovden, Robert Hutchins, Julia and Wilfred P. Iltis, Leavenworth Jackson, Peacock R Janet, Christopher Jones, Paul Jorjorian, Jane Ruth Kaplan, Anthony Kavanagh, Jane Kelly, Joan Kelly, Shirley Kessler, Dorothy Kidd, Robert Kimberling, David G. Kirby, Alice D. Kisch, Liana and Jack Kornfield, Gina Green Kozak, Jonel Larson,

Lesley Lathrop, William J. Lawler, Harold Lecar, Gale Jennings Lederer, Margaret Lee, Changchuan Alex Lee, Leon Lefson, R. Leong, Henry C. Levy, Mary Jane Lillard, Emily and John Lockett, Susan D. Long, Grace Longeneker, Jeanne L. Lovasich, Evelyn C. Lundstrom, Richard G. Lustig, Gloria McClain, Paulette C. McDevitt, Per Madsen, Mary C. Magee, Philip Maldari, John V. Maria, Stacey and Gerald Martin, Jill Martinucci, Brian Mauck, Gerald B. Merrill, Chad Michel, Carolyn J. Miller, R. L. Miller, John H. Mitchell, Alex Morrison, Barbara C. Moulton, Rowena Muirhead, Scott T. Murphy, Sylvia Grissim Murphy, Lari P. Mussatti, Clark L. Natwick, Dr. G. Hoke Ned, Florence C Norman, William D. North, Wanda Nusted, Diana L. Obrinsky, Jeanne O'connor, Beth C. Olson, Laurie Olson, George Orelian, Philip J. Osegueda, Robbie Osman, Edward A. Parks, Leslie W. Partridge, Yevgeni Philipovitch, Norman R. Powers, L. Darlene Pratt, Sylvia R. Ramirez, Barbara Rasmussen, Linda Ray, Janette M. Reid, Carol Requadt, Margaret A Richardson, Christopher Ris, J. M. Rosenmeier, Susan M. Rouzie, Anthony H. Sacco Jr., Farid Saleh, Mark Sapir, Dianne Savory, Jerry F. Schimmel, David Schneider, Phyllis Schneider, Veronica Selver, Susan Severin, Eugene Sharee, Irwin Silber, Leslie B. Simon, Leonard O. Smith, Veronica A. Smith, S.H. St. George, George W. Starke, Brown Stephen, J.B. Stewart, Susan Stone, Dorothy A. Stroup, F. Jeffrey Sturm, Tim Sullivan, Susan Supriano, Marge Sussman, Marnie Tattersall, Trevor L. Thomas, Patricia Ann Thompson , Celia B. Thompson-Taupin, Murray Tobak, Marsha Torkelson, Roy Tuckman, Judith M. Turley, Carl W. Tusch, Debra Valov, Shirley L. Van Bourg, Nancy Waidtlow, Howard Waite, Steven and Ruth Robert Weintraub, Brian L. West, Timothy West, Harry Wiener, John L. Wiens, John A. Wiget, Susan Wilder, Farrar M. Wilson, Sara Wilson, William Witter, Leon Wofsy, Michiyuki L. Yamaguchi, Rhodes Young, Carol Lou Young-Holt, and Mary Louise Zernicke.

1   Rita Lasar, quoted in Barbara Kingsolver, *Small Wonders: Essays* (Perennial, 2003), p.193.

A Note on Sources

Aside from interviews, the materials used for this book come from a wide variety of sources that I have collected over the years and most of which I possess. These include minutes, correspondence, newspaper articles, taped programs, and many screeds, statements, and other artifacts from the Internet, where much of the Great Pacifica Fight took place. I have tried to establish an orderly paper archive at Pacifica at various times, but the instability of the organization has made that difficult. In the mid 1990s former executive director Pat Scott asked me to assemble what became the Pacifica National Office Papers (PNOP), an indexed collection of board minutes, correspondence, and other documents from the 1940s through the 1980s. It appears that in late 1999, during the KPFA crisis, executive director Lynn Chadwick hurriedly moved these materials to Washington, D.C., in relocating the Pacifica National Office there from Berkeley. The papers were subsequently sent to the Pacifica Archives in Los Angeles. In 2002, I traveled to Washington, D.C., to create a new archive of PNOP materials from the 1990s, and I mention several boxes from this venture in my notes to this volume. However, those containers have also been relocated and stored in various places unknown to me since Pacifica moved back to Berkeley.

The good news is that I have kept copies of most of the documents cited in this book, as well as the private papers of Lewis Hill, Pacifica's founder, which were given to me by his close friend Eleanor McKinney. I refer to these in the notes to Chapter 1 as the Lewis Hill papers (LHP). Eventually I plan to give these materials to a library which, we must hope, will not have an internecine crisis requiring them to relocate every few years.

Printed in the United States
74186LV00001B/1-30

9 781900 355520